COMPUTER
BOOK SERIES
FROM IDG

BBSs For Du...

MW00845021

Quick Reference — Basic BBS Vocabulary

Get a jump on the jargon that permeates the world of BBSs.

BBS	Abbreviation for Bulletin Board System — a computer that your computer can call to communicate with others and get free software.
commercial service	Encompasses America Online, CompuServe, Prodigy, GEnie, and the other larger, nationally known commercial online service providers.
cyberspace	The online dimension — the next-to-the-final frontier.
download	Get a file from the BBS computer.
E-Mail	Abbreviation for Electronic Mail — messages sent through cyberspace.
FAQ	A file containing a list of Frequently Asked Questions.
flame	To engage in contentious behavior while online.
Internet	A vast collection of university, government, business, and personal computers from around the world that exchange information, research, ideas, and silly conversation — the so-called Information Superhighway. It defies defining.
logging off	The process of telling the BBS that you want to leave and then hanging up.
logging on	Identifying yourself to the BBS computer by typing in your name and password.
lurker	Someone who reads public messages, but doesn't participate.
newbie	A person who's "new" to BBSs.
offline mail reader	A program that lets you call a BBS and quickly retrieve all messages so you can read and reply to mail while not online.
online	Being connected with the BBS computer.
shareware	Software available for downloading and trial usage. If you like the program, you are honor-bound to register it with the author.
Sysop	Abbreviation for System Operator — the person who runs a BBS.
thread	A series of public messages connected together by the same subject.
Zip files	Files that have been "freeze-dried" using a special, clever program that squishes files. Zip files all end in .zip.

. . . For Dummies: #1 Computer Book Series for Beginners

BBSs For Dummies®

COMPUTER
BOOK SERIES
FROM IDG

Cheat Sheet

The Ten Commandments of BBSing

1. Thou shalt use thy real name when logging on.
2. Thou shalt help others as others' have helped you.
3. Thou shalt not TYPE MESSAGES IN ALL CAPS, because IT READS LIKE SHOUTING.
4. Thou shalt compress any files thou uploadest to the BBS.
5. Thou shalt not laugh at nor make fun of typographical errors in others' messages.
6. Thou shalt change thy password frequently.
7. Thou shalt read all the messages in an ongoing debate before responding.
8. Thou shalt not flame other users.
9. Honor thy Sysops by offering tribute in the form of cold hard cash in support of the BBSs you frequent.
10. Thou shalt remain on-topic in forums.

Rosetta Stone for Online Hieroglyphics!

Shorthand and symbols you'll bump into when you start reading messages online:

IMHO	In my humble opinion
FWIW	For what it's worth
BTW	By the way
TTFN	Ta-Ta for now!
OTOH	On the other hand
PITA	Pain in the a*
RTFM	Read the f* manual!
<ROTFL>	Rolling on the floor laughing
<Grin> or <G>	Grin
smileys or emoticons	Little faces inserted into messages to express feelings. Like a :-) for a smiling face and a :-(for a sad one.
asterisks	Used for emphasis because boldface and underline don't work online. Example: He said *what*?

WARNING!

While it's okay to talk to strangers online, don't give them personal or financial information. Never, ever give anyone your secret passwords. Unless you're in an online shopping mall, never give out your credit card number or address. Parents, be sure to check out where your kids hang out online — just because it's on a computer doesn't make it educational.

List your favorite BBS numbers here.

. . . For Dummies: #1 Computer Book Series for Beginners

References for the Rest of Us

COMPUTER BOOK SERIES FROM IDG

Are you intimidated and confused by computers? Do you find that traditional manuals are overloaded with technical details you'll never use? Do your friends and family always call you to fix simple problems on their PCs? Then the . . . *For Dummies*™ computer book series from IDG is for you.

. . . *For Dummies* books are written for those frustrated computer users who know they aren't really dumb but find that PC hardware, software, and indeed the unique vocabulary of computing make them feel helpless. . . . *For Dummies* books use a lighthearted approach, a down-to-earth style, and even cartoons and humorous icons to diffuse computer novices' fears and build their confidence. Lighthearted but not lightweight, these books are a perfect survival guide for anyone forced to use a computer.

> *"I like my copy so much I told friends; now they bought copies."*
>
> **Irene C., Orwell, Ohio**

> *"Quick, concise, nontechnical, and humorous."*
>
> **Jay A., Elburn, Illinois**

> *"Thanks, I needed this book. Now I can sleep at night."*
>
> **Robin F., British Columbia, Canada**

Already, hundreds of thousands of satisfied readers agree. They have made . . . *For Dummies* books the #1 introductory level computer book series and have written asking for more. So, if you're looking for the most fun and easy way to learn about computers, look to . . . *For Dummies* books to give you a helping hand.

IDG BOOKS WORLDWIDE

BBSs
FOR
DUMMIES®

by Beth Slick and Steve Gerber

IDG
BOOKS
WORLDWIDE

IDG Books Worldwide, Inc.
An International Data Group Company

Foster City, CA ♦ Chicago, IL ♦ Indianapolis, IN ♦ Braintree, MA ♦ Dallas, TX

BBSs For Dummies®

Published by
IDG Books Worldwide, Inc.
An International Data Group Company
919 E. Hillsdale Blvd.
Suite 400
Foster City, CA 94404

Library of Congress Catalog Card No.: 95-76824

ISBN: 156884-900-1

Printed in the United States of America

10 9 8 7 6 5 4 3 2 1

1E/QW/QW/ZV

Distributed in the United States by IDG Books Worldwide, Inc.

Distributed by Macmillan Canada for Canada; by Computer and Technical Books for the Caribbean Basin; by Contemporanea de Ediciones for Venezuela; by Distribuidora Cuspide for Argentina; by CITEC for Brazil; by Ediciones ZETA S.C.R. Ltda. for Peru; by Editorial Limusa SA for Mexico; by Transworld Publishers Limited in the United Kingdom and Europe; by Al-Maiman Publishers & Distributors for Saudi Arabia; by Simron Pty. Ltd. for South Africa; by IDG Communications (HK) Ltd. for Hong Kong; by Toppan Company Ltd. for Japan; by Addison Wesley Publishing Company for Korea; by Longman Singapore Publishers Ltd. for Singapore, Malaysia, Thailand, and Indonesia; by Unalis Corporation for Taiwan; by WS Computer Publishing Company, Inc. for the Philippines; by WoodsLane Pty. Ltd. for Australia; by WoodsLane Enterprises Ltd. for New Zealand.

For general information on IDG Books Worldwide's books in the U.S., please call our Consumer Customer Service department at 800-762-2974. For reseller information, including discounts and premium sales, please call our Reseller Customer Service department at 800-434-3422.

For information on where to purchase IDG Books Worldwide's books outside the U.S., contact IDG Books Worldwide at 415-655-3021 or fax 415-655-3295.

For information on translations, contact Marc Jeffrey Mikulich, Director, Foreign & Subsidiary Rights, at IDG Books Worldwide, 415-655-3018 or fax 415-655-3295.

For sales inquiries and special prices for bulk quantities, write to the address above or call IDG Books Worldwide at 415-655-3200.

For information on using IDG Books Worldwide's books in the classroom, or ordering examination copies, contact Jim Kelly at 800-434-2086.

For authorization to photocopy items for corporate, personal, or educational use, please contact Copyright Clearance Center, 222 Rosewood Drive, Danvers, MA 01923, or fax 508-750-4470.

About the Authors

Beth Slick

BBSs For Dummies is Beth Slick's fourth book for IDG Books Worldwide.

Beth joined the computer revolution in 1982 when she bought her first computer, which eventually led to a seven-year stint as a computer store manager where she was in charge of training and phone support.

Even while running the computer store, Beth was writing articles for computer magazines, completed two other computer books, and wrote two episodes of *Star Trek: The Next Generation* — one of them with Steve Gerber.

In addition to computer writing, Beth has written a novel, several TV shows, and even spent four days rewriting a Mickey Mouse cartoon.

Steve Gerber

Steve joined the computer revolution in 1984 when Beth *sold* him his first computer and taught him how to use it. *BBSs For Dummies* is his first effort for IDG Books and his first foray into the field of computer writing.

Most of Steve's time is spent writing comic books. He created *Howard the Duck* for Marvel Comics, *Sludge* for Malibu Comics, and, over the past 20 years, has contributed to the adventures of Superman, Spider-Man, Dr. Strange, the Hulk, and many other characters. He has also worked extensively as a writer and story editor in television animation on such series as *Thundarr the Barbarian*, *G.I. Joe*, and *Dungeons & Dragons*.

He is currently writing *Codename: Stryke Force*, *Cybernary*, and *Pitt* for Image Comics.

...together

Beth and Steve wrote the second-season episode of *Star Trek: The Next Generation*, entitled "Contagion." Much of that collaboration was conducted on Steve's Bingo Bango Bongo BBS, as was their work together on this book.

Welcome to the world of IDG Books Worldwide.

IDG Books Worldwide, Inc., is a subsidiary of International Data Group, the world's largest publisher of computer-related information and the leading global provider of information services on information technology. IDG was founded more than 25 years ago and now employs more than 7,500 people worldwide. IDG publishes more than 235 computer publications in 67 countries (see listing below). More than 60 million people read one or more IDG publications each month.

Launched in 1990, IDG Books Worldwide is today the #1 publisher of best-selling computer books in the United States. We are proud to have received 8 awards from the Computer Press Association in recognition of editorial excellence, and our best-selling ...For Dummies™ series has more than 17 million copies in print with translations in 25 languages. IDG Books Worldwide, through a recent joint venture with IDG's Hi-Tech Beijing, became the first U.S. publisher to publish a computer book in the People's Republic of China. In record time, IDG Books Worldwide has become the first choice for millions of readers around the world who want to learn how to better manage their businesses.

Our mission is simple: Every one of our books is designed to bring extra value and skill-building instructions to the reader. Our books are written by experts who understand and care about our readers. The knowledge base of our editorial staff comes from years of experience in publishing, education, and journalism — experience which we use to produce books for the '90s. In short, we care about books, so we attract the best people. We devote special attention to details such as audience, interior design, use of icons, and illustrations. And because we use an efficient process of authoring, editing, and desktop publishing our books electronically, we can spend more time ensuring superior content and spend less time on the technicalities of making books.

You can count on our commitment to deliver high-quality books at competitive prices on topics consumers want to read about. At IDG Books Worldwide, we value quality, and we have been delivering quality for more than 25 years. You'll find no better book on a subject than an IDG book.

John J. Kilcullen

John Kilcullen
President and CEO
IDG Books Worldwide, Inc.

IDG Books Worldwide, Inc., is a subsidiary of International Data Group, the world's largest publisher of computer-related information and the leading global provider of information services on information technology. International Data Group publishes over 235 computer publications in 67 countries. More than sixty million people read one or more International Data Group publications each month. The officers are Patrick J. McGovern, Founder and Board Chairman; Kelly Conlin, President; Jim Casella, Chief Operating Officer. International Data Group's publications include: **ARGENTINA'S** Computerworld Argentina, Infoworld Argentina; **AUSTRALIA'S** Computerworld Australia, Computer Living, Australian PC World, Australian Macworld, Network World, Mobile Business Australia, Publish!, Reseller, IDG Sources; **AUSTRIA'S** Computerwelt Oesterreich, PC Test; **BELGIUM'S** Data News (CW); **BOLIVIA'S** Computerworld; **BRAZIL'S** Computerworld, Connections, Game Power, Mundo Unix, PC World, Publish, Super Game; **BULGARIA'S** Computerworld Bulgaria, PC & Mac World Bulgaria, Network World Bulgaria; **CANADA'S** CIO Canada, Computerworld Canada, InfoCanada, Network World Canada, Reseller; **CHILE'S** Computerworld Chile, Informatica; **COLOMBIA'S** Computerworld Colombia, PC World; **COSTA RICA'S** PC World; **CZECH REPUBLIC'S** Computerworld, Elektronika, PC World; **DENMARK'S** Communications World, Computerworld Danmark, Computerworld Focus, Macintosh Produktkatalog, Macworld Danmark, PC World Danmark, PC Produktguide, Tech World, Windows World; **ECUADOR'S** PC World Ecuador; **EGYPT'S** Computerworld (CW) Middle East, PC World Middle East; **FINLAND'S** MikroPC, Tietoviikko, Tietoverkko; **FRANCE'S** Distributique, GOLDEN MAC, InfoPC, Le Guide du Monde Informatique, Le Monde Informatique, Telecoms & Reseaux; **GERMANY'S** Computerwoche, Computerwoche Focus, Computerwoche Extra, Electronic Entertainment, Gamepro, Information Management, Macwelt, Netzwelt, PC Welt, Publish, Publish; **GREECE'S** Publish & Macworld; **HONG KONG'S** Computerworld Hong Kong, PC World Hong Kong; **HUNGARY'S** Computerworld SZT, PC World; **INDIA'S** Computers & Communications; **INDONESIA'S** Info Komputer; **IRELAND'S** ComputerScope; **ISRAEL'S** Beyond Windows, Computerworld Israel, Multimedia, PC World Israel; **ITALY'S** Computerworld Italia, Lotus Magazine, Macworld Italia, Networking Italia, PC World Italia; **JAPAN'S** Computerworld Today, Information Systems World, Macworld Japan, Nikkei Personal Computing, SunWorld Japan, Windows World; **KENYA'S** East African Computer News; **KOREA'S** Computerworld Korea, Macworld Korea, PC World Korea; **LATIN AMERICA'S** GamePro; **MALAYSIA'S** Computerworld Malaysia, PC World Malaysia; **MEXICO'S** Compu Edicion, Compu Manufactura, Computacion/Punto de Venta, Computerworld Mexico, MacWorld, Mundo Unix, PC World, Windows; **THE NETHERLANDS'** Computer! Totaal, Computable (CW), LAN Magazine, Lotus Magazine, MacWorld; **NEW ZEALAND'S** Computer Buyer, Computerworld New Zealand, Network World, New Zealand PC World; **NIGERIA'S** PC World Africa; **NORWAY'S** Computerworld Norge, Lotusworld Norge, Macworld Norge, Maxi Data, Networld, PC World Ekspress, PC World Nettverk, PC World Norge, PC World's Produktguide, Publish & Multimedia World, Student Data, Unix World, Windowsworld; **PAKISTAN'S** PC World Pakistan; **PANAMA'S** PC World Panama; **PERU'S** Computerworld Peru, PC World; **PEOPLE'S REPUBLIC OF CHINA'S** China Computerworld, China Infoworld, China PC Info Magazine, Computer Fan, PC World China, Electronics International, Electronics Today/Multimedia World, Electronic Product World, China Network World, Software World Magazine, Telecom Product World; **PHILIPPINES'** Computerworld Philippines, PC Digest (PCW); **POLAND'S** Computerworld Poland, Computerworld Special Report, Networld, PC World/Komputer, Sunworld; **PORTUGAL'S** Cerebro/PC World, Correio Informatico/Computerworld, MacIn; **ROMANIA'S** Computerworld, PC World, Telecom Romania; **RUSSIA'S** Computerworld-Moscow, Mir - PK (PCW), Sety (Networks); **SINGAPORE'S** Computerworld Southeast Asia, PC World Singapore; **SLOVENIA'S** Monitor Magazine; **SOUTH AFRICA'S** Computer Mail (CIO), Computing S.A., Network World S.A., Software World; **SPAIN'S** Advanced Systems, Amiga World, Computerworld Espana, Communicaciones World, Macworld Espana, NeXTWORLD, Super Juegos Magazine (GamePro), PC World Espana, Publish; **SWEDEN'S** Attack, ComputerSweden, Corporate Computing, Macworld, Mikrodatorn, Natverk & Kommunikation, PC World, CAP & Design, Datalngenjoren, Maxi Data, Windows World; **SWITZERLAND'S** Computerworld Schweiz, Macworld Schweiz, PC Tip; **TAIWAN'S** Computerworld Taiwan, PC World Taiwan; **THAILAND'S** Thai Computerworld; **TURKEY'S** Computerworld Monitor, Macworld Turkiye, PC World Turkiye; **UKRAINE'S** Computerworld, Computers+Software Magazine; **UNITED KINGDOM'S** Computing /Computerworld, Connexion/Network World, Lotus Magazine, Macworld, Open Computing/Sunworld; **UNITED STATES'** Advanced Systems, AmigaWorld, Cable in the Classroom, CD Review, CIO, Computerworld, Computing Client/Server Journal, Digital Video, DOS World, Electronic Entertainment Magazine (E2), Federal Computer Week, Game Hits, GamePro, IDG Books Worldwide, Infoworld, Laser Event, Macworld, Maximize, Multimedia World, Network World, PC Letter, PC World, Publish, SWATPro, Video Event; **URUGUAY'S** PC World Uruguay; **VENEZUELA'S** Computerworld Venezuela, PC World; **VIETNAM'S** PC World Vietnam.
05/17/95

Credits

Acknowledgments

The Authors would like to thank...

From IDG Books: John Kilcullen, David Solomon, Megg Bonar, and Kathy Cox.

Also, thanks to our gentle copy editor, Shannon Ross, the rigorous tech editors, Dave Bennett and Mike Lerch, and copy editors Diana Conover and Tammy Castleman.

Thanks to the production staff, especially Tyler Connor, Chris Collins, Cameron Booker, Carla Radzikinas, and Gina Scott.

Thanks to Lee Goldberg for his time and words.

Boundless appreciation to the fine folks at Mustang Software, Inc., publishers of the Wildcat! BBS software, and especially Jim Harrer, Rick Heming, and Scott Hunter. Special recognition to Jack Rickard, editor of *Boardwatch Magazine,* to his staff, and in particular to Brian Gallagher — keeper of the list.

A special thank you and much gratitude to the hard-working Sysops who generously made time where none existed to respond to our survey and provide war stories, hints, and encouragement to those just starting out with BBSs.

Finally, a very special tip o' the modem to Mark Evanier and Suzanne Weiss, for their gracious donation of silicon organs from their dear, departed computers to keep Steve Gerber's Bingo Bango Bongo BBS alive — without which this book could not have been written.

(The Publisher would like to give special thanks to Patrick J. McGovern, without whom this book would not have been possible.)

Contents at a Glance

Foreword xxiv

Introduction 1

Part I: On the Road to Cyberspace 7
Chapter 1: What the Heck Is a BBS? 9
Chapter 2: Logging On 15
Chapter 3: Snagging Files and Bringin' 'em on Home 41
Chapter 4: Zippity Doo Dah! 61
Chapter 5: Communicating in Cyberspace 71
Chapter 6: Modeming Defensively 85
Chapter 7: Looking at the Dark Side 103

Part II: I Don't Think We're in Kansas Anymore 111
Chapter 8: Finding and Retrieving the Truly Great Files 113
Chapter 9: Electrifying E-Mail 131
Chapter 10: Confabulating in Conferences 147
Chapter 11: Striking up a Chat Session 165
Chapter 12: Playing Games, Shopping, and Doors 177
Chapter 13: Changing the System 185
Chapter 14: Introducing the Internet Connection 191
Chapter 15: Reading Mail Offline 197

Part III: I, Sysop 209
Chapter 16: Hosting Your Own Mini-BBS 211
Chapter 17: Running Your Own BBS? 219
Chapter 18: Setting Up a Wildcat! BBS 231
Chapter 19: Exploring a BBS behind the Scenes 277

Part IV: The Part of Tens 299

Chapter 20: Top Ten Secret Commands 301
Chapter 21: Ten Files to Download First 305
Chapter 22: Ten Ways to Get Out of Trouble 309
Chapter 23: Top Ten Hints from Sysops 315

Part V: Appendixes 321

Appendix A: Getting to the Starting Line 323
Appendix B: The Complete Top 100 BBSs 329
Appendix C: Putting the Global in Global Village 339
Appendix D: I Want My ANSI.SYS! 345

Index 351

Cartoons at a Glance
by Rich Tennant

Page 111

Page 87

Page 7

Page 209

Page 321

Page 230

Page 299

Page 154

Page 62

Page 190

Table of Contents

Foreword .... *xxiv*

Introduction **1**

About This Book 2
One Small Step 2
The Ping Pong Gambit 3
Do You Have What It Takes? 4
So What's the Plan? 4
    Part I — On the Road to Cyberspace 4
    Part II — I Don't Think We're in Kansas Anymore 4
    Part III — I, Sysop 5
    Part IV — The Part of Tens 5
    Part V — Appendixes 5
Icons Used in This Book 5
Different Strokes 6
Out-of-Body Experience 6

Part I: On the Road to Cyberspace **7**

Chapter 1: What the Heck Is a BBS? **9**

Exploring Cyberspace 9
Uncovering BBS Kinships 10
    Closing in on content 10
    Sizing up the structure 11

Chapter 2: Logging On **15**

Logging on for the First Time 16
    Dialing the phone 16
    Making the connection 17
    Introducing yourself 19
Setting up an account 28
Becoming an unverified new user 29
    Finishing up the logon job 30
    Saying good-bye — logging off 31
Getting Validated 32
    Rambling through Other Systems 33
    Same question, new words 33

Making the case for default 34
Taming tech topics 34
Set screen width 35
Check out the top 35
Stop the pages 35
Use an editor 35
Going for graphics 36
Finding hotkeys 36
No nulls is good nulls 37
Scrollin' on the river 37
Donning a secret disguise 38
Logging on the Second Time 38

Chapter 3: Snagging Files and Bringin' 'em on Home **41**

Introducing Capture and Download 42
Making a Home for Your Booty 42
Remedial DOS 43
Directories 43
Filenames 44
Wildcards 44
Putting it all together 45
Developing a download directory 45
Creating a corner for captured characters 46
Capturing Files 47
Planning ahead 47
Grabbing text retroactively 49
Using captured files 50
Downloading Files 51
Downloading 101 51
Doing the download 53
Uploading Files 59

Chapter 4: Zippity Doo Dah! **61**

Putting Zip in Your Life 61
UnZipping: The Concept 64
Doing it itself: the self-extracting file 65
Doing it yourself 65
Setting Up Zip 67

Chapter 5: Communicating in Cyberspace **71**

Exchanging E-Mail 72
For your eyes only 74
Getting on a soap box 75
Chatting up a Storm 79
Are you talking to me? 79
Joining the conversation 81

Minding Your Ps and Qs on BBSs 81
    Keeping your elbows off the table 81
    Keeping it short 83
    Using virtual body language 83
Putting an angle on it 83
Smiling faces 84

Chapter 6: Modeming Defensively **85**

Microscoping Out a Computer Virus 86
Taking Preventive Action 86
Staying Current with Virus Checkers 88
    Updating Microsoft Anti-Virus 89
        Downloading the update 89
        Updating the program 92
    Connecting with McAfee AntiVirus 94
        Getting McAfee AntiVirus 94
        Installing McAfee AntiVirus 96
    Checking for Viruses 97
        Using Microsoft Anti-Virus 98
        Using McAfee VirusScan 99
Getting a Red Alert 100

Chapter 7: Looking at the Dark Side **103**

Telling the Truth 104
Avoiding a Scam 104
Remaining Anonymous 105
Stalking Online 106
X-Rated Chat 106
Protecting Your Kids 107
Protecting BBSs from Your Kids 108
Dealing with Hackers 108
Looking on the Bright Side 109

Part II: I Don't Think We're in Kansas Anymore **111**

Chapter 8: Finding and Retrieving the Truly Great Files **113**

Finding the File Menu 114
Searching for a File 116
    Grazing files 117
        Poking through file directories 117
        Checking out what's new 118
    Searching with a purpose 120
Retrieving Files 123
    Getting immediate gratification 124
    Tagging now, downloading later 125

Putting Your Booty to Work — or Not 126
    Putting a file in its place 127
    Banishing files 127

Chapter 9: Electrifying E-Mail 131

Responding to New E-Mail 132
    Disentangling attachments 133
    Replying to the missive 134
    Disposing of the message 134
    Moving on 135
Writing a Message 136
    Pressing the go button 137
    Putting keyboard to screen 140
    Replying to sender 141
    Sending the message 143
Retrieving Mail 145

Chapter 10: Confabulating in Conferences 147

Characterizing Conferences 148
    Going national — and beyond 149
    Getting to the basics 151
Tapping into Conferences 153
    Choosing a topic 155
    Choosing a topic, part deux 156
    Rounding up messages 157
    Reading messages 160
    Posting your own messages 160
    Keeping your head when all about are losing theirs 162
Flame wars 162
Rules of debate 162
Abandoning a Conference 163
Selecting Conferences 163

Chapter 11: Striking up a Chat Session 165

Classifying Chat 166
Entering the Chat Menu 168
    Paging 172
    Responding 172
Chatting Rooms 173
    Introducing Chatting Room commands 173
    Leaving 174
    Getting help 175
    Looking around 175

Squelching others 175
Private message 175
Beyond Chatting 176

Chapter 12: Playing Games, Shopping, and Doors 177

Playing Games 177
Single-user games 178
Multiline games 179
MUD games 179
Going Shopping 180
Walking through the Door 181
Searching databases 182
Reading magazines 182
Making a love connection 183

Chapter 13: Changing the System 185

Assessing Your Setup 185
Making Needed Changes 187
Password 187
Protocol 187
ANSI graphics 188
Full-Screen Editor 188
Using Other Utilities 188
Time online 189
Your statistics 189
Who's online 189
Chat status 189

Chapter 14: Introducing the Internet Connection 191

The Bad News 192
The Good News 193
Internet Features Coming to a BBS Near You... 195

Chapter 15: Reading Mail Offline 197

Using Offline Readers 197
Preparing for the Installation 199
Putting the Offline Reader in Its Place 200
Setting OLX Up 201
Configuring the Online System 203
Downloading the E-Mail Packet 203
Reading and Replying on OLX 204
Uploading Your Reply Packet 206
Looking to the Future 207

Part III: I, Sysop *209*

Chapter 16: Hosting Your Own Mini-BBS 211

Hosting a CyberParty 211
Preparing Your System 212
    Making the guest list 213
    Answering the call 213
    Disarming call-waiting 215
Invoking the Host 215
Receiving Guests 216
Moving the Party 218

Chapter 17: Running Your Own BBS? 219

Ruling Your Own Cyberspace Realm 220
    My Problem 220
    The Solution 220
    I was hooked 221
Doing Business Electronically 221
Reading, Writing, and Logging On 222
Keeping Yourself off the Streets 223
Abdicating the Throne 224
    Cashing in — or costing out? 224
        Hardware 225
        Software 226
        Hidden costs 226
        "The Time Tunnel" 227
        Murphy's Law 227
    Sharing, caring — and repressing your urge to kill 228

Chapter 18: Setting Up a Wildcat! BBS 231

Planning Your BBS 232
    Organizing your board 232
    Framing the file areas 233
Installing Your BBS 234
    The Wildcat! installation screen 235
    The WINSTALL window 238
Making Notes and MEMories 240
Making Wild(cat!) 241
    Creating your board's blueprint 243
        The first General Information screen ... 243
        Third and final General Information screen ... 248
    Battening down the hatches 251
    Introducing Wildcat! to your modem 254
The second Modem Settings screen 256

The third and fourth Modem Settings screens 256
Reaching outside Wildcat! 257
Profiling your users 257
Invoking manual override 265
Fiddling with file areas 265
Profile Access window 266
Conference Area Access window 267
Cranking up your conferences 269
Opening doors 272
Hooking the big one 273
QWKening your callers' mail 273
Chatting, idling, and speaking in tongues 275
Calling it quitsville 275

Chapter 19: Exploring a BBS behind the Scenes **277**
Taking Command of Your BBS 278
The New User Main Menu 279
The Security Change window 280
Peering behind the Curtain behind the Curtain 283
"Status, Mr. Data...base?" — Pressing S 284
Taking a walk on the file side — Pressing F 285
Browsing through your users' lives — Pressing U 287
Following your users' footprints — Pressing A 293
A fistful of commands — Pressing $, !, *, N, and B 294
Overtaking events — Pressing E 295
Taking the plunge to DOS — Pressing D 296
Custom-tailoring your BBS 297

Part IV: The Part of Tens **299**

Chapter 20: Top Ten Secret Commands **301**
A Bit of History 301
The Ten Commands 302
Pause — Ctrl+S 302
Restart — Ctrl+Q 302
Cancel — Ctrl+C 303
Abort — Ctrl+X 303
Suspend — Ctrl+K 303
Help — ? or H 303
<CR> or Enter 303
Top — * or 0 304
Backward and Forward — – and + ... 304
Global — / 304
Read the Screen 304

Chapter 21: Ten Files to Download First 305

PKZ204G.EXE 306
DOSAV.EXE or WINAV.EXE 306
QM46TD-1.EXE and QM46TD-2.EXE 306
OLX-TD.EXE 307
LIST90H.ZIP and WINLIST.ZIP 307
VPIC61.ZIP 307
SHEZ106.ZIP 308
DRAGFL.ZIP 308
WINPRN15.ZIP 308
TIMESET7.ZIP 308

Chapter 22: Ten Ways to Get Out of Trouble 309

Read 310
Jump to the Top 310
Ask Another User 311
Voice Support 311
Use a Screen Command 311
Try Something Different 311
Visit the Past 312
Page the Sysop 312
Leave a Comment 313
Hang Up on the BBS 313

Chapter 23: Top Ten Hints from Sysops 315

Set Your Communications Software Properly 315
Read the Instructions on the Screen 316
Don't Be Afraid to Ask Questions 316
Remember, the BBS Is Run by a Hobbyist 316
Be Familiar with Zmodem 317
Correct External High-Speed Modem Drop-Outs 317
Don't Blame the Sysop for Line Noise 317
You Can't Hurt the BBS 318
Don't Just Download Files 318
Use Offline Readers 318
Give Help to Other Users 318
Bonus: Hints for Dealing with Sysops 319

Part V: Appendixes *321*

Appendix A: Getting to the Starting Line 323
Picking a Phone Line 323
Hunting Down the Modem 324
Sleuthing Out Your Software 326
Dealing with the Dialing Directory 327

Appendix B: The Complete Top 100 BBSs 329

Appendix C: Putting the Global in Global Village 339
Getting the International Online 339
And Now a Word for Our Sponsor... 343

Appendix D: I Want My ANSI.SYS! 345
Finding ANSI.SYS 345
Installing ANSI.SYS 347
Troubleshooting 348

Index *351*

Foreword

· ·

*T*he foibles that probably afflict a writer most are isolation, insecurity, and procrastination. You write by yourself, and, convinced that you're lousy at it, you put it off as long as you can.

Nothing exploits those foibles better than a modem and a BBS. Except, perhaps, a strike.

In early 1988, a week after I bought my first modem, the Writers Guild of America, the union for screen scribes, went on strike for six months. Thousands of writers were suddenly even more alone and insecure than before. But around the same time, the Guild launched its own BBS. It became a lifeline, a way to feel connected to other writers, even when sitting at your desk in your underwear, eating Doritos and guzzling Diet Coke.

For hours I'd sit there, bathed in amber, talking to people I had never met — writers I had either long admired or never heard of. But, in that virtual meeting hall, we were all equal, venting our fears and frustrations, sharing information, trading gossip, offering advice, and arguing about such weighty issues as who was the best James Bond.

Suddenly, my computer wasn't just a writing tool. It was an *avoid*-writing tool. Best of all, you could look like you were writing while using it ("No, honey, I can't empty the garbage. Can't you see I'm *writing*?").

Emboldened and with plenty of time to kill, I started exploring other BBSs (including one run by Steve Gerber, the co-author of this book). I discovered there was a BBS for every conceivable interest, from the mundane to the profane, and I logged onto them all, especially since most of them were absolutely free.

Then I got my phone bill.

Ouch.

But by then I was hooked. I found, to my surprise, that starting the day with a few minutes BBSing actually helped my writing. It got me to the keyboard, my fingers flying across the keys, and jump-started my creativity. To get around those wallet-ripping phone bills, I concocted a cunning plan. I'd start my own BBS. Then I could sit back while everybody called *me*.

It worked. And my BBS for writers, The Idle Gossip (818-342-7808), is still up-and-running today.

At their best, BBSs are like a non-stop party among friends, where challenging debates, stimulating conversation, and interesting gossip are shared. At their worst, BBSs can become an electronic cockfight, where the anonymity and facelessness of the medium encourages the vicious, the lurid, and the cruel.

Happily, the best far exceeds the worst — which is why I'm still BBSing today, and why this book is so long overdue.

Thanks to Beth Slick and Steve Gerber, you can find the BBSs where people just like you gather to talk about the things that interest you most.

And now you, too, can sit at your desk and pretend to be working when it's your turn to walk the dog.

Lee Goldberg

Lee Goldberg is a writer/producer whose work includes *Diagnosis Murder, Sliders, The Cosby Mysteries,* and *Baywatch.*

Introduction

Remember the first time you crossed the street all by yourself? Your first time at the wheel after scoring your driver's license? Your first apartment? And, of course, no one forgets the first time — well, I think we've got enough examples. The point is, all of those were personal, world-expanding moments. If you're in business and up on all the current buzz-words, you may know them as *paradigm shifts*.

If you haven't been online — other than waiting for a movie — yet another one of those life-changing experiences awaits you. Whether you've got an IBM-type computer, an Apple Macintosh, or even an Amiga or CP/M-based system, you are eligible to join a community of people bounded by neither geography nor time zones. The citizens of this community are diverse, yet are brought together by intense passions for concerns ranging from sewing to global peace to, of course, computers.

Don't run away because you don't have a clear mental picture of what *going online* means, exactly, or what a BBS is. In a few pages I'll start from ground zero, and you'll not only find out what BBSs are — other than an abbreviation for Bulletin Board Systems — but why you want them and how they're changing the world.

And, even if you've been online via CompuServe, America Online, or Prodigy, you've only had part of the experience. Limiting your online time to these commercial services, as excellent as they are, is like only eating at Sizzler's and ignoring all the great local restaurants. Not that there's anything wrong with Sizzler's, of course.

However, venturing into an unfamiliar area, much like trying out a new restaurant, can be a frustrating experience. The maitre'd doesn't seem to treat you with respect, you don't know if you'll like the food, and it's a crapshoot what will be on the menu. Then, when the main course arrives, you learn that *calamari* is not a new kind of pasta.

That's where *BBSs For Dummies* steps in. I'll gently, carefully, and *safely* walk you through the wild, wacky, and, yes, even sexy world of home-brew bulletin boards.

You'll be using the *Boardwatch Magazine* list of the Top 100 BBSs as your launching point. This *best of* list gives recognition to deserving BBSs operated by dedicated cyberheads and is much like a *best restaurant* list from truck drivers. Or, if you prefer, a Zagat's Guide. Though, of course, these aren't the only really terrific BBSs on the planet. This list is just a good place to start.

And don't worry, I absolutely will not let you order the *escargots* unless you really want snails.

About This Book

What you'll find here is all the information you'll ever need to know about logging on and using a Bulletin Board System, plus a boost for those in business — or for fun — who want to start their own BBS but assumed it was far too complicated to attempt.

This book assumes you know nothing about BBSs and want to know only as much as you need to join the party. In other words, we'll take something that looks convoluted and straighten it out. Your friends will be coming to you for advice.

The rest of this introduction explains how *BBSs For Dummies* works and what you are supposed to be bringing to the table.

One Small Step

Occasionally you'll find a list of step-by-step instructions, telling you precisely what you need to do to achieve computer nirvana.

To keep the steps as concise as possible, I'll be using a shorthand way of telling you what to do. I'm sure you won't find it startlingly different from what you're used to, but here goes:

- Select **File**⇨**S**ave.

  Implicit in this kind of instruction is the option to use either the mouse or the keyboard — your choice. If you were using a mouse, then you'd slide your mouse pointer to the top of the screen and click once on the word File. The single click reveals the pull-down menu. One of the options on that menu is Save. Click on Save.

  If you prefer a keyboard approach, press the Alt key on your keyboard to access the menu on top. Then press the letter F — see how it's bold-faced in my instruction . . . that's what tells you to press the F. After the File drop-down menu reveals itself, press the letter S. Why S? Same reason as the F; it's bold-faced in the instruction.

- Type **PKUNZIP GAMES.ZIP** and press Enter.

This is what's known as a command line. No mice allowed. In this case, you would start out by typing PKUNZIP — again, you're typing the bold-faced stuff — press spacebar on your keyboard, type GAMES.ZIP, and then bring it on home by pressing the Enter key, also on your keyboard. That's not too bad, is it?

✔ When you are asked [N]o, [Y]es, or [C]ontinuous? press Y and press Enter.

The important thing to notice here is that [N]o, [Y]es, or [C]ontinuous? is in a completely different typeface than anything surrounding it. Whenever you see words in that different kind of typeface, you are looking at text being beamed straight from the BBS's computer to your computer. In short, it's something you can expect to see on your computer screen. It's like a direct quote from the BBS. Except, instead of using quotes, we set it off with the special typeface.

The long-winded version of the above example is: Wait until the BBS computer sends you the following message: [N]o, [Y]es, or [C]ontinuous? After that message appears on your computer screen, respond by pressing the letter Y.

✔ Press Alt+F1 for Help.

When you see something like this, I want you to depress the Alt key on your keyboard and keep holding it down while you hit the F1 key. Then release Alt and F1. You do not type the letters A, L, T or the plus sign or F or 1. If this is confusing, look at it this way. Pretend you're instructing someone else on how to make an uppercase J. You'd say, "Press Shift+J." See? Hold down the shift key and keep holding it down while you press the letter J. You should probably make sure you know where the Ctrl key is on your keyboard, too. We'll be using it later on.

The Ping Pong Gambit

Unlike a novel, _BBSs For Dummies_ doesn't have to be used in a linear fashion. If you know all the stuff in Part I already, skip on. Or maybe you're eager to get started sending mail and getting programs, as featured in Part II. If something in Part II turns out to be a little more advanced than you expected, you can go back to Part I and pick up what you need to know. There's no wrong approach.

Do You Have What It Takes?

As I mentioned before, this book is about everything you need to know to log on and use a BBS. This assumes your modem is saddled and mounted. To get to the starting gate, you must have a computer, a phone line, a modem, and installed modem software champing at the bit. If you aren't sure whether you do or don't have any of these elements, skitter over to Appendix A for a helping hand.

Other than that, you have to be able to follow instructions and know how to turn the computer on. That's it! Oh, except for the most important thing of all — have a good sense of humor.

So What's the Plan?

To get to this page, you had to pass by a detailed, and perhaps intimidating, Table of Contents. Here's an easier-to-digest description of what to expect once we get beyond this introduction.

Part I — On the Road to Cyberspace

This is where you can gain the foundation — if you don't already have it — for what to expect over the rainbow in BBS-land. Part I is like the classroom portion of driver education. It's good to be aware of the rules of the road before zooming down the freeway (or expressway, or autobahn, or whichever is applicable in your corner of the world). Knowing how to navigate the curves makes the difference between smooth traveling or crashing and burning. First, you drive around the parking lot just to get the feel of things.

Part II — I Don't Think We're in Kansas Anymore

In Part II, school's out and it's time to explore strange new worlds, seek out new life and new civilizations, and boldly go online! Each chapter uses real-life experiences from Bulletin Board Systems listed in the *Boardwatch Magazine* Top 100 BBS list. After going through these chapters, you'll have enough cyber-smarts to figure out any system you bump into. It's the same as how, after taking a driving course, you can expect to jump into any car and drive it.

Part III — I, Sysop

Start your *own* BBS? Is this remotely realistic? Absolutely! And it doesn't have to cost very much, either. Steve Gerber, who has run BBSs for many years, shows you two ways. And, even if you never plan to set up your own BBS, Steve's behind-the-scenes tour makes it easier to understand why BBSs work the way they do.

Part IV — The Part of Tens

Who doesn't like top-ten lists? They're fun and to the point. In the Part of Tens, you see lists like: ten ways to look like an expert, ten ways to get out of trouble, and even top-ten hints from the people who run BBSs.

Part V — Appendixes

Don't ignore these Appendixes! They contain some important stuff — not the least of which is the entire *Boardwatch Magazine* Top 100 list (find one near you), a list of international BBSs, and a few technical hints in case you find yourself wrestling a bit with your modem and your computer.

Icons Used in This Book

Part of the charm of the *...For Dummies* series is its use of little pictures, called icons in the computer biz, in the margins to emphasize what you're reading. The icons are self-explanatory. However, in the interest of completeness, here they are, and here's what they are telling you.

A shortcut or labor-saving secret that will save you time. As in, "Have the waiter instruct you on using the tiny fork that comes with escargots."

Sometimes it's interesting to know the why or how of what's going on. In case you're curious, visit these technical side roads. If you don't care, then you can skip them, no harm done. Example: "Escargots, or helix Pomatia to their friends, are not the same basic types as found under a rock in your garden. They have been grown and cultivated for sale to restaurants."

This is a little factoid to consider before taking the next step, like, "remember that escargots are easy to cook badly. How familiar are you with this restaurant?"

If you see one of these, you know you're swimming in dangerous waters; be aware of your surroundings. For instance, "If your date makes gagging sounds when you order escargots, rethink your ordering decision."

This flags a comment, testimonial, hint, or observation — sometimes humorous — from some of the hard-working people who operate one of the Top 100 Bulletin Board Systems.

Different Strokes

Bulletin board systems are designed with you in mind — whatever your interest — by people like you who share that interest. BBSs are as varied as the people who use them. In order to select good examples of ways BBSs can do things, I use screen shots from various BBSs on the *Boardwatch Magazine* Top 100 List. A very few of these examples are from adults-only BBSs. I mark these with the words "Adults Only" in the caption or sidebar where the BBS is named. To be sure that the BBS you call has material that you're comfortable with, check out the description of the BBS in the Top 100 list before dialing in. Those with only adult-oriented materials are marked with a dagger (†).

Out-of-Body Experience

The only truly verifiable out-of-body experience is the one you have when you go online. You can be at home wearing sweats, with your hair sticking out in that funny way, while at the same time romancing the person of your dreams, collecting new software, or consulting professionals who would charge you an arm and a leg for their advice in the outside world.

How do you do all this and more? I thought you'd never ask.

Part I

On the Road to Cyberspace

The 5th Wave   By Rich Tennant

"WHAT CONCERNS ME ABOUT THE INFORMATION SUPERHIGHWAY IS THAT IT APPEARS TO BE ENTERING THROUGH BRENT'S BEDROOM."

In this part...

*I*f you were planning a visit to another country, you'd probably prepare for the excursion by studying a map, learning local customs, and memorizing a few key phrases. Your impending foray into the online dimension should likewise trigger a few moments of contemplative advance study. Unless, of course, you prefer the macho-but-stupid *sink or swim* approach. If you do, plunge straight into Part II. For those of us who want to reduce the long-distance floundering to a minimum, Part I covers the concepts and philosophies of the BBS world — including the all-important issue of *What the Heck Is a BBS?* Once you know what to expect online and have some of the terminology under your belt — or wherever you carry your terminology — you'll be issued a passport and be certified to travel around the world.

Chapter 1

What the Heck Is a BBS?

In This Chapter

▶ Uncovering BBS kinships

▶ Closing in on content

▶ Sizing up the structure

A BBS — shorthand for Bulletin Board System — is, minimally, a lonely computer and a trusty modem hooked up to a phone line. The computer and its faithful modem sidekick wait patiently for other computers to call. Often, the BBS computer and modem live in the den of the perhaps equally lonely hobbyist who assembled the system.

Your mission, should you decide to accept it, is to call that lonely BBS computer. Under the direction of your telecommunications software, your computer and your modem can reach out. Then, once the BBS computer answers the phone, you are officially *online*. If this were a horror movie, a wild-haired fellow would start screaming, "It's alive!"

Real life, in this case, is much more interesting than fiction. Once you are online — or, if you want to be hip, once you are in *cyberspace* — you have remote control over the BBS computer sitting in someone's den a thousand miles away! Maybe this *is* a science-fiction movie, after all. So what happens next? Everything!

Exploring Cyberspace

Once online, you may browse around the BBS to see if there's any new free software that whets your appetite, say howdy to the other users who are simultaneously online, pick up the threads of several conversations and toss your two cents in, and then write a letter home to Mom — in Australia — at no extra charge. Or perhaps today you're online to defend your status as top space warrior against an up-and-comer who has foolishly challenged you to one-on-one combat in space . . . from the comfort of your keyboards, of course.

This is just one possible scenario, one version of what the heck a BBS is. There are millions of stories in the cybercity — and you can participate in all of them.

Uncovering BBS Kinships

Although every BBS has a unique personality, after trying out a few systems and adjusting to the initial thrill and confusion, your keen mind will detect a pattern. That's right; all BBSs sport the same basic components. How those ingredients are arranged and emphasized is what distinguishes one BBS from another.

It's easier for you, as a first timer, to understand what the heck a BBS is if you familiarize yourself with the system's basic building blocks — the DNA, if you will — of a BBS. The chromosomes shared by all BBSs fall into two general categories: *content* and *structure*.

Closing in on content

Content is what each system offers in terms of services and fun things to do. In 25 words or less, sort of, here are the broad categories of resources you'll grow to expect from BBSs:

- **Low cost, high performance:** BBSs are, without a doubt, the bargain of the 1990s. A BBS is often a professional service run as a hobby. Money that's requested helps defray costs. Some BBSs, of course, are businesses with employees, rent, insurance, and all the responsibilities of a grown-up venture. But for the vast majority of *Sysops* — the system operators who own BBSs as a labor of love — the fantasy is just to break even one day.

- **Free software:** The number-one reason people use BBS systems is to try out free software. BBSs serve as the distribution channel for programs created by hobbyists. Just because these programs are free, or nearly free, doesn't mean that they're junk. In fact, ProComm and Doom were first made available on bulletin boards. You'll be astonished at what you can find.

- **Public forums and chatting:** Because computer users are often stereotyped as nerdy, antisocial misfits, it may be a major revelation to you that one of the most popular aspects of BBSs is the opportunity to meet and chat with people who have like interests. In fact, the people who use BBSs are, themselves, part of the package that draws others to the system. It's not uncommon for BBSs to connect with other BBSs and share their messages on public forums, so that your comments are transmitted, literally, around the world.

✔ **Electronic mail:** Commonly referred to as E-Mail, a BBS's electronic mail system enables you to send a note or file to other people who use the system — and perhaps beyond — whether or not they are currently online. When they do check in, the BBS notifies them that the "flag is up" on their mailbox. With E-Mail, you can stay close to people you can't visit or who are on the road.

✔ **Games:** I'm not just talking about downloading games to play on your computer at home — that comes under the heading of free software — I'm talking games played against other BBS users while you're all online together. You have to see to believe.

✔ **Internet:** More and more BBSs are providing some kind of access to the Internet — the so-called Information Superhighway that everyone keeps talking about. If you've never heard of the Internet, that's fine — I tell you what it is in Chapter 14. If you *do* know what it is, but are intimidated just by the thought of on-ramps merging into the Information Superhighway, you'll find that a BBS can provide shuttle service on and off the highway. Leave the driving to us.

✔ **News and information:** Some BBSs are connected to news services that provide access to weather, current news, stocks, and so on.

Sizing up the structure

Every time you contact a BBS, you can rely on a certain sequence of events occurring. Knowing how these events are arranged reduces the confusion factor. Here, in Part I, you spend some quality time with each of these events, or modules. In Part II, you see how each module fits together, like Legos, to create an entire BBS experience. Sort of a gestalt kind of thing.

Does it charge $2 an hour?

Early on in my career as a Sysop, my wife became jealous of the time I gave the BBS and threatened to throw the computer out the window. Several years later, on one of those frustrating nights when everything goes wrong — databases becoming corrupt, monitor giving up the ghost in the middle of a database repair, the delivery of a $500 phone bill — I decided to throw the computer out the window myself.

My wife looked shocked, and then, after a long pause, she sternly said, "Don't you dare! That BBS is the best baby-sitter I've ever had. I can go out and not worry about where you are or what you might be up to. I know you'll still be sitting right in that chair when I get home. You throw the computer out the window and there's going to be trouble around here, Buster!"

Chip North, Sysop, The Source BBS

✔ **Logging on:** Ever see those speakeasy movies where the gangster knocks on an unmarked door and then, if he knows the secret word, is allowed in? You get to do a cyberversion of that every time you call a BBS. After first connecting, you're asked to type your name and to give the secret password. If you do it correctly, the BBS doorman admits you to the system. This process is called *logging on.*

✔ **Welcome Screen:** The Welcome Screen is pretty much what it says. The system identifies itself — usually with a flashy logo — and announces any impending special events, changes in the system, or what have you. Often the Welcome Screen states the BBS's mission — why it exists or what it intends to do.

✔ **Bulletin Menu:** The Bulletin Menu is where you can find all sorts of information about the system you just logged onto. You get a sense of what the system is going to be like by how the bulletin topics are worded. Typical bulletin items include system statistics: who called when, what files are most popular, rules of conduct, frequently asked questions (known as FAQs), and so on. Figure 1-1 is a typical array of just-in bulletin items. The BBS tells you which bulletins are new or different since the last time you logged on.

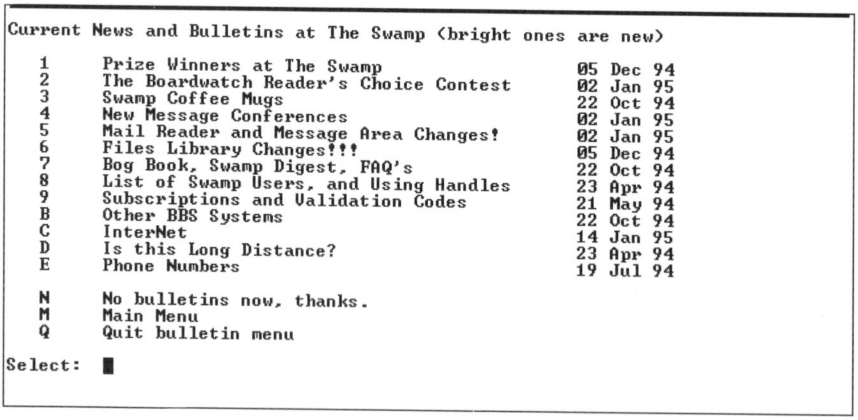

Figure 1-1:
The Bulletin
Menu for
The Swamp
offers a
range of
activities
from
ordering
coffee mugs
to getting a
list of other
BBSs.

```
Current News and Bulletins at The Swamp (bright ones are new)

   1     Prize Winners at The Swamp                      05 Dec 94
   2     The Boardwatch Reader's Choice Contest          02 Jan 95
   3     Swamp Coffee Mugs                               22 Oct 94
   4     New Message Conferences                         02 Jan 95
   5     Mail Reader and Message Area Changes!           02 Jan 95
   6     Files Library Changes!!!                        05 Dec 94
   7     Bog Book, Swamp Digest, FAQ's                   22 Oct 94
   8     List of Swamp Users, and Using Handles          23 Apr 94
   9     Subscriptions and Validation Codes              21 May 94
   B     Other BBS Systems                               22 Oct 94
   C     InterNet                                        14 Jan 95
   D     Is this Long Distance?                          23 Apr 94
   E     Phone Numbers                                   19 Jul 94

   N     No bulletins now, thanks.
   M     Main Menu
   Q     Quit bulletin menu

Select:  █
```

✔ **Main Menu:** Once you leave the Bulletin Menu, you're deposited at what's called the Main Menu. The Main Menu is command central for the whole BBS. By typing one of the commands displayed on the Main Menu, you are whisked to the feature of your desires. Figure 1-2 and Figure 1-3 are Main Menus from two different BBSs. Although the menus are different, they share some features and even share some commands.

If you're brand new to computers and are only familiar with Windows and its so-called *graphical user interface* (that's what the experts call Windows' on-screen design), you may never have encountered a Main Menu system before. Windows programs all have menu categories across the top with drop-down options. With a Main Menu like those used on a BBS, though, every current option is visible in a center-of-operations screen. What you see is what you can get. No point and click. No pop-up help. This is what we old-timers had to deal with in the days before Windows.

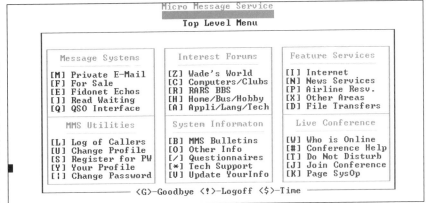

Figure 1-2:
Micro
Message
Service's
Main Menu
is command
central for
this system.

Figure 1-3:
The
Pegasus
Project BBS
Main Menu
is another
example of
how to
organize a
BBS.

✔ **Logging off:** When you're done, you need to politely say good-bye. Just as in real life, it is considered very rude to just hang up the phone with no warning. Usually, there's a Good-bye command from the Main Menu that you need to activate. After confirming that you really want to hang up, the BBS says farewell and hangs up for you. Sometimes, you get a thought for the day — just in case you didn't have one of your own.

Okay, now that you've done a BBS flyby, you're ready to start flight school — which is a lame way of herding you along to Chapter 2, where you can get logged on for the first time.

Speaking of flight school, remember how in the movie "Top Gun" everyone had a compelling nickname like Maverick, Goose, Iceman, and Viper? You'll also need a cool nickname when you log onto some of the systems in this book. So start working on a good one now, because you don't want to settle for a weak nickname simply because you're unprepared. "Top Gun" would have been a completely different movie if Tom Cruise's name had been Botanist rather than Maverick. And Sysops really hate changing nicknames once you've made a commitment to one.

Chapter 2
Logging On

- -

In This Chapter

▶ Logging on for the first time

▶ Getting validated

▶ Rambling through other systems

▶ Logging on the second time

- -

As space launches go, zooming into cyberspace is a space walk.

The first time you knock on the door of any BBS, though, expect to spend 10 to 20 minutes — depending on your words-per-minute keyboard stats — answering questions. In addition to name, rank, and serial number, the BBS has a checklist of geeky inquiries like, Do you want clearing codes sent? And you do, by the way. Want clearing codes sent, that is. But I'll talk about that later.

The point is that passing through that initial gauntlet of inquiries can be intimidating. So, by no mere coincidence, that's what this chapter is about: calling in — also known as logging on — for the first time and taking on cyberspace *mano-a-mano*.

And, because life should be faced straight on, you can actually go online with me for your very first time right now. Live. Together. Don't chicken out now! Take this book, sit down in front of Mr. Computer, and follow the bouncing cursor.

Of course, if you've done so much logging on that people are beginning to think you're a lumberjack, you should go find a chapter that covers something you're not quite so confident with. Let the rest of us take things at our own pace — one step at a time.

Logging on for the First Time

Since you're going online, you have to actually call someplace. Unless you have someplace else in mind, why not start at the top of the heap by logging on to the number-one BBS on *Boardwatch Magazine*'s Top 100 BBS list? That would be a bulletin-board system called Software Creations. (The complete Top 100 list appears in Appendix B.)

Software Creations is a BBS that bills itself as the *home of the authors* because more leading program authors, graphics artists, sound-effects engineers, musicians, story writers, creative directors, vendors, distributors, reviewers, and magazine editors/publishers use this system as their base than any system in the world. Basically, if it's cool, Software Creations has it first. That's why they're number one. Unlike the lonely little computer sitting in a hobbyist's den, Software Creations has walls of floor-to-ceiling computers, state-of-the-art phone systems, and professional technical-support personnel, all dedicated to running the system.

If you use Windows or work with software that makes it possible to run several programs at the same time, it's a good idea to save whatever you have open before cranking up your communications software. Voyaging into cyberspace can, though not often, freeze up the computer. If that happens, sometimes the only way to thaw the system is with a swift kick in the reset button. The problem with this kind of shock therapy, though, is that you lose whatever was in your computer's memory. If you didn't save your work, it's gone. Frequent saving is never bad advice.

As I mention in the Introduction — you did read that, didn't you? — because there are literally dozens of different communications programs out there, I hope you can understand the impossibility of including specific, step-by-step commands for each of them. The good news is that communications programs often use the same terminology, and sometimes even the same commands. That means that I can often point you in the right direction. The other good news is that fewer than a half-dozen communications software commands are needed to successfully navigate cyberspace. With my hints, you'll be able to fake your way through.

Dialing the phone

The first step in logging on is to dial the phone number of the BBS you want to call. In order to dial the phone number, you have to know how to do the following:

1. **Get your favorite telecommunications software in gear.**

2. **Open its *dialing directory*—a phone book containing BBS numbers.**

   Usually the command for this is Alt+D. Or try clicking on the icon of a phone book, if you're using a Windows program.

3. **Add the number you want to call, if it's not already in your dialing directory.**

   In this example, you want to call Software Creations at 508-368-7139. Chances are, you don't have that number — or any other number — in your dialing directory at this point.

4. **Give the dial command.**

   Programs vary, but usually you do this by highlighting the entry you want to dial and pressing Enter.

If this business of dialing directories and dialing commands has the room spinning and you gasping for air, warp on over to Appendix A. There's a section in there about Dueling with Dialing Directories to get you started. Breathe into a paper bag for a minute first, though.

Once you issue the dial command, whatever yours happens to be, a bunch of letters and numbers may flash across your computer screen. That's good. That's what's supposed to happen. You should also hear a dial tone and the sound of dialing.

If you do not hear a dial tone or the sound of dialing, your modem may not be working or may be hooked up improperly. I predict some troubleshooting action with the modem in your near future. Modem fixing is another thing I can't help with — especially at arm's length. Get a friend or a professional to lend a hand. If you're feeling particularly adventurous, you might want to pick up a copy of *Modems For Dummies*, also published by IDG Books Worldwide, and take a crack at it yourself. I'll still be here when you get the modem going.

After dialing Software Creations, don't be too surprised if you receive a busy signal. That's why your modem software has automatic redial. Usually only a few redial attempts are necessary before you get through.

Making the connection

When the BBS answers the phone, you hear some awful squawks and screeches. Although not fun to listen to, these noises are what you want to hear. They're the sounds of your modem wrestling with the BBS modem, trying to figure out how to communicate. Once they settle their differences, the modems go silent, the screen clears, and messages begin to appear. You may get the sensation that someone else is typing at your computer . . . which is not far from the truth.

After the squawks and screeches quiet down, if nothing else appears to be happening, then slowly count to ten. Sometimes the BBS can be a little slow on the uptake even after it answers the phone. If, after several seconds, you're still waiting expectantly for messages to begin, press Enter twice. This lets the other system know you're there. Then wait for signs of life.

If, after a minute or two, nothing streams in from *the other side*, then you can assume that it's time to hang it up and try again. When you dial up and get nothing, it doesn't mean you did anything wrong. Not by a long shot. Yes it's very disappointing to do everything right and not get rewarded, but silence is not sinister. It might just mean that the BBS system has a broken computer, that the phone line is bad, or that the BBS modem is not fully functional. That's why the proper response is a shrug of the shoulders and a redial.

It's also possible to get too much of a good thing — a flood of stuff appears on the screen, but it's gibberish. That is also grounds for hanging up and trying again. These things happen. Again, don't freak. Just hang up the connection and try again. If you get a lot of screen gibberish the second time you call, take a quick look at the sidebar in this chapter called "Taking out the garbage."

If you don't know how to get your modem to hang up, here are some things to try:

- In ProComm for Windows, the command to hang up the phone is to press Alt+F2 — or click the little hang-up-the-phone icon. Many DOS-modem programs use Alt+H — as in Alt+Hang up.

- Still stuck? The next option is to type three plus signs: +++. Then, after a second, the word OK should appear on the screen. That's your modem talking to you. Type **ATH** and press Enter.

- If the keyboard locks up as well, you have no choice but to press the computer's reset button. It may be nerve-racking to do this, but think of it as a rite of passage. As long as you saved before you started your online session, you won't lose anything. No reset button? Then shut off the computer. Be sure to wait a minute before turning it back on.

Whatever communications software you're using, don't forget to consult the wisdom stored in its help command — especially if you're using a Windows telecommunications program with search capabilities. Create a self-esteem-building moment for yourself by looking something up and then solving a problem using nothing more than your own keen intelligence. Aw, c'mon — give it a shot. The worst that can happen is that you'll verify your hypothesis that help systems are utterly worthless. But you *might* get lucky and find they are helpful after all. People have spent money on the lotto with slimmer odds. Besides, once you *try*, at least you can stop feeling guilty that you never tried. And that certainly builds self-esteem right there.

Taking out the garbage

If you're making the connection to that BBS out there — you can hear the other modem making mating calls to your modem — but keep getting meaningless symbols and letters on the screen, then it's time to put on the rubber gloves. You'll have to mess with the guts of your communications software.

The issue is that your protocol may be improperly set. A _protocol_ determines the basic ground rules for how the modems talk to each other. What the BBS expects and what your modem does have to match. If they don't match, you get garbage on the screen.

You take out the garbage by changing the protocol. Generally, the protocol you want is 8-N-1.

Right now, it might be incorrectly set to 7-E-2 or even 7-E-1. Although every communications program has a different approach, try looking in the following places to adjust your protocol:

✔ The Dialing Directory — the option for protocol may be right there next to the phone number.

✔ The configuration part of the program.

If you're having problems finding this, call the manufacturers of the modem software. They can help you out. They may not be of much help in general, but _this_ question they can answer.

Introducing yourself

Digressing for a moment, I want to reveal, for the first time ever, the top suggestion Sysops have for first-timers — _pay attention to the BBS screen and follow instructions._

People waste gobs and gobs of hours every year — according to official government tallies — figuring out how to do things that are already explained in detail two feet from their faces. Although _you_ would never ignore the instructions, I mention this only so you might do a good deed and warn your less-diligent friends.

Okay, one more aside, and then I'll continue. Some people believe that, even if they do figure out how to get online, the BBS itself is a huge, clumsy thing to use. As it turns out, on a BBS you have, at any given moment, maybe 25 choices. Tops. Compare that to the software you're used to using like Word for Windows, which has literally hundreds of options at any given moment. The software system that runs the BBS is very simple to use — especially if you pay heed to the instructions on the screen. So don't go into cyberspace with the mindset that it's more than you can handle.

Picking a language

Speaking of instructions, if you've been following mine for logging on to Software Creations, you should be staring at something like Figure 2-1 on your very own computer screen. What you see is the very first question in your logon lineup. If you're not actually following along, that's okay; you can experience the thrill vicariously and apply what you read to logging on to another system.

```
Enter Language # to use (Enter)=no change?
```

If you want English, just press Enter. You can get away with a simple Enter response for this option because, if you look at Figure 2-1 again, you see that English is the *default* option. The default is what you get if you make no other selection. It's the go-with-the-flow option. (Enter)=no change means that if you press Enter, the default is selected for you.

- ✔ For fun on Software Creations, try the Startrek option, Number 16, sometime.

- ✔ In case you're wondering, selecting Portuguese, for example, doesn't mean that E-Mail conversations and online activities are translated into Portuguese on the spot. No. Selecting Portuguese just causes system prompts and menus to appear in Portuguese. After that, you're on your own. Hopefully, you can find someone to send you a message in the language of your choice.

Figure 2-1:
Parlez-vous français?
You can if you log onto Software Creations, the number-one BBS on the *Boardwatch* Top 100 list.

```
CONNECT 2400/ARQ/LAPM/V42BIS
CONNECT 2400 / 03-06-95 (10:26:44)
(Error Correcting Modem Detected)

«     Software Creations BBS     »
PCBoard (R) v15.2/250 - Node 32

Operational Languages Available:

1  - English  (Default)
2  - Novice prompts
3  - RoboComm/1stReader
4  - Dutch
5  - Deutsch
6  - Danish
7  - Español
8  - Francais
9  - Norwegian
10 - Portuguese
11 - Finnish

Enter Language # to use (Enter)=no change? █
```

Using graphics

Usually, the next question on any BBS is about your graphics capabilities. Software Creations is no different.

```
Do you want graphics (Enter)=no?
```

Graphics, in the context of a BBS, can mean anything from attractive, colorful screens to cool online games. The safest answer is to press Enter and not use graphics.

There are two reasons for not using graphics. One is that it takes more time to send a graphic screen from the BBS computer to yours. You have to trade off your desire for color with the sluggish response. The sluggish response isn't just a matter of annoyance, it's also a matter of dollars and sense, since the longer you're online waiting for another pretty screen, the bigger the phone bill. The faster your modem, though, the smaller the time lag. Look on your modem or in your modem manual. If you see 2400, your modem is slow. If you see 9600, 14.4, or 28.8, your modem is fast.

The second reason for just saying no to graphics is that your computer may not be set up for them. Anyway, even if you pass on graphics now, you can always change your mind later. This is not a permanent-record kind of choice.

  ✔ If you want to try out the graphics, then press Y, for Yes, and Enter.

  ✔ Are you seeing _[and ^[or even Ü and Ä on your screen? If so, chances are you've taken the graphics option, and your system isn't set up to handle it. See Appendix D, "I Want My ANSI.SYS!," for some tips. Even if your screen looks funny, you can still finish the logon process. The extra junk on the monitor won't impede functionality. In other words, it looks bad but still works fine.

After you make your graphics decision, the BBS displays its logo, tells you a little about itself, and then asks you to share a little about yourself, as in Figure 2-2.

The next two questions are simple. When asked, type your first name and press Enter; then type your last name and finish it up with the traditional Enter. I wonder what Cher does about a last name when she logs on? Such are the mysteries that make BBSing so exciting.

If you make a typo, backspace over the error and type the correct character. Once you've pressed Enter, there's no way to scroll back and fix it. But don't panic. Eventually, you are asked to review your responses to check for accuracy. Then you can step forward to clear your name. So to speak.

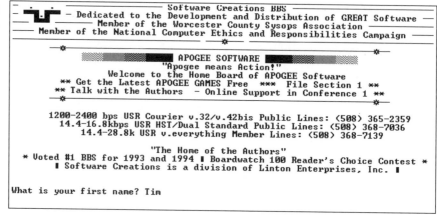

Figure 2-2:
This BBS's
opening
screen
provides
information
about its
mission and
pedigree—
and asks
who you
are.

```
 ┌────────────────────── Software Creations BBS ──────────────────────┐
 ── ⌐⌐ ── Dedicated to the Development and Distribution of GREAT Software ──
 ──────────── Member of the Worcester County Sysops Association ────────────
 ── Member of the National Computer Ethics and Responsibilities Campaign ──

       ※                                                           ※
                ▨▨▨▨▨▨▨▨▨▨▨ APOGEE SOFTWARE ▨▨▨▨▨▨▨▨▨▨▨
                         "Apogee means Action!"
                 Welcome to the Home Board of APOGEE Software
          ** Get the Latest APOGEE GAMES Free  ***  File Section 1 **
          ** Talk with the Authors  - Online Support in Conference 1 **
       ※                                                           ※

      1200-2400 bps USR Courier v.32/v.42bis Public Lines: (508) 365-2359
         14.4-16.8kbps USR HST/Dual Standard Public Lines: (508) 368-7036
          14.4-28.8k USR v.everything Member Lines: (508) 368-7139

                         "The Home of the Authors"
      * Voted #1 BBS for 1993 and 1994 ▮ Boardwatch 100 Reader's Choice Contest *
          ▮ Software Creations is a division of Linton Enterprises, Inc. ▮

 What is your first name? Tim
```

Registering

After you press Enter at your last name, the BBS attempts to find you in the user membership rolls. Guess what? You're not there. So the computer says

```
YOUR NAME not found in USER's file.
If you have entered your name correctly and wish to log on as
          a new caller, type (C), otherwise type (R) to re-
          enter your name: (C)
```

You want to register as a new caller: C. This response initiates the process of introducing yourself to the system. The BBS assumes you want to register — 'cause if you don't, the call is over — and even supplies the C for you. How's that for friendly? The only action you need to take is a confident upward movement of the right pinkie finger, followed by a firm, downward stroke upon the Enter key.

However, if you get a message back from the BBS repeating your name and asking if you're from Nome, Alaska, or if Software Creations tells you how many times you've called before and asks for your password, don't worry. You don't have a twin or a clone running around in Alaska. It just means that someone with the same name as you has logged on to the system before. If your name is Bob Smith, you're probably used to stuff like this. Here's what to do:

✔ If the BBS asks, `Are you So-And-So from Nome, Alaska, Y or N?` Simply press N. You are then asked if you want to log on as a new user. Press Y and this time, when asked for your first name, enter a variation on the name from Nome. Bobby Smith or Robert Smith.

✔ If the BBS simply assumes you're from Nome and wants a password, hit Enter. Do that a few times, and the BBS will hang up on you — which is what you want. Call in again. This time, when it asks for your name, enter a variation on the name from Nome. Bobby Smith or Robert Smith.

Next, Software Creations gives you an informational screen, as in Figure 2-3.

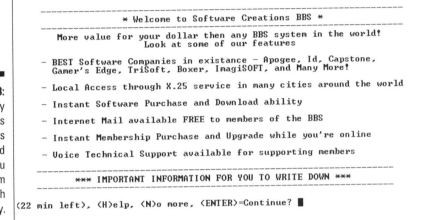

```
---------------------------------------------------------------
            * Welcome to Software Creations BBS *
---------------------------------------------------------------
     More value for your dollar then any BBS system in the world!
                   Look at some of our features

  - BEST Software Companies in existance - Apogee, Id, Capstone,
    Gamer's Edge, TriSoft, Boxer, ImagiSOFT, and Many More!

  - Local Access through X.25 service in many cities around the world

  - Instant Software Purchase and Download ability

  - Internet Mail available FREE to members of the BBS

  - Instant Membership Purchase and Upgrade while you're online

  - Voice Technical Support available for supporting members

---------------------------------------------------------------
      *** IMPORTANT INFORMATION FOR YOU TO WRITE DOWN ***
---------------------------------------------------------------
(22 min left), (H)elp, (N)o more, (ENTER)=Continue? █
```

Figure 2-3:
Every system is proud of its features and tells you about them at each opportunity.

Okay, it's a bragging screen. When you've got cool stuff, why not flaunt it? But notice that, at the bottom, there's a mysterious query.

```
(22 min left), (H)elp, (N)o more, (ENTER)=Continue?
```

You often see this kind of message on BBSs. Take a second to examine the parts of speech in this message to better understand what it's trying to say.

✔ (22 min left)

Did you know that your call was being timed? Every minute you spend on this or any other BBS is on the clock. Your time card gets punched the moment you type your name. After your allotted visiting time has expired, you are dropped — in a nice way, of course — and the system hangs up on you. Don't dawdle.

✔ (H)elp, (N)o more, (ENTER)=Continue?

The letter in parentheses is the character that activates that command. H gives you Help. N selects the No More — or stop — option, and pressing the Enter key means "please give me more." This is how it works: Suppose you've pressed H to get a screenful of information explaining your options.

> After you read one screen, pressing Enter advances the text to the next screenful. Once you're done reading this help topic, you can press N to stop and move to the next option.

Should you `Continue` or is it time to `No more`? What would Superman do? The answer depends on whatever is on the screen at the moment. In Figure 2-3, there's a line that implies that Important Information is coming up. I guess this means you better press Enter to continue.

Then, as promised, after you get around to pressing Enter, the important information about the system is displayed. If you are actually logging on right now, be sure to read the instructions and caveats.

At the bottom of the screen is another question:

```
Would you like to register with us, Timmy? (Enter)=yes? (Y)
```

Except, of course, your name will be in the place of Timmy. The answer is Yes. You do want to register. Press Enter for Yes.

- ✔ Registering doesn't cost any money or obligate you in any way.

- ✔ Registering means that you intend to give the BBS a try. For the privilege of kicking their tires, you must reveal your address, phone number, and some other information about your computer and modem. This is the only legitimate time you will be asked for personal data. Good Sysops want to know who is using their system. Since Software Creations is one of the BBSs on the Top 100 list, you can assume they do their best to guard your privacy.

- ✔ No BBS can absolutely guarantee your privacy, however, or the confidentiality of anything you do online. Many systems have a warning up front reminding you of that very fact. On a BBS of quality, it's an acceptable risk. It's less of a risk than using a cellular phone, where people with the right equipment can listen in or even clone your account.

Selecting a password

After agreeing to register, you have to come up with a password. In one way, the password is like your personal identification number (PIN). It is secret. The password is what confirms that it's really you calling in. Otherwise, anyone could log on with your name, eat up your time, act boorishly, and leave you to deal with the consequences. Talk about an evil twin! One thing that separates passwords from PINs is that you can and should change your password often.

So you need a good password. People tend to get lazy when concocting a password. Not you, of course, but friends of yours may. Tell them to put a little backbone into the effort and come up with something better than using a firstandlastname mushed together as a password. Other password faux pas include using your phone number, birth date, spouse's name, or anything else that someone could easily guess. Got it? Okay.

```
Password (One word please!)? (          )
```

Don't be startled, while typing the password, to see periods instead of the letters you thought you were typing. This is part of the secrecy. No one looking over your shoulder can see what you're doing! After inputting the secret word, press Enter.

```
Re-enter password to verify? (........ )
```

This isn't the same question as the other password question. This one asks you to type the password a second time just to make sure you didn't make a typo the first time — but couldn't see it because of the periods instead of the letters. Retype your password and press Enter when done. If you get it wrong, you get a chance to do it all over again. Remember to remember your password. You'll need it whenever you log on to this system.

Entering your personal information

During the registration process, it's okay to give the BBS personal information. And, when the BBS asks for information in a certain format, please help out by honoring the request.

```
Enter your city and state information in the format CITY,
                STATE
```

This is a short version of the next question. In Figure 2-4, you can see what your screen looks like after you enter your password twice and then move on to the name-and-address phase. In this case, you type the names of your city and state with a comma separating them.

```
Please enter your daytime phone number in the format XXX-XXX-
                XXXX
```

Want to get off to a bad start with the Sysop? Simply ignore the format instructions and enter something that looks like this: (310) 555-4567 or this: 310.555.4567. Neither one of those is what the Sysop's looking for, now is it? Either of these entries will gum up the system. Since the instructions specify XXX-XXX-XXXX as the desired format, make sure your response looks like: 310-555-4567. Of course, use your own phone number. But you knew that, didn't you? When the answer is complete, press Enter.

Name your CPU and have your druthers

The next three questions are illustrated in Figure 2-5.

```
        -  Use your real name, address, and phone number
        -  Check all files before you upload, we do not accept
           RETAIL FILES, PIRATE or HACKING files, or ADULT files.
Would you like to register with us, Timmy? (Enter)=yes? (Y)

Password (One word please!)? (........    )

Re-enter password to verify? (........    )

┌─────────────────────────────────────────────────────────────────────┐
│ Enter your city and state information in the format CITY, STATE       │
│ Callers from outside the United States, please include your country.  │
│ Please do not abbreviate your city - you may know what it is, but we won't. │
│     ** Do not enter fake information or we cannot validate you **     │
└─────────────────────────────────────────────────────────────────────┘
? (Anytown, CA              )

┌─────────────────────────────────────────────────────────────────────┐
│ Please enter your daytime phone number in the format XXX-XXX-XXXX     │
│ Callers from outside the US/Canada, please include country code.      │
│ ** Do not enter fake information (555-1212) or we cannot validate you ** │
└─────────────────────────────────────────────────────────────────────┘
? (█          )
```

Figure 2-4:
When
entering
data, do so
in the format
requested.
Passwords
appear as
dots to
protect
privacy.

```
Brand of CPU you are using? (         )
```

What the question is asking, in English, is for the type of computer you've
got. You can be as specific or generic as you like. You can even leave this one
blank. It would be neighborly if you'd put IBM, Macintosh, or something in
the spot — even if all you can manage is the type of processing chip that runs
your computer, like 486/66, Pentium, or whatever. If you don't know what
chip you've got, that's okay. Stick with the kind of computer. Anyway, when
done, press Enter.

```
Clear the screen between each message? (Y)
```

The question is whether you want the BBS to automatically tidy up instructions
and junk at the bottom of the screen before scrolling on to another screen. This
is a buttons-and-bows kind of option. It's also the kinder and gentler way of
asking if you want clearing codes sent. Press Enter for the Y response.

```
Default Protocol Desired (Enter)=no change? (N)
```

Figure 2-5 shows the whole question. The protocol has to do with getting and
sending files to and from the BBS. The usual answer is pressing Enter to go with
No Default Protocol (ask each time). Chapter 3 illustrates in more
detail how to get and receive files. I even explain what a protocol is. For now,
press Enter, and you see, as in Figure 2-5, something like this:

```
Please wait - Adding TIMMY THOMERSON to Quick Index File ...
Thanks, Timmy, your registration information is saved.
```

```
 Brand of CPU you are using? <IBM                             >

Clear the screen between each message? <Y>

   <A> ASCII            <Text files only>
   <X> Xmodem           <Windows Terminal>
   <C> Xmodem-CRC
   <O> 1K-Xmodem        <Procomm's Ymodem>
   <F> 1K-Xmodem/G
   <Y> Ymodem           <Batch U/L and D/L>
   <G> Ymodem/G         <Batch U/L and D/L>
   <Z> DSZ Zmodem       <Batch U/L and D/L>
   <H> HS/Link Bi-directional Protocol
=> <N> No default protocol <ask each time>

Default Protocol Desired <Enter)=no change? <N>


Please wait - Adding TIMMY THOMERSON to Quick Index File ...

Thanks, Timmy, your registration information is saved.
```

Figure 2-5:
So many
protocols,
so little time.
I'll deal with
them in the
next
chapter.

Two things. One, you see your name in this message, not the name of Timmy Thomerson. Two, this doesn't mean you're finished. Not by a long shot. You're almost halfway through, though, if that's any consolation.

Subscribing?

You see some screens go by. Finally, you get the following opportunity:

```
Would you like to subscribe? (       )
```

Subscribe is an altogether different word from register. Subscribe means you're ready to increase your debt-load. You don't have to subscribe just to try the system out. So, for now, press N for No and then press Enter to get the next question.

```
Press (ENTER) to continue or (G) to log off and change num-
               bers ? (       )
```

Press Enter so you can continue on the BBS. If you say good-bye to the system, you won't finish the entire initial logon process and will not be entered into the system.

Getting into the system

After you press Enter, Software Creations starts scrolling a bunch of advertisements for games and stuff available on the BBS. If you've logged on with me, you can read the ads on your own time, okay? Let's press onward. Oops, no, there is no *onward* key, I just mean let's continue.

When the Software Creations screen stops scrolling, look at the bottom of the screen to see what it wants now. If it says to press any key, then press something on your keyboard. If you see `(N)o more, (ENTER)=Continue?`, press N and then press Enter to put an end to the commercials.

```
Scan Message Base Since 'Last Read' (Enter)=yes?
```

You don't want to scan for messages at this juncture. Reply with N and press Enter. I'll deal with messages later on. If you have run ahead and actually logged on to Software Creations and pressed Enter for yes, you find two automatic welcome messages from the Sysop waiting for you. The messages will still be there the next time you log on. For now, just finish the logging process. The kids are starting to get cranky.

Setting up an account

After you press Enter, the BBS tells you that it's making a user's account for you. No obligation. The user's account is just the record of who you are. BBS operators like to track who's traipsing through their system — both for personal and legal reasons.

Read the screens. In turn, you are asked for your first name, middle initial, and last name. If you're not sure of the answers, take a look at your driver's license. It has all that stuff.

Don't put that license away too quickly; next the system wants to know your address and zip code. Please pay attention to the way the BBS wants to receive the data. City only. Then state only. Read what's on the screen. Even if you make a typo, relax. Once everything has been entered, you get a chance to look at what you've written and make changes.

```
Is the above information correct Y)es N)o?
```

If your name, address, and phone number are all in the right places, press Y — which is sometimes considered a vowel, by the way — and then press Enter. If you've made an error or if the cat ran across the keyboard when you were filling out this form, press N and then Enter, and you can make it right.

Are we there yet? No. But at least most of the questions are easy to answer. Date of birth — in the correct mm/dd/yy format — is next. Each of these inquiries is self-explanatory. There are no wrong answers, so do your best and press Enter when done typing. One question may make you pause.

```
Are you a Shareware Author Y)es N)o? (   )
```

It shouldn't surprise you too much to discover that you are not a shareware author. Press N and then Enter.

```
Are you a Graphic Artist Y)es N)o? (    )
```

If you don't know whether you're a graphic artist or not, chances are you are not. Press N and then Enter.

```
Do you have a CD-ROM drive Y)es N)o? (    )
```

Type the appropriate response — Y for Yes or N for No — and press Enter.

```
Have you ever registered a Shareware program Y)es N)o? (    )
```

Answer N if you don't understand the question. I cover shareware in the next chapter. Someday you'll not only understand the question, but you'll be able to proudly respond, Yes!

```
Are you a SYSOP (If yes do SYSOP registration - Type DOOR 3
             at menu) Y)es N)o? (    )
```

Probably you're not a Sysop quite yet. However, in Part III of this book, you can find out how to become one. Who knows? I may be logging on to your BBS soon! Right now, however, you're almost finished with your first logon.

Becoming an unverified new user

After answering the last question and pressing Enter, you get a notice from Software Creations that you must read Bulletins 1 through 4 if you want to be upgraded.

- ✔ Upgraded? Yeah. When you first log on, you're at the very bottom of the BBS-user hierarchy. You are what is called an *unverified new user*. That means two things. One, it means that you can't do very much for very long. Basically, you can look, but don't touch. Two, to the Sysop it means that you're an unknown quantity — hopefully friend, but potentially foe.

- ✔ To become verified, expect a phone call, letter, or some other contact from the Sysop. Once they verify that you're not the guy seen on "America's Most Wanted," they give you more time and access to more features.

- ✔ If you support the system with money, you get even more time and are free to roam the system.

- ✔ Although a little inconvenient, it's a good sign when a BBS won't give you full access without attempting to verify that you are the person you say you are. It shows that the Sysop cares who's on the system and is doing everything possible to keep the riffraff to a minimum.

After pressing Enter to continue, you see the final question about saving money on long distance. As much as we all want to save money on long distance charges, for now resist the impulse to read about it. Press N and then Enter.

Congratulations! You have done it. After answering all those questions, you have now crossed the border into cyberland. Your decoder ring is in the mail. Now you can, for free, use this BBS for 40 minutes every day (thanks to the courtesy of Software Creations).

Every BBS has its own formula for granting online time and resources. You will find that most BBSs generously grant some free access time. If you find yourself logging on a lot, then do the right thing and support the system. If you are using the system for free, it's considered good manners to drop the Sysop a thank you note every now and then.

After yet another welcoming screen and a request to Press any key to continue..., the sky opens up, and, even though it's the dead of winter, birds begin to sing. Huzzah! The Main Menu! (See Figure 2-6.)

Finishing up the logon job

If you are now actually online with Software Creations, take a moment to scan the four bulletins the Sysop politely asked you to read. The Sysop checks to see if you've read them — they have their ways — and awards extended online time if you have. Think of this as a bonus round. Besides, the reason the Sysop is insisting you read the bulletins is that they actually help you use the system. It's a crazy thought.

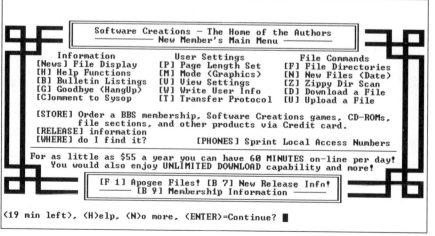

Figure 2-6:
After burrowing through a maze of questions, the New Member's Main Menu is, at last, revealed!

```
        Software Creations - The Home of the Authors
                 ── New Member's Main Menu ──

      Information           User Settings          File Commands
  [News] File Display    [P] Page Length Set    [F] File Directories
  [H] Help Functions     [M] Mode (Graphics)    [N] New Files (Date)
  [B] Bulletin Listings  [V] View Settings      [Z] Zippy Dir Scan
  [G] Goodbye (HangUp)    [W] Write User Info    [D] Download a File
  [C]omment to Sysop     [T] Transfer Protocol  [U] Upload a File

  [STORE] Order a BBS membership, Software Creations games, CD-ROMs,
          file sections, and other products via Credit card.
  [RELEASE] information
  [WHERE] do I find it?        [PHONES] Sprint Local Access Numbers

  For as little as $55 a year you can have 60 MINUTES on-line per day!
      You would also enjoy UNLIMITED DOWNLOAD capability and more!

           [F 1] Apogee Files! [B 7] New Release Info!
              ── [B 9] Membership Information ──

<19 min left>, (H)elp, (N)o more, <ENTER>=Continue? ▮
```

To read the bulletins, the first step is to ask for the Bulletin Listings. From the New Member's Main Menu, press B and then Enter. In a moment, you see something like Figure 2-7.

After getting the Bulletin Listings menu, press 1 and Enter to see Welcome to the BBS information. After reading a screenful, press Enter to continue until you've read the entire document. Then, still at the Bulletin Listings Menu, press 2 and Enter to read the Privacy Act Notice. Continue the process with Bulletin 3 — User Agreement — and Bulletin 4, Access Information.

If you accidentally hit Enter twice, you may find yourself back at the New Member's Main Menu instead of the Bulletin Listings Menu. To get back to the Bulletin Listings Menu, press B and then Enter.

When finished with the required reading (there will be no quiz), you see the prompt `(H)elp, (1-30), Bulletin List Command?`. Press Enter to flip back to the New Member's Main Menu.

Saying good-bye — logging off

When you're ready to bid adieu to your cyberconnection, it is considered bad form to just hang up without going through the good-bye ritual. However, if you must hang up on a BBS without the ritual, you won't blow up the BBS computer or hurt anything. But don't be an Ugly Cyberian unless it's an emergency. Besides, going through the process ensures that your time card is punched out properly.

Figure 2-7: Most BBSs have some variation of this Bulletin Listings menu to provide instructions, notices, and help.

```
┌─────────────────────────────────────────────────────────────┐
│   ┌──────────────────────────────────────────────────┐       │
│   │   Software Creations - The Home of the Authors    │      │
│   │   ───────────── Bulletin Listings ─────────────   │      │
│   └──────────────────────────────────────────────────┘      │
│        (1) Welcome to the BBS     (3) User Agreement         │
│        (2) Privacy Act Notice     (4) Access Information      │
│   ┌──────────────────────────────────────────────────┐       │
│   │  6) Apogee Catalog!    7) Coming Soon From Apogee! │      │
│   └──────────────────────────────────────────────────┘      │
│   10) ASP Approved BBS    17) Important Names    24) Real Names │
│   11) What is Shareware   18) Sprint Local Access 25) PC Catalog │
│   12) Nodes Caller Log    19) Become a Dist HUB!  26) Summer Camp! │
│   13) Download Violation  20) Unzipping Files    27) Retail Uploads │
│   14) Download Problems?  21) Upload Guidelines  28) Where to find it │
│   15) Modems/Phone Lines  22) Files by mail      29) BBS Direct! │
│   16) Distribution Sites  23) Your Statistics    30) Dream Forge │
│   ┌──────────────────────────────────────────────────┐       │
│   │  Read Bulletin (9) for information on membership! │      │
│   └──────────────────────────────────────────────────┘      │
│   (H)elp, (1-30), Bulletin List Command? █                   │
└─────────────────────────────────────────────────────────────┘
```

To signal that you're ready to hang up now, at the `Main Board Command?` prompt, press G — for Goodbye — and then press Enter. Complicated, huh?

How do I know that G is the command for hanging up? Simple. I looked at the instructions on the screen. On the New Member's Main Menu, certain letters are enclosed in [brackets]. Typing the letter shown in the bracket and pressing Enter activates the command to the right of that letter. In this case, [G] means Goodbye (HangUp).

Before you can leave, though, Software Creations makes another pitch at getting you to subscribe — that is, pay money. Since you haven't had a chance to try anything out yet, no one is really expecting an affirmative response at this point. So press N for No and then press Enter.

The last message you see before going **hasta la bye-bye** is: `Press (ENTER) to continue or (G) to logoff and change numbers ? (   )`.

Press G to *log off* — which is computer for hang up the phone. I bet that on the Star-Trek-language version you'd see `Beam me out of here, Scotty`, instead of the more nerd-like command to log off.

Normally, as the system hangs you up, you see a report of the amount of time you've just spent online. It's amazing how time flies!

After issuing the logoff command, make sure the other system actually hangs up. I've been on systems where the line stays un-hung for several minutes before the connection actually terminates. After you give the BBS a chance to finish its cycle, issue your own hang-up command — try clicking on the hang-up icon if you use Windows, or pressing Alt+H if you're a DOS diehard.

That's it. You are now a citizen of cyberspace!

Getting Validated

As I said before, when you first log on you are an unknown quantity until someone from the BBS contacts you. This contact can take many forms.

- ✔ You may receive a normal, voice phone call from the Sysop. It's quick and painless. The Sysop just asks you to repeat some of the personal data you left online. That's it.

- ✔ The BBS computer might call your computer and ask you to verify personal information.

- ✔ You might be asked to call a computerized phone system to verify your data.

✔ You may get a letter in the mail, asking you to fill out a form and maybe send a copy of your driver's license.

✔ Some systems can actually handle credit-card payments. If you're willing to subscribe, you get instant access to the system. Money talks in cyberspace just as in the real world.

Be prepared for the inevitable lag time between your first logon and getting your BBS pit pass. No matter what the validation method, getting verified may take time. If the system uses an automatic method, the delay is slight. Otherwise, it may take anywhere from a few hours (to receive a validation phone call) to a week (for snail mail). It is unrealistic to expect, on your first phone call (to have 100 percent access to everything and be able to use the system into the wee hours of the night.

Rambling through Other Systems

In your little field trip to Software Creations, you saw one version of the first-time logon. When you call another BBS, you'll notice that, although the logon steps may not be exactly the same, the issues you encounter during the process are not too far afield. After all, there are only so many things a BBS could possibly be interested in about you.

Same question, new words

Sometimes another system asks a question that seems familiar — like, Do you want graphics? — in a new way. The graphics issue can be broached as Do you want ANSI? or Do you want color?, or you may even be shown a blinking word and asked if you can see that it's blinking. No matter how it's phrased, you should be able to deal with it.

Déjà log on

If you log on to DSC, deltaComm Online, or PC-Ohio — their descriptions and numbers are listed in Appendix B — you notice that their logon sequence is amazingly close to Software Creations' logon sequence. Were these Sysops mind-linked when they set up their systems? Is this one of those Unsolved Mysteries? Perhaps. It is more likely, however, that these fine Sysops have all selected the same brand of BBS software to run their systems. It's called PCBoard. But PCBoard isn't the only BBS software out there. Other favorite programs include Wildcat!, TBBS, MajorBBS, and many others. The point is, even though there are thousands and thousands of BBSs, you'll find many of them have an identical logon mechanism and command structure.

Multiple personalities

While I'm sure you would never do a thing like this, some people attempt to extend their complimentary time ad infinitum by logging on under a series of different names. It's the oldest trick in the book. Putting aside that it's dishonest and rude, it's also the number-one thing that drives Sysops crazy, because of the time it wastes. So tell your friend who's thinking of doing this to forget it and get a life. Besides, you might as well know right now that, as one Sysop put it, "We can usually spot them [the multiple loggers], since a person's typing style and usage patterns are about as individual as fingerprints."

Making the case for default

Also, Software Creations makes it very clear, at every question, what the default is. `Enter=Yes` or `Enter=Default` is spelled out each time. Other systems may indicate the default, or normal, response in a more subtle way.

```
Do you want this? (Y/n)
```

From reading the question above, can you figure out whether the default answer is Yes or No? Look carefully at the question. Okay, I'll give you a hint. Look at the capitalization. See how the Y is uppercase? The n is lowercase? The capital-letter response is the normal response, and it's the choice that is invoked if you press Enter. Keep an eye open for that uppercase/lowercase business. You'll see it a lot.

The following sections cover some common first-logon questions you didn't encounter during your foray into the land of Software Creations.

If you are online and get confused by a question you don't understand, your best bet is to simply press Enter and accept the default. Chances are, it's what you want anyway. Besides, if it isn't, you can always change it later. The point is to move forward.

Taming tech topics

There are a few traditional technical questions that are bound to make a high-tech appearance at some point. There's no avoiding these oldies but goodies.

Set screen width

Straight from the Top Ten Antique Technical Questions is that old favorite:

```
How many characters fit on one line?
```

This isn't a twist on the philosophical debate about dancing angels on the head of a pin. The *characters on one line* question refers to the width of your screen. Why is this even an issue? Back in the days of the pioneers, computers could display only 40 characters on one line at a time. Nowadays, the answer is 80. Always 80. Granted, with small fonts and a good monitor, 80 is not the real answer, but it's the correct answer in this situation.

Check out the top

Typically, the next question appears after a list of numbers has just slithered up the side of the screen.

```
What is the number at the top of your screen (Usually 24
                lines)
```

The number at the top of the list is the answer. As indicated by the question, the answer is usually 24. Don't argue. Just type that in and press Enter.

Stop the pages

Nothing is more frustrating than reams and reams of information whizzing by before you can read it. That's what this next question wants to fix.

```
Do you want page pausing (Y/n):
```

The question means: When there's more than one screenful of information on a topic, do you want the computer to stop after one screen and wait for you to enter a command before displaying the next screen? This is called *page pausing,* and your answer should be Yes. It's the civilized approach.

Use an editor

Here are two versions of the same burning question — do you want to use a full-screen editor?

```
Would you like to use a Full Screen Editor (Y/n)
Use the MaxEd full-screen editor [y, N, ?=help]
```

"What is a full-screen editor?" is more to the point. Full-screen editors have to do with message writing. This question is not about whether you do or don't want to write messages. It's about *how* you're going to write messages. Have you heard of E-Mail? That's what this question's all about. E-Mail is coming up in Chapter 5.

For now, just to show you how different two systems can be, notice that the top question indicates that the default answer is yes. In the bottom question, no is the norm. Which is right? As it turns out, this is a personal-taste question, and you won't know which you prefer until later. Also note that in the second question you have a new option. If you type a question mark, this system explains exactly what the choice you're making is all about. Say yes for now; you can always make adjustments later.

```
Would you like to be prompted for Prepared Message Text
        (y/N):
```

This is another E-Mail-related question. Press Enter and accept their No suggestion. I cover this in Chapter 9 in more detail.

Going for graphics

Here are three more ways to ask the familiar question: Do you want graphics?

```
Does your system support ANSI Screen controls (Y,n,?=help)
Use IBM-PC characters [y,N,?=help]?
ANSI codes/terminal emulation allowed.
```

When Software Creations asks the question, the answer depends on the speed of your modem and the setup of your computer, and that's the case with all BBSs. To be honest, fewer things can go wrong if you choose no. On the other hand, if aesthetics are important to you, or if you intend to play games, say yes. Either way, you can always change your mind later.

Finding hotkeys

A hotkey sounds like something stolen, so you may wonder if the system is accusing you of thievery when you encounter this question:

```
Use 'hotkeys' [Y,n,?=help]?
```

Actually, hotkeys are supposed to be a labor-saving feature. Here's how the hotkey works. Remember the New Member's Main Menu with the letters in brackets? Pressing G and Enter meant Good-bye? If you turn hotkeys on, you don't have to press Enter any more when the computer is waiting for a one-letter command. If you press G, it automatically goes to Good-bye. No Enter required. This is another personal-taste issue — there is no right answer — but we should all have a hotkey at least once in our lives.

No nulls is good nulls

My personal favorite BBS question is

```
How many Nulls?
```

The answer is 0. I don't know if no nulls is a double negative. What's the old saying, two nulls don't make a right?

Scrollin' on the river

When you're logging on for the first time, the Sysop needs to present you with a great deal of information and instructions. As you saw in the Software Creations logon, screens and screens of stuff scrolled by, but you had the option to press Enter to continue or N for no more. Sometimes the way to indicate to the BBS that you're done reading isn't so clearly spelled out. Raising your hand in cyberspace doesn't work very well.

Here are some clues:

✔ `(19 min left). (H)elp, More?`

This is a typical message at the bottom of the screen. It is a puzzle because it's asking if you want more, but gives no clues about how to say yes or no. The secret is that the system assumes you do want more. Therefore, if you just press Enter, you get the next screen. However, you can also press N for No and then press Enter; when you do that, it's like yanking the cord on a train. You get no more screens on that topic.

Sometimes pressing N doesn't work. In that case, try Q for quit.

Sometimes you can press Ctrl+C to stop a scrolling screen.

✔ `More - [Y]es, [N]o, [C]ontinuous`

If you can read faster than a speeding bullet, or if scanning the material is all that's needed, press C and then Enter for the material to scroll by without stopping at every screen.

To freeze a runaway scroll, try Ctrl+S. To unfreeze or restart the scroll, press Ctrl+Q.

✔ `<CR> to continue`

You may run into the <CR> instruction.

> <CR> is short for Carriage Return, which is what the Enter key was called on typewriters in the days of yore. The above instruction is another way to tell you to press the Enter key.

Donning a secret disguise

The Lone Ranger, Batman, and Zorro would not necessarily be welcome on every BBS system. While some systems do not allow their users to hide behind the anonymity of an alias or, borrowing from CB-radio jargon, a *handle*, others do.

Some believe that allowing handles protects privacy. After all, who wants to broadcast their name to everyone who logs on? Also, handles are a method of making it safe for people to open up, speak what's on their mind, and stimulate the flow of debate. Sometimes, though, shielded by a secret, anonymous name, the impulse to become rude and abusive can become irresistible.

To alias or not to alias, that is a question the Sysops answer when setting up their systems. Whether 'tis nobler or not depends completely on the personalities of those using the system. If, however, you want to play on a board that allows handles, at least try to come up with something fun that reflects a bit on who you are. My handle could be DumWriter. On second thought. . . .

```
By what Handle/alias will you be known to us?
```

This is just one way the question may be phrased. But it is phrased in the form of a question. Your response? Type your alias and press Enter. Often, you'll find that someone is already using your first choice. Be prepared with a couple of names. Once you make a choice, though, you are absolutely stuck with it — unless you have impressive skills at begging piteously and throwing yourself prostrate before the Sysop.

Logging On the Second Time

The second time you call into a system, it's like walking into Cheers — everybody knows your name. After prompting you to enter your name and secret password, the BBS verifies your answers with its database files. Once it determines that everything matches, it whisks you straight to the menu. No more questions, no nothing — just glad to see you, and you've got a message waiting . . . though the system may still ask you if you want to subscribe.

On some systems, you can save yourself a few keystrokes and log on faster. Here's how: When the BBS asks for your first name, type your first name, last name, and password all on one line, separating each with a space. Then press Enter. For example, our fictitious Timmy would type the following and press Enter:

```
Timmy Thomerson fullmoon
```

This doesn't work for every system, but it won't hurt to try. The only drawback is that your secret password appears on the screen, unprotected, in all its glory. If you're sitting home alone, this may not be a problem.

When you've actually coughed up the cash, you see the Subscriber's Main Menu, Figure 2-8, when you log on.

While you're waiting to get upgraded, why not go through the rest of this book and see what you've gotten yourself mixed up with.

Figure 2-8:
The Subscriber's Main Menu reveals Software Creations' bizarre "pay more/get more" philosophy that has corporate America terrified.

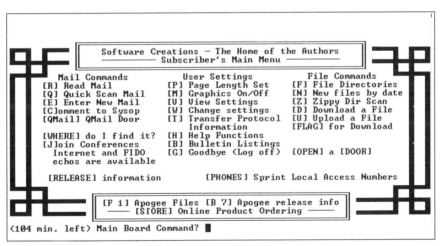

Advice for newbies

The best advice that we can give any newbie is simply... "The only stupid question is that which you do not ask." I encourage people to speak up with their particular problem. And then we can come to their rescue.

Jan Metzger, Sysop — Crafts BB, Prodigy

Chapter 3

Snagging Files and Bringin' 'em on Home

- -

In This Chapter

▶ Introducing capturing and downloading

▶ Making a home for your booty

▶ Capturing files

▶ Downloading files

▶ Doing the download

- -

*W*hile you're online, they sit tauntingly on the screen before you: a helpful tip sheet, a cool game, a clever little program that will solve all your computer problems, or even a program that can inject a little humor into your daily routine. Sure you can see them on the BBS-system computer, but you want them on your own computer so you can print them out, install them, play them, or whatever. How do you reach through the line and pull the stuff back through the looking glass and onto your system?

The answer should be simple. Parts of it actually are simple. The easiest part is moving the goods from where they are to where you are. What happens next can get tricky.

The trickiness factor is directly connected to how much you already know about directories and copying files. If you've managed to avoid understanding these DOS concepts by relying on the kindness of strangers or, worse yet, crossing your fingers and hoping nothing goes wrong, well—you're busted. Because you have an honest face, however, this time I'll let you off with a warning, and I'll show you how to do what you need to do. Next time I may not be in such a good mood.

In this chapter, I cover the theory and the steps for harvesting material found online. You also get a chance to take another brief foray online to get in some more practice. Part II of this book supplies additional details on what you can do once you know how to lasso a file and bring it on home.

After all, as no one has ever said before, "It's better to learn about horses *before* riding in the rodeo."

Introducing Capture and Download

From a big-picture perspective, material on a BBS is offered in two ways.

The primary way you see material online is when text — words and numbers — scrolls before your eyes onscreen in a readable format. If you want to, you can actually save that onscreen stuff to a file on your own hard disk using a process called *capturing*.

The second way material is presented on a BBS is through a *directory* or list of files. This list of files consists of programs, games, or text that can be selected from one or more online catalogs and *downloaded*. Downloading is not unlike copying something from your hard drive to a floppy drive. Except, of course, downloading is the process of copying a file from the BBS computer, through the phone line, onto the hard disk of your own computer. It's magic, isn't it?

If you're like everyone else — not to diminish the incredible uniqueness that is you — you'll do a lot more downloading than capturing. Each process has its place, though.

Making a Home for Your Booty

Do you think of your hard disk as a vast pit into which you toss files, not sure if tomorrow the Great God of the Pit will graciously return them to you? If so, please take a moment to talk *game plan* before capturing or downloading new stuff into your pit.

If you've ever purchased a new program, you may recall that during the installation process the program makes a new place for itself on the hard disk. That's because standard computer practice is to keep separate programs, well, separate.

When you capture or download online material, it's also a good idea to keep these new programs corralled in an area separate from the programs you use every day. If you don't, disorganization will multiply exponentially. Trust me on this one.

Newly immigrating files need temporary housing on the hard disk until you can determine whether they are keepers or losers. Basically, you need a sort of Ellis Island for your downloads.

This Ellis Island is a *download directory*. If you're not too clear about the difference between files and directories, take a moment to read the following section, "Remedial DOS." Otherwise, move right along to the next section. If you don't know as much as you thought, you're still welcome back to "Remedial DOS" at any time.

Remedial DOS

While some claim that superior graphics is what sells Macintosh computers, I disagree. What really sends people fleeing into the Apple computer camp is the DOS organizational system. Dealing with directories and files has sent more than one PC user into cross-eyed paralysis. And once you've tried to get the system and don't, it's human nature to give up. But let's gird our loins and give these concepts another try. C'mon. Please?

A *directory* is a place on the hard disk where stuff is stored. A *file* is material you create with a program — like a letter to your Aunt Bea — or even a program itself. There's a consensus, sort of, among software makers to use the analogy that directories are like file folders, and files are like pieces of paper that go *into* the folders.

Directories

If you take a stroll through File Manager in Windows (or Explorer, in Windows: The Next Generation), you can see this file-folder/files analogy in pictures. Actually, you'd see it in almost any disk-management program. Your hard disk will be neatly divided into directories symbolized by little file folders. And if you double-click on one of those folders, it opens up and a list of the files contained within that folder appears to the right.

So far, so good. It's at the next step, unfortunately, where the file-folder/files analogy crumbles.

✔ The first problem is that, in computers, file folders often contain not only files, but more file folders. In the workplace, you'd never stick one manila file folder inside another manila file folder. In computers, you can. You just have to accept that in computers, directories can contain both files *and* more file folders.

✔ The second confusing thing about files and directories is the way they are referred to when no folder and file icons are around to help out. In other words, going from pictures to the written word can lose something in the translation. And who decided to go with this nutty business of a backslash (\ ) and a colon? Admittedly, it's about as unintuitive as you can get. It is, however, learnable.

For example, on your hard disk, probably known as drive C, is a directory called WINDOWS. The way to write that down is: C:\WINDOWS. In the Windows directory is another directory called SYSTEM. If you wanted to write that down, you'd do this: C:\WINDOWS\SYSTEM.

Every time you see a backslash, substitute the word *within*. To read C:\WINDOWS\SYSTEM you start at the right and read to the left saying, "System is a directory within another directory named Windows, which is within the hard disk named C." If you've ever sung "Knee bone's connected to the thigh bone," then you can do this.

The colon — as in C: — is used to let you know that you're talking about a drive rather than a file. Drive A would be A:.

Filenames

All right, let's move on to the rules for filenames. A filename is up to eight characters long followed by a period, and then by a tag that's up to three characters strong. No spaces are allowed in filenames.

Let's say there's a file in the System directory called ARIAL.FOT. If you need to leave a note to tell someone where to find the file, you write C:\WINDOWS\SYSTEM\ARIAL.FOT. See? That's much easier than writing, "Dear Aunt Bea, The file called Arial.fot is within the System directory, which is within the Windows directory, which is within the hard disk named C."

Wildcards

Okay, one last concept.

Sometimes you need to make sweeping generalizations. Like, instead of talking about one crummy file ending in FOT, you may want to copy or delete all files that end with FOT. It's not practical to copy two dozen or more files one at a time. So the great computer gurus invented a shorthand way of saying *every file that ends in FOT* using an asterisk — *.

The asterisk means, literally, *anything*. So to indicate all files that end in FOT, you'd write: *.FOT. Substitute the word "anything" for the asterisk, and you get *anything that ends in FOT*.

Putting it all together

Can you figure out, then, what this means: C:\WINDOWS\SYSTEM*.FOT?

If you said, "Anything ending in FOT, within the System directory, which is within the Windows directory, which is on drive C," you just earned your GED for DOS. If you didn't, you might read through this section again. Many of these DOS concepts are used in this book. Some appear in the very next section.

Developing a download directory

The idea to have a download directory — an area on the hard disk created to hold downloaded files — wasn't mine originally. Nearly all communications programs automatically create a download directory for you during the installation process. Which means you may already be the proud owner of a download directory — and not even know it.

You can try to confirm this hypothesis by going into your communications software and looking.

- ✔ If you use Qmodem for DOS, check out Config ➪ Files ➪ Path Definition. Look at Download.
- ✔ For ProComm for Windows, look at Online ➪ Receive Files.
- ✔ If you're using HyperTerminal with Windows 95, look at Transfer ➪ Receive File.
- ✔ Any other program, you're on your own. A logical place to start your investigation might be in the setup part of the program. Alternatively, try activating the download command now, while you're still in dry dock, and see if it points to a particular directory.

When you discover the secret location of your download directory, write it down. Knowing where your computer is sending those downloaded files should make it easier to find them. In essence, you can greatly reduce that *vast pit* feeling.

If you are that unlucky someone with old software that didn't set up a download directory, you'll have to make one yourself. It's not a big deal.

1. **Get to the system prompt, which looks something like this:**

```
C:\
```

If you're using DOS — in other words, not Windows — just quit whatever you're doing. Save first, of course.

If you use any version of Windows, you can get your very own system prompt by clicking on the MS-DOS icon. If you can't find the MS-DOS icon, use the Run command — in Windows 3.1, select File ⇨ Run, and in Windows 95 you'll find the Run command right above the Start button on the Taskbar. Once you see the Run... dialog box, type **command,** if it isn't already typed for you, and press Enter.

2. **Once you can see the system prompt, type** MD \DOWNLOAD **and press Enter.**

If you get `bad command or filename` from the computer, you've made a typo. I'm sure it was a charming and clever typo, but you'll have to try again.

In case you're interested, MD is the command to make a directory. Typing MD \DOWNLOAD creates a directory named DOWNLOAD.

3. **Make a note of the location of your download directory (C:\DOWNLOAD).**

4. **That's it!**

Unless you need to retire back to Windows; in which case, just type **EXIT,** click your heels together three times, and press Enter to slip into the comfort and safety of the Windows environment.

Now, one way or another, you've got a download directory, and you know where it is. I'm glad that's settled.

Creating a corner for captured characters

I don't know why, but most communications programs want to put captured files in a different directory from downloaded files. I'm not sure what they think will happen if captured files are allowed to touch downloaded files. Maybe there are some things humans are not meant to know. Actually I'm sure it's just a pathetic attempt at keeping things further confused and/or organized, depending on your point of view.

If your communication software does not automatically provide a hard disk haven for wayward captured files, then we'll stick 'em in the download directory. We're wild and free and willing to take chances. Don't even try to hold us back.

Capturing Files

Capturing files, that is, collecting text as it scrolls by on the screen into a file on your hard disk, is not the best way of moving stuff from the BBS computer to yours. Besides, capturing only works with text; it's useless for getting 98 percent of the stuff you'll want from a BBS.

Capturing is slow, compared to downloading, and it is subject to the slings and arrows of phone static. Even the phone company that claims you can hear a pin drop on their service must deal with weather problems and sunspots just like everyone else. Whatever is on the screen, including garbage and instructions from the BBS, is included in the captured file. The resultant captured file always requires a bit of plastic surgery — snipping extra characters here, removing sagging characters there — to put it in a presentable format.

So why bother with capturing? Simply because sometimes the only way to save information into a file is to capture it. Here are some examples of when capturing may be necessary:

- ✔ In Chapter 2, you encounter screens and bulletins chock-full of helpful instructions. Unless you've got a black belt in Evelyn Wood's speed reading class, you can't read and remember all the information as it scrams past you on the screen. Quickly trying to jot it all down can be a drag. Instead, just capture the text as it flows by. Then, after you've hung up, read the captured file.

- ✔ In an upcoming chapter, I talk about electronic mail messages; capturing is often the only way to save those incoming missives. This is especially important if you do any business online using electronic mail. Keeping a record of correspondence is critical.

- ✔ If you're doing research and ask to see an old magazine article, the text of the article will scroll by like any other message. You'll need to capture it so you can read it later when you're not on a ten-cents-a-minute — or more — clock.

File capturing can be accomplished in a couple of ways. Again, you'll have to look up some commands in your communication software, and you should handle that before going online.

Planning ahead

Pretend you see a bulletin entitled "How to Do Everything Online." Wow, you think to yourself, I want to read that. In fact, I probably need to *study* that. But I don't want to study that while the online clock is ticking. Oh, you say to yourself, woe is me. What to do? Could the answer be to capture the file? Very good.

You see that "How to Do Everything Online" is bulletin item Number 1 on the — need I say fictitious — Wacky Wally BBS. Anyway, you know that the moment you press 1 and then Enter, the "How to Do Everything Online" bulletin will scroll by faster than you can read and comprehend. So before pressing 1 and Enter, you need to tell your communications software to capture the bulletin.

1. **Turn on the Capture Mode in whatever way your communications software requires.**

   In ProComm for Windows, that would be Alt+F1; in Qmodem for DOS it's Ctrl+Enter. HyperTerminal uses Transfer⇨Capture Text.

2. **A window may pop up asking you to name the file into which the about-to-be-flowing text will be funneled.**

   This window also tells you which directory the file is being saved to. Make a note of it — in ProComm for Windows, it's usually C:\PROWIN2\CAPTURE; Qmodem for DOS uses C:\QMPRO\MSG; HyperTerminal goes for C:\WIN95\HYPERTRM. Whatever directory your system uses, you'll need to know this later.

   If you're using ProComm for Windows, it automatically creates a file with the name of the BBS you're calling, so you can skip Step 3.

3. **Type a filename, like** BULL1.DOC**, or any other filename that you'll recognize later, and press Enter.**

   It makes it easier on you later if you give your file a name that ends in DOC.

   If you wish to be a bit more adventuresome, you can take the ultimate make-it-easy choice by beaming your captured file straight into your word processor's directory. If you use Word for Windows and have a DOCS directory, you might save your BULL1.DOC to C:\WINWORD\DOCS. That way the file will be right there when you get into Word.

4. **Give the BBS the command to start the text flowing.**

   In this pretend example, it'd be 1 and Enter.

5. **When the text has finished flowing, repeat Step 1.**

   The Capture Mode is a toggle, like a light switch. You turn it on and everything that happens gets recorded until you turn it off. Actually, it's really more like a tape recorder than a light switch. It's kind of both.

You can capture an entire online session or turn capture on and off as many times as needed during your online stint.

You don't always know in advance when something you want to capture is about to scroll by. More often than not, material scrolls by, and then you realize you want it. Or maybe you just forgot to turn on capture. That's when you need to grab text retroactively which is, strangely enough, the next topic.

Grabbing text retroactively

The text just scrolled by. The message of a lifetime. Because this is a make-believe situation, we're going to pretend that we can't just ask that the BBS redisplay the message, which usually you can do.

Instead, let me tell you about another way to get the message back. In just about all communications programs, there is a feature known as a *scrollback buffer*. A scrollback buffer is a holding tank for the last half-dozen — sometimes more — screens of BBS information. You can scroll this holding tank backwards, like scrolling towards the top of a document in a word processor, and go back in time with the BBS. The scrollback-buffer size is limited, however, and eventually the oldest stuff gets kicked out in favor of the new.

So, if you view a message or bulletin, and it scrolls off the screen, you haven't lost it yet. Just invoke the scrollback buffer, scroll backwards, and then read the message. Again, each communications package has its own command for viewing the scrollback buffer.

- In Windows-based programs, scrolling back is a matter of using the vertical scroll bar.
- In DOS-based programs, the scrollback command varies. In Qmodem, Alt+up-arrow is the key.

The scrollback buffer ain't no little look-but-don't touch affair. Anything in the buffer can be funneled into a file on the disk. That's what I mean by capturing stuff retroactively.

When you're viewing the contents of the buffer, activate the communications program's save command and name the file into which you want to pour the buffer's contents. Be sure to take careful note of the directory and file the buffer is being saved into.

- In Procomm Plus for Windows, the command to save the buffer is Alt+F11.
- In Qmodem for DOS, once the scrollback buffer has been activated with Alt+up-arrow, the contents can be saved by pressing S, for Save, and then typing a filename in which to save it. Be sure to note the directory the material is being saved in and don't forget the filename you select.

All bulletin boards have some variation of a dead-man's switch. If you haven't typed a key or issued a command within a certain time period — sometimes as short as five minutes — the BBS assumes you're done and logs you off. You'll get a beep and a warning before this happens. The reason I'm bringing this up now is that, if you start reading your scrollback buffer, you aren't issuing BBS commands. The BBS might think you've gone to answer the door and aren't coming back. You could find yourself logged off if you don't pay attention.

You don't have to be online to read your scrollback buffer. After hanging up, the contents of the buffer are still there for perusal. You can also decide, even after you've logged off, to save the buffer. The material in the buffer stays there for retrieval until you exit the communications program. Then, and only then, do the buffer's contents byte the big one.

Using captured files

Once the deed is done, and you've wrestled yourself a file, what do you do with it? You can do anything with it you can do with any other text file. You can open it, edit it, and print it with a word processing program, whether you're using Microsoft's Word for Windows or Novell's WordPerfect 5.1. You can even open captured files in Windows NotePad or DOS's Edit — if the files aren't too big. Here's how:

1. **Get into your favorite word processing program (or NotePad or whatever).**

2. **Use the program's equivalent of the File➪Open command.**

3. **Either browse or type the path and filename of the captured file.**

   The filename and path are, hopefully, what you made note of when you were naming the file. If you failed to name the file with a DOC ending, you may not see the file listed in your word processor. To correct that, put your cursor where you see *.DOC and change that to *.*. Then you'll see everything.

4. **Highlight the file and press Enter or click OK to bring up the file.**

Once the file is under your control, you can read it, print it, or perform on it whatever acts you had in mind when you captured it. As cautioned before, you may want to grab a bucket and a broom because there will be some cleanup work — not the least of which is the enter command the computer puts at the end of every line, which may cause some very short lines.

Sending a captured file to the printer

If you are a DOS rat and live life on the edge, you can print any captured file simply by going to the directory where the file is located and typing the word **PRINT**, then a space and finally the name of the file to print. This incantation is put into action by pressing Enter. When you see a message on the screen, press Enter again. Here's how to print out a file named CAPTURE.DOC. Type **PRINT CAPTURE.DOC** and press Enter. When you see a question about list device, press Enter again. Out comes the file in all its glory. Look, Ma, no word processor!

Downloading Files

Although many bulletin board systems are discussion-based, as you see later in the book, most people admit that they are BBSing for the files. It's the continuing, ongoing, great-white-shark-like obsession for new files that keeps them coming back.

The general term *files* covers a lot of turf. Files can be technical papers and instruction guides. Files can be utility programs, database programs, financial management programs, games, communications programs, and many other things you can't find at the local computer store. Files can be fix-it and upgrade patches direct from the manufacturer (for example, did you know that the upgrade from DOS 6.0 to 6.22 was available free from Microsoft's BBS?) Files can even be something I need to send to you before next week's meeting.

Downloading is the process of cloning what's on a BBS computer onto your computer. Downloading is what you do with programs, images, and formatted text files. As I said before, downloading is much like copying a file from the hard disk to drive A.

Downloading 101

Before you do a download, try to get a picture of the download process using a silly, noncomputer example. Say you want to arrange for one friend, Steve, to give another friend, Bonnie, a book. You tell Steve to meet Bonnie at Sunset and Vine and give her the book. Steve agrees and goes to Sunset and Vine and waits for Bonnie.

In this scenario, Steve is going to be waiting a good long time to give Bonnie the book because you never informed Bonnie that Steve is waiting to give her a book. In order to get the two parties together, you must not only tell Steve to meet Bonnie and give her the book, but also tell Bonnie to go to Sunset and Vine to get the book from Steve. Only then can a connection be made and the book be transferred.

Downloading works the same way.

You start by issuing a command to the BBS to send a file (that's the Steve half of the equation). Then you tell your communications software to receive the file (that's the Bonnie half).

As it happens, when Steve and Bonnie meet, they have to communicate with each other to work out the details of the file exchange. The behind-the-scenes structure for downloading is called a *protocol*. Just to confuse things, there are a lot of different protocols. Flip back to Figure 2-5 for a typical list of the little buggers.

Although at first glance protocol names look like so much alphabet soup, take a closer look and you see that they all just have an X, Y, or Z stuck in front of the word modem. Not too creative. We forgive whoever named them, though, because it must have been exhausting just to invent protocols in the first place.

Here's the good news. You don't have to understand a darn thing about what a protocol does or how it works or anything else about it, except the following two simple things:

- ✔ Whatever protocol you tell Steve to use, you must tell Bonnie to use the same protocol. If you tell the BBS you want Zmodem, tell your communications software to use Zmodem. If you don't match protocols, the download will never happen: You've got your basic "failure to communicate."

- ✔ When deciding which protocol to use, select Zmodem first. If your communications software doesn't know about Zmodem, then use Ymodem. If you can't use Ymodem, select Xmodem.

Still with me? Okay. In techno-talk, here are the steps you take to perform a download:

1. **Go online.**

2. **Select an interesting, must-have file on a BBS to download.**

3. **Activate the BBS download command.**

4. **Tell the BBS which download protocol you prefer.**

5. **Wait for the BBS to tell you it is downloading the file.**

6. **Tell your communications software you want to download something.**

7. **Tell your communications software the protocol you prefer.**

8. **Tell your communications software the name of the file to download and where to put it on the hard disk.**

9. **Wait for the BBS and your software to synch up, and then the file is downloaded.**

Do nine steps seem complicated? Overwhelming? The first step, going online, you have to do whether you want to download or not. I shouldn't count that as a step. Also, two of the remaining steps are *Wait for. . .* steps, so actually there are only six action steps. Plus, many communications programs — including ProComm, Qmodem, and HyperTerminal — automatically perform Steps 6 through 8 for you. That leaves only three action steps and two wait steps. Now that's not too bad, is it?

Sure, someday it'll all be automatic, and nobody will have to worry about protocol and download directories and all that. You'll just tell your computer — verbally — the kind of stuff you're interested in, and the computer will gather and download files before you even think to ask for them.

But right now, the reality is that you do have to pay attention to those things. That is part of the price for being on the cutting edge.

One last moment of preparation before Doing the Download. Please take the time now to determine what the download command is in your communications software. You will have to know. Look it up or call technical support, but find out. You can't download without it.

- ✔ The download command in ProComm for Windows and HyperTerminal is to click the file folder icon with a down arrow in it. Down arrow for download, get it?

- ✔ In Qmodem for DOS and many DOS programs, press the PgDn key — also known as the PageDown key — to activate a download.

Doing the download

All BBSers, whether they are plotting total global domination from their bedrooms or log on only when television goes into summer reruns, need a program called PKZip. You may have heard of it — or not. PKZip kind of sounds like one of those stay-awake-all-night products loaded with caffeine, doesn't it? Actually, without PKZip, very little of what you download is usable. PKZip is that important. I'm even devoting the next chapter to it.

What we're going to do right now is go fetch us a copy of PKZip by calling the PKWare BBS — the official home of PKZip. This mission, and I assume you've decided to accept it, will give you another chance to go through a logon with the group as well as experience your first download. I'll tell you why you need PKZip and what it does after you get it.

It's fun to build a little drama and suspense into this, isn't it?

Ready to get PKZip? Then let's go talk to Steve and Bonnie:

1. **Crank up your communications software and dial** 414-354-8670.

   When you've connected, you see something like Figure 3-1. Note that you need to enter both your first and last names.

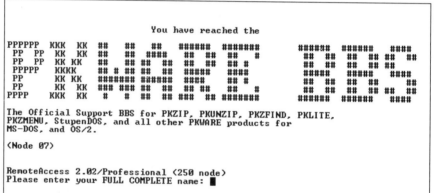

Figure 3-1: PKWare BBS is the home address of PKZip, the key to unlocking files.

```
                        You have reached the

PPPPP   KKK  KK  ##     ##  ######  #######        ######  ######  ####
PP  PP  KK  KK   ##     ##  ## ##   ##    #        ##  ##  ##  ##  ## ##
PP  PP  KK KK    ##     ##  ## ##   ##             ##      ##  ##  ## ##
PPPPP   KKKK     ## # ## ## ##  ##  #####          #####   #####   ####
PP      KK KK    ####### ###### ##   ####          ##  ##  ##  ##   ##
PP      KK  KK   ### ### ##  ##  ##   #            ##  ##  ##  ## ## ##
PPPP    KKK  KK   #   #  ##  ## ### ## #######     ######  ######  ####

The Official Support BBS for PKZIP, PKUNZIP, PKZFIND, PKLITE,
PKZMENU, StupenDOS, and all other PKWARE products for
MS-DOS, and OS/2.

<Node 07>

RemoteAccess 2.02/Professional <250 node>
Please enter your FULL COMPLETE name: █
```

2. **Log on as a new user.**

   Since you're new to the BBS, and it doesn't have you in its database, you have to make friends via the logon route. Although I've listed all the logon questions and the appropriate answers below, try to do it by yourself before looking in the book. The book is here if you need it, but this is a fairly short logon process, and I'm sure you can do it.

   Remember that pressing Enter alone selects the uppercase option; for example, pressing Enter on (Y/n) selects the yes response.

```
Select your preferred language: 1
Did you enter your name correctly (Y/n)? Yes
Would you like ANSI color and graphics (Y/n)? No
Do you want to use the ANSI full-screen editor (Y/n)? No
How many lines does your display have (10-66, Enter=24):
          <Enter>
Would you like to pause after each screen page (Y/n)? Yes
Do you want screen clearing codes to be sent (Y/n)? Yes
Where are you calling from? Yourcity, ST
Please enter your home/voice phone number:
```

```
Number: XXX-XXX-XXXX
Number entered: XXX-XXX-XXXX
Is this correct (Y/n)? Yes
Please enter your business/data phone number:
Number: XXX-XXX-XXXX
Number entered: XXX-XXX-XXXX
Is this correct (Y/n)? Yes
Please enter your date of birth (MM-DD-YY): XX-XX-XX
Enter your password to use: ********
Please re-enter for verification: ********
Did you enter all the above information correctly (Y/n)? Yes
```

Congratulations! You are logged on!

3. Press Enter at each welcoming screen.

You end up pressing Enter four times before your find yourself at the Top Menu (see Figure 3-2). Take special note of the very first option at the top: `D>ownload PKZIP 2.04G`. That's what you're going to do.

Figure 3-2:
The PKWare BBS menu doesn't look the same as Software Creations, but is similar. Look —there's even a Bulletins option.

```
              PKWARE BBS Top Menu
D)ownload PKZIP 2.04G (PKZ204G.EXE!) - Newest version of PKZIP/PKUNZIP/etc.
L)ist latest version of PKWARE software
R)elease dates for upcoming PKWARE software

######## F)ile Area #####        ----- MISC. -----        ##### M)essage Area ########

P)KWARE files section       O)ther/Utility        1) PKWARE Messages
I)BM/MS-DOS file section     B)ulletins            2) IBM/DOS Messages
A)miga file section          w(H)o's On-Line       3) Data Compression Library
W)indows file section        G)oodbye (HANGUP)     4) Email/Comments to PKWARE
u(N)iversal file section                           5) Combined Message Area
Z)ip/PKWARE related files    S(T) Atari Files
U)pload to PKWARE BBS        O(S)/2 File Area       6) TOP 20 Downloads

+) Order a PKWARE Product On_Line with VISA, MasterCard or AMEX

7) Download a complete file listing for PKWARE BBS
8) Download a list of only newer files (15 days old)


Command: █
```

4. Press D.

You are presented with a list ending with `Protocol (Enter=quit):`. The one you want is Zmodem.

5. Press Z.

6. When you see `(D)elete or (C)lear all (Enter to continue):`, **press Enter to continue.**

Above this message should be a brief, cryptic note about PKZ204G.EXE. That tells you what file they are going to send. That's the one you want.

7. When you see `(S)tart transfer, (L)ogoff after transfer, (N)ew protocol, (A)bort:`, **press S and Enter.**

This is, basically, the *go* command. If something is wrong or you've changed your mind, pressing A and Enter will cancel the whole process — you can start again if you want.

The BBS will now calculate how long it will take to download your file so you have some idea how long a normal transfer time is for you. On my system it takes about two minutes. This note ends with `Start receiving now, or press <Ctrl-X> several times to abort.`

8. Enter the download command on your communications software.

If your communications software suddenly starts doing things on its own — popping open a window and telling you stuff — you can skip this and the next few steps. Rejoin the rest of us down at Step 12.

9. Select the same protocol — Zmodem — as you did in Step 5.

You will probably be shown the download directory and asked if that's where you want the file to go. Press Enter to confirm.

If your communications software is clueless and is asking for the name of a download directory, type the directory you created earlier — **C:\DOWNLOAD**. Press Enter.

If you didn't create a download directory, but have to come up with one right now, type **C:\DOS**. Press Enter.

10. Look to see that something is happening with your communications software.

There should be a window telling you stuff is coming and how much is remaining, something like Figure 3-3.

If nothing is happening — except maybe a stream of garbage as in Figure 3-4 — you need to bring this operation to a halt and start again. The stop command is Ctrl+X. Press Ctrl+X a bunch of times in a row. You won't see anything, but the BBS will. It should abort the streaming mess. If it doesn't, you have to hang up and start again.

When the transfer is successfully completed, your system beeps at you, waves a flag, launches fireworks, or in some way indicates that the job is done. If you have a lump of sugar handy, feed it to the computer and pat its head while the PKWare Top Menu redisplays itself.

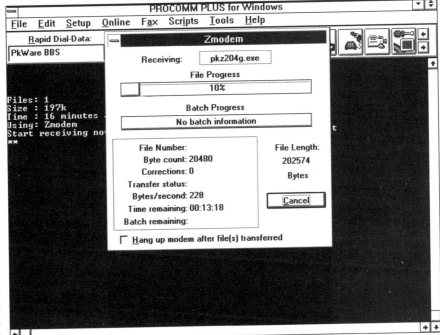

Figure 3-3:
Downloading
in all its
glory! The
download
countdown
stats keep
you
informed.

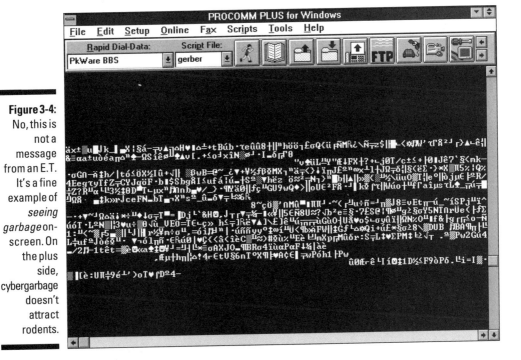

Figure 3-4:
No, this is
not a
message
from an E.T.
It's a fine
example of
*seeing
garbage* on-
screen. On
the plus
side,
cybergarbage
doesn't
attract
rodents.

11. **To wrap up this session and say good-bye, press G and then Enter — just like you did with Software Creations when you were ready to split.**

12. **At the little Logoff Menu, press N and then Enter to hang up without leaving a love letter to the Sysop.**

13. **Make sure you've been disconnected.**

As PKWare BBS says farewell, it offers a thought for the day — in case you didn't have one of your own. When you see the words NO CARRIER, you have been disconnected from PKWare. If you don't see those words after a short time, issue a hang up command on your communications program.

Now it's done. And now I'll warn you: Downloading files is like that potato-chip commercial where you can't eat just one. You may have gone and made yourself a download junkie.

So now that you've got PKZ204G.EXE, what do you do with it? That's what the next chapter's all about.

Yes, Virginia, there is free software...

...kinda. I mentioned before that there were lots of programs and goodies available for downloading. When you recover from the shock that there's so much cool stuff, you may begin to wonder where it all came from. A lot of those programs come from the minds of skilled amateur programmers, or perhaps even professional programmers who do their own thing on the side. It's like somebody who writes advertising copy during the day and a novel at night. Novelists, though, have to convince a publisher to print and distribute their work. Programmers can go straight to the public by posting their efforts on BBSs.

Programs found on BBSs are referred to as *shareware* — a variation on the term *software*. The idea is, you download a shareware program and try it out for free. If you decide to keep and use it, you are honor bound to send a registration fee to the author. Registration fees typically range from $5 to $75. Once you register the program, its author will send an enhanced version of the program with a few more features, maybe a manual, and an offer of telephone support.

Some shareware titles include *nag screens* that prod you, upon entering or exiting the program, to register it. Once registered, the nag screens disappear. Another variation on the shareware concept is *crippleware* — programs that have a key feature, like Save, turned off. Once you've registered, you receive the fully functioning version. Finally, there are *freeware* programs that have no price tag at all — kind of like your neighbor who makes bird houses for fun and then gives them away.

Part of being a good cybercitizen is to register the shareware programs you couldn't live without.

Uploading Files

There are two important sayings that explain uploading. First, Sir Isaac Newton's, "What goes down must come up." The other is the phrase which no child below the age of eight understands — especially around Christmas, "'Tis better to give than to receive."

In other words, it's possible to *send* files to a BBS as well as to get files. In fact, you're encouraged, if you find something cool on one system, to upload it to another. Some BBSs do more than just encourage you to upload new stuff. They make it a rule.

Your *upload/download ratio* may be monitored carefully. Some systems will even cut you off if you download excessively more than you upload. Although all Sysops assume you'll download more than you upload, some insist on a five-to-one ratio, some ten-to-one. In other words, for every five or ten bytes you download, you need to upload one byte. On the other hand, some Sysops couldn't care less what your upload/download ratio is and don't keep statistics. Again, this is where the tone is set by the Sysop.

During your early, formative days on BBSs, you won't be doing much uploading. By the time you're ready to start uploading, you'll have done a volume business in downloading, and uploading won't be such a mystery. Actually, already it's not too much of a mystery because the process is almost exactly the same as downloading.

1. **Make a note of the exact name and location, on your hard disk, of the file you want to upload.**

2. **Go online.**

3. **Activate the BBS upload command — you'll be asked for the name of the file and for a brief description.**

4. **Tell the BBS which protocol you prefer.**

5. **Wait for the BBS to tell you to upload the file.**

6. **Tell your communications software you want to upload something.**

7. **Tell your communications software the protocol you prefer.**

8. **Tell your communications software the name of the file to upload and where to find it on the hard disk.**

9. **Wait for the BBS and your software to synch up, and then the file is uploaded.**

We may sneak in an uploading experience later on, but for now you don't absolutely, positively have to know all about it. There are far more important things to deal with at the moment. I just thought the symmetry of downloading would be out-of-whack if I didn't, just once, mention uploading. So consider it mentioned.

Chapter 4
Zippity Doo Dah!

In This Chapter
- ▶ Putting Zip in your life
- ▶ Unzipping: the concept
- ▶ Setting up PKZip

There's a famous scene in *Paper Chase* — either the movie or the TV show — where the law professor says to his students, "You come in here with a skull full of mush and come out thinking like lawyers." You may feel as though BBSs do the opposite.

You start out thinking like lawyers, and after messing with downloads, logons, ANSI graphics — and in this chapter, Zip — you wind up with a skull full of mush.

Rest assured. Zipping is the last of the new, really weird things you have to know about. But it is important. No pressure, though. We take it real slow. Besides, you're still in the relative safety of Part I — the Theory Zone.

And I promise after this chapter we go on to something more normal . . . like writing messages. I'm sure you've done that at least once in your life, even if it was only to send a Hallmark Card or write home for money.

So, what the heck is Zip?

Putting Zip in Your Life

You have, no doubt, been at a party when someone handed you a can of peanuts. As you innocently unscrewed the lid, out flew coiled snakes, causing you to scream or jump and everyone else in the room to laugh. It's just one of those normal rites of passage, like learning to play 52 Pickup.

My guess is that the can o' snakes was the inspiration for Zip. Remember how the volume of the snakes, once uncoiled, seemed a lot bigger than the inside of the can? But then, when carefully compressed, the snakes magically fit inside the can? And then you probably handed the can to someone else and laughed at *them*.

Anyway, that's the idea behind the concept of *compressing files*. Computer files, it seems, have lots of empty space inside. And, with the proper software prestidigitation, files can be deflated 10 to 90 percent smaller — just like that commercial where they remove the water from the coffee and leave behind a tiny pile of freeze-dried crystals. Later, the files are restored by adding water — so to speak.

The 5th Wave   By Rich Tennant

Once Sysops realized that deflated files not only reduce download time by 10 to 90 percent, but also increase their available disk space by a like amount, they deflated all the files on their BBSs, and the concept of file compression was an overnight smash hit.

But there's more! The software that compresses files also solves another complication. You see, most programs consist of more than one file. Using a half-dozen files for one program is not considered excessive. But who would want to go through the process of downloading 10 or 20 little files? Not me.

The compression software handles this problem by placing the files it compresses into a single file for easy transport. Like putting those joke snakes in a can or, more pleasantly, clothes in a suitcase. Then, you and I can simply download the one suitcase file — or can — and unpack and rejuvenate the contents once we're at home.

As you may have surmised, the responsibility for decompressing downloaded files rests with you. As you'll soon see, however, *how* to inflate the files is simple. Simpler, even, than *where* to inflate the files.

And now I'd like to introduce you to the program that compresses and consolidates files — a big hand for PKZip! Virtually every file stored on a BBS has been compressed and consolidated with PKZip. Or, as they say, the files have all been *zipped*. When we go back online in Part II, you'll know which files are zipped by the ending of their file names. Zipped files end with ZIP. As in DOOM.ZIP, FANTASY.ZIP, or CARDS.ZIP.

The program that *decompresses* files and restores them to normal is called, naturally enough, PKUnZip. And that's the program you need to make sense of all the fabulous files you're downloading.

 To recap, PKZip both compresses and consolidates files. PKUnZip both decompresses and unpacks files. Both of these programs were invented by a fellow named Phil Katz. He's the man who put the PK in both PKZip and PKUnZip. Check out Figure 4-1.

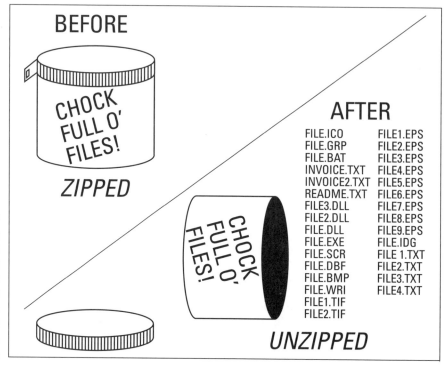

BEFORE

CHOCK FULL O' FILES!

ZIPPED

AFTER

FILE.ICO	FILE1.EPS
FILE.GRP	FILE2.EPS
FILE.BAT	FILE3.EPS
INVOICE.TXT	FILE4.EPS
INVOICE2.TXT	FILE5.EPS
README.TXT	FILE6.EPS
FILE3.DLL	FILE7.EPS
FILE2.DLL	FILE8.EPS
FILE.DLL	FILE9.EPS
FILE.EXE	FILE.IDG
FILE.SCR	FILE 1.TXT
FILE.DBF	FILE2.TXT
FILE.BMP	FILE3.TXT
FILE.WRI	FILE4.TXT
FILE1.TIF	
FILE2.TIF	

CHOCK FULL O' FILES!

UNZIPPED

Figure 4-1:
How do all those files fit in one tiny can? It's easy with PKZip and PKUnZip.

UnZipping: The Concept

The process of removing and inflating files contained in a zipped file is called either *unzipping* or *extracting*.

And, again, here's where another analogy bites the dust. The business of zipped files being likened to suitcases, cans o' snakes, and freeze-dried coffee doesn't match what happens next. When files are extracted from the zipped file, they aren't taken out of the file like you take clothes out of a suitcase or coffee from the jar. The files get *copied* or *cloned*. Unzipping a file is actually copying what's in the suitcase and reconstituting it. So you've still got your freeze-dried crystals and also your cup of coffee.

I mention this because, logically, you'd expect the zipped file to be empty — maybe even shriveled up and gone — once you've finished unzipping it. Don't be surprised or think you did something wrong when you finish extracting a zipped file . . . and still have a big ole zipped file sitting there!

There are two approaches to extracting files. One is *do it yourself* and the other is to let the file *do it itself*.

Doing it itself: the self-extracting file

The do-it-itself approach is when the zipped file has imbibed the knowledge to unpack and rejuvenate itself. Wouldn't it be great if you could come home from a vacation and have the suitcase unpack itself? There's something so depressing about unpacking from a vacation. Anyway, this kind of zipped file is known as *self-extracting*.

Don't get your hopes up. Self-extracting files are not the norm. In order to make a file self-extract, you've got to shove the self-extracting engine into the file — which makes the file bigger. Sometimes, the engine makes the suitcase file bigger than it was before starting the compression process. It's just not always practical. Especially when unzipping files is so easy.

Programmers create self-extracting files only when they don't have any faith that you know how to deal with a compressed file. Self-extracting files are advertised as such, and the name of the file always ends in EXE rather than ZIP.

You already have one self-extracting file sitting on your hard disk, if you followed along in the last chapter and downloaded PKZ204G.EXE — or whatever the current version is at the time you download the file. PKZ204G.EXE is a self-extracting file, which you can see in action, shortly.

Doing it yourself

Most of the time you have to roll up your sleeves and do the extracting all by yourself. Basically, all you have to do is type **PKUNZIP**, a space, the name of the file to be unzipped, and then press the magic Enter key. Honest. It's that simple. All the complicated stuff is done by the unzipper.

So, if you download several files like DOOM.ZIP, FANTASY.ZIP, or CARDS.ZIP, to unzip them you drop to a DOS prompt and type PKUNZIP DOOM and press Enter. Then you sit back and watch the files necessary to play Doom appear from, seemingly, nowhere. Then you type PKUNZIP FANTASY and press Enter, and the files that compose Fantasy appear. Finally, you type PKUNZIP CARDS, press Enter, and you should be able to guess what happens next.

Here's the caveat, though. Just as you can get into trouble downloading files willy-nilly onto your hard disk if you don't organize them into a download directory — as in Chapter 3 — you can also wreak havoc on your computer by unzipping files in the wrong directory.

An example would be if, for some reason, you decide to unzip a file in the directory where Word for Windows is stored. It takes more than two-dozen files to run Word for Windows. If you unzip a file in the Word for Windows directory, that tosses another half-dozen files into that directory. At first, you don't have a problem.

But what if, after using the downloaded program for a while, you realize it's not doing what you had hoped. Reeling from the disappointment, you want the new program never to darken your doorstep again. But which files belong to the downloaded program and which belong to Word for Windows? You don't know. The files are commingled. Any good lawyer will caution against commingling your assets.

Wouldn't it make more sense, she asks (leading the witness), to make a special directory just for that one downloaded program and, after moving the zipped file into that directory, to unzip the file in that contained arena? Later, if you want to nuke the file, it's easy to do so because that program's parts are the only things to be found in that particular space-and-time continuum. And, gosh, that's what directories are all about — to keep things separate and organized.

To recap, here's the broad-strokes process we go through to download and unzip a file:

1. **Download into the download directory — the temporary holding tank — one or more zipped files from a BBS (as in Chapter 3).**

2. **When ready to play with one of the downloaded files, or to make a permanent new home for a zipped file, create a new directory and copy the zipped file into it.**

3. **Extract the zipped file by typing** PKUNZIP **and the name of the file to unzip and pressing Enter.**

4. **Use the extracted files and have fun!**

You should know how to do Step 1 either from Chapter 3 or from your own vast life experiences. Before moving to Steps 2 through 4, though, you first have to attend to the minor detail of setting up PKZip and PKUnZip on your computer.

Enjoys helping

Don't fret that, because you're new to BBSing, you're not welcome. Many fellow users and Sysops are there to help. Many enjoy helping. "A brand-new modem user... they are the most fun. To watch their eyes light up when they *chat* for the first time or *download* their first file... it's awesome! When they finally find a BBS that will actually help them learn, they go nuts!"

Don Presten, Sysop, West Coast Connection

Setting Up Zip

Before we move on, it's time for a reality check.

To start zipping, you need to have PKZ204G.EXE downloaded onto your very own computer. If you haven't done that yet, zip on back to Chapter 3 and do your duty. This is one program you absolutely, positively have to have.

If you skipped downloading PKZ204G.EXE because you already have PKZip and PKUnZip, please make sure you have the latest and greatest version by typing **PKZIP** and pressing Enter at the system prompt. At the top of the screen, on the right, the version number appears. If you don't have the current version — PKZ204G — please go back and download it directly from the horse's mouth. About-face to Chapter 3.

Be sure you know the name of the directory you downloaded the file into. Knowing the name of the download directory is very important. If you really don't remember, or can't figure out, where your download directory is — and if you use Windows — use File Manager's Search command to solve the riddle once and for all. Here's how:

1. **To get to the File Manager, double-click on the Main group icon and then double-click on File Manager's two-drawer file-cabinet icon.**

2. **Once in File Manager, select File⇨Search to activate a Search dialog box.**

   The Search command is like a crystal ball. It can tell you where anything is on your computer if you ask correctly.

3. **In the text box to the right of Search For, type PK204G.EXE.**

4. **Make sure that Start From says** C:\, **and that** X **is marked in front of Search All Subdirectories.**

5. **Press Enter or click OK, and wait a few seconds.**

   Eventually, a Search Results window appears, telling you where PKZ204G.EXE is located. Everything in front of PKZ204G.EXE is the download directory. Like, if you see C:\PROWIN2\DNLOAD\PKZ204G.EXE, then you know C:\PROWIN2\DNLOAD is the download directory.

Installing PKZip is a one-time process, and it's no big deal. You can stick the program into your DOS directory and then let it extract itself. There are any number of ways to do this — with Windows and without. Since some of you may not have Windows, I'll show you how to do it sans Windows so that everyone has a fair shot. Okay. Ready?

1. **Get to the DOS prompt.**

   If you're currently using a DOS program, exit. If you're using Windows, you can either exit Windows — save your files first, of course — or, from Program Manager, select File ⇨ Run and, in the Run dialog box, type **command** and press Enter. If you're running Windows 95, select Run from the Taskbar.

   One way or the other, get to the bloomin' prompt so you see something like C:\.

2. **Type** CD\[name of download directory] **and press Enter.**

   Remember when you wrote down the name of your download directory? Now's the time you need it. If you use ProComm for Windows, for example, type: **CD\PROWIN2\DNLOAD** and press Enter. For Qmodem for DOS, it'd be **CD\QMPRO\DOWNLOAD** and Enter. If you had to make your own download directory, it'd be **CD\DOWNLOAD** and, of course, Enter.

3. **Once in the download directory, Type** COPY PKZ204G.EXE \DOS **and press Enter.**

   If, after a moment, you see a message on your screen about one file(s) being copied, then you were successful. If instead you're harassed with bad command or filename, invalid number of parameters, or invalid directory, double-check your typing. Try again.

4. **After the file is copied, type** CD\DOS **and press Enter.**

   After performing this step, you should be looking at C:\DOS or something close to it.

5. **Type** PKZ204G **and press Enter.**

If everything is moving as scheduled, the joint should be jumpin'! You have something very close to Figure 4-2, with files inflating and stuff coming at you. You don't have to duck, all is happening as it should.

You have now done all you need to set PKZip and PKUnZip to work on your computer. That makes you totally prepared to work with downloading for the rest of your life.

```
Searching EXE: C:/TEMP/PKZ204G.EXE
  Inflating: README.DOC    -AV
  Inflating: SHAREWAR.DOC  -AV
  Inflating: WHATSNEW.204  -AV
  Inflating: V204G.NEW     -AV
  Inflating: HINTS.TXT     -AV
  Inflating: LICENSE.DOC   -AV
  Inflating: ORDER.DOC     -AV
  Inflating: ADDENDUM.DOC  -AV
  Inflating: MANUAL.DOC    -AV
  Inflating: AUTHVERI.FRM  -AV
  Inflating: PKZIP.EXE     -AV
  Inflating: PKUNZIP.EXE   -AV
  Inflating: PKZIPFIX.EXE  -AV
  Inflating: ZIP2EXE.EXE   -AV
  Inflating: PKUNZJR.COM   -AV
  Inflating: OMBUDSMN.ASP  -AV

Authentic files Verified!   # PKW655
PKWARE Inc.

Thank you for using PKWARE!  PKWARE Support BBS (414) 354-8670

C:\TEMP >
```

Figure 4-2:
A self-extracting file in action is a thing of beauty and a joy for moments.

 Because you *copied* the PKZ204G.EXE file to the DOS directory, that means you have two copies of PKZ204G.EXE now — one in the DOS directory and one in the infamous download directory. Because the PKZip and UnZip files have been extracted from PKZ204G.EXE, you don't need them any more. If you want — and you should — you can delete both copies of those files.

1. **While you're still in the DOS directory, type** DEL PKZ204G.EXE **and press Enter.**

If the computer doesn't talk back at you, the file was deleted.

2. **Now move back to the download directory by typing** CD\[download directory] **and pressing Enter.**

This is just like what you did in Step 2 in the previous set of instructions, and it will again take you back to the download directory.

3. Type DEL PKZ204G.EXE **and press Enter.**

If you use Windows and are more comfortable using File Manager (or Explorer) or have another program you use for disk management, by all means go ahead and use it to move and copy files.

Anyway, let's zap on out of Zip and move on to Chapter 5.

Getting ZIP together!

Although we're concerned mostly about using PKUnZip in this book, you may find that PKZip is very handy to have around the computer. Separate from BBSing, PKZip can save space and help organize files... if you're into that sort of thing.

For example, say you produce a spreadsheet for every quarter. At the end of the year you have four spreadsheet files: MAR.XLS, JUN.XLS, SEP.XLS, and DEC.XLS. If you don't need those files every day, why not zip them together in a single file called YEAR.ZIP — or whatever makes sense to you. If you need to access one of the files in the YEAR.ZIP file, you can unzip the YEAR.ZIP file and reconstitute the four worksheet files using the same process as with a down-loaded file.

To create your own zipped file, type PKZIP and then the name of the file you want to create — like YEAR.ZIP — and the names of the files to be put into the main zipped file. Separate each filename

with a space. Here's how the command would look for this example. Don't forget to press Enter after the last filename.

```
PKZIP YEAR.ZIP MAR.XLS JUN.XLS
     SEP.XLS DEC.XLS
```

You see action on the screen telling you that the file is being squished and mooshed, and then you have YEAR.ZIP, which is smaller than the total of the four files combined.

If you are familiar with using wildcards (*) — see "Remedial DOS" in Chapter 3 if you aren't — you'll be happy to discover that you can use them to create a zipped file. In the spreadsheet example, you could save yourself plenty of key-strokes by issuing this command instead: PKZIP YEAR.ZIP *.XLS and pressing Enter. Of course, you'd want to make sure that only those four files were in the current directory or *all* XLS files would be included.

Chapter 5

Communicating in Cyberspace

In This Chapter
▶ Exchanging E-Mail
▶ Chatting up a storm
▶ Minding your Ps and Qs on BBSs

*W*hether it comes in a bottle, through the grapevine, over the wire, or even via satellite, it's fun to receive a message. The need to make contact is so basic, even computer geeks feel compelled to reach out now and again. Hence, electronic messaging. Now nongeeks have also discovered that electronic messaging is compelling, fun, efficient, and world-expanding.

Granted, some people never participate in electronic messaging because they are shy, believe they have nothing to say, or are intimidated by the fact that it takes place on a computer. That's okay as long as they support the BBSs they use in at least a monetary way. Maybe someday, after they feel more comfortable going online, they'll give messaging a try.

For many, though, messaging *is* BBSing. Sure, they enjoy downloading files, but the people they "meet" are even more important. To these folks, it's a simple question of, "Where would you rather be — the party with great food and bad guests or the party with bad food and great guests?" What's great and what's bad, of course, is subject to your own interpretation. And that's what makes it all the more interesting.

So what the heck is messaging on a BBS? I'll start off with the two basic types of communication online. One is called *E-Mail*, the other *Chat*. Both Chat and E-Mail can be either *public* or *private*. Once you learn how Chat and E-Mail work, I'll send you to finishing school so you can learn about online etiquette. Finally, you'll find out what <ROTFL> and ;-] mean — two things you'll be seeing and doing once you start sending messages.

Exchanging E-Mail

E-Mail is shorthand for *electronic mail*. As with most noncybermail, the point is to write down a thought or a feeling and then transmit it.

Everyone has a story to tell . . . including *you*. And we want to hear it. Even if the only thought in your head is, "Help, I'm confused," it's worthy of E-Mail. You may get help, or you may get a response from some guy who sympathizes because he's also feeling confused.

After letting the BBS know you want to write a message, you are asked to whom you want to send the message and what the subject matter will be. This works just like an office memo.

Next, the BBS provides you with a miniature word-processing program for composing your thoughts. These BBS word processors are very simple . . . almost typewriter-like. If you can type a message and backspace over errors, you are now an expert. It's that simple. Figure 5-1 shows a typical blank message screen.

After a moment, you see something close to Figure 5-1 — which is an E-Mail message waiting to happen.

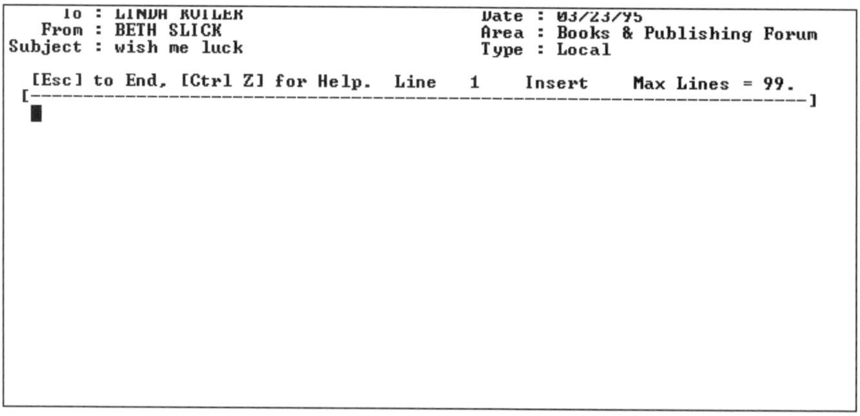

Figure 5-1:
The BBS
provides
pen and
paper —
actually a
mini-word
processor
— to
encourage
sending of
electronic
mail. E-Mail
for short.

```
  To   : LINDA KOILER              Date : 03/23/95
  From : BETH SLICK                Area : Books & Publishing Forum
Subject : wish me luck            Type : Local

  [Esc] to End, [Ctrl Z] for Help.  Line   1     Insert     Max Lines = 99.
  [--------------------------------------------------------------------------]
  █
```

Unlike with a major word-processing program, where you are supposed to save often, on a BBS you do not save your message until you are completely, finally, and unalterably finished. That's because, on a BBS, saving and sending are the same thing.

When you have finished composing, you must issue an I'm-done-writing command of some sort, like pressing Esc once or Enter twice. If you look carefully at your BBS word-processor screen, you will find an end-of-message command displayed somewhere, though not always in the most obvious way. In Figure 5-1, just above the cursor you see the phrase [Esc] to End. That means press Esc when you decide to end the message.

After you unburden yourself and indicate you're all done writing, you get a list of message-handling options. The minimal range of command choices facing you includes

- ✔ **Save:** This really means send the message.

- ✔ **Abort:** This is your chance to change your mind and forget the message.

- ✔ **Edit:** This lets you go back and change something.

- ✔ **Continue:** This one may be confusing. Continue doesn't mean, as it often does, go on to the next step. In E-Mail, Continue means that you want to go back to the message and continue writing. So, if you just remembered something you wanted to add, then you use Continue.

Once you tell the BBS to save/send your witty message, it is instantly delivered. E-Mail is nothing like the U.S. Post Office — often referred to online as *snail mail* — which must be collected, sorted, routed, re-sorted, and delivered. And that's only if everything goes right.

When I say instant, I'm not using hyperbole. From personal experience, I know this to be true. I was talking to a friend in Paris, France, while we were both online — yes, I have two phone lines into my apartment — and he said, "There, I just sent you a file." Ten seconds later, I received a beep tone on my computer in Venice, California, indicating that the message had just arrived. E-Mail on a BBS won't take even that long.

Once the message is sent, where does it go?

For your eyes only

The most traditional landing spot for a piece of E-Mail is in the mailbox of another user of the BBS. To visualize this, think of the BBS system as a building containing lots of post-office boxes. Every person who signs up with the BBS has a box. Messages sent person-to-person are called *private mail*.

Unlike a physical mailbox, where you go peek through the glass or open it with a key, you're dependent on the BBS to notify you that there is mail. In fact, the BBS automatically checks every single time you come online. If you've got mail, you are told.

If you do have a message, some BBSs ask if you want to read it immediately and offer to take you to your mail via a shortcut. Or, you may have to take a moment to select E-Mail from the Main Menu to get to your mailbox menu, like the one in Figure 5-2.

Figure 5-2:
My own private Mailbox on Monterey Gaming System.

```
** Beth's private Mailbox **
1. Read your private messages
2. Quick Scan Message Headers
3. Write a private Message
4. Delete a Message
5. User Search

U. Utilities   M. Main   P. Previous   G. Goodbye
```

Although other system users cannot read private, person-to-person messages, the Sysop and the Sysop's heirs and assigns have access to everything on the board, including your mail. Most Sysops have better things to do than read other people's mail. Also, many Sysops pride themselves on the privacy granted to their users. However, the bottom line is that Sysops are legally accountable for *whatever* happens on their BBSs — whether it occurs in public forums or private E-Mail.

Getting on a soap box

I've often wondered what soap boxes looked like at the time the phrase "getting on a soap box" was coined. My little box of Tide would crumble under the weight of my cat, much less a human. They must have made some serious soap boxes back then.

Even though soap boxes have changed, the need to stand up and speak your peace hasn't wavered. And BBSs know that. That's why they provide an opportunity for public opinion-expressing.

A major part of every BBS is the *conferences*. Conferences go by many names, including forums, special interest groups (SIGS), or message bases. Each conference has a theme or suggested topic. Figure 5-3 shows a group of topics available on the Monterey Gaming System.

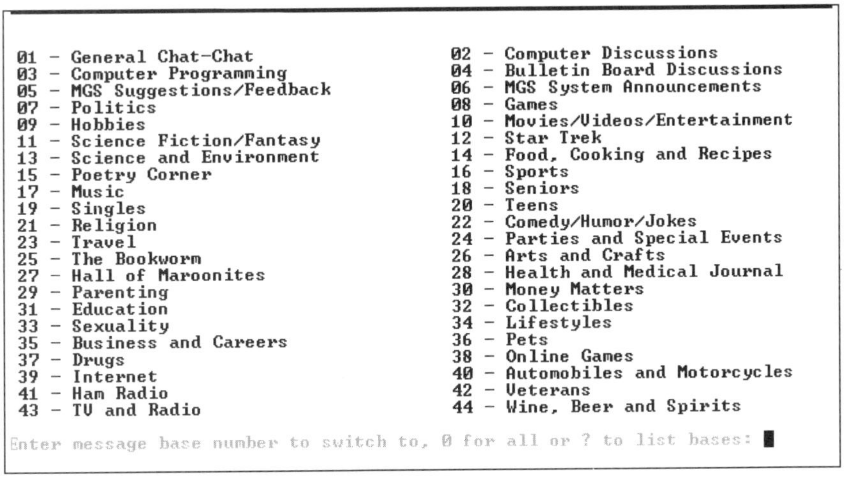

Figure 5-3:
Want to talk about Poetry, Politics, or Pets? Join like-minded types in a conference.

```
01 - General Chat-Chat            02 - Computer Discussions
03 - Computer Programming         04 - Bulletin Board Discussions
05 - MGS Suggestions/Feedback     06 - MGS System Announcements
07 - Politics                     08 - Games
09 - Hobbies                      10 - Movies/Videos/Entertainment
11 - Science Fiction/Fantasy      12 - Star Trek
13 - Science and Environment      14 - Food, Cooking and Recipes
15 - Poetry Corner                16 - Sports
17 - Music                        18 - Seniors
19 - Singles                      20 - Teens
21 - Religion                     22 - Comedy/Humor/Jokes
23 - Travel                       24 - Parties and Special Events
25 - The Bookworm                 26 - Arts and Crafts
27 - Hall of Maroonites           28 - Health and Medical Journal
29 - Parenting                    30 - Money Matters
31 - Education                    32 - Collectibles
33 - Sexuality                    34 - Lifestyles
35 - Business and Careers         36 - Pets
37 - Drugs                        38 - Online Games
39 - Internet                     40 - Automobiles and Motorcycles
41 - Ham Radio                    42 - Veterans
43 - TV and Radio                 44 - Wine, Beer and Spirits

Enter message base number to switch to, 0 for all or ? to list bases: █
```

To participate in discussing a specific topic, you need to join the appropriate conference. If you have a question about God, for example, you should join the Religion forum. Actually, if you have an answer about God, you should also join.

Joining a conference is not like joining a gym or joining a book club or even joining someone for a cup of coffee. The word *join* on a BBS is roughly a euphemism for *go to*. Joining a conference is no more a commitment than going to a different directory or folder on a hard disk. Every time you go to a conference, you join it. When you're ready to leave, you either join another conference or quit all the conferences and go back to the Main Menu.

Say you've had a disappointing week and could use some cheering up. Spending time in the Comedy/Humor/Jokes conference might be just the cure.

When you join a conference, you will discover how Bulletin Board Systems got named. They borrowed the term from businesses that attached cork bulletin boards to a prominent wall for their customers to post notices for their own business services, lost dogs, goods for sale, and other items of public interest.

In a conference, instead of papers stuck on a bulletin board, E-Mail is *posted* by other BBS members for general consumption, such as the message in Figure 5-4, which appeared in a Comedy conference.

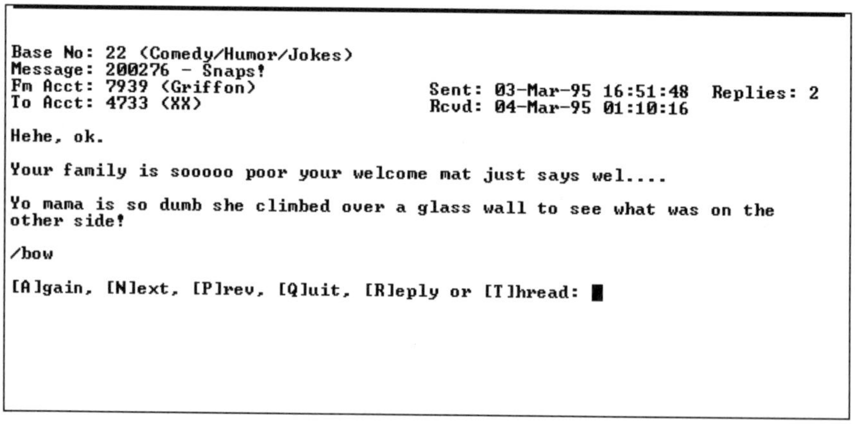

Figure 5-4:
Snaps online? In the Comedy/ Humor/ Jokes conference on the Monterey Gaming System, you may run into the next David Letterman or Martin Lawrence.

```
Base No: 22 (Comedy/Humor/Jokes)
Message: 200276 - Snaps!
Fm Acct: 7939 (Griffon)                Sent: 03-Mar-95 16:51:48    Replies: 2
To Acct: 4733 (XX)                     Rcvd: 04-Mar-95 01:10:16
Hehe, ok.

Your family is sooooo poor your welcome mat just says wel....

Yo mama is so dumb she climbed over a glass wall to see what was on the
other side!

/bow

[A]gain, [N]ext, [P]rev, [Q]uit, [R]eply or [T]hread: █
```

E-Mail posted in a conference is created, written, and saved just like private E-Mail. The main difference is that E-Mail in a conference ends up on a public bulletin board instead of a private mailbox.

If you join a Parenting forum, you may see E-Mail messages asking questions about child-rearing, the efficacy and dangers of vaccines, and so forth. People with questions or issues post them and then wait for a reply from someone else who's come by to browse the postings.

You may even come across a message with a question that *you* can answer. In that case, jump in with a public reply. Then, anyone else who joins in can benefit from your knowledge. Or, if you prefer, you can reply using the security option to mark the reply as private — only to be read by the addressee.

One side note. Some BBSs don't have private mailboxes, per se. What they do instead is dedicate a conference to the topic of Private Mail. Everyone who wants to send someone else a message that doesn't pertain to a particular ongoing topic sends the E-Mail in the Private Mail conference, being sure to mark the missive as Private. If other people join that conference, they cannot read any of the messages there except the ones addressed to them.

There is no limit — other than your overall time limit — to the number of conferences you can join and messages you can read and reply to. You'll find that almost any question you have, someone either has an answer, will point you in the right direction, or can commiserate with you over the problem.

If you just read messages but never respond, you are known as a *lurker*. Usually it's a good idea to lurk for a while to see what's going on. After all, you'd never walk up to several people at a party and immediately try to monopolize the conversation. First you'd listen, see what the conversation was about, determine the flow, then jump in and make your point if you have one.

In any conference, as in any good party, several conversations take place simultaneously. Unlike any party, you can participate in all of the conversations, if you are that much of a party animal.

The messages posted in a conference appear in chronological order. For example, here's a summary of some messages you may encounter if you join the Singles forum (although the structure of these messages would probably look more like the Comedy Chat shown in Figure 5-4):

Message:	#51
Subject:	Newly single
	Newly-single man wondering about being single after twenty years of marriage

Message:	#52
Subject:	Pizza Party
	BBS member putting together a party for singles on the BBS

Message:	#53
Subject:	Adult Ed
	Message about which adult education classes are good for meeting singles

Message:	#54
Subject:	Singles with kids
	Complaints about the problems of being a single parent and trying to find a new mate
Message	#55
Subject:	Pizza Party
	Someone confirms they can make the party
Message	#56
Subject:	Adult Ed
	A list of four adult education classes where people met future mates
Message	#57
Subject:	Newly Single
	A message from a newly-single woman wondering about being single after twenty years of marriage

Although this isn't how you're used to talking, the progression of each conversation can be easily followed. In BBS-speak, each of these conversations — the Pizza Party, Newly Single, Adult Ed, and Singles with Kids — is called a *thread*.

If you take a close look at Figure 5-4, bottom right, you'll see an option called Thread. When you use that option, it takes you to the next message with the same subject line. In Figure 5-4, the subject is Snaps. If you want to follow that conversation and ignore the others, you have that option.

It's the all-important Subject line that strings messages together in a thread. Part of your duty as a message-writer is to keep the integrity of the Subject line so others can follow the thread.

Sometimes a conversation evolves into a different topic, but everyone continues using the original Subject line from the source conversation so that latecomers can follow the whole thread. At some point, someone will notice the conversation and the subject line no longer resemble each other and start a new thread. Usually, though, a thread runs its course and dies a natural death.

There are a number of mind-bending aspects to conferencing:

> ✔ *Time doesn't matter.* The conversation is always going on, and you don't have to miss a moment of it. Whenever you log onto the BBS it will show you, at your request, all the new messages posted since your last logon.

✔ *Geography doesn't matter.* If you live in a small town, you may have a hard time meeting fifty people who want to talk Ham Radio. On a BBS, you're not restricted by where you live or your ability to get out and around. On a BBS, it's a Ham Radio convention every day. Or, if you can clear a room by bringing up the topic of Star Trek, you'll find a Star Trek conference where you're applauded for knowing who poisoned the quardotriticale, rather than being told to get a life by the shockingly inferior life forms in your family.

✔ *You never see whom you're exchanging messages with.* Stereotyping based on corporal appearance is impossible. Your judgment of people will be based on what they say and do, not on age, career choice, or pierced body parts.

✔ *It's virtual reality.* Just as people supply mental pictures for radio, you'll supply pictures and sound for the conference participants. Eventually the BBS seems like a world crowded with people — some with sexy voices, some loud and boisterous, others with great laughs. You hear the champagne pop and the glasses tinkle; but, of course, it's all in your head.

Chatting up a Storm

If you've ever participated in one of those telephone Party Lines, then you understand the verbal version of how chatting on a BBS works.

Many BBSs — the bigger ones anyway — allow for more than one caller at a time to be on the system. Someone got the idea that if two people are simultaneously online, they may want to talk to each other in real time — rather than leaving E-Mail to be read later.

Instead of actually talking, though, chatting on a BBS involves typing messages back and forth to each other. What one person types, the other person sees at the same moment. It's as though they have one computer screen with two keyboards.

Are you talking to me?

A typical scenario for chatting might work like this: You log on and check out who's online right now by giving a command at the Main Menu. One of the people online goes by the handle of Mouse. You and Mouse have had a few discussions via E-Mail, and you want to clear something up. A quick Chat session could save several E-Mail exchanges. So you give another command that sends a message, called a *page*, directly to Mouse — interrupting Mouse's current activities — which says you want to chat. After a few seconds, Mouse agrees to chat, and the BBS puts you both in Chat mode.

As you type, Mouse sees the letters as they form words and sentences. Although you may make typos, if the word is understandable, it's best not to worry about correcting errors. After you give the signal that you've finished typing, Mouse gets a turn to type a response while you patiently wait. After receiving a *go ahead* signal from Mouse, it is again your turn to type a message.

And so it goes until you both agree the conversation has come to an end. Then, you terminate Chat mode and continue using the BBS.

Anyway, that's the G-rated version of what happens in private chat. Often, though, the conversation takes a steamier turn — just like the Party Line phone calls. You didn't think all those Party Line callers were just exchanging recipes did you? Hardly. Just remember

✔ BBSs with Chat features give you the option of indicating that you don't want to chat and blocking anyone else's ability to hook you into Chat. (Figure 5-5 shows a Chat menu with many options.)

✔ If you're in Chat and find the content turning distasteful, pull the plug. Exit Chat.

✔ If you are looking for a hot Chat session, just browse around, and I'm sure you can find one spicy enough for any palette.

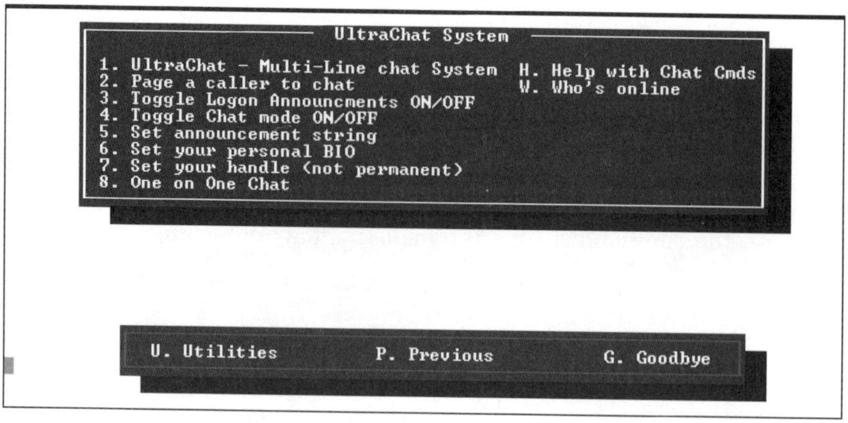

Figure 5-5:
A chatting menu on the Monterey Gaming System with all the bells and whistles. Wouldn't it be nice if you could select who you chat with in real life?

```
                        UltraChat System
    1. UltraChat - Multi-Line chat System    H. Help with Chat Cmds
    2. Page a caller to chat                  W. Who's online
    3. Toggle Logon Announcments ON/OFF
    4. Toggle Chat mode ON/OFF
    5. Set announcement string
    6. Set your personal BIO
    7. Set your handle (not permanent)
    8. One on One Chat


    U. Utilities         P. Previous          G. Goodbye
```

Joining the conversation

A Chat session needn't be limited to two people. Depending on the number of phone lines coming into the BBS, of course, you can have half a dozen or more people in the same Chat session. Again, you'll find a number of conversations going on at the same time, and it can be tiresome to wade through all the stuff that appears.

However, people can have online meetings. The Pizza Party committee can get together and make their decisions from the comfort of their own homes. It's not unlike setting up a conference call at the office. The only difference is that people are typing, not talking.

Minding Your Ps and Qs on BBSs

As you might imagine, if you have time to imagine at all, communicating online has evolved into an art form. A minor one, but still an art form. There are certain rules of etiquette and methods of getting a point across that you just don't encounter offline — that wouldn't even make sense offline.

Keeping your elbows off the table

Etiquette online is like nothing you've ever encountered. For example, it is permissible to chew with your mouth open, scratch wherever it itches, and make all the rude noises you want. The height of boorish behavior, though, is to type your messages all in uppercase letters. Why? Because IT LOOKS LIKE YOU'RE SHOUTING. And that is rude.

Other quick tips include:

- Conference messages are usually composed online and not by professional writers. People make mistakes. You will make mistakes. Don't be a jerk and post messages that correct the spelling and grammatical content of someone else's message. I guarantee you that if you do that once, you'll find every one of your own messages scrupulously dissected for errors for a long time to come.

- Read all the messages in a thread before replying. You may find that someone has already said what you wanted to say. Please participate, but don't cover the same ground. Remember, everyone is on a time clock and some are paying long distance. Don't waste time.

- Keep your messages relevant to the topic of the conference. It would be scary if you left a question about baby care in the Pets Conference.

- Avoid meaningless messages. If your message only contains a reaction, like "Yippee!" or "You sure told him!," then don't bother. If you have something to add to the thread, great. Another type of meaningless message reads something like, "I agree with Bob." Not only don't the rest of us have a clue which one of Bob's points you're agreeing with, but, what's worse, you've added nothing to the discussion.

- Keep arguments above the belt. It is better to say, "That is a stupid idea," than to say "You are a stupid person." Please, keep discussions from degenerating into name-calling slugfests. It makes you look bad, and no one wants to read message after message reminding us that human beings still have lots of evolving to do. People who leave messages intended to enrage or just plain dump all over someone are engaging in an activity called *flaming*. Generally, flaming is frowned upon.

- Remember that your tone of irony and dry wit may not come across in a message unless you've worded it very carefully. If you're not used to writing, keep to simple, direct sentences at first. With a little practice, you'll be able to get your meaning across. Sincerity, enthusiasm, and clear thinking are welcome on any BBS. Witty phrases can backfire.

- Since you can't underline, boldface, or mess with fonts and font size, the text in your messages will look unadorned. To combat this, people use different characters to emphasize their words. You might see, That's an *incredible* idea — using the asterisks in place of an underline. As you read messages, you'll get new ideas.

TIP

Asking for help

If you run into problems, you can find people online willing to help, if you send a message to ALL in the appropriate conferences. Everyone online has gone through what you're going through and sympathizes. However, there's a right way and a wrong way to ask for help. See if you can guess which of these two examples is the recommended approach: Sample #1: "This BBS is stupid and complicated. I've tried to download a file 100 times and every single time I run into the same problem. And don't tell me to read the instructions, I never understand them. Just tell me what to do." Sample #2: "I've read the bulletin on downloading but still have a problem. The instructions say to press <CR>, but I don't know what that means. Please help."

Obviously the first sample is written by a jerk. No one who's ever done technical support will be eager to help that person. They will be on the receiving end of ten minutes of verbal abuse before the helpee calms down enough to listen to the helper.

The second sample is a polite, *specific* request for information. We can see this person has tried to help him- or herself but just hit the glass ceiling of current knowledge. A quick E-Mail explaining that <CR> means carriage return, or Enter, is all that's needed. As a Sysop, I would probably also thank the individual for asking, because it reminds me to go back into that bulletin and change all those cryptic <CR>s into Enters — which I've been meaning to do for some time.

Keeping it short

I'm sure you've received a party invitation with RSVP written on the bottom or a memo from the boss with ASAP or FYI written on the top. And all of us who work Monday through Friday sport tattoos that read TGIF. These are all common abbreviations.

BBSers also draw from a stock of accepted acronyms to get their points across. You'll find many messages polka-dotted with these acronyms, in order to save keystrokes and time. Acronyms are especially useful during Chat sessions, when speed of typing really counts. A few of the most common ones follow:

- **IMO:** In my opinion. Also seen as IMHO — in my humble opinion. Usage: This book was a big help, IMO.

- **FWIW:** For what it's worth. Usage: FWIW, I thought Ishtar was a funny movie.

- **BTW:** By the way. Usage: This isn't the first time you've done this, BTW.

- **TTFN:** Ta ta for now. Usage: Someone's at the door, TTFN.

- **RTFM:** Read the F******* Manual. A gentle suggestion that if you would only look at the instructions, all will be explained.

You'll run into established acronyms and may witness the birth of new ones. Don't be afraid to ask what they mean.

Using virtual body language

Experts agree that body language and tone of voice carry most of the content in communication. With those key elements absent from electronic communications, cybercitizens have invented some crazy new ways to get their points across while still maintaining the intimacy and fun of a coffee klatch.

Putting an angle on it

One way to indicate your body language is to write down what you're doing and set it off with angle brackets. Angle brackets indicate a physical action, separate from the text. For example

- I'm so happy for you <grin>.

    This one is used so often that it's often abbreviated: <G>.

- Have you seen the latest <sigh> Brad Pitt movie?

- Hi everyone <sniff>. Don't get too close <sniff> I have a terrible cold.

✔ Good to see you again <wink>.

✔ <ROTFL>

Sometimes you see this by itself. It means *rolling on the floor laughing*. If someone says something funny, this is a way to let them know you enjoyed it. Again, especially helpful during Chat.

Smiling faces

The second way to indicate what your face is doing while your fingers are typing is to use *smileys* or *emoticons*. A smiley is a little typewriter-drawn face that represents your emotions.

I have seen books filled with examples of smileys in a range of shapes and sizes. The number of characters and emotional states simulated by a little creative typing is astonishing. If you run across someone with a talent for it, it's a lot of fun.

Your basic have-a-nice-day smiley looks like this: : -) . If you don't see the smiling face immediately, try looking at it with your left ear to your shoulder. Imagine the colon as two eyeballs, the hyphen is the nose, and the parenthesis as a smile; you'll see how it works. Here's a frowning face: : - (. This smiley did not have a good day.

Some examples of smileys in action:

✔ Hey, good-looking ;-)

✔ What great news :-)

✔ I hate cooked mushrooms :-s

✔ You remember Kramer . . . ##:-) Seinfeld's neighbor?

SYSOP SEZ

It's a cyberworld after all

"People call Crystal Quill to be with other people and with telnet access from anywhere on the planet, we get fascinating personalities from every culture in the world — all meeting on a small silicon chip 15 minutes from the capital of the United States. It is truly amazing."

Pamela Stewart, Sysop, Crystal Quill

Chapter 6
Modeming Defensively

. . . .

In This Chapter

▶ Microscoping out a computer virus

▶ Staying current with virus checkers

▶ Checking for viruses

▶ Getting a Red Alert

. . . .

Super Nova, Black Holes, Warp Engines, — all words designed to bypass brain-taxing scientific explanations by painting intriguing mental images. The average man-on-the-street may have heard of a Black Hole, but he'd be hard-pressed to come up with a cogent explanation of it.

"Well, it's a hole and it's black, right?"

You can add *computer virus* to the list of meaningless terminology.

Unlike those other highfalutin ideas, though, computer virus is one term that you'd better understand and be able to explain to your friends when they say, "Well, it's a virus and it's in a computer, right?"

You should be able to sit straight in your chair, raise an eyebrow, and tell them that they are correct only to the extent that any parasitic biological microorganism can thrive in a nonbiological medium. Which is to say, *no*, they are not right.

So what the heck are computer viruses, and how much of a problem are they really?

Microscoping Out a Computer Virus

A so-called computer virus is a program, a wee bit o' software, with three basic missions:

- To burrow its way into the soft underbelly of your computer system — like the program that controls and starts the computer or keeps track of where all the files are

- To clone a copy of itself onto every program stored in the computer, and onto every program that leaves the computer via a floppy disk or backup tape, or that is uploaded via a modem

- To destroy, at a predetermined time, the vulnerable spot of the computer, which usually wipes out everything on the system; often, the destruction is accompanied by a taunting note to let you know you've been trashed by a certain virus or person

A computer virus also has a another, secondary directive — to avoid detection. The bad guys who create these destructive programs design their viruses to mimic normal computer activities or functions. But ultimately, no matter how hard the virus may try to maintain a low profile, each virus has a detectable *signature,* or modus operandi. As fast as evil programmers turn out viruses, the resistance in white lab coats is working out ways to detect and destroy them.

And, if you haven't guessed by now, the reason these destructive programs are called viruses is because of the way they are designed to replicate themselves and spread out like a virus in a living creature.

Taking Preventive Action

The only way to completely avoid a virus is to never download files and never copy files from a disk onto your computer. This includes disks from manufacturers; disgruntled employees have done a lot worse than infect master disks. I even heard a story about a man who sent an infected disk to his ex-wife, promising that it would fix her computer problems.

Horror stories aside, I hope you decide against the monastic approach and opt to learn how to be safe while enjoying the great software and fun activities going on in cyberspace. Personally, and I may be tempting fate, I have never encountered a virus in almost a decade of using modems and BBSs.

The 5th Wave
By Rich Tennant

Although computer viruses are certainly a fact of life, many protective measures are in place to shield you, even if you never lift a finger on your own behalf. But you should. Lift a finger, that is.

Here are three things you can do to reduced the risk of catching a virus (if you noticed there are *four* items in this list, that last one doesn't reduce the chance of *getting* infected; it's simply a good way to prepare just in case):

✔ Download files from BBSs that automatically run virus checkers on every uploaded file. Running virus checkers on all uploaded software is no more than a simple act of self-preservation for a BBS. The bottom line is that if a Sysop isn't bright enough to run a virus check, the board won't last too long anyway.

✔ Take a few seconds every day to run a virus checker on your computer. You probably already own a virus checker if you have the current version of DOS.

✔ Frequently download new virus signatures to keep your virus-checker software aware of the current "most wanted" list.

✔ Back up often. Having a current backup makes it possible to recover from a virus disaster cheaply, easily, and without having that oh-so-inconvenient heart attack when you realize *everything is gone*. Although I'm sure *you* back up every day, be sure to caution your friends to adopt good back-up habits. Isn't the information on your computer worth the few minutes it takes to back up?

Don't leave backing up on your permanent *tomorrow* list. DOS comes with easy-to-use backup software — look for Microsoft Backup for either DOS or Windows 3.1. If you don't have Microsoft Backup, a kajillion backup programs are available at your local software store. You can also download a backup program from a BBS — Chapter 8 shows you how to search for helpful files on BBSs. The computer you save may be your own.

Staying Current with Virus Checkers

Because new viruses are being invented all the time, half the battle is to stay on top of all the latest virus signatures. You can, of course, download signatures. Each virus-checker software package has its own way of doing things, so you have to know what virus checker you're using to discover where to get the updates.

✔ You may own a commercial, off-the-shelf virus checker. If you haven't updated it since you first brought it home, now's a good time to look in the manual for instructions on getting the latest in sneaky virus signatures.

✔ With Version 6 of MS-DOS, you'll find a virus checker called Microsoft Anti-Virus in the package — both an MS-DOS and a Windows 3.1 version. To discover if you have Microsoft Anti-Virus, get to the system prompt — which means save your files and quit everything — type **MSAV** and press Enter.

If you see Microsoft Anti-Virus come to life, you can assume that you own Microsoft Anti-Virus. Skip on down to "Updating Microsoft Anti-Virus" or "Using Virus Checkers" for more information.

If, on the other hand, you get the dreaded bad command notice from your computer, then you don't have Microsoft Anti-Virus. Your last hope lies with Windows 3.1. Check around for the Microsoft Anti-Virus icon. If you find it, double-click to make sure that the program works. If that doesn't work either, Don Pardo has some nice parting gifts for you. You'll have to either, ahem, buy a virus checker or run on down to the section "Connecting with McAfee AntiVirus."

Updating Microsoft Anti-Virus

Microsoft Anti-Virus, for those who care about these things, was not invented by Microsoft. It was licensed from a fine organization named Central Point Software. Central Point Software, which had purchased XTree systems earlier, was itself purchased by Symantec, which had also purchased Norton Utilities some years earlier. You think soap-opera families are twisted — just try keeping up with the software industry for a while.

The only reason we care that Central Point Software is the maker of Microsoft Anti-Virus software is that, if you want to get the latest virus signature updates, who you gonna call? The Central Point BBS.

If you belong to CompuServe, you have the option to call them and explore Symantec's online forum over the phone. But it's a toss-up as to which is more expensive — the on-line fee or the long distance call. Once on CompuServe, GO SYMVIRUS. Search the Library to find either DOSAV.EXE, which contains the virus signature updates for the DOS version, or WINAV.EXE for the Windows 3.1 update.

Downloading the update

If you're the type that flips ahead instead of letting the mystery unfold, you may have discovered that, beyond this page, are a lot of numbered steps. But don't assume, just because there are many steps, that downloading the update is going to be unbelievably complicated. Sometimes more steps is actually less complicated than fewer steps. Although that belies common sense, here's why it's true.

For example, I can explain the whole procedure in two steps (I feel like I'm on Name That Tune). Step 1: Call the Central Point BBS. Step 2: Download the current virus signature file. Now that sounds easy, right? However, if you're a little nervous about downloading, you may find it simpler to have detailed help along the way. Hence, more steps is less complicated than figuring it out yourself.

Just for the record, you can figure out every step of the way simply by reading the instructions onscreen. Honest. No special knowledge is required. See if you can pick up the clues from what's onscreen. Just to make sure you remain on the right trail, I've provided you with clues of my own:

1. **Call the Central Point BBS at 503-984-5366 and log on.**

   You have to go through a short, first-time logon process. You can handle it. Just follow the instructions. Eventually, you are delivered to the Main Menu.

2. **Press F and Enter to select Files from the Main Menu.**

   After each step, you see some sort of change to the screen. Remember not to continue with the next step until that option becomes available. You may notice a small lag between when you type a command and when the BBS carries it out. It's easy to forget that, when you type a command, you're telling your computer to send a message across thousands of miles to another computer, which has to carry out that command and then send a new screen to your computer. Have patience.

3. **Press either D for DOS or W for Windows and then press Enter.**

   Whether you press D or W depends on which version of Microsoft Anti-Virus you want to use. The version that starts from the system prompt is the DOS version. If you started the program from Windows 3.1 . . . well, you get the idea.

4. **Press A for Central Point Anti-Virus and then press Enter.**

5. **Press F for Find Files and then press Enter.**

6. **Press D and then Enter to request files be shown by date — the newest first.**

   This makes it easier to find the latest version.

7. **When asked which libraries you want, press C for Current and then press Enter.**

   You see a list of files including DOSAV.EXE for DOS or WINAV.EXE for Windows 3.1.

   Nothing changes faster than the computer industry — except for maybe the new fall TV lineup. Between the time this book is written and the time it arrives in your hands, the Central Point BBS may be different, and the exact names of the files to download may have changed. So, if you find some modifications, just take a deep breath, carefully examine your options, and make your best guess.

8. **Using your arrow keys, highlight the file of your choice.**

9. **When the file is highlighted, press Ctrl+D to initiate the download sequence.**

   Gosh, doesn't that sound like something out of NASA? Actually, it just brings the basic list of protocols to your screen.

10. **Type Z for Zmodem when presented with the basic list of protocols.**

    Remember that you don't need to know what a protocol is or does at this point, you just need to choose one.

11. **Enter your communication program's download command and select the same protocol you used in Step 10 — hopefully Zmodem.**

    Remember, the download command varies depending on which telecommunications program you're using. In many programs, it's the PageDown key. In Procomm Plus for Windows, it's a matter of clicking the down-arrow file icon.

12. **Wait while the file downloads. It's a big one.**

13. **After the download is finished, press C to Continue.**

    This takes you back to the list of files.

14. **Press X — without pressing Enter afterwards — to exit the list of files.**

    This starts the process of floating back up to the top of the Central Point BBS menu system and exiting.

15. **Press X to ignore the next list of options.**

16. **For a change of pace, press * and then Enter to quickly get back to the top menu.**

17. **Press X and then Enter to log off . . . almost.**

18. **When you're asked if you really want to log off, press Y and then Enter.**

19. **Quit your telecommunications software, quit Windows, quit everything, and get to the system prompt (C:\).**

Getting the virus-signature update file safely home in your download directory — we talked about download directories in Chapter 3 — is a victory. But it's not the end of the story. We have yet to actually update the Microsoft Anti-Virus program with the new signatures.

However, if you need a cup of coffee at this point, you can take a break. I'll be waiting.

Updating the program

To recap, you have the Microsoft Anti-Virus update signatures in your hard disk's download directory. Now you're going to copy them from the general download directory to their own little examining room. Once the files you downloaded update the Microsoft Anti-Virus program, you won't need the update files any more. You can nuke 'em, which is the next-to-the-last step.

1. **At the C:\ prompt, type** CD\[download directory] **and press Enter.**

   You have to type in your own download directory, like CD\PROWIN2\DNLOAD for Procomm Plus for Windows or CD\QMPRO\DOWNLOAD for QmodemPro. Or, if you made your own download directory back in Chapter 3, you would type **CD\DOWNLOAD.**

2. **After you get to your download directory, type** MD TEMP **and press Enter.**

   This makes a temporary holding tank to put the program into while you examine it.

3. **Next, copy the file into the temporary directory by typing** COPY DOSAV.EXE TEMP **and pressing Enter.**

   If you copied the Windows version, then trade WINAV.EXE for DOSAV.EXE in the preceding instruction.

4. **Go to the temporary directory by typing** CD TEMP **and pressing Enter.**

5. **Type** DOSAV **and press Enter.**

   Or, if you've got the Windows version, don't type DOSAV; type **WINAV** and press Enter.

You get 50 extra bonus points if you noticed that the file you downloaded ends in EXE. Remember, EXE at the end of a filename tells you two things. First, you know for sure it isn't a ZIP file. Why? Zip files all end in ZIP. Second, it is a safe assumption that this file is a self-extracting file. That is, this file decompresses itself for you.

If you performed Step 5, then you've just seen the file decompress. If this seems confusing, that's only because you've just started doing it. Pretty soon it'll all be second nature. Remember how driving a car used to seem so complicated — so many things to remember — and now you can do it in your sleep? Well, almost, anyway.

You can find the how-to for the next step in the file named — appropriately enough — README.TXT, which is one of the files that extracted itself. Every compressed program comes with a *readme* file. It's where the instructions are. You can play with readme files when you download files in Chapter 8. For now, I've already read README.TXT and distilled the instructions for you.

Use Step 6a for DOS or Step 6b for Windows.

6. **Perform the update.**

a. If you have the DOS version, you see a note telling you what to do. Basically, just type **UPDATE** and press Enter. Then, when prompted for a Path, type **C:\DOS** and press Enter, just like the example on your screen. After a few seconds, you see Update Successful.

– or –

b. If you have the Windows version, you need to copy two files. Type **COPY MWAVSCAN.DLL C:\DOS** and press Enter. After you get a 1 file(s) copied message, move on to the next file. Type **COPY MSAVIRUS.LST C:\DOS** and press Enter.

Step 6 performs the update, so you won't need those files or the temporary directory anymore. Because the instruction for Step 7 deletes everything in the current directory, you want to make sure you're in the right directory. If you type **DIR** and press Enter, you get a list of files. If you've been using the Windows update, and you see eight files listed (or if, in DOS, you see ten), then you're in the right place. Go ahead.

If you get more than ten files, you may have accidentally extracted the files in the wrong directory. Don't do the next two steps until you troubleshoot what happened — which you'll have to do by yourself or with a little help from your friends. Because Steps 7 and 8 are, essentially, clean-up steps, if you stop now and skip the rest of these steps, no harm will come to you.

7. **To delete the update files, type** DEL *.* **and press Enter.**

You are warned that all files will be deleted. Go ahead and press Y and then Enter.

8. **Now, type** CD .. **and press Enter to back out of the temporary directory and get to the download directory where you started.**

9. **Get rid of the temporary directory by typing** RD TEMP **and pressing Enter.**

That's why it's called a temporary directory. We only needed it for a little while.

You may recall that the original file you downloaded is still in the download directory. Step 10 gets rid of that file, too.

10. **Type** DEL DOSAV.EXE **and press Enter or, if you have the Windows version, type** DEL WINAV.EXE **and press Enter.**

The worst part of getting a program is setting the darn thing up. Using Microsoft Anti-Virus is very simple. Leapfrog over the following McAfee sections, and you'll be checking for viruses in no time.

Microsoft Anti-Virus also comes with a program that works like a radar — always sweeping your system for something that looks like a virus. If that program detects a virus trying to sneak by, it beeps like crazy. Because this book isn't called *Virus Protection For Dummies*, I'm not going to drag you through the setup, usage, and problems with VSAFE (that's what it's called). If you are determined to use this program, look it up in the manual or get help from Microsoft. My goal in this chapter is to give you *some* protection, not set you up like Fort Knox.

Connecting with McAfee AntiVirus

McAfee Associates has a virus checker called Scan that you can download right this very minute.

If you currently have no virus checker and are using the less-than-current version of MS-DOS, McAfee Associates is a good place to start (I mean, of course, other than your local computer software store, where they will be more than happy to disinfect your wallet along with your hard disk). You don't want to be flying into this BBS business with no virus checker, unless you're willing to leave your destiny to the fates.

Hurry, hurry, hurry! Try Scan for 30 days at no charge. However, if you decide to add Scan to your permanent library, you need to register the program and pay a fee — currently, $25.

Scan comes in an MS-DOS and Windows version. For the sake of simplicity — and because everyone has DOS but not everyone has the current version of Windows — I just cover getting the MS-DOS version. If you prefer Windows, you may download that version instead.

If you belong to CompuServe, you can type GO MCAFEE and get the same files. I don't know which is worse, the online fee or the long distance; you'll have to do the math. America Online users can type the keyword MCAFEE. Same caveat.

Getting McAfee AntiVirus

For those of you planning to call McAfee, here's how. By the way, see how far you can get on your own, just by reading the instructions on the screen before you start using the steps below.

1. Call McAfee Associates' Homebase Bulletin Board at 408-988-4004.

   Once connected, you see that you don't have to go through a long logon process. In fact, if you're there to download — which you are — you can use a Guest User account.

2. **When prompted for your first name, type** GUEST **and press Enter.**

3. **When prompted for your second name, type** USER **and press Enter.**

4. **When asked to confirm that you're calling from anywhere, press Y and then press Enter.**

5. **When asked to** Press Any Key, **press S for Stop and then press Enter.**

   McAfee acts as though you didn't tell it to stop and tries again with additional information. But again, respond with S when asked to press any key. After receiving several S commands, McAfee finally believes you, stops with the advertisements, and gets down to the Main Menu.

6. **When you see a long list, choose 1 for McAfee AntiVirus.**

7. **When told to** Press Any Key, **do so until you see the screen that announces Current McAfee AntiVirus Programs.**

   Make a note of the name of the current version of ViruScan for DOS.

   As the great philosophers Sonny and Cher once said, *The Beat Goes On* — which means that change is constant and inevitable. The overall impact of Windows 95 will continue to pound a rhythm to the brain for some time to come (though some might characterize that pounding as a headache). The file name used in Step 10 may not be the same by the time you are ready to download. In fact, I'd be surprised if it is. Be sure to carefully read the list of Current Software in Step 7 and confirm that it matches your reality — be it DOS, Windows 3.1, or Windows 95.

8. **After you've written down the file name, press S the next time the system tells you to press any key.**

   That oughta show 'em.

9. **When you're presented with several options — the first of which is** <D>ownload — **press D and then Enter.**

10. **At** File name?, **type the name of the file you wrote down in Step 7.**

    Currently that would be SCN-217E.ZIP; but, since this file is constantly updated, it will be something different by next week — not to mention by the time you have this book. Oh, and press Enter.

    Now comes the traditional march of the protocols. You still don't need to know what protocols are or what they do.

11. **Just press Z, for the Zmodem protocol, and then Enter.**

    Now the file is on its way.

12. **Tell your telecommunications program to download.**

    In many programs, that means hitting the PageDown key. In Procomm Plus for Windows, it's a matter of clicking the file icon that has the down arrow. Be sure to select Z as your download protocol.

13. **When the file is done downloading, you get that long list again. Press L and then Enter to log off (or, as** *they* **call it, terminate the connection).**

14. **As usual, you get an are-you-sure question. Press Y and Enter to formalize your decision.**

You'll want to repeat these steps to download the program called Clean. If you do find a virus, you'll need the Clean program to put things right.

Installing McAfee AntiVirus

Getting McAfee up and running requires unzipping and copying. If you need help on unzipping and copying, the dirty details are back in Chapter 4.

1. **At the C:\ prompt, type** CD\[download directory] **and press Enter.**

   You have to type in your own download directory, such as **CD\PROWIN2\DNLOAD** for Procomm Plus for Windows or **CD\QMPRO\DOWNLOAD** for QmodemPro. Or, if you made your own download directory as discussed in Chapter 3, it would be **CD\DOWNLOAD.**

2. **After you get there, make a temporary holding tank to put McAfee in while you examine it by typing** MD TEMP **and pressing Enter.**

3. **Next, copy the file into the temporary directory by typing** COPY SCN-217E.ZIP TEMP **and pressing Enter.**

4. **Move to the temporary directory by typing** CD TEMP **and pressing Enter.**

5. **Type** PKUNZIP SCN-217E.ZIP **and press Enter.**

   See the files decompressing themselves before your very eyes?

   The how-to for the next step can be found in the file named — appropriately enough — README.TXT, which was one of the files that extracted itself. Every compressed program comes with a *readme* file. It's where the instructions are. You can play with readme files when you download files in Part II. For now, I've already read README.TXT and distilled the instructions for you.

6. **Type** COPY SCAN.* C:\DOS **and press Enter.**

   After you get a 2 file(s) copied message, move on to the next step.

7. **Type** COPY NAMES.DAT C:\DOS **and press Enter.**

   This step puts the Scan engine into the DOS directory with other important files. You are through with the files in the temporary directory. You *should*, however, print out a copy of REGISTER.TXT so you can register the program later on — just call up the file in your word processor or using Edit. There's also a 100-page manual, if you happen to have some free time on your hands. In the next step, you erase the files in the temporary directory and then get rid of the temporary directory itself.

Because the instruction for Step 8 deletes everything in the current directory, you want to make sure you're in the right directory. Type **DIR** and press Enter, to get a list of files. If you've downloaded the DOS version along with the rest of us, you see 18 files listed. You're in the right place. Go ahead.

If you get more files than 18, you may have accidentally extracted the files in the wrong directory. Don't do the next few steps until you troubleshoot what happened — which you'll have to do by yourself or with a little help from your friends.

8. **To delete the McAfee files, type** DEL *.* **and press Enter. You are warned that all files will be deleted. Go ahead and press Y and then press Enter.**

9. **Now, type** CD .. **and press Enter to back out of the temporary directory up to the download directory where you started.**

10. **Get rid of the temporary directory by typing** RD TEMP **and pressing Enter.**

That's why it's called a temporary directory. You only needed it for a little while.

11. **As you may recall, the original file you downloaded is still in the download directory, so get rid of it too by typing** DEL SCN-217E.ZIP **and pressing Enter.**

McAfee AntiVirus comes with a 100-page manual and another program that works like a radar — always sweeping your system for something that looks like a virus. If the program detects a virus trying to sneak by, it beeps like crazy. Because this book isn't called *Virus Protection For Dummies*, I'm not going to drag you through the setup, usage, and problems with VSHIELD (that's what it's called). If you are determined to use this program, look it up in the manual or get help from McAfee. My goal in this chapter is to give you *some* protection, not to set you up like the Pentagon.

Checking for Viruses

Congratulations, if you've just successfully installed an antivirus program, you've made it through the circle of fire. Scanning for viruses is nothing in comparison to getting to this point. Now, with the program all set up, all you have to do is give a Scan command of some sort, and a couple minutes later you've got your, hopefully clean, bill of health. And that's it!

Using Microsoft Anti-Virus

The two anti-virus programs, Microsoft and McAfee, are fairly close in terms of which commands do what — though the layout is different. And, of course, the Windows version is prettier.

To check for viruses:

1. **For DOS users, at the system prompt type** MSAV **and press Enter.**

   – or –

   For Windows users, double-click on the Microsoft Anti-Virus group icon and then double-click on the Microsoft Anti-Virus icon.

   If you don't have Microsoft Anti-Virus in Windows, try the first part of Step 1. When you get the opening screen, something like Figure 6-1 for Windows users, you're in the right place.

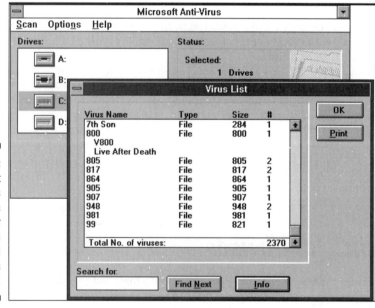

Figure 6-1: Microsoft Anti-Virus for Windows reporting for duty to wipe out evil viruses everywhere!

2. On both versions, select Options.

For maximum protection, the following items need to be selected: Verify Integrity, Create New Checksums, Anti-Stealth, and Check All Files.

However, selecting all these options makes running the program the first time a real pain. The checker compares each file to one on a list. Since you don't have a list yet, the checker goes to every file and tells you that it has *changed* since the last time, and do you want to update — that is, create — the list. Say yes, and the list is created as you go along. Next time you scan, the checker will use this list as a point of comparison.

If your patience wears out, you can stop the virus check at any time. You can also decide to uncheck those items — I recommend not using the Check All Files, at least — and still have *some* virus protection. Click OK when done.

3. Back at the menu, select Detect (for DOS) or Scan ⇨ Detect (for Windows) and let the program rip.

4. When it's all done, select Exit or press F3 to get out.

Using McAfee VirusScan

The DOS version of this program is not about to win any beauty contests. You'll just have to be happy that you have something that really does the job.

To check your disk

1. Get to the system prompt, usually C:\.

In other words, save your files and exit all your programs, including Windows.

2. Type SCAN /ADL **and press Enter.**

Scan first checks the memory for viruses, and then all the files on your disk. After a minute, you get the results, something like Figure 6-2.

```
Summary report on C:

File(s)
           Analyzed: ..............    7443
           Scanned: ..............    1265
           Possibly Infected: .....      0
Master Boot Record(s):..........      1
           Possibly Infected:......      0
Boot Sector(s):................      1
           Possibly Infected:......      0


Time: 00:00.48

Thank you for choosing to evaluate VirusScan from McAfee.  This version
of the software  is for Evaluation Purposes Only and may be used for up
to 30 days to  determine if  it meets your requirements. To license the
the software, or to  obtain assistance  during the  evaluation process,
please call (408) 988-3832, or  contact  your  local  authorized  agent
(see the file  AGENTS.TXT for a  current  list).  If  you choose not to
license the  software, you need to remove it from your system.  All use
of this software  is conditioned upon compliance with the license terms
set forth in the LICENSE.TXT file.

C:\ >
```

Figure 6-2:
McAfee's
AntiVirus
reports that
I have zero
possible
infections.

Getting a Red Alert

If the Microsoft or McAfee program alerts you to a virus, that doesn't necessarily mean you have one. Virus detectors are a little like car radar detectors; they are prone to sending back false alarms — the idea being, *better safe than sorry*. If you do get a virus alert

   ✔ Make a note of what the alert is telling you.

   ✔ Turn off the computer. Don't run any other programs — even programs to eradicate the virus — it will only spread the virus.

   ✔ Call the appropriate technical support number and get some help.

Making a boot disk

If you find yourself infected with a virus, you'll be told to start your computer with a *clean boot disk*. A clean boot disk is a disk with enough smarts to start up your computer. Because you keep this disk in a box someplace, it won't be infected with the virus.

Naturally, this is something you have to make *before* the virus hits. You should have a clean boot disk anyway. There are many computer emergencies that can be more easily resolved if you have one. Here's how to make one:

1. Get a floppy disk that fits in your A drive. Select a disk that you know is blank or that you don't mind erasing. Put a label on the disk that says "Boot Disk." Neatness does not count.

2. Put that disk in the A drive.

3. From the system prompt, type **FORMAT A:/S** and press Enter.

   The computer warns you that all the files on drive A will be erased, but you knew that already. Select yes to continue.

4. When the computer is finished formatting, it asks if you want to give the disk a volume label—computer-speak for *naming the disk*. Just press Enter.

5. The computer asks whether you want to format another; press N for No.

6. Before removing the disk, type **COPY \DOS\SYS.COM A:**, press Enter, and wait for the computer to tell you that one file has been copied and give you the system prompt again.

Remove the disk, do the Hokey Pokey, and that's what it's all about!

You may want to stick your clean boot disk in the A drive sometime and do a CTRL-ALT-DEL reboot just to make sure the computer will start up on the power of that disk. If you see `bad or missing command interpreter` on the screen, then you need to take another shot at making a boot disk. If you end up with an A:> system prompt, you have graduated from boot-disk-making school—with an A.

In either case, to restore the computer to normal, remove the disk and reboot again.

Once you have a good boot disk, save it and hope you never need it!

Chapter 7
Lookin at the Dark Side

In This Chapter

▶ Telling the truth

▶ Avoiding a scam

▶ Remaining anonymous

▶ Stalking online

▶ Chatting with adults

▶ Protecting your kids

▶ Dealing with hackers

▶ Looking at the bright side

*1*n one of the color episodes of the 1950s TV series, Dragnet, Sgt. Joe Friday apologizes to a Los Angeles citizen for the behavior of a cop gone bad. Friday delivers one of his patented, monotone litanies listing each and every step, test, review, probe, analysis, and subanalysis a police recruit is subjected to before winning a badge. Even with all that, Friday concludes, a bad cop is bound to slip through the cracks because of the one problem the police department can't lick.

The spellbound citizen asks, "What problem is that?"

Close-up on Sgt. Joe Friday; "We still have to recruit from the human race."

The same goes for the online world. The skills required to go online are no litmus test to reveal evildoers and angels. Once online, you encounter a demographically appropriate number of jerks, nutcases, and crooks — just like in real life.

However, because of the excitement of going online and the friendliness of the people you encounter there, it's easy to forget that a dark element is always prowling in the background.

Telling the Truth

The first thing to remember is that people are almost programmed to respond factually to a directive or question posed by a computer. If a computer asks, "How old are you?" it is more likely to get an honest reply than a human being asking the same question. It's a fact that people are often more truthful with computer terminals. Go figure. Psychiatrists and potential employers know this and often use computers in the get-to-know phase. What does this mean to you? It means that if someone online asks for private information, you're likely to comply without reflection simply because you read the question on a computer screen. So don't do it.

Giving your information to one person is bad enough. What's worse is that, often your information is then reposted on other BBSs and accessed by dozens or hundreds of other shady characters. And they pass the information on to others. And on and on.

The easiest way to avoid being victimized is by checking in with your common sense when a situation presents itself. Don't leave your street smarts at home just because you're traveling in cyberspace. Never give your personal or financial information to anyone you don't know well, and maybe not even then.

Avoiding a Scam

Say you're sitting at home and someone from your bank calls. The person explains that, because of a system failure, all bank-customer records are scrambled, and now they are trying to reconstruct the data. Would you kindly help by telling them your secret PIN and ATM numbers so they can put you back in the system?

Oh, yeah, right. What you'd better do is hang up on this bozo in a nanosecond and wonder who'd fall for such an obvious scam.

Yet, not too long ago, subscribers to a large online service were called and told that the system had lost some customer records. These subscribers were asked for their user IDs and secret passwords so the service's database could be restored. Amazingly, they complied. A month later, when billings were mailed, hundreds of hours of online time appeared on their accounts, and they realized they'd been ripped off.

The three basic, common-sense rules are

- **Never give out your password**. Remember, a password is like a PIN. After you log on, it is not possible for anyone to have a legal reason to request it from you.

- If someone asks you for any kind of personal data, financial or otherwise, run it through the "Would I give this information to a stranger on the street?" test before responding.

- Don't give out credit-card information unless you're in a section designed to take credit card orders and you want to place an order. Even so, if you can, you may want to consider getting a voice number and giving that information in person.

Remaining Anonymous

One of the intriguing aspects of online communication is the *anonymity factor*. People are judged by what they say, not by their appearance or status in society. A few celebrities have found that online, under the guise of a nonfamous name, they can finally have normal conversations with people. However, not every unmasking is going to reveal Brad Pitt or Pamela Anderson. Here are three scenarios to keep in mind.

- You can be talking to a prison inmate, a stalker, or other deviant. This isn't an inherently terrible thing — these people must have a mighty interesting perspective on life. However, keep in mind that since you don't know to whom you're talking, you shouldn't make public knowledge of the specific details of your life.

- Imagine spending an evening mouthing off about your crummy job to a sympathetic online pal. You find out later that your cyberconfidant turns out to be best friends with your boss — or the person you're competing with for a promotion. Be circumspect about what you say. Remember that whatever scrolls by on the computer screen can be saved, printed, and distributed.

- Another way anonymity can work out interestingly is in the area of human relations. Don't assume the person you've been flirting with who goes by the name of "FunGirl" is either fun or a girl.

Stalking Online

Stalking happens.

Online stalking often takes the form of excessive message-sending. That may sound like three lashes with a wet noodle, but going online and seeing 100 messages waiting for you with the subject heading of "I hate you" can be disturbing, to say the least. Many systems require that a message be read before it can be deleted. So even if you were to ignore the content of these messages, who wants to waste online time deleting all those messages?

Stalkers may spend all day roaming the system, waiting for their victims to log on; the stalkers then bombard their victims with chat requests or, if they know their phone numbers, phone calls. If you're lucky. There have been cases in which people gave enough personal information to a stalker that he or she was able to locate the victim and begin stalking them physically.

No one really knows what triggers this obsessive behavior. The only advice I can give is that you remain polite and keep people at arm's length until you've had a chance to spend time exchanging messages. If someone seems friendly beyond the norm, check that person out with the Sysop. Whoever is annoying you now has probably done it before, and the Sysop can intervene.

Keep in mind that you are never obligated to respond to any message or Chat request. The best response is to ignore the stalker, alert the Sysop to the harassment, and move on. When stalkers continue to get no response, they will move on to a more *excitable* victim.

X-Rated Chat

Whether or not so-called adult BBSs are part of the dark side of online life is completely a judgment call. The fact is, sexually explicit discussions and images do exist online. Some people believe this sort of activity is an embarrassment to the online community. Others, of course, think it's the greatest thing since sliced bread.

No matter what your opinion, you have control over what you see and what you don't. All Adult BBSs and conferences are clearly marked and advertised as such. If you see a BBS advertising "Open-minded adults," "Hottest system ever," or "XXX," you can guess what you'll find there. On the other hand, if one part of the system is *adult*, you can reliably assume that the remaining portion of that BBS will not be as risqué. It's a lot like cable TV. Just because such a thing as the Playboy Channel exists, doesn't mean other cable shows are affected. You didn't stop using the telephone when 900 numbers started appearing, did you?

Protecting Your Kids

Would you let your child spend hours at a friend's house without ever meeting the friend or the parents? Of course not. So don't let your kid stay online for hours without knowing exactly what kind of service has your child so riveted. Just because it's on the computer doesn't mean it's educational. Two things to watch out for are

- ✔ **Graphic material:** Many online libraries include adult photographs. It's a lot easier to hide a file on a computer than to hide magazines under the mattress. Especially if mom and pop aren't exactly Brainiac when it comes to the computer.

- ✔ **Talking to strangers:** The whole point, almost, of going online is to talk to new people. So where does that leave the old don't-talk-to-strangers edict? You need to discuss this with your child. It is not unheard of for an adult to claim to be a teen online. Pedophiles can go online as easily as anyone else. Sometimes they even coax the kids into face-to-face meetings.

Parents need to discuss these issues with children. Use the same common-sense approach you use when you explain to your children that they shouldn't tell strangers on the phone about who is or is not at home.

- ✔ Discuss the rules for not giving out personal information to strangers. Make sure you and your child discuss concrete examples of what personal information is — including their telephone number, home address, and the name of their school.

- ✔ Make sure your child knows that if someone is sending them messages they don't like, they can come to you to make it stop.

- ✔ Also, tell your child not to send his or her photograph online, and, if someone requests it, to tell you at once.

- ✔ Set guidelines for computer usage just like you would for excessive television usage. You may want to keep the computer in the family room or den, rather than in the child's bedroom.

- ✔ Again, the child should know never to arrange a meeting with an online correspondent.

For more information about online concerns for parents, contact The National Center for Missing and Exploited Children at 800-843-5678. For those who cannot call the 800 number, use 703-235-3900. Ask for their pamphlet entitled *Child Safety on the Information Highway*.

Do you know where your kids are?

There was a kid who was calling at all hours of the night to play games online. It concerned me that a 13-year-old was on the computer at 3:00 a.m. playing games. I left him a message about it. The short version is that eventually, with his permission, I contacted his parents and we set up a reward system consisting of extra privileges and eventually some extra responsibilities on the BBS based on his report cards. He's been a real plus to have around and will be going to college next year.

Chip North, Sysop, The Source BBS

Protecting BBSs from Your Kids

The other side of the parental-duty coin is to ensure that your kids aren't the ones exhibiting obnoxious behavior online. If little Johnny has demonstrated antisocial tendencies in the real world, chances are he's doing it online, too. Also, the anonymity factor can bring out the worst in the nicest people. With seemingly no consequences for bad behavior, the temptation to run wild may be too great for some kids.

Introduce yourself to the Sysops on your children's favorite online haunts. Log on and check in with the Sysops, asking if little Johnny is behaving properly and letting them know you're a concerned parent.

Dealing with Hackers

Everyone has heard about hackers: the Twinkie-chomping, socially awkward people who spend all their waking hours breaking into computers and stealing data or starting World War III. Does going online make you vulnerable to hackers?

First of all, and I mean this in the kindest way, hackers don't give a byte about your home computer. They are on the hunt for systems with thousands of long-distance calling-card numbers, bank accounts, and personal identification numbers. They are also looking to earn bragging rights for hacking into mega-systems and tweaking the nose of the giant. Your little PC is of no interest.

Second, even if your computer contains an irresistible mother lode of data, hackers can't get into your computer unless it is first configured to receive callers (as described in Chapter 16). Computer hackers rely on phone lines to gain entry to systems. If your computer doesn't know how to answer the phone, you're safe.

Actually, hackers are less likely to present a threat to your credit report than those white-collar types who are breaking into your credit-card company's system looking to make a lot of money and hightail it to Rio.

Until you know what you're doing, stay away from BBSs that cater to hackers. If you find yourself on a BBS that features tips on Phone Phreaking (basically, stealing from the phone company) and breaching Firewalls (circumventing security systems), then you're in a Hacker Zone. Quietly leave.

Looking on the Bright Side

You, me, and all the other folks online are figuring out, everyday, how a cybercommunity works. No simple set of rules exists, online or off, that effectively protects good people from bad. One of the major stumbling blocks to creating such rules is that most people cannot agree on what is *good* and what is *bad*. I mean, we can't even get a consensus on whether it's "E-mail," "email," or "E-Mail." Sigh. Democracy is a messy business.

Just because some nuts are out there, you don't need to live in fear. Just as on the TV news, the bad guys get the headlines. What isn't reported are the millions of hours people spend online each year helping each other out, the wonderful friendships forged every day, the intense exchange of ideas going on around the world, and the vital information being distributed.

To miss out on the good because you might encounter the bad is like never driving a car because you might have an accident. In fact, I've read that your chances of becoming involved in a car accident are greater than your chances of encountering any of the problems mentioned in this chapter.

Feel better? Good. Now let's go online!

Part II
I Don't Think We're in Kansas Anymore

The 5th Wave   **By Rich Tennant**

"GARY AND SOME OF HIS FRIENDS WANTED TO BOB FOR APPLES THIS YEAR. I GUESS IT CAN'T HURT AS LONG AS THEY'RE NOT PLUGGED IN."

In this part...

1 f Dorothy had been briefed in advance about Munchkins, good and bad witches, that man behind the curtain, and how to click her heels, her stopover in Oz probably would have been a lot less nerve-racking and a lot more fun.

Whether you were introduced to downloading, E-Mail, Chat, conferences, zipped files, and virus checkers from Part I or knew all about them already, you now have had enough pre-flight training so that your trip into cyberspace shouldn't feel like a house just dropped on you. Heck, you might even start to feel as though your life is changing from black and white to color.

Chapter 8

Finding and Retrieving the Truly Great Files

● ●

In This Chapter

▶ Finding the File Menu

▶ Searching for a file

▶ Retrieving files

▶ Putting your booty to work — or not

● ●

Downloading software — jump back to Chapter 3 if you need a refresher — is quickly becoming the new great American pastime.

Some Sysops hook juke-box-like CD-ROM towers to their BBS computers so that callers can mainline an unbelievable array of shareware programs. Once you get started, you're hooked for life!

Exec-PC BBS, acknowledged king of the hill for maintaining one of the largest shareware collections known to man or woman, boasts more than 80 gigabytes of files available online. Eighty gigabytes is roughly equivalent to filling 57,143 floppy disks — the 3 1/2-inch, high-density kind. If you stacked those disks flat, one atop the other, you'd have a pillar of disks over 211 yards tall. That's more than what you'll find at the local computer store.

Worrywarts amongst you may already be getting concerned about the daunting task of finding *anything* on a BBS, when the options are so overwhelming. After all, if it's a challenge to find that file you saved five minutes ago on your own hard disk, what are the odds of tracking down something stored on a dinosaur-sized BBS?

Don't hyperventilate.

First of all, one big difference between finding files on a BBS and finding something on your computer is that the BBS *wants* you to find the file. Although the exact commands vary from system to system, every BBS provides searching tools. And, with a little practice, you'll be navigating the nooks and crannies of the system like a pro.

Second, and don't take this personally, the BBS folks organize their files a lot better than you organize yours. Files are arranged by topic into what are usually called *file directories*, *file libraries*, or *file areas* (Exec PC BBS calls them *file collections*). Notice the word *file* appears in all those names. That's the word to remember.

Once you ask for a listing of files within a file library on a BBS, you see that, in addition to the file's name and size, is a sort of a thumbnail description of what that file does and whom it's for. If the file sounds interesting, you can often ask for more-detailed information before committing to downloading the thing.

This chapter shows you how to be a cyberbloodhound when it comes to tracking down and retrieving a file or a piece of shareware that will change your life — or at least make it more fun.

Finding the File Menu

The first step in finding and retrieving files is to determine how the BBS has organized its file commands. This is an obvious-sounding, but important, step.

After logging onto a BBS, you eventually end up at a Main Menu — command central . . . the bridge of the starship Enterprise if you prefer.

Each BBS system has, in its Main Menu, an option called File Menu, File Directories, just Files, or something very close to that. Again, the key word to look for, as you inspect the Main Menu, is *file*.

BBSs have two general approaches to offering file commands on their Main Menus:

- ✔ The first, as in Figure 8-1 and Figure 8-2, is to have a single file command on the Main Menu that will take the caller to a menu listing a bunch of file-command options.

- ✔ The second approach offers callers an assortment of favorite file options right on the Main Menu, as in Figure 8-3, as well as a file submenu.

Yes, having different approaches to file commands is confusing. Because Sysops can customize their BBSs to suit their own tastes, file commands can appear on the top Main Menu in some systems, or buried below three layers of submenus in other systems. But once you know what to look for — like the word *files* — with a small amount of effort, you can find the menu or option that puts you where you want to be.

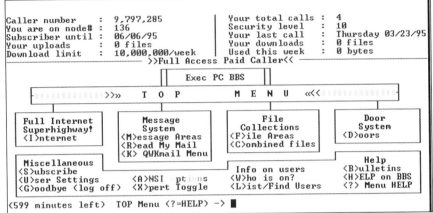

Figure 8-1:
Exec-PC
BBS's Top
Menu,
from which
all good
things — on
that system
— flow.

```
Caller number     :  9,797,285       Your total calls :  4
You are on node#  :  136             Security level   :  10
Subscriber until  :  06/06/95        Your last call   :  Thursday 03/23/95
Your uploads      :  0 files         Your downloads   :  0 files
Download limit    :  10,000,000/week Used this week   :  0 bytes
                    >>Full Access Paid Caller<<
                         ┌─────────────────┐
                         │   Exec PC BBS   │
                         └─────────────────┘
<::::::::::::::::>>»   T  O  P        M  E  N  U   «<<::::::::::::::::>
┌──────────────────┐ ┌──────────────────┐ ┌──────────────────┐ ┌──────────────┐
│ Full Internet    │ │   Message        │ │     File         │ │   Door       │
│ Superhighway!    │ │   System         │ │   Collections    │ │   System     │
│ <I>nternet       │ │ <M>essage Areas  │ │ <F>ile Areas     │ │ <D>oors      │
│                  │ │ <R>ead My Mail   │ │ <C>ombined files │ │              │
│                  │ │ <K> QWKmail Menu │ │                  │ └──────────────┘
└──────────────────┘ └──────────────────┘ └──────────────────┘ ┌──────────────┐
┌──────────────────┐                                           │   Help       │
│ Miscellaneous    │                      Info on users        │ <B>ulletins  │
│ <S>ubscribe      │                      <W>ho is on?         │ <H>ELP on BBS│
│ <U>ser Settings     <A>NSI ptions       <L>ist/Find Users    │ <?> Menu HELP│
│ <G>oodbye (log off) <X>pert Toggle                           └──────────────┘
<599 minutes left>   TOP Menu (?=HELP) -> █
```

Figure 8-2:
Blue Ridge
Express's
no-fat, low-
cholesterol
Main Menu.
Can you find
the file
command?
It's there
under
Elsewhere,
over on the
right.

```
          ------*>>>   BRE's Main Menu    <<<*------
----- Mail ----------- System ---------- Utilities ------ Elsewhere ---
                   [B]ulletins         [H]elp (or ?)      [F]iles
 [R]ead Mail       [C]omment to Sysop  [J]oin Sub-Board   [G]oodbye
 [P]ersonal Mail   [I]nitial Welcome   [U]iew User Statu  [Q]uit To
                   [W]ho's on With You [X]pert on/off      [U]tilities
                   [N]ew Sub-Board Mail
                     * = unavailable
---------------------------------------------------------------------
   Current time:  8:20 PM  Minutes remaining: 26      Security: 30
---------------------------------------------------------------------
MAIN: 26 min left
MAIN command <?,B,C,F,G,H,I,J,K,M,N,P,Q,R,U,U,W,X>? █
```

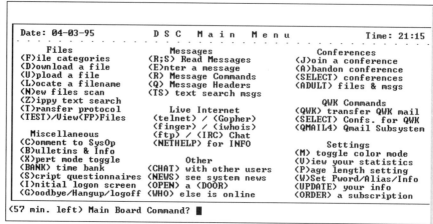

```
Date: 04-03-95            D S C   M a i n   M e n u            Time: 21:15

        Files                     Messages                    Conferences
(F)ile categories          (R;S) Read Messages          (J)oin a conference
(D)ownload a file          (E)nter a message            (A)bandon conference
(U)pload a file            (R) Message Commands         (SELECT) conferences
(L)ocate a filename        (Q) Message Headers          (ADULT) files & msgs
(N)ew files scan           (TS) text search msgs
(Z)ippy text search                                        QWK Commands
(T)ransfer protocol             Live Internet           (QWK) transfer QWK mail
(TEST)/View(FP)Files       (telnet) / (Gopher)          (SELECT) Confs. for QWK
                           (finger) / (iwhois)          (QMAIL4) Qmail Subsystem
     Miscellaneous         (ftp) / (IRC) Chat
(C)omment to SysOp         (NETHELP) for INFO                   Settings
(B)ulletins & Info                                      (M) toggle color mode
(X)pert mode toggle              Other                  (V)iew your statistics
(BANK) time bank           (CHAT) with other users      (P)age length setting
(S)cript questionnaires    (NEWS) see system news       (W)Set Pword/Alias/Info
(I)nitial logon screen     (OPEN) a (DOOR)              (UPDATE) your info
(G)oodbye/Hangup/logoff    (WHO) else is online         (ORDER) a subscription

(57 min. left) Main Board Command? ▮
```

If you're frustrated after reading and rereading a menu without finding any mention of the word *files*, here's a wild thought: Are you looking at the Main Menu or are you looking at something else? Could it be that you're stuck at the Bulletin Menu? Check the top of the screen, and if you're in a Bulletin Menu, select the option to Quit or Exit the Bulletin Menu. That ought to take you to the Main Menu. Now do you see a Files option?

In a BBS, selecting Quit or Exit takes you out of the current menu back to the previous menu — which is usually the Main Menu. Quit and Exit do not generally mean to quit or exit the BBS. Just like in a voice phone call, Good-bye is what you say before you hang up.

If the file-search options are not in front of your face on the ever-popular Main Menu, you can bet it's a part of the File Menu itself. Use whatever available files command you can find on the Main Menu and see where that takes you. It never hurts to go exploring.

Searching for a File

According to my observations, when it comes to shopping — whether they're searching for a new car or a new file — people fall into two basic personality classifications.

Type One is the Sortie Shopper. This self-disciplined breed comes to the store with a specific purchasing mission. After executing the assignment, the Sortie Shopper immediately returns to home base.

The second type is the Butterfly Buyer. Shoppers in this category often don't have an exact idea of what they want, but rather flit from one item to another until something strikes their fancy.

When it comes to finding files online, you need to decide which shopping plan works for you. Do you want a specific type of program to do a particular job — like a billing program or a home inventory database? Or, do you just want to check in and see what's new? Just between you and me, eventually you'll end up using both approaches.

Grazing files

Grazing through a list of files is the preference of the Butterfly Buyer whose philosophy is, "You don't know what you want until you find it." There's wisdom in there — someplace — especially if you don't classify yourself as an A-1 computer genius.

By thumbing through the list of available files, you find out about all the great shareware available and what it can do for you. You'll probably think of new ways your computer can simplify your life. Going online and checking out new files is like having Christmas every day. Or, perhaps, it's more like a box of chocolates — you never know what you're going to get.

There are two ways to skim through files. The first is to look at all the files stored in a certain topic, and the other is to examine files by date.

Poking through file directories

To look for files stored by topic on a BBS, the first step is to ask the BBS for a list of available storage topics, such as the ones in Figure 8-4.

Figure 8-4: GLIB's list of File Areas. Interested in Games for Windows? Try area 34.

```
Select File Area

[ 1] ASP Related Files              [20] Hobbies
[ 2] Business                       [21] Home
[ 3] Collecting                     [22] Lottery
[ 4] Communications                 [23] Music
[ 5] Database Applications          [24] Programming
[ 6] Education - History/Geography  [25] Religion & Philosophy
[ 7] Education - Language           [26] Scouting
[ 8] Education - Mathematics        [27] Sports
[ 9] Education - Other              [28] Utilities - Disk/File
[10] Education - Science            [29] Utilities - Hardware/System
[11] Education - Teachers           [30] Utilities - Other
[12] Education - Trivia             [31] Utilities - Printer
[13] Engineering                    [32] Windows - Business
[14] Finances                       [33] Windows - Education
[15] Games - Arcade                 [34] Windows - Games
[16] Games - Board                  [35] Windows - Other
[17] Games - Card                   [36] Windows - Utilities
[18] Games - Other                  [37] Writing Applications
[19] Graphics
 Cursor keys = Move highlite bar        0-9 = Enter file area #
 S = Search files by name or keyword  <Enter> = Select file area
 N = New files by date                    ? = Help, <Esc> = Exit
```

Sometimes, to get a file directory, you have to select the *list of files* option. The BBS then asks you which directory you want a list of files from, and it is at that point that you get to request a list of directories from which to choose. It's a little backwards, but that's the way it works a lot of the time.

Then, once you find an area of interest, ask for a list of the files stored under that topic. While reading the listing, you may run across a file that solves a current problem or lets you do something you didn't know you could do.

Checking out what's new

New Files Since or *New Files Search* is probably the command most oft-used right after logging on. This command takes advantage of the BBS recording the last time you called in. With that information, it's easy for the system to figure out and display a chronological list of all files added to the BBS library since your last call — organized by category or lumped together in a combined group. After giving the New Files Since command, you're given the choice of whether you want all or some files listed.

You don't *have* to use the date of your last call; if you prefer, you can search *since* another date. Pick any date at all. Perhaps you noticed a file two weeks ago and now realize that you desperately need it. Just search *since* two weeks ago. The New Files Since command gives you an opening to adjust the date slot to your liking.

After selecting your search-since date, the BBS goes to work and, after a few seconds of due consideration, assembles a list of files that match your date-search criteria, something like Figure 8-5 or Figure 8-6.

Figure 8-5:
Exec PC lists the first screen of all the new files added to the system since March 28.

```
  Collection:  MS Windows
  Showing   :  All files AFTER 03/28/95
  Filename     Size   MMDDYY Description ("+" means there is extra info)
  ───────────────────────────────────────── Total Files: 6,983 ─────────
A TELIX.TXT       144 021495 Do not upload Telix for Windows (see FREE area)
B UBRUN30.EXE  246805 041594 LATEST (3/7/94) UBRUN300.DLL FROM MICROSOFT D.S.
C UBSTUFF.ZIP  865730 011094+UPDATED VISUAL BASIC FILES (UBRUN100.DLL & UBX)
D NONONO.TXT     1933 072993 NO WAV/BMP/DOS/FONT/ICON/MIDI OR AVI FILES HERE!
E UBRUN200.ZIP 220049 111792+UBRUN200.DLL.  RUNTIME FOR VISUAL BASIC 2.0
  ─────────────────────────────────────────────────────────────────────
F ISPY216.ZIP  429080 040495+InfoSpy - The Complete Windows Utility
G ECLITE.EXE  2771931 040495+PIM, calendar,phone dir, etc. by NETMANAGER CORP
H N32E11B3.EXE 862747 040495 Win95/Win NT 32-bit-Netscape Navigator 1.1  Beta
I N16E11B3.EXE1562809 040495 WIN/WfWg 3.1x 16-bit-Netscape Navigator 1.1 Beta
J WSFTP195.ZIP 116700 040495 Winsock FTP Client vesrion 95.01.22  **FREEWARE**
K WBE42B.ZIP   138788 040395+WINBOND-E V4.2b WINDOWS application to track
L HEXER11.ZIP  127904 040395+HEXER1.1 MS WINDOWS FILE AND DISK EDITOR
M GC221.ZIP    475828 040395+THE GROCERY CONSUMER 2.21 - Most powerful
N CDQCK111.ZIP 141176 040395+CD-QUICK Cache v1.11 <ASP> Now smaller and
O ACDC123B.ZIP 119468 040395+! -=- ACDSee v1.23b for Windows -=-  !
P WRLE13.ZIP   971284 040395+WRITER'S CRAMP LE v1.0 <ASP> -
Q TC46MIN.ZIP  414607 040395+TIME AND CHAOS v4.06  The Award Winning
R AUTOWN13.ZIP 531717 040395+AutoWinNet 1.3 - Complete Internet Automation!
>>More? ([Y]/Stop/Continuous/^/DL/UL/Remem/Aces/Extra/Type/Who/Fiddle/?=help)
```

```
 1 KABBALAH.ZIP  395k 04/01/95 KABBALAH: THE PROPHECY OF THE CHARIOT
                               Shareware E-book. Traces Nostradamus'
                               source of inspiration to the medieval
                               Kabbalah. With hypertext file viewer
                               and self-displaying illustrations.

 2 2CLUSTER.ZIP  249k 04/01/95 This NASA Hubble Space Telescope <HST>
                               image shows rich detail, previously only
                               seen in neighboring star birth regions,
                               in a pair of star clusters 166,000
                               light-years away in the Large Magellanic
                               Cloud <LMC>, in the southern
                               constellation Doradus.  The field of
                               view is 130 light-years across and was
                               taken with the Wide Field Planetary
                               Camera 2.
 3 95_GUIDE.ZIP   40k 04/01/95 95_GUIDE.ZIP - The lowest
                               price magazine subscriptions
File area #   1 ... Recent Uploads by our Users
<A>rea, <D>ownload, <P>rotocol, <S>earch, <E>xam, <N>ew, <J>ump, <H>elp, <Q>ui
Enter Command letter or  <CR>  to continue list : █
```

Figure 8-6:
The Kabbalah, NASA photos, and magazine subscriptions — all New Files Since.

Although the listings in Figures 8-5 and 8-6 use a different format, you can see, if you look very carefully, that the *elements* in both Figure 8-5 and Figure 8-6 are virtually identical. Both figures include

- A sequential number or letter to the left of the filename
- The filename
- Size and date of the file
- A description of the file

Some files stored on a BBS are several years old and may no longer work with your computer or software. In general, avoid downloading anything more than two years old. Specifically, as an example, if you use Word for Windows 6.0, don't download a file that's designed to work with Word for Windows 2.0. Unless, of course, you're enough of a Word for Windows wizard that you can take the older file as a starting point and update it.

Another way to stay current and find out what the newest, hip files are is via the *system statistics*. This may sound like a big yawn, but BBSs maintain all kinds of information about the system including Top File Downloads; in other words, the files most frequently downloaded by your fellow users. Take a look at what everyone else on the BBS is downloading and — despite the childhood warnings about, "If little Bobby down the street jumped off a bridge, would you do that too?" — download it too. Or at least consider downloading it. If system statistics aren't an option on the Main Menu, then you can find them in the Bulletin Menu. Usually.

Searching with a purpose

If you are a Sortie Shopper and know what you want, all you need to learn now is how to ask for it.

You can narrow your search in two ways: by ordering the computer to cough up a particular file that you already know the exactly name of, or by coaxing the BBS to search through the file descriptions to find the ones that contain your search word.

Naming names

Say a friend tells you, "Be sure to download calculat.zip; it's a very cool calculator that pops up in Windows." You simply jump into cyberspace, go to the File Area, issue the Download command, and, when asked for the name of the file to download, type in **CALCULAT.ZIP**. You're done. A perfect Sortie-Shopper experience.

Sifting through descriptions

Unfortunately, not everyone is *that* specific. You'd be lucky if someone said, "Hey, dude, there's, like, a totally cool calculator for Windows online. I can't remember what it's called, but I know you'll like it."

Here's the logic needed to get what you want.

Your first brainstorm may be to get a list of files in the category most likely to have the calculator. Good thought. But sometimes that doesn't work. After a quick gander at a typical File Directory, as in Figure 8-4, you'd realize that the calculator program could be in any one of several areas — Business, Windows-Business, or even Windows-Other. And, yes, you can look through every file in every area if you want to do it the long way.

But you don't.

Finding the search command

What you need is a search command. Just like a word processor can be told to search for a word in a document, BBSs know how to search for file names and the text in file descriptions, like the ones in Figures 8-5 and 8-6.

The search command is another option that is placed wherever the Sysop or the BBS software manufacturer deems most convenient. That means you have to look around some — but not a lot — to find the search command on a BBS. The keyword here is *search*. Can you find *search* back in Figures 8-3, 8-4 and 8-5?

✔ Figure 8-3 has the Zippy text search command on the Main Menu, under the Files options on the left.

✔ Figure 8-4 has a Search Files by Name or Keyword command at the bottom of the screen File Area screen.

✔ Figure 8-5 shows the search command at the bottom of the file-listing screen.

Framing the search

Once you're in a position to use the search command, you are asked, of course, what you're searching for. What do you hope to find? This question isn't posed in English, though, it appears disguised as something like Figure 8-7.

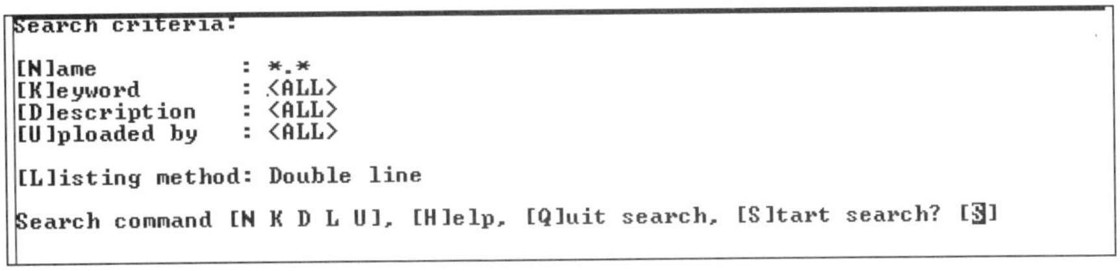

Figure 8-7:
If you know
how to
phrase a
search, the
BBS will
find the file
you want.

```
Search criteria:

[N]ame           : *.*
[K]eyword        : <ALL>
[D]escription    : <ALL>
[U]ploaded by    : <ALL>

[L]isting method: Double line

Search command [N K D L U], [H]elp, [Q]uit search, [S]tart search? [S]
```

The search engine in Figure 8-7 allows the kind of sophisticated search needed to separate the junk mail from the Sizzler coupons. Typical search options, no matter how the BBS asks for them, include

✔ **Name of file:** What *exactly* is the file called? This is often not what the program is called after it's been downloaded and unzipped. This is the *before* name.

✔ **Keyword:** This is one or more words used by the Sysop to classify the program.

✔ **Description:** This is the recommended search option, mainly because a description is usually several sentences long, and you've got more of a chance to make a match between your search word and the BBS's description. In our calculator example, I'd select Description and type in **calculator** as the search word.

✔ **Uploaded by:** This is the name of the person who put the program on the BBS. Boy, talk about esoteric information! Don't worry about this. I guess some of these programmers have fans. Does the phrase "get a life" mean anything to anyone out there? Yikes.

Once you've finished outlining your search request, be sure to press the proverbial go button by selecting the Start Search option or its equivalent. After a few seconds, the computer is proud to present the list of files that meet your specs, as in Figure 8-8.

Figure 8-8:
Advanced searching via Exec PC's Hyperscan™ on Exec. What do these files have in common? They have calculator and Windows in their descriptions. Cool.

```
 Collection:  ALL files                COMBO
 Showing   :   Search for:  CALCULATOR & WINDOWS
 Filename       Size    MMDDYY Description ("+" means there is extra info)Exec-P
                                         ── Total Files: 337,481 ──
B 12CPP.ZIP    322851 040295+WIN 12C++, HP 12C Calculator for Windows 100%
C 12CPP.ZIP    324322 031495 12C++, HP 12C Calculator for Windows 100%
D BCALC2.ZIP   192799 072894 WIN Business Calculator V2.00 for Windows 3.1
E SMTSUM12.ZIP  67061 060194 WIN SmartSum 1.2 - Windows Printing Calculator
F EQUATR13.ZIP   7675 050294 WIN RPN Calculator for Windows
G WINDLR13.ZIP  99922 030594+WIN Windows financial calculator.
H BCALC210.ZIP 206129 030594+WIN Business Calculator V2.10 for Windows 3.1
I OKNA_WIN.ZIP 132328 030494+WIN Windows for Windows (Books,calculator Etc.
J XCALC12.ZIP  105191 030494+WIN Highly Configurable Calculator For Windows1
K WINTEM.ZIP     2367 030494+WIN Temperature Calculator for Windows that
L ICALC.ZIP     28758 030494+WIN An Icon Sized Calculator for Windows.
M FATYC136.ZIP 329329 030494+WIN Fatty Calc v1.36: MS-Windows calculator w/a
N CALCU1.ZIP    30075 030494+WIN The Moosie Calculator is a Word for Windows
O CALCTAPE.ZIP 310134 030494+WIN Windows calculator with built in tape that is
P BCALC22.ZIP  222894 030494+WIN Business Calculator V2.20 for Windows 3.1
Q ADDER21.ZIP   59561 030494+WIN Windows calculator specialized to show
R 4ACAL310.ZIP  47635 030494+WIN 4A Calculator v3.10: MS-Windows math
S CCCALC10.ZIP   4040 021594+WIN Credit Card Calculator for Windows.
>>More? ([Y]/Stop/Continuous/^/DL/UL/Remem/Aces/Extra/Type/Who/Fiddle/?=help)
```

Until you log a few hours of BBSing and get the lay of the cyberland, keep search benchmarks simple. If you get too fancy, you could finesse yourself out of hitting a bull's eye. If you consistently get hundreds of files in response to your search criteria, though, then it's time to get more specific.

Wildcard and Boolean

Wildcard and Boolean sound like two characters in the next Batman movie — or a TV series starring Jack Scalia. However, wildcard and Boolean *searches* are just two fancy tricks some BBSs stock to both widen and narrow the scope of a search … all in the name of making it easier to find what you need.

The first trick is a card trick — a *wildcard* trick. A wildcard search lets you ask the BBS to find a file name even if you don't know the whole file name. You do have to know some of the filename, but the trick is in using the asterisk character to fill in the blank parts of the name that you don't know. For example, if you're looking for an astrology program, try looking for astr*.*. Searching on astr*.* turns up all files beginning with astr — like astro1.zip, astrlgy.zip, or even, of course, astronat.zip, which has nothing to do with astrology but which does begin with astr.

The second trick, nothing up my sleeve, is not available very often. When it is available on a BBS, you are told that Boolean searches or Boolean Logic is allowed. Boolean Logic is named after a guy called George Boole who, apparently, could teach Mr. Spock a thing or two. You definitely need to check the Help files for details on how Boolean Searches work on your favorite BBS, if they work at all. The basic idea behind a Boolean Search is to refine your search request by using the words AND, NOT, and OR. If you're

looking for an astrology program that runs in Windows, you might search for "astrology and Windows." If you wanted one that didn't run in Windows, try "astrology not Windows." If you wanted "astrology or astrological," you'd put the OR to work. Then there's a whole other complication with parentheses and — you don't want to know . . . there may be children reading this book. If it makes it easier, think of it as Wayne's World logic. Not!

Don't worry about wildcard and Boolean searches until you're more comfortable with BBSs and searching. I just wanted you to know they're out there in case you need them or in case you're feeling smug about using BBSs.

Retrieving Files

The resolution to bring a file home for a trial spin is usually made when the file and its description are staring you in the face. Visions of using it are dancing in your head. Good news — once the file is in your sights, it is yours.

You now have two choices — do you want the file now or later?

If you lust after a file that will take 20 minutes to download, make sure you've got enough time left on your clock. Computers, it turns out, are aces at math and will not let you start a download that exceeds your allotted time.

Jurassic BBS: the Sharewareasorus

"We have 350 phone lines up and running. We currently receive 10,000 phone calls per day. We receive well over 100 new files per day. Also, on your first call you can download a few hundred megabytes of files from our very popular Free file collections. We've been the world's largest BBS since 1983."

Bob Mahoney, Sysop, Exec-PC BBS

Getting immediate gratification

If you're staring at a file listing that contains an irresistible file, lower your vision to the bottom of the screen for the command to put a download into gear. Refer to Figures 8-5 and 8-6, which use the commands DL or D, respectively — I always wanted to use respectively in a sentence — to start a download.

You are asked for the name of the file to download. This is not a test; the correct name is there on the screen. Just copy it. If the name scrolled off the screen, use your communications software scrollback buffer to refresh your memory.

If you want to save a few keystrokes, type in the number or letter of the file to the left of the filename instead.

You are shepherded through the hopefully now-familiar download process; if you need a refresher, check back to Chapter 3.

1. **Select a download protocol on the BBS — Zmodem is the best choice.**

   If you preselected, as your default, Zmodem protocol — which is not a bad idea — you are not asked for a download protocol. The BBS assumes you want to use Zmodem. Instead you are asked if you want to download a file in addition to the one you've already selected. Press Enter when the BBS asks if you want to download another file.

2. **Decide whether or not to log off.**

   The computer may ask if you want to log off automatically after you finish downloading. That's up to you and whether you're done BBSing for the moment.

3. **When asked to initiate the download process, type the download command for your communications program.**

4. **If needed, type the name of the download directory on your hard disk that will temporarily hold your new file.**

5. **Watch the file download.**

When the file is finished downloading, the screen changes, and you find yourself back where you started before the download. You can continue on your merry way, or you can pick another file for downloading, if you want.

Tagging now, downloading later

Many BBSs offer the luxury of *tagging files* — also known as *flagging files* or *marking files* — *for download*. It's a way of putting several files into your electronic shopping cart and then checking them all out later. Tagging is most helpful when you want to download more than one file. It's far more convenient than searching, downloading, searching, downloading, searching, and downloading.

If the BBS supports tagging, you'll find the the actual "tag-you're-it" command displayed at the bottom of the screen — under the filenames and descriptions.

If you've got an older communications program that does not know about Z latest styles in Zmodem, you'll find that you cannot perform a tagged download — or, as it's actually known, a *batch download*.

As you travel on BBSs, you'll encounter two schools of file tagging:

- ✔ After you issue the tag command, the system asks you for the name or number — the number listed to the left of the filename — of the file to be tagged. Once you type in your selection, press Enter. The BBS makes an internal record of your choice and then delivers you back to the file-listing screen.

- ✔ The other file-tagging philosophy uses the newer, more, as they say, graphical interface, shown in Figure 8-9. Doubtless you'll see more systems sporting this style of file listing because it's a lot more intuitive. Simply highlight the name of the file you want to tag and press the space bar. Usually an asterisk will appear next to the filename as confirmation of your decision.

After tagging all the files you want and getting emotionally ready, select the download command — either from the Main Menu or the File Menu, depending on the system.

Once you issue the command to download the tagged files, you're shown the complete list of files you've selected, with an estimate of the download time. You have an option to edit — or remove — items from the tagged files list if you've changed your mind or are going to exceed your time limit before the download is over.

Figure 8-9:
The Index
BBS allows
file tagging
by high-
lighting
and then
pressing the
space bar.
Here the
first file has
been tagged
— see the
asterisk? In
the upper
right is how
long the file
will take to
download.

```
Area: Recent Uploads                        Batch: 1 files, 42k
                                            Xfer: 0:15 Zmodem-90
[ 1]* COLORTST.EXE   42k  3-30-95 this is a fun little personality tester.
                                  Try it, then you'll try it on all your
                                  friends
[ 2]  FRAINT19.ZIP  568k  3-28-95 Fractint version 19.0.  The latest version
                                  of the classic fractal generation program.
[ 3]  NGROUPS.ZIP    82k  3-26-95 A list of all newsgroups available by name
                                  only, no descriptions.
[ 4]  GAMEREV1.TXT    6k  3-23-95 Game Reviewer-- electronic gaming mag!
                                  issue #1, apr/may.  Covers most popular and
                                  new age systems and developments.




<Space> = Add/Del file to/from batch   ^D/D = Download file/batch now
<Enter> = Display file info            * after number = file is in batch
      O = Other commands available     ? = Help, <Esc> = Exit to area list
```

Once the BBS starts the download, if you don't see some kind of dialog box on the screen counting down the bytes as they arrive on your computer, then you have to manually issue the download command from your communications software and select Zmodem as the download protocol.

If you can't get everything in one trip — because of time constraints — make a note of the file that you're leaving behind. Then, next time you're online, you can cut to the chase by downloading that file by name.

Putting Your Booty to Work — or Not

Once the thrill of a successful download has faded, you are left with your online booty sitting uselessly on your computer like Charlie Brown's lump of coal.

What to do next shouldn't be a big challenge, especially if you have read through downloading and zipping and that stuff in Part I. However, I'll go ahead and give you a quick refresher on what to do next. After all, it's just *so* exhausting to flip back a few pages. Besides, I'll stick in a couple of new tricks to help make things easier.

Putting a file in its place

For the sake of an example, pretend we downloaded CALCULAT.ZIP. No such file really exists, so don't waste your time looking for it. There *are* calculators, but I just made up CALCULAT.ZIP so I'd have something to talk about.

1. **Get to the system prompt — C:\.**

   Exit your communications software; exit Windows if you have to.

2. **Go to the download directory where the file is located.**

   That is, type **CD \[name of download directory]** and press Enter.

3. **Make a temporary directory to hold the zipped file.**

   You just type **MD TEMP** and press Enter. Or you could type something more meaningful like MD CALC. You can have only one directory named TEMP at a time, so you may have to be creative in naming temporary directories.

4. **Copy the zipped file into the temporary directory.**

   In this example, you'd type **COPY CALCULAT.ZIP TEMP** and press Enter. Except, of course, you don't really type CALCULAT.ZIP; instead, type in the name of the real file you downloaded.

5. **Go to the temporary directory.**

   Type **CD TEMP** and press Enter.

6. **Unzip the file.**

   Type **PKUNZIP CALCULAT.ZIP** and press Enter.

7. **Find the file named README.1ST — or something similar to that — and read it.**

   You can call the readme file up in a word processor or in Windows Write, or you can even print it out by typing **PRINT README.1ST** and pressing Enter twice. This is the file with the instructions for setting up and using the program. And, unfortunately, it is at this point that you are now on your own. Each program has its own instructions and setup procedures. With luck, you won't encounter anything too complicated.

Banishing files

If you realize the program you downloaded is more powerful than a locomotive when all you need is a pushcart, or the other way around, you can delete the unneeded program to avoid clutter. You will find that at least two-thirds of the stuff you download just won't work out. As they say, you have to kiss a lot of frogs before you find Prince Charming. It's in the rules.

Here's how to delete the file, assuming it's still in its temporary directory (if you moved or installed the file elsewhere, substitute that directory name):

1. **Per usual, get to the system prompt by saving and then quitting everything.**

2. **Type** CD \[download directory]\[temporary directory] **and press Enter.**

   Using the example of installing the calculator, you type **CD \[download directory]\temp.**

3. **Check to make sure you're in the right place by typing** DIR **and pressing Enter.**

   Ask yourself, are these the files that belong to the program I want to delete? If yes, proceed.

4. **Type** DEL *.* **and press Enter.**

   This is the delete-everything-in-this-directory command. That's why you had to do Step 3 first, to make sure you were deleting the right things.

5. **You are warned that** all files will be deleted **in this directory. Press Y and Enter.**

6. **Type** CD .. **and press Enter to move up one directory level.**

7. **Type** RD [temporary directory] **and press Enter.**

   For example, if you want to remove a temporary directory named TEMP, you type **RD TEMP** and press Enter.

8. **If the original zipped file is still in the download directory, be sure to delete it by typing** DEL [file].ZIP **and pressing Enter.**

   That would be **DEL CALCULAT.ZIP** and Enter to nuke our imaginary file.

If you are familiar with and prefer to use Windows File Manager or Explorer or any other hard disk-management software to delete files or make and remove directories — be my guest. Those programs are made for jobs like this. They make the process less, as they say in the computer biz, *keystroke intensive.*

Another way to simplify things is, after performing Steps 1 and 2 in the preceding list, to use PKUnZip to extract only the readme file for perusal. You'll get a sense of the program from the readme information. You can decide from your reading whether or how to continue with the installation. Here's how:

1. **Perform Steps 1 and 2 from the preceding instructions.**

2. **Type** PKUNZIP -V CALCULAT.ZIP **and press Enter, substituting, of course, the name of the real program for our fake one.**

   The -V stands for View. What it means to you is that you get a list of all the files in the zipped file. Make a note of the file that's named closest to README.1ST.

3. **Type** PKUNZIP CALCULAT.ZIP README.1ST **and press Enter.**

   Again substitute your zipped file name for CALCULATE.ZIP and the actual name of the readme file, discovered in Step 2, for README.1ST.

One small peck for mankind

"We know how difficult it can be to start out fresh, with a new computer, knowing little about DOS and communications. We were all there at some point in time. The questions are hard to deal with sometimes, and we know the only way users are going to learn is if someone is there by their side, taking one step at a time. But, the *pecker* is the worst. What is a pecker? A pecker is the newcomer, not only to computers, but also to a keyboard. You get them into a Chat seeing they are having a difficult time navigating the BBS. Uh, oh. There he goes. Peck (one key press), peck peck (a couple more), now what does that word mean? Backspaces realizing the word made no sense. Meanwhile a minute has gone by and the only thing you can make out is the "I" that has been typed. You know you are in for an hour-long session helping this poor person out. If the Sysop has helped and leaves Chat knowing the User has a better idea of DOS communications or utilizing the BBS, it is a moment of triumph and a good feeling for the Sysop."

Don Habegger, Sysop, YA! WEBECAD! BBS

Chapter 9
Electrifying E-Mail

● ●

In This Chapter
▶ Responding to new E-Mail
▶ Writing a message
▶ Retrieving mail

● ●

*W*hen you were nine or ten and wondered why the letter carrier never brought you any mail, a parental figure probably commented, as they opened the latest utility bill, that they wished *they* never got any mail.

If you were lucky, though, someone patiently explained to you that for every action there is an equal and opposite reaction. In short — you have to write a letter to get a letter.

Sending E-Mail is how you make friends online.

So, even though learning to send mail to online friends when you don't have any online friends seems like putting the cart before the horse, it really isn't. Sending E-Mail is the action that you must take to generate a reaction, both in the public forums and in the personal mailboxes. The only difference between public mail and private mail is the destination.

> ✔ **Private E-Mail:** Messages exchanged between you and another person. These communiqués are generally meaningful only to you and the recipient, or are not items about which you want to debate publicly. An example of private E-Mail would be messages regarding bowling plans or about a book you both read.

> ✔ **Public E-Mail:** Messages dealing a with a broader scope of topics, like the merits of certain presidential candidates, which computer is the best, and who is stronger — Batman or Spider-Man. Public E-Mail is used in Conferences, which is what the next chapter is about.

E-Mail is so important that industries, both large and small, have grown around ways to make online E-Mail faster, better, cooler, and even easier.

Responding to New E-Mail

You may have expected the first topic in a chapter about E-Mail to be about how to write a message. That would be a logical assumption. Apparently you have forgotten you're in the Computer Zone. Nothing works as you assume it should.

By the mere act of registering with a BBS, you may automatically trigger an electronic-mail message from the Sysop that welcomes you to the system and probably also gives you some hints about learning the ropes. If you don't receive this message the first time you log on, it can make its appearance the second time. Therefore, odds are you'll have to respond to E-Mail even if you never spawn a single message of your own.

You find out that you have mail waiting for you after you finish your logging on ritual. You are presented with a screen something like Figure 9-1, asking if you want to read your new mail. Yes or no?

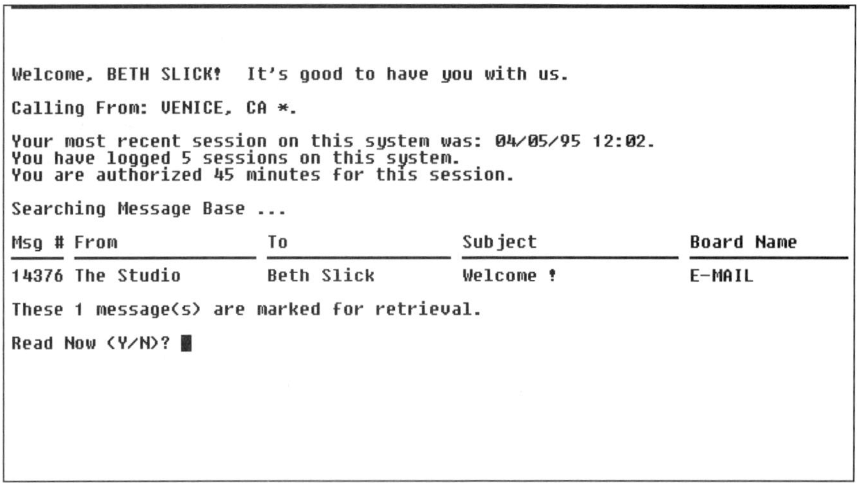

Figure 9-1:
After you log on, BBSs automatically notify you if you have new mail waiting and give you the chance to read it immediately.

```
Welcome, BETH SLICK!  It's good to have you with us.

Calling From: VENICE, CA *.

Your most recent session on this system was: 04/05/95 12:02.
You have logged 5 sessions on this system.
You are authorized 45 minutes for this session.

Searching Message Base ...

Msg # From              To              Subject          Board Name
14376 The Studio        Beth Slick      Welcome !        E-MAIL

These 1 message(s) are marked for retrieval.

Read Now <Y/N>? █
```

Who can resist new mail? Who would want to? Press Y and Enter to say yes to reading all personal mail. You may get a couple more questions:

- ✔ "Do you want to pause after each message?" Yes. That will give you a chance to read and respond.

- ✔ "Do you want to read all new messages?" No. All new personal mail, yes. All the new messages from the entire system, no.

Once the BBS stops bugging you with questions, you receive something like Figure 9-2.

```
 Welcome

 Welcome to GLIB!

 While your surfing through all the great stuff available here, don't
 overlook POWERPLAZA and The Studio-Print Shop. Down load our SOURCE1.ZIP
 file and check out some of the treasures available from gifts to Rainbow
 flags!

 All pricing is exceptional and GLIB receives a generous contribution
 from every order. You save, GLIB benefits and your purchasing from a gay
 owned & operated business.


 <B>ack, <W>ait, <C>ubby, <F>wd, <D>el, <R>eply, <A>gain, <N>ext, or <S>top? █
```

Figure 9-2:
Cubby, Del,
or Stop? Are
these
Mickey
Mouse Club
members or
mail-
command
options?

Once you finish reading your glad-to-have-you message from the Sysop, you are faced with a question mark and some options. *If* you're lucky enough to get options.

If there's one thing to learn in this book, it's the fact that BBSs are like snowflakes — no two are exactly alike. It comes as no surprise, then, to learn that each BBS puts its own spin on message-handling commands. However, we can categorize the approach BBSs take to the end-of-message mania into two groups.

> ✔ **The multiple choice:** Where there are a number of possible responses thoughtfully laid out for you, like in Figure 9-2.

> ✔ **The single question:** One message, one question — what's your End of Message Command? Speak now or forever hold your peace. Daunting, to say the least.

In either situation, you need to run through a little mental checklist as you decide how to proceed.

Confused about your next move? Remember to try pressing H and Enter, or ? and Enter, to get help. Even if help is not an official option, sometimes typing an H or a ? works anyway.

Disentangling attachments

Before you leave the message, take a close look at the options at the bottom of the screen — always a good plan. Some BBSs permit message senders to *attach* or *enclose* files with their messages. This means that, in addition to the message you can see, there is a file set up for you to download.

It's not unusual for the Sysop to attach a file containing the BBS's manual, registration forms, and what have you to the welcome message. This is a good thing. You want to download this so you can print it out and review it later.

Among those commands at the bottom of the screen is an offer to download the attached file — if there is one attached. If you say yes, the BBS asks for a download protocol and the usual download process commences. If you feel a little hesitant about downloading, take a quick refresher in Chapter 3.

Once the file has been downloaded, or if you decide not to download the file, then move on to the next item in your mental checklist. In Figure 9-2, there is no file attached, so it's a nonissue.

Replying to the missive

Do you want to send a message right back to the author of this message? If you do, then select the Reply option — press R and then, if necessary, press Enter. If you do want to reply, you should jump ahead a few pages in this chapter to "Writing a Message." However, let's assume you don't have anything to say to the Sysop. Move to the next decision.

Disposing of the message

You laughed, you cried, it became a part of you. Now it's time to erase the message using the delete, or kill, command.

Each message takes up space on the BBS computer, so it is considered good etiquette to erase messages that are no longer needed, so that you don't clog up the system. Generally, you give the command to delete, or kill, the message. Once you delete the message, you get to move forward.

If you need to keep the message for reference, then don't delete it. Some BBSs, like GLIB — the Gay and Lesbian Information Bureau, which came in at the third spot in the Top 100 — allow you to sock away special messages in a personal cubbyhole. Don't regard a BBS as a filing cabinet, though. Many systems purge messages after they start to grow beards. It's best to capture or download the file to your home computer. That's the only way to be sure you've saved it.

A quick-and-dirty alternative to capturing or downloading messages is to turn on the printer and, when the message you want to save is onscreen, press Shift+PrtScr to print the screen. This sends everything that's on the computer screen to the printer. If you're using Procomm Plus for Windows, pressing Alt+L sends the contents of the screen to the printer.

Moving on

If your messages-waiting screen — refer to Figure 9-1 — indicated more than one message was pending, you'll want to continue on to the next message.

Or, if you have read your last personal message, you are asked if you want to continue on to the Main Menu. If you select yes, or continue, you go out of mail-message madness and back to the Main Menu.

If you don't get multiple choice options at the end of a message and have to deal with the dreaded End of Message Command?, your potential responses — other than pressing H, for Help, and Enter to get a full list of options — are

  ✔ Type **RE** and press Enter to Reply.

  ✔ Press Y and Enter to read messages addressed to you.

  ✔ Press K and Enter to kill the message.

  ✔ Press N and Enter to quit reading messages.

Thankfully, you usually see the multiple choice setup at the end of a message. That way you don't have to actually memorize anything, you just have to be able to pick the right option out of the lineup.

After you declare you are finished reading your personal messages, the BBS may have more side tours for you to take.

  ✔ Do you want to read new bulletins?

  ✔ Do you want to look at new files?

  ✔ Would you like to know who else is online right now?

  ✔ Are you interested in learning who read your bio while you were away?

You may say yes or no as you wish. If you get stuck in a Bulletin Menu, remember that to get out you select the command to quit. This quits the Bulletin Menu and takes you to the Main Menu. Don't forget that Goodbye or Logoff are the only commands that end your BBS session. *Quit* is the command to leave the current menu.

Congratulations, you have just handled your first E-Mail. Of course, all this applies to reading any new E-Mail messages.

Common sense. I talk about it in Chapter 7. It's time I bring it up again, because you're playing in the number-one place on a BBS where you need to use it. Remember, there is no legitimate reason for anyone to be asking for your password via E-Mail. Don't give out personal information or financial data that would give someone access to your goods. Always keep the Sysop informed of any improper communications.

Writing a Message

Although using a BBS involves a lot of new concepts, the arena of message writing should be as familiar as the stern look you got from the teacher after getting caught passing notes — again.

BBS E-Mail is no-frills word processing coupled with only an occasional nod to the principles of grammar, spelling, and punctuation. E-Mail is a little unkempt because it's usually composed online under the pressure of waning moments of allotted time and the growing size of the phone bill. All that's important is that you move the conversation forward and get off as quickly as possible. No one will subtract points for spelling.

Later on, in Chapter 15, I talk about a type of software that has a tricky way of letting you read and respond to online messages while not online. But you're not there yet. First you have to learn how to read and respond to messages while online.

When you feel compelled to write a message to someone online, the process is spectacularly unsurprising:

1. **Issue the BBS menu command to start the E-Mail program.**

2. **You are asked to whom you want to write the message, what the subject is, and whether the message is public or private.**

3. **Write and edit the message.**

4. **Save — which means send — the message.**

5. **Exit the E-Mail program.**

6. **Wait for a response.**

Now that you've got the big picture, you can move in for the details.

Generally speaking, it's a good idea to know exactly to whom you're going to write before starting your E-Mail maneuvers. For practice, try writing a note to yourself. But in the future, as you'll see shortly, if you don't have the person's name exactly as the BBS lists that person's name, the BBS won't accept the mail message. If you need to look up the person's name, do it before you give the E-Mail command.

E-Mail experiences

"On my BBS — The Swamp — I have a five year old who is learning to spell. I have a caller with a tattoo on his arm from Treblinka. I have a gay teenager who decided to come out to some of his BBS friends, and discovered that he still had friends afterwards. I have a woman who could not talk about her rape until she found BBSing and was able to confide in others and get support.

I have a mother and son who could not get along until he left home for college, and *now* they can talk to each other on the BBS. I have many, many callers that could not write a sentence a year or two or three ago, but now have become rather good writers. And on and on and on..."

David Bushard, Sysop, The Swamp

Pressing the go button

When the compulsion to write a note must be satisfied, the first step is to find the E-Mail command on the BBS Main Menu.

If you don't see the word E-Mail right way, it's also known as *private mail*, *local mail*, *your mailbox*, or sometimes just plain, old *messages*. Every system has its own way of hiding . . . er, uh . . . I mean, *offering* the E-Mail command, as you can see in Figures 9-3 and 9-4. No matter how they disguise it, though, you can pretty much depend on pressing the letter E to start E-Mail.

Figure 9-3: The Main Menu for GLIB places its E-Mail command in the lower right. Press E to get to the local E-Mail commands.

```
GLIB-The Main Menu

   <Q>uit, sign off    <Y>our membership access level?    <#>Utilities
   <=> CESF WeatherGraf    <Z> ! POWER PLAZA !    <^> GLIB Phone Numbers
   <H>ow to Use GLIB - Your User's Manual <<-- New member?  Look here first!
                  "Sharing Our Loss" <M>emorial Section

   - THE GAY DATABASE <sm> -                  - COMMUNICATIONS -

<O>nLine Magazine - News, Events, USA     <R>eaders - QSO Offline Support
   Today, Weather, Boardwatch             <A>ll GLIB Message Bases Combined
<B>ulletin Board, Information Files       <P>ublic Messages/Conferences
   Events, Groups, What's Happening?      <S>tored Messages - Your Cubbyhole
<L>eisure Lounge - Laughs, Fun Stuff
<G>LIBnews - What's new on GLIB?          <E>-Mail, Private, LOCAL ONLY
<U>iew GLIBFLASH again - Say What?        <I>nternet e-mail & Other Services
<C>omputer SIGS, Info, ShareWare          <N>etworks - Other International Net

Command: █
```

Figure 9-4:
Even though
Aquila BBS
puts its
E-Mail
commands
right on top
and in the
middle —
it's the letter
E, again,
that whisks
you into
message
mode.

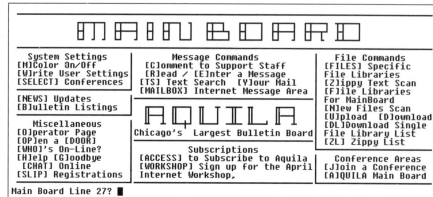

```
 ┌──────────────────────────────────────────────────────────────┐
 │          MAIN BOARD                                           │
 │   System Settings      Message Commands         File Commands  │
 │  [M]Color On/Off     [C]omment to Support Staff  [FILES] Specific │
 │  [W]rite User Settings [R]ead / [E]nter a Message File Libraries │
 │  [SELECT] Conferences [TS] Text Search [Y]our Mail [Z]ippy Text Scan │
 │                      [MAILBOX] Internet Message Area [F]ile Libraries │
 │  [NEWS] Updates                                  For MainBoard │
 │  [B]ulletin Listings                             [N]ew Files Scan │
 │                         AQUILA                   [U]pload [D]ownload │
 │     Miscellaneous                                [DL]Download Single │
 │  [O]perator Page     Chicago's Largest Bulletin Board File Library List │
 │  [OP]en a [DOOR]                                 [ZL] Zippy List │
 │  [WHO]'s On-Line?          Subscriptions                       │
 │  [H]elp [G]loodbye   [ACCESS] to Subscribe to Aquila  Conference Areas │
 │    [CHAT] Online     [WORKSHOP] Sign up for the April [J]oin a Conference │
 │  [SLIP] Registrations Internet Workshop,          [A]QUILA Main Board │
 │ Main Board Line 27? █                                          │
 └──────────────────────────────────────────────────────────────┘
```

What happens next depends on the BBS you're using. That single letter E could either start the E-Mail engine, or it could take you to a message menu where you have to select something else, like Write a Message, to get the ball rolling.

Once you do get the E-Mail program in gear, you get a series of questions that includes:

✔ Who do you want to send the message to?

Type the recipient's name and press Enter. If you have misspelled the name, or if the person is not in the BBS database, you are told just that and not allowed to proceed until you enter a name that is listed in the system.

✔ What's the subject?

Type something brief, but as meaningful as possible — "stuff" is not very revealing, but "lunch plans" is — and press Enter.

✔ Is this correct (Y/N)?

Here's your chance to change the subject.

✔ Message Security (Y/N)?

This is where you indicate whether or not the message is for the eyes of the addressee only. Usually the choice is simple enough: No Security (public) or Yes Security (private). Make sure you pick the right one! Remember how much fun it was having your note read out loud to the class?

> ✔ Use Full Screen Editor (Y/N)?

After you say yes or no to this question, you find yourself in the editing program and can start writing.

But how should you respond to the offer of a full-screen editor? What *is* a full-screen editor? First of all, BBS word processors are generally referred to as *editors* or *text editors*.

The editor with the fewest number of word processing-like options is called a *line editor*. A line editor can only change, or edit, text that's on the same line as the cursor. Once you've gone on to the next line, you can't go back up and fix anything. Well, you can, but it's very tedious. Figure 9-5 is an example of a line editor in action.

Figure 9-5:
At the top of the screen are the questions any BBS editor would ask. Below, however, is what a text editor looks like in action.

```
To: Beth Slick
Subj: computers
Is this correct <Y/N>? Y
Use Full Screen Editor <Y/N>? N

Enter text of message.
<CR> by itself ends input.

01: Dear Beth:
02:
03: I can't believe you decided *not* to use the full screen editor <G>.
04:
05: You can't believe the problems you have to go through to edit text once
06: you've gone to the next line!  If you try to use the arrow/cursor keys to
07: move around you get weird things like [D[D[C[C on your screen.  The only
08: key that works is the backspace -- and then only on the current line!
09:
10: *Plus* I have to remember to put a space between each paragraph or the
11: stupid editor thinks I'm finished with the message.  Yikes!
12:
13:

<L>ist, <U>iew, <E>dit, <R>cpt, <F>ile, <Q>uit, <S>ave, or <H>elp? █
```

A *full-screen editor*, as shown in Figure 9-6, empowers the cursor to travel up, down, left, right — all over the entire screen. And that, boys and girls, is why they call it a full-screen editor — you can edit any place on the full-screen — not just on the current line.

Who wouldn't want a full-screen editor? Why ask why? In the olden days, with slower modems and computers, using a full-screen editor could be painfully slow. Nowadays, there is almost no reason not to take advantage of the full-screen editor option — if it's offered.

Say yes to the full-screen editor.

Figure 9-6:
The
message in
Figure 9-5 is
now in a
full-screen
editor —
meaning the
cursor is
free to roam
the entire
screen.

```
┌──────────────────────────────────────────────────────────────────────┐
│ To: Beth Slick          Subj: computers              Mode:Insert       │
│ Dear Beth:                                                             │
│ I can't believe you decided *not* to use the full screen editor <G>.  │
│                                                                        │
│ You can't believe the problems you have to go through to edit text once you've │
│ gone to the next line!  If you try to use the arrow/cursor keys to move around │
│ you get weird things like [D[D[C[C on your screen.  The only key that works is │
│ the backspace -- and then only on the current line!                    │
│                                                                        │
│ *Plus* I have to remember to put a space between each paragraph or the stupid │
│ editor thinks I'm finished with the message.  Yikes!                   │
│                                                                        │
│ Fortunately, you can switch back to full screen editing at any time....│
│                                                                        │
│ *whew*                                                                 │
│ █                                                                      │
│                                                                        │
│ <Esc>=Exit  Ctrl-V=Overwrite  Ctrl-Z=Help              Line:17         │
└──────────────────────────────────────────────────────────────────────┘
```

Putting keyboard to screen

Once you've got your editing screen up, as in Figure 9-6, take a moment before you begin composing to look at what it's telling you. Usually you see at least two very important commands. Take note of them before your start writing, because sometimes these options scroll off the screen as your message gets longer.

✔ How to stop editing: `Esc = Exit`

Pressing the Esc key is how you tell the editor that you are done writing and want to either send or do something with the finished message. You can even throw it away if you want. But first, you must press Esc. It's not too much to ask.

✔ How to get help: `Ctrl-Z = Help`

Use the help command on your editor to discover what the actual editing commands are on the BBS you're using. Pressing delete, delete, delete not only gets old very quickly, but is a big waste of time — especially when you've got Ctrl+Y waiting in the wings eager to wipe out the whole line in one keystroke.

When you issue the help command, you may be startled to see the screen clear, your message disappear, and a list of editing commands take its place. Don't worry, after you finish scrolling through the editing commands, your composition reappears and you are put back exactly where you were when you asked for help.

Also, just to make things more interesting, your help screen may be packed with caret symbols (^). That ^ is geek-speak for Ctrl. So ^Z means *press Ctrl+Z*. I know it's weird. In fact, it's totally out of ^!

While the look of every BBS full-screen editor isn't exactly the same, the Esc and Ctrl-Z commands are comfortingly universal. It's nice to know there are some things you can count on. But always double-check, just to be sure.

Replying to sender

Remember that stuff about equal and opposite reactions? It can happen to you.

Sometimes you read a message and it generates, within you, the desire to react. Hopefully that reaction manifests itself in the form of a desire to answer the message. The BBS system encourages the impulse to respond by offering a Reply option conveniently located at the end of every message you read, as shown in Figure 9-2.

If it seems as though you see something different at the bottom of every E-Mail screen, you're not going crazy. Yes, the options at the bottom of the screen change. They are what is called *context sensitive*. In other words, the options at the bottom of the screen apply to what you're doing. If you're reading a message sent to you by someone else, you get one set of options — like Reply, Delete, and Stop. If you are *writing* a message and issue the stop-editing command, you see another set of options — like Send, Abort, Attach, and so on. The options match what you're doing.

Giving a line editor that blank look

If you end up on a BBS that has, let us say, *limited resources*, the luxury of a full-screen editor may not be available. You'll have to make do with the line editor. There is one particularly frustrating line editor trap that you should know about if you find yourself roughing it.

The problem is that pressing Enter twice in a line editor is the signal that you're finished writing.

Unfortunately, pressing Enter twice is also what you do if you want to put a blank line between two paragraphs.

What to do? The solution is to trick the computer. Press Enter at the end of the first paragraph, type a single space on the line you want to appear as blank, and then press Enter again. The computer thinks of the space as a character and continues editing. The reader won't know the difference.

Meanwhile, back at the ranch. . . .

Once you select the Reply option — usually by pressing R and Enter — the BBS immediately hooks you into the online text editor. Since the editor is very smart, it fills out the addressee and the subject for you, assuming that you want to reply to the person who wrote you the message and use the same subject. You get a yes-or-no chance to make corrections.

Once you're in the, I assume, full-screen editor, you can write your letter as described in the previous section. However, since your are in reply mode, a bonus command is now at your fingertips to make your reply easier to write and less confusing for your correspondent to read.

We are talking about the mystical *quote command* — usually Ctrl+Q.

Pretend a friend writes to you asking this disturbing question, "Why did NASA name their monster space telescope after Robert Redford's character, Hubbel Gardiner, in *The Way We Were?* If they want to name it after a movie character, why not Klattuu?"

In a normal conversation the lag between a question and an answer is measured in seconds. In E-Mail, days could pass between the question and the answer. When you reply, it's a good idea to phrase the answer to remind your correspondent of what he or she said. Everyone, at one time or another, has received a message saying nothing more than, "You're right. Let's do it." — and not had a clue what it's about. In this example, you'd have to write, "NASA did not name their Space Telescope after Hubbel Gardiner in *The Way We Were.* It was named after Edwin P. Hubble, the noted astronomer."

But the quote command allows you to quickly copy the question from your correspondent's message and paste it into your reply message. Then, all you need to do is type a quick answer under the quoted question, like, "More likely it was Edwin P. Hubble, the astronomer."

It takes a little patience to get this primitive cut-and-paste to work, but it's worth the effort.

1. **Type the reply command and start your message.**

2. **Put your cursor where you want the quoted material to appear and press Ctrl+Q to activate the quote command.**

3. **Some sort of note appears at the bottom of the screen asking** `Beginning from line # or <L>ist:`

4. **Press L and Enter to get the BBS to repeat the message you're replying to, as in Figure 9-7, with numbers assigned to each line of text.**

Figure 9-7:
Here's the
message I'm
replying to,
listed with
line
numbers.
Lines 7-8
are the ones
I want to
quote first.

```
Beginning Line # or <L>ist: 1

1:    Beth --
2:
3:    Although I wouldn't normally write a letter to myself, I just can't
4:    let this situation continue unchecked.
5:
6:    Computers are a very serious business and I think you take them far
7:    too lightly.  Simply put, computers are not a laughing matter and I
8:    think you are being far too cavalier on the topic.
9:
10:   You have ten days to repair your ways.
11:
12:   Beth
13:

Beginning Line # or <L>ist: █
```

5. **Once you see the phrase in the message you want to put in your reply, type the line numbers in which the phrase appears.**

   In this case, I'd type **7-8** and press Enter.

6. **The phrase you requested appears in the message.**

   Don't worry about the extra words, the person reading the message will be able to figure it out. If you really want to make it neat, you can do so manually. But it's a waste of time, in my opinion.

7. **Continue writing your response, calling the quote command into play as needed.**

   You end up with a message looking something like Figure 9-8. Notice the quoted material is set off by angle brackets (>). Sometimes the quoted material has a box around it and the name of the person who said it. More often you see the first name or initials of the person being quoted.

Sending the message

When you're all done crafting your E-Mail, then it's time to send it.

1. **Issue your I'm-all-done command — usually Esc or pressing Enter twice.**

2. **Select the save command and press Enter.**

   Once the message is sent, you can't unsend it or change your mind. It's gone. When the addressee logs on next time, they'll be told they have mail waiting.

3. **Once the message is sent, the message you're responding appears again. If it's no longer needed, go ahead and delete — or kill — it.**

Figure 9-8:
The first two lines were quoted from the message I am responding to. The angle brackets remind you what was said in the original message.

```
Msg#:29368 *E-MAIL*
04/14/95 02:08:43
From: Beth Slick
  To: Beth Slick
Subj: REPLY TO MSG# 29309 <an example>

 > too lightly.  Simply put, computers are not a laughing matter and I
 > think you are being far too cavalier on the topic.

Well, I think you take them far too seriously!

 > You have ten days to repair your ways.

You needn't wait ten days.  I will not change.  Computers are definitely a
laughing matter!

Sincerely,

Beth

<->, <B>ack, <W>ait, <C>ubby, <F>wd, <D>el, <R>eply, <A>gain, <N>ext, or
<S>top? █
```

TIP

If you accidentally hit Esc, use the continue command to return to the E-Mail message and continue editing. If you decide not to send the message, press Esc and then select Abort.

In addition to just a plain-vanilla sending of the message, many BBSs have additional twists and turns to the E-Mail story — soon to be a major motion picture. As always, all these options are not available on every system.

✔ Send a file with your message. In the Hubble case, you can send a bio of Edwin Hubble and his work with red shifts, other galaxies, and the expanding universe. After issuing the Esc — I'm-all-done — command, you see an option to *attach a file*. Use that command and you are prompted to type in the name of the file and upload it. When the recipient gets the message, they have the option to download the file. If they prefer gazing at Hubbel Gardiner to reading about Edwin Hubble, they may opt not to download the bio.

✔ Use the *receipt command* to get a message informing you as to the exact nanosecond when the recipient accessed your message.

✔ You can send a copy of your message to someone else using a *carbon command.*

✔ In addition to replying to a message, you can also *forward* the original message to someone else — which may prompt you to wonder how private, private mail really is. The only guarantee is that it starts out private.

Retrieving Mail

Every time you log onto a BBS, you may be asked if you want the system to scan the message base. What that means, in real life, is that the BBS will search high and low to find any messages that are addressed to you.

Mail to you can be sitting in a public conference or in a private mailbox.

There are dozens of ways this information can be displayed, ranging from the appropriate message numbers appearing with asterisks next to them to a list of conferences that contain messages addressed to you.

Mail can either be marked for later retrieval — when ready, you hit a *marked command* and your messages are presented one after the other. Or the BBS can display each message one at a time before you even get to the Main Menu.

In the beginning, I highly recommend you accept any BBS invitation to read mail now. Let the BBS take you straight to your messages so you can read and respond to them with minimal muss and fuss.

If you don't read the mail when the BBS offers to show it to you, you'll have to learn how that particular system retrieves and displays mail for reading. Here are some things to look for:

> ✔ If the BBS has a personal or private mailbox, enter the command that accesses it. You are then shown a submenu with options that let you read your new mail, something like the one in Figure 9-9.

Figure 9-9:
A nice, handy private mailbox courtesy of America's Suggestion Box BBS. Basically, everything you need to get your private mail.

```
** Beth's private Mailbox **

1. Read your private messages
2. Quick Scan Message Headers
3. Write a private Message
4. Delete a Message
5. User Search



   U. Utilities    M. Main    P. Previous    G. Goodbye
```

✔ Sometimes reading new mail is an option from the Main Menu. Look for commands like *read new mail*, *scan for unread personal mail*, *retrieve marked mail*, and so forth.

✔ If the system doesn't have private mailboxes, you may have to join a private-mail conference and search for your mail there. Since the next chapter is about conferences, that's where you should go next.

One new job, hold the mayo

One of our subscribers who currently works as a diner cook and would like a career change, gave 24th Street Exchange credit for his recent positive job outlook. It seems he was recently offered a part-time computer programming apprenticeship by a fellow subscriber.

Jackie Kuhwarth, Sysop, 24th Street Exchange

Chapter 10

Confabulating in Conferences

In This Chapter
▶ Characterizing conferences
▶ Tapping into conferences
▶ Choosing a topic
▶ Rounding up and reading messages
▶ Posting your own messages
▶ Keeping your head
▶ Abandoning a conference
▶ Selecting conferences

C onfabulation!

Say it loud enough and someone is likely to respond with *gesundheit!* Actually *confabulation* means an informal chat or conference. It's the perfect word to describe what goes on inside online public forums — which have come a long way since, "Friends, Romans, and countrymen!"

However, computer people prefer to call it a *conference,* and we have to go along with them. The starting-from-ground-zero definition of a conference is that it's a predefined place on a BBS where people discuss a particular topic via E-Mail. The name of the conference lets people self-select what they want to talk about and, in some ways, with whom.

A real-world comparison would be a group of people that meets to discuss movies or poetry. In a conference, though, you don't have to all get together in order to have the meeting. You can step in at any time, catch up on E-Mail left since you last checked in, make your comments, and leave.

Characterizing Conferences

There's no doubt that conferences can initially be confusing and maze-like. There are a couple of reasons for this.

First, unlike downloading and E-Mail, which are presented in a comparatively uniform fashion from BBS to BBS, conferences appear in several guises. They can be called such things as

- *Conferences*
- *Public forums*
- *Mail or mail area*
- *Message bases/menu*
- *SIGS* — short for *Special Interest Groups*

The second reason conferences can cause consternation is that there are just so many of them. A single BBS can have hundreds of conferences. Figure 10-1 shows just one page of conference listings — and we're not even out of the "A"s yet! How are you ever going to look at them all?

- You can't look at them all. Nobody can. You don't feel compelled to be on a first-name basis with every single book in a bookstore, or know what's going on at any given movement on every one of those famous 500 channels, do you? Of course not. Same thing with conferences.

- Scan a few of the topics and then pick two or three and start reading and participating. If that isn't enough, you know there's a lot more where those came from. Conferences, after all, are not a homework assignment. They are supposed to be *fun*.

Finally, just to make things as confusing as possible, the term *conference* is also sometimes used in conjunction with a group Chat (Chatting is covered in the next chapter). The major difference between a conference in Chat and the type of conference or public forum we're talking about here is that, in the Chat version, everyone who wants to participate must be there at the same time — like that poetry group or movie club. In a public forum, the conversation builds as people come to the forum, read messages, leave one of their own, and then leave.

Figure 10-1:
What do
Japanese
animation,
Africa, and
King Arthur
have in
common?
They are all
discussion
topics on
the Aquila
BBS.

```
 General Discussion Topics  || I=Ilink F=FidoNet R=RIME NX=Annex
 #    | Name        | Echo | Description
 425  | ACOA        | R    | Adult children of alcoholics
 226  | ADMIN       | R    | Rime Network Administration Conference
 687  | AFRICA      | I    | Africa and African Culture
 669  | AIDS        | I    | AIDS Discussions
 456  | AIDS-HIV    | R    | Aids virus discussion
 454  | ALT-ENT     | R    | Off-beat and unusual TV series
 205  | ANIME&MANGA | I    | Japanese Animation and Comics
 450  | ANIME       | R    | Animation discussion
 449  | ANIMLRTS    | R    | Animal rights discussion
 685  | AQUARIUM    | I    | Aquarium Environment Talk
 452  | AQUARIUM    | R    | Care of your salt,freshwater fish
 633  | ARCHIVES    | PB   | Retailer "Archives" Provides Book Lists
 295  | ARTHUR      | R    | Discussion centering around king arthur
 634  | ARTISTS     | PB   | Traditional, Classical, Graphical; Art and Mechs
 308  | ASTROLOG    | R    | Discussion centering around astrology
 678  | ASTRONMY    | I    | Current astronomical news & events
 420  | ASTRONMY    | R    | Stars, physical laws & announcements
 679  | ATHLETICS   | I    | Sports topics & discussion
 477  | AUDIO       | F    | Sound Discussion Conference
[Y],[N],[NS],[S]earch ? █
```

Going national — and beyond

Instead of being organized by topic first, some public message bases are organized first by their intended audience, then by topic. You may assume that the intended audience for a message base is anyone using that BBS. You would be logical, but wrong. Not all messages remain confined to the BBS that spawned them. Often they are distributed far and wide. The intended audience is defined by these basic groups:

✔ **Private:** If the BBS doesn't have mailbox facilities, then one conference is declared private, and that's where people go to leave messages. If someone were to try to read all the messages there, they'd be told that all the messages stored there, except the ones addressed to them, are private.

✔ **Local:** These are the public conferences that have meaning to the local area — basically the city where the BBS is — and not the rest of the world. This is where you'd see the conference covering the Fourth of July plans in your city, or business groups grappling with a postage increase.

✔ **Network or Echo:** Your local BBS can have alliances with a number of BBSs in other cities. All the BBSs in an alliance — or network — agree to have one or more conferences with the same topics in common.

Then, at a prearranged time — usually in the wee hours — each computer in the alliance calls up the other, and the messages in their aligned conferences are distributed or echoed to all of the computers in the network. At the end of the exchange, each conference would contain, not only its own messages, but all those on that topic from the network BBSs.

The advantage of this is that it effectively makes the BBS look bigger, allows you to confer with others without paying long distance, and increases your chances of gathering enough people willing to discuss, for example, Forensic Forestry.

There are lots of different networks. You see them listed in the conference areas, mostly as either somethingNet or somethingLink. There's even one network called ThrobNet, and you can guess what the conferences in *that* network deal with. If you can't guess, never mind. Figure 10-2 shows a series of network names and their last mail exchanges.

Figure 10-2:
Mail Call!
Network
East
displays a
list of
current mail
runs so you
know how
up-to-date
the
conferences
are.

```
Last Mail Runs:

NETWORK        DATE       TIME     SENT     RECEIVED

RelayNet       04-19-95   01:56     16         816
MetroLink      04-17-95   22:19      1         241
SmartNet       04-18-95   22:31      2          66
ILink          04-19-95   07:08      2         835
ThrobNet       04-18-95   22:52      8         560
U'NI-net       04-18-95   22:13      1        1202
NANet          04-18-95   16:11      2        1420
FidoNet        04-19-95   02:35     19        5802

Last Internet Mail Exchange:    04-19-95 at 12:34
Last Usenet Newsgroup Mail:     04-18-95 at 15:42

Latest Weather Maps:   04-18-95 at 17:14 - Type MAPS for the Weather Center
Sports News Updated:   04-19-95 at 12:51 - Type SPORTS for Sports Connect
```

If the BBS has a theme, then the Sysop could elect to participate only in the network conferences that synch up with the mission of the BBS. For example, the Sysop of the OS/2 Shareware BBS has culled every OS/2 Conference out of several networks, including Internet, to provide his users with a one-stop OS/2 Shareware conference shop — or close enough to it.

Back in Figure 10-1, you can probably now figure out what those letters in the Echo column mean. This is another way of indicating that the conference is distributed on a network. The key to the abbreviations in that Echo column are listed at the top of the screen — ILink, FidoNet, RIME, and Annex.

✔ **Internet:** A growing number of BBSs have set up links to the Internet. If you think BBS conferences are overwhelming, welcome to the really big time on the Internet. There are more than 7,000 ongoing conferences on the Internet. On the Internet, they're called newsgroups instead of conferences. It seems as though there's a newsgroup covering every conceivable human thought ranging from parenting to business news. You can read Introducing the Internet in Chapter 14 for a little more info. Figure 10-3 offers a Message Menu with a variety of options, including Internet E-Mail.

Figure 10-3:
The spa!
Message
Menu
where all
things
message
originate—
including
private,
public, and
Internet
E-Mail.

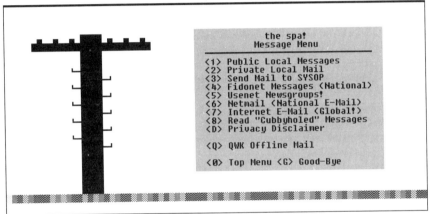

```
                              the spa!
                             Message Menu

              <1> Public Local Messages
              <2> Private Local Mail
              <3> Send Mail to SYSOP
              <4> Fidonet Messages <National>
              <5> Usenet Newsgroups!
              <6> Netmail <National E-Mail>
              <7> Internet E-Mail <Global!>
              <8> Read "Cubbyholed" Messages
              <D> Privacy Disclaimer

              <Q> QWK Offline Mail

              <0> Top Menu <G> Good-Bye
```

Getting to the basics

Even though conferences are organized differently and referred to on each BBS by a disparate collection of names, like a rose, they all still smell as sweet. Once you actually get down to the conference area itself, you find that conferences on all BBSs work in basically the same way:

✔ Each conference has its own topic.

The first step in using conferences is to find a topic that really turns you on. Hobbies or pet interests are good places to start. Figure 10-1 is just the first screen of many listing typical conference discussion topics. Eventually you realize that experts in fields you know nothing about are willing to give help if you ask. For example, if you want to give someone a nice bottle of wine, the habitués of the wine forum will be glad to give you some great advice.

✔ Asking the BBS to let you see the messages in a particular conference is called *joining* a conference, as in Figure 10-4.

You can't watch a TV show without going to and "joining" the channel that's got the show. Joining a conference is akin to switching channels on a TV set. No commitment. Once you've joined a conference, you can read, write, and search for messages.

Figure 10-4:
Network
East
displays a
screen of
conferences
and asks
which one
you want to
join.

```
┌──────────────────────────┐
│ ELECTRONIC MAIL │          Current Mail Network:
└──────────────────────────┘
                                       RelayNet

See <B>ulletin 63 for complete conference details

4DOS.................1    ARJ..................15   BiModem..............3
Abortion.............2    Asia................145   Biology..............3
ACOA.................3    ASP Support..........17   Birth................3
Agriculture..........4    Astrology............18   Black Experience.....3
Alarm/Security.......5    Astronomy............19   Barbershop Harmony...2
Amiga................7    Atari-ST.............20   Batch Files..........2
AmiPro.............333    Audio................21   BBS ADS..............2
Animal Rights........8    Aviation.............22   BBS Caller's Digest..2
Anime................9    BBS Doors............42   BBS Trade Assns.....34
Ansi Codes..........10    BBS Issues...........27   Boating..............3
Apogee..............11    BBS Software.........28   Boston Computer......3
Apple...............12    Beer.................29   Boyan................3
Aquariums...........13    Bible Studies........30   Brief Text Editor....3
Archivers...........14    Bicycles.............31   Broadcast Prof.......4

Conference # to join <Enter>=none, <R)elist?
```

✔ The entire content of a conference is E-Mail written for public viewing and pertaining to the topic of the conference.

✔ Users come into the conference, read all the messages, and then add their own, if they have something to say.

A lot of people just read conference messages and don't publicly participate. Those people are known as *lurkers*. While it's not exactly flattering to be called a lurker, there are far worse insults.

✔ Users can also write private E-Mail in conferences, if an aside to another user would be of no general interest.

✔ Unlike private E-Mail, messages in the conferences should not delete your messages unless they are inaccurate, you've changed your mind, or you realize the phrasing of the message is unnecessarily inflammatory.

The whole idea of public discourse is that everyone can see the progression of the argument — whether they follow it day by day or check in once a week. Besides, your advice to another user may be read and appreciated by hundreds or thousands of others. You just never know.

A level playing field

One of the best things that a BBS can do is allow people who normally couldn't, to "get out" and "meet people." We have users online with handicaps ranging from cerebral palsy to being legally blind, from being wheelchair bound to being paraplegic. Some of our most popular users are handicapped, but no one knows it until they meet.

And then, they are treated the same as anyone else. Getting online puts you on a level playing field with everyone else. No prejudice on race, sex, age, physical impairment, background, financial status, educational level, or anything else.

Rodney A. Aloia, Sysop, The INDEX System ™

Tapping into Conferences

E-Mail is the primary coin in public conferences. Since you already know how to use E-Mail, you're posed to make your debut in the conversational fray. The only problem is finding the conferences in general and the conference you want in particular.

If it makes it more fun for you, you can pretend you're a spy, searching for the secret messages hidden on the BBS.

Your first clue to the mystery of the hidden messages is to look at the Main Menu for any of those magic words I mentioned earlier — like conference, message base, mail menu, and so forth. Can you find the right command in Figure 10-5? If you don't look carefully, you might choose the wrong one.

Figure 10-5:
Okay, boys and girls, can you find the menu choice that will take you to the public forum?

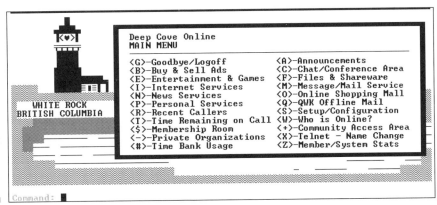

```
Deep Cove Online
MAIN MENU

<G>-Goodbye/Logoff              <A>-Announcements
<B>-Buy & Sell Ads              <C>-Chat/Conference Area
<E>-Entertainment & Games       <F>-Files & Shareware
<I>-Internet Services           <M>-Message/Mail Service
<N>-News Services               <O>-Online Shopping Mall
<P>-Personal Services           <Q>-QWK Offline Mail
<R>-Recent Callers              <S>-Setup/Configuration
<T>-Time Remaining on Call      <W>-Who is Online?
<$>-Membership Room             <+>-Community Access Area
<->-Private Organizations       <X>-Telnet - Name Change
<#>-Time Bank Usage             <Z>-Member/System Stats

Command:
```

WHITE ROCK
BRITISH COLUMBIA

In Figure 10-5, did you choose C, Chat/Conference? Oops — wrong answer. Remember, right now we're talking about conferences that take place via *mail*. So, the right choice is M for Message/Mail. I told you this could get tricky.

Even if you had chosen C and gone off to that menu, you would have quickly realized you were in the wrong place because the choices there all have to do with chatting, and none of them have to do with reading messages. So, you'd have simply returned to the Main Menu and kept on reading. No harm done. Plus, now you know where Chat is on that system.

The 5th Wave   **By Rich Tennant**

"IT'S THE BREAK WE'VE BEEN WAITING FOR, LIEUTENANT. THE THIEVES FIGURED OUT HOW TO TURN ON ONE OF THE STOLEN VIDEO CONFERENCING MONITORS."

Choosing a topic

Once you find the public-forum area, the BBS will assume you want to join one. Sometimes it says Conference # or L to list, which is one way of saying that if you already know the assigned number of the conference you want to join, then type it now. If you don't, then press L and press Enter to get a list of conferences.

I'll share with you the sad and pathetic fact that I know the numbers of my favorite conferences on the BBS I frequent most — 53 and 105. If you hang out someplace often enough, you'll start memorizing their numbers too. And before you start laughing at me for being a geek, remember that even Olivia Newton-John referred to her favorite song by its jukebox number — E17.

However, for the first time out, you want to press L and Enter to get a list in English, like the one back in Figure 10-1 and the one in Figure 10-6.

Figure 10-6:
From the
Springfield
Public
Access
BBS, the
beginning of
their
Message
Board
topics. Note,
you can
search for a
topic or
scroll
through
the list.

```
┌─────────────────────────────────────────────────────────────────────┐
│ Springfield Public Access BBS! (The Spa!) Individual Message Board Area │
├─────────────────────────────────────────────────────────────────────┤
│  000 Mystery Science 3k    000 Mystery Science 3k    000 Mystery Science 3k │
│  101 Advanced D&D          102 Amiga                 103 Amiga Games   │
│  104 Amiga-New England     105 Amiga For Sale-N Eng  106 Apple (Pre-Mac) │
│  107 Atari ST              108 Audio                 109 Autoracing    │
│  110 Beyond War            111 Biking                112 Blue Wave Support │
│  113 Broadcasting          114 CD ROMs               115 Chess         │
│  116 C Language            117 Comics                118 Consumer Reports │
│  119 Controversy           120 Cooking               121 Diabetes      │
│  122 Ecology               123 Electronics           124 FCC Discussion │
│  125 Feminism              126 For Sale (National)   127 Funny Stuff   │
│  128 Gaming                129 Genealogy             130 Genea-Who's Got What │
│  131 Gourmet               132 HAM                   133 HAM - For Sale │
│  134 HAM - Tech            135 Humor                 136 Indian Affairs │
│  137 LAN Discussion        138 Mac - Communications  139 Mac - Development │
│  141 Mac - For Sale        142 Mac - Games           143 Mac - General │
│  144 Mac - Hype            145 Mac - Macwoof         147 MIDInet       │
│  148 Military People       149 Motorcycle            150 Native Americans │
│  151 Neural Nets           152 New Age               153 News Chat     │
│  154 OS/2                  155 Packet Radio          156 Pascal        │
│ Enter a Board Number, <CR> Continue, <G>o To, <R>elist, <S>earch, <Q>uit: █ │
└─────────────────────────────────────────────────────────────────────┘
```

Because the volume of specific topic options can be more than people will wade through, another approach, as in Figure 10-7, is to display a general subject list. Once you make a choice, like Professions, for example, type the number next to the area of interest and press Enter. Voilà, you've joined. Kind of anticlimactic, huh?

Figure 10-7:
Pick an area
of interest,
and the
Deep Cove
Online
system
shows you
specific
topics within
the group.

```
┌─────────────────────────────────────────────────────────────────────┐
│     Deep Cove Online - Personal Message Group Selection/Editing       │
│    1 E-MAIL            3 LOCAL MAIL            4 COMMUNICATIONS         │
│    5 APPLICATIONS      6 BUSINESS             7 PERIPHERALS            │
│    8 PROGRAMMING       9 DISCUSS-ARGUE       10 ENVIRONMENT            │
│   11 GENEALOGY        12 HAM RADIO           13 HEALTH ISSUES          │
│   14 HOBBIES          15 CHATTER             16 INFORMATION            │
│   17 MACINTOSH        18 MUSIC               19 NOVELL & UNIX          │
│   20 OS/2             21 IBM-NET             22 PERSONAL               │
│   23 RELIGION         24 SCIENCE             25 SPORTS                 │
│   26 SCIENCE FICTION  27 PROFESSIONS         28 BUY & SELL             │
│   29 TRANSPORTATION   30 NOAH'S ARK          31 HOME & GARDEN          │
│   32 ENTERTAINMENT    33 POLITICS            34 EMPLOYMENT             │
│   35 RACENET                                                          │
│ <A>dd, <R>emove, <E>dit, <L>ist All Available Boards, <Q>uit          │
│ Select a Group ID Number or Enter a Group Command: █                  │
└─────────────────────────────────────────────────────────────────────┘
```

Choosing a topic, part deux

On some systems, there's another way to find a conference using a secret shortcut. Usually, if this option is available, it will be advertised on the Main Menu as a hint. This may not be for everyone, but it's definitely for those who like to know the sneaky way to do things.

Instead of making a choice from the Main Menu to join a conference and then scrolling through the list of conferences, you can ask the system to search through all the conferences for you — right from the Main Menu.

Just type the bizarre-looking formula: **J;S;[what you're looking for]** and press Enter — capitalization doesn't matter.

In a real example, if I wanted to find all the conferences dealing with pets, I'd type **J;S;pets** and press Enter. Don't be frightened by the semi-colon. It's just a way of saying "space" to the BBS. In Figure 10-8, I conducted a search for pets and found five Pets conferences on as many networks. Here's my chance to talk to others about my precious little kitties. For some reason everyone in my family is sick of hearing about them.

Figure 10-8:
This is really
a two-part
picture of
the Network
East Main
Menu
where I
typed
j;s;pets to
find all the
pets
conferences.
Below is the
result of the
search and
an offer to
join them.

```
All NETWORK commands are shown in brackets: <H>elp

ELECTRONIC MAIL         OTHER COMMANDS              UTILITIES & GAMES
                        <B>ulletin list            <RUN> online programs
                        <G>oodbye <logoff>         <SPORTS> Connect!
<C>omment to Sysop      <H>elp
<E>nter messages    --> <KEYWORD> Access List       SOFTWARE LIBRARY
<FAX> a message         <M>ode <color on/off>
<J>oin mail area        <P>age length setting      <D>ownload files
<K>ill messages         <T>ransfer protocols       <F>iles Menu
<Q>uick message scan    <U>iew your settings       <N>ew software
<R>ead messages         <W>rite your info          <SEARCH> for files
<RE>ply to messages     <X>pert mode <on/off>      <U>pload files
<SEL>ect area scans

<51 min. left> NETWORK Command? j;s;pets
   475> I-Pets
  1510> N-Pets
   212> R-Pets
   734> S-Pets
   909> U-Pets

Mail Area number to join <Enter>=none?
```

The great thing about conferences is that there is no wrong place to start. Just pick a topic that sounds intriguing and join. You may not like the first six places you try. That's okay. You may even have to try conferences on several BBSs before you find your home. That's okay, too. The only wrong move is not to try.

Rounding up messages

When you've found and joined a conference topic, you are poised to read the messages that have been posted there. After you join a few conferences, the process becomes second nature.

After you join a conference, you are also rewarded with a set of message-handling tools. You may get a list, like the one in Figure 10-9, or you may have to look closely at the bottom of the screen. Either way, the basic setup will be similar.

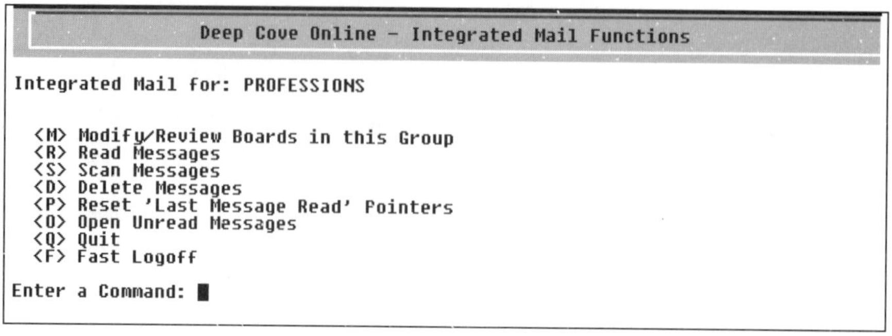

Figure 10-9:
The basic
tools for
handling
conference
messages
include
Reading,
Scanning,
and
Deleting.

```
┌─────────────────────────────────────────────────────────────────────┐
│            Deep Cove Online - Integrated Mail Functions               │
│                                                                       │
│ Integrated Mail for: PROFESSIONS                                      │
│                                                                       │
│    <M> Modify/Review Boards in this Group                             │
│    <R> Read Messages                                                  │
│    <S> Scan Messages                                                  │
│    <D> Delete Messages                                                │
│    <P> Reset 'Last Message Read' Pointers                             │
│    <O> Open Unread Messages                                           │
│    <Q> Quit                                                           │
│    <F> Fast Logoff                                                    │
│                                                                       │
│ Enter a Command: █                                                    │
│                                                                       │
└─────────────────────────────────────────────────────────────────────┘
```

✔ **Read messages:** You can either begin with the last message you read and work to the present moment, or read messages from the present moment back to the last one you read.

✔ **Scan messages:** Scanning enables you to find out who wrote messages to whom and on what topic, as shown in Figure 10-10.

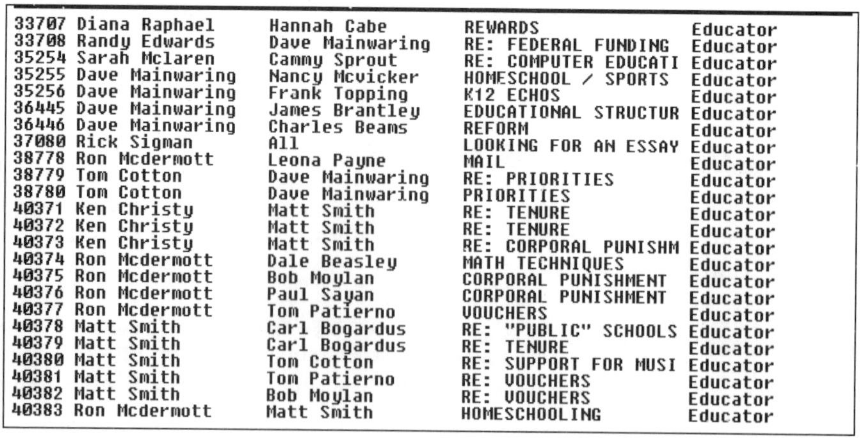

Figure 10-10:
Apparently
Educator
is a
profession,
according to
Deep Cove's
definition,
anyway.
This is a
scan of
messages
showing
addresser,
addressee,
and topic.

```
┌────────────────────────────────────────────────────────────────────────────┐
│ 33707 Diana Raphael    Hannah Cabe      REWARDS                  Educator    │
│ 33708 Randy Edwards    Dave Mainwaring  RE: FEDERAL FUNDING      Educator    │
│ 35254 Sarah Mclaren    Cammy Sprout     RE: COMPUTER EDUCATI     Educator    │
│ 35255 Dave Mainwaring  Nancy Mcvicker   HOMESCHOOL / SPORTS      Educator    │
│ 35256 Dave Mainwaring  Frank Topping    K12 ECHOS                Educator    │
│ 36445 Dave Mainwaring  James Brantley   EDUCATIONAL STRUCTUR     Educator    │
│ 36446 Dave Mainwaring  Charles Beams    REFORM                   Educator    │
│ 37080 Rick Sigman      All              LOOKING FOR AN ESSAY     Educator    │
│ 38778 Ron Mcdermott    Leona Payne      MAIL                     Educator    │
│ 38779 Tom Cotton       Dave Mainwaring  RE: PRIORITIES           Educator    │
│ 38780 Tom Cotton       Dave Mainwaring  PRIORITIES               Educator    │
│ 40371 Ken Christy      Matt Smith       RE: TENURE               Educator    │
│ 40372 Ken Christy      Matt Smith       RE: TENURE               Educator    │
│ 40373 Ken Christy      Matt Smith       RE: CORPORAL PUNISHM     Educator    │
│ 40374 Ron Mcdermott    Dale Beasley     MATH TECHNIQUES          Educator    │
│ 40375 Ron Mcdermott    Bob Moylan       CORPORAL PUNISHMENT      Educator    │
│ 40376 Ron Mcdermott    Paul Sayan       CORPORAL PUNISHMENT      Educator    │
│ 40377 Ron Mcdermott    Tom Patierno     VOUCHERS                 Educator    │
│ 40378 Matt Smith       Carl Bogardus    RE: "PUBLIC" SCHOOLS     Educator    │
│ 40379 Matt Smith       Carl Bogardus    RE: TENURE               Educator    │
│ 40380 Matt Smith       Tom Cotton       RE: SUPPORT FOR MUSI     Educator    │
│ 40381 Matt Smith       Tom Patierno     RE: VOUCHERS             Educator    │
│ 40382 Matt Smith       Bob Moylan       RE: VOUCHERS             Educator    │
│ 40383 Ron Mcdermott    Matt Smith       HOMESCHOOLING            Educator    │
└────────────────────────────────────────────────────────────────────────────┘
```

- ✔ **Delete messages:** You can kill messages that were either written to you or by you.

- ✔ **Reset 'Last message read' pointers:** This lets you tell the BBS that you want to start reading messages from October 1, instead of September 1, for example. This is not a command that you need to worry about initially, but it's an option you'll see on almost every system.

Just when you think you're home free, you're about to choose the Read command and expect the parade of messages to begin, the BBS — like Columbo — has just one more question. W*hich* messages in this topic do you want to read?

You have the chance to specify — and it all depends on where you are and what you want at the time — which of the options to put into action.

- ✔ **To you?** As in, do you want to see all the messages addressed to you — be they public or private?

- ✔ **From you?** Do you want to review the posted messages you wrote — again, public or private?

- ✔ **Unread Personal Mail?** That's all the secret, private E-Mail that you haven't read yet.

- ✔ **All new mail?** This includes all messages written and posted in this conference since the last time you logged on. If you follow a conference closely, this is the one you want to choose when you log on once a day to see what's happening.

- ✔ **Start at what number? (98-251)** That number to the right of the question tells you that the messages in the conference start with Msg. #98 and the last message is Msg. #251. If you press Enter, the BBS will assume — always a dangerous thing — that you want to start reading with Msg. #98. You probably don't want to read 154 messages in one sitting. Trust me. You don't. Make sure you start at a reasonable spot, like 220. If the messages are that compelling you can always come back and read 98-219. In case you're wondering where messages 1-97 are, they have probably been purged from the system — as most messages are, after a certain amount of time has elapsed. Don't expect to find messages more than a couple of weeks old on any system.

- ✔ **TS, Text Search, or Search?** Some systems allow you to look for text in the header or subject of a message — sometimes even within the body of the message itself. So if you want to see whether anyone here in the Educator forum has discussed fund raising, select the search option and the system asks you one last question — search for what? Type in your search word and press Enter.

You know, I bet you thought I was kidding about that spy stuff in the beginning. And yet, I brought you straight to the secret message base headquarters of EDUCATOR — Euro-Disney United Corps of Action to Overcome Rejection. I can trust you to keep this secret, can't I?

Reading messages

Once you go through the steps, you finally get to see the messages you've fought so long and hard to receive. As the messages present themselves, usually in the order in which they were received, you can handle them as you would any other E-Mail.

This is where all those carefully laid E-Mail building blocks finally come to bloom. I think I'm mixing metaphors, here. But you understand.

There are a couple of differences between public E-Mail and private. In public E-Mail

✔ You shouldn't delete messages after you read them. Actually, you really *can't* delete them. Unless you wrote a message, you cannot delete it.

✔ An option appears at the bottom of the screen letting you read forward or backward along a thread — or subject — of the E-Mail. It can make it easier to follow a complex topic to just stay on one subject.

✔ When you get to the end of the message thread, you may even be asked if you want to add your thoughts.

Posting your own messages

Not everyone who reads messages posts responses. Sometimes it's fun to just read a discussion. Other times, people are saying what you would have said anyway, so there's no need to jump in with a redundancy. It's even possible that you're just shy.

If you're the type who's always got something to say, that's great too. However, before posting your first message, you may want to do the following:

✔ Just read messages for a couple of days to get into the swing of things and see how things work.

✔ Before responding, make sure you've read *all* of the thread you're reacting to. It's kind of a pain to have someone espouse an opinion or ask a question that's already been handled ten messages back. I'm sure it's happened to you in real life. Someone asks a question — why is the sky blue — and after 15 minutes of explaining, another person walks into the room, hears the words "blue sky," and then says, "Yeah, why is the sky blue?"

However, when you've got something new to say, we can hardly wait to see what you post. Nothing is more exciting than new members posting their first messages. When it comes time to post your own message, you do it one of two ways:

✔ Replying to what someone else has said

  After reading a message from another user, press R for Reply, and you get an E-Mail screen in which to compose your response. This is the same E-Mail system covered in Chapter 9.

  Your reply, even though addressed to someone by name, is public. Everyone can read it. The only way to change that is by selecting Private or Restricted when you are prompted by the Security option.

✔ Originating a new topic of your own

  Entering a message — which is usually done by pressing E — lets you start a message subject of your own choice, like asking everyone about fundraising for public schools. When writing a message in a public forum, if you don't specify an addressee by name, the system assumes you want to send the message to All. This means, of course, that the message will be visible to everyone who enters the forum.

  The BBS also prompts you to set the subject heading. Keep it specific enough so that people who scan the message base, as we did in Figure 10-10, will be able to get the gist of your message by reading the subject.

As a small example, I've written a message in a Windows conference. As you can see in Figure 10-11, the E-Mail in the message base is the same old E-Mail you've already grown to love.

Figure 10-11:
Asking for
help by
leaving a
public
message in
the
Windows
conference
on
AlphaOne
Online.

†Adults-only BBS.

```
 To: All                    Subj: I'm new here                Mode: Insert
Howdy --

I've just started using this system and I have a question.  Actually, this is
the first BBS I've ever called, so be gentle.  I noticed in your messages that
you're using a Windows program to retrieve mail off line -- but I didn't catch
the exact name of the program, or the file name to download.  Help!

Thanks!
█




              



 <Esc>=Exit  Ctrl-V=Overwrite  Ctrl-Z=Help                        Line:10
```

Keeping your head when all about are losing theirs

If you get two people together, eventually you'll have disagreement.

If you get hundreds of strangers together, all safe from the possibility that an argument could devolve into a fist fight and cloaked in the anonymity of an alias name, you'll likely have some serious disagreement at times.

Fortunately, most people can agree to disagree and appreciate the opportunity to view things from another perspective.

Flame wars

At some point on every system, though, two people who have nothing in common but a hair trigger, a bizarre sense of righteous self-indignation, and the inability to step away from a slight — imagined or not — begin an exchange of vitriolic messages. In intellect and intensity, this is a lot like those stories you see on talk shows about feuding neighbors who come to blows over whose dog did its business on the other's lawn.

When people get into these sorts of exchanges, it's called a *flame war*. Online, the word *flame* is used as a verb. In English class, we'd learn to conjugate it. I flame. He flames. Yesterday she got flamed. We are all sick of these guys flaming each other.

At a certain point, the Sysop has to douse the flames. The rest of us don't like our precious on-line time and long-distance fees wasted on this sort of nonsense.

Rules of debate

Disagreement is not a bad thing, as long as it's kept civilized. As English author Samuel Butler put it, "It is not he who gains the exact point in dispute who scores most in controversy — but he who has shown the better temper." I suspect Butler's first draft of that eloquent quote was, "Nobody likes to watch a screed fest!"

SYSOP SEZ

The perfect spot

I'm surprised by the number of posts on Prodigy Travel BB that deal with romance: "I am searching for ideas on the best ways to propose marriage to my girlfriend." Or, "I'm trying to help my brother find the perfect romantic setting to ask his girlfriend to marry him." Messages like these usually get useful responses.

Jack Adler, Sysop, Prodigy Travel

Keep these points in mind as you begin your debating career:

- ✔ There is a subtle and very important difference between, "That *idea* is dumb," and "*You* are dumb." Besides, if you really do believe, sincerely in your heart, that this person is impossibly worthless, why are you wasting your time trying to educate him or her? Let it go.

- ✔ Don't buy into the Ace Ventura Pet Detective philosophy of life, which categorizes people into two camps — winners and losers. Sometimes you win by *learning* — not by making another person a loser.

- ✔ Carefully read the other person's message. Flame war messages invariably degenerate into fights over what was really said and what was really meant in previous messages.

- ✔ You can't hear if you're talking.

- ✔ It takes two to tango.

Abandoning a Conference

At some point, when you're done reading and writing messages, you want to leave a conference. Leaving a conference is known as *abandoning* a conference.

Although it sounds kind of cruel to join and then abandon a conference, just keep in mind that *joining* wasn't too much of a commitment, so *abandoning* isn't that much of a dumping.

To abandon a conference, you can usually find an option on the conference, message, or Main Menu that says just that. If nothing seems to say abandon, then just return to the Main Menu.

If you want to join another conference at this point, then go for it. You can join and abandon as many conferences as you have time for.

Selecting Conferences

Selecting a conference is not just a semantic variation of the phrase *joining a conference*. Selecting a conference not only has its own meaning, but it has its very own command — on the systems that support conference selecting, that is.

Whenever you log onto a BBS, it scans the message base looking for mail addressed to you. You know something about the messages in the message base that the BBS computer doesn't know. You may know, for example, that there will never be any messages for you in the Oboe conference, in the Zoos conference, or even in the Punk Rock conference. You may know that if there are any messages for you, they'll be in the Private Mail conference, the Educator conference, and the Blackjack conference. You know that because those are the only conferences you visit.

Gosh, you may be thinking to yourself, how can I tell the BBS that it needn't scan all those messages in the entire message base? How can I tell the computer only to search through those three conferences?

Funny you should ask.

That's where selecting a conference comes in. You can *select* the Private Mail, Educator, and Blackjack conferences. Then, when it's time to scan, the system is guided by your selections.

If Selecting a Conference is an option offered on the BBS you favor, you can probably find it as a command on the Main Menu. After you issue the Select command, the BBS prompts you to enter the conferences that you wish to select. And that's about it.

You won't want to select a conference until you've had some experience with the system.

If conferencing lacks a sense of instant gratification, you may want to try Chat. That's what the next chapter is about.

Reach out and touch...

"Having a BBS is a lot of fun, but we also try to give back something to the community.

Just before Christmas, one of our staff told us about a young girl with a rare disease that attacks bone, nerve and muscle, and who was rapidly outgrowing the old computer she had. We discussed this a bit, then put out a public notice on our Board, and to make a long story short, within 27 hours of posting that notice, we had resources and parts committed to be able to present the girl with a custom-built 486-50 multimedia computer setup, with about a bushel of educational software!

We met her and her parents the week before Christmas and presented her with all this.

There wasn't a dry eye in the house. It was very gratifying!

Now we've just managed to scrounge a laptop for her to use for the times when she's in the hospital and can't use her new 'puter."

Stan Shelhamer, Sysop, Hello Central

Chapter 11

Striking up a Chat Session

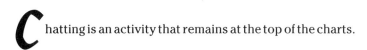

In This Chapter
- ▶ Classifying Chat
- ▶ Entering the Chat menu
- ▶ Paging
- ▶ Responding
- ▶ Chatting commands

C hatting is an activity that remains at the top of the charts.

What happens — computer-wise — when two people go into Chat is that both their computer screens synch up, and whatever is typed on either keyboard appears simultaneously on both screens.

If both people typed at the same time, there would be total chaos. So they have to take turns. If this was a lesson you missed in kindergarten, now's as good a time as any to make up the course.

In Chat, one person types while the other watches. When person number one has completed a thought, he or she presses Enter twice. Sending a blank line is the signal that person number two may jump in and respond, also following up with two Enters when done.

And so on.

This process is what is known as real-time Chat, because it is happening as you see it. Probably someday they'll rename it CNN Chat.

Chatting got its start, as most BBSing did, from a similar activity on the monster-system called the Internet (for more about the Internet, see Chapter 14). With the Internet, a scientist at the Jet Propulsion Laboratory and another at MIT can talk to each other, via keyboard, with neither one incurring long-distance charges. It's a way to meet and confer on the cheap.

Now Chatting is mostly a social activity.

When people log onto their favorite BBS, they go over to Chat to see who, if anyone, is hanging out there. There's a certain element of luck, spontaneity, and anonymity that defines how Chatting works.

Chat is simply one of those activities that some folks absolutely cannot get enough of, while others wonder why these people don't just pick up the phone or meet for a cup of coffee.

There is no doubt, though, that this unique way of communicating is more popular than ever. You can find it on every Main Menu, like the one in Figure 11-1. This chapter gives you the absolute basics for entering into and surviving a Chat session. Getting an invitation to Chat can be disconcerting if you don't know what to expect.

Figure 11-1:
The
Chrysalis
Main Menu
offers a Chat
Area.
Selecting
Chat from a
menu is the
most
common
first step to
making an
online
connection.

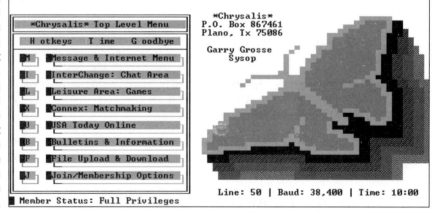

```
        *Chrysalis* Top Level Menu          *Chrysalis*
                                            P.O. Box 867461
         H otkeys   T ime   G oodbye        Plano, Tx 75086

    M   Message & Internet Menu             Garry Grosse
                                               Sysop
    I   InterChange: Chat Area

    L   Leisure Area: Games

    X   Connex: Matchmaking

    U   USA Today Online

    B   Bulletins & Information

    F   File Upload & Download

    J   Join/Membership Options

    Member Status: Full Privileges      Line: 50 | Baud: 38,400 | Time: 10:00
```

Classifying Chat

Chat isn't always just two people. More likely than not, you have a group of people in Chat simultaneously — everyone pitching in comments and responses. It can get messy as several conversations continue on top of one another.

With a small amount of practice, you can sort things out. It's certainly easier to follow several online conversations than to sort out screaming panelists on your average afternoon talk show. Besides, most people are very slow typists, and it's almost necessary to have more than one thing going on, or things would get very dull very quickly. In terms of excitement, watching someone type is a seven on the Watching Paint Dry scale of interest.

The typical sorts of cyberyakking include:

- ✔ **Public Chat:** This is a lot like those party lines you see on TV, where a number of people are simultaneously online. People come in and drop out at will. Whatever they talk about can be seen by anyone who joins the Chat. The conversations vary widely and are G-rated — unless it's an adult board.

- ✔ **Conference:** This is a public Chat with either a topic or rules. Rules of conduct and a strict moderator are only necessary if there's a guest speaker, and some sort of order must be maintained. A Chat conference is not the same as a message conference — as discussed in Chapter 10.

- ✔ **Private Chat:** Others cannot join unless those already Chatting approve. The messages inside the private Chat are seen only by those in the private Chat. Private Chat is often used as a place for virtual sex (kind of like those 976 lines, except via typing). This is steamy stuff. Could *this* be why some people love Chat so much?

The meeting places for these encounters, be they G- or X-rated, go by a couple of names that mean the same thing.

- ✔ **Rooms:** This name comes from the metaphor of a meeting room. Or, I suppose, a hotel room.

- ✔ **Channels:** The original metaphor for Chat was the Citizen's Band radio, which allows traveling truckers — or anyone with a CB radio — to join others and chat on various channels.

- ✔ **Lobby:** This is an area where people can congregate and make connections. Sometimes a lobby is the gateway to the other online rooms. It's still the same thing as a room or a channel.

These rooms come in two basic flavors:

- ✔ **Structured:** These rooms have a self-selecting theme, like the ones in Figure 11-2 from the Chrysalis BBS. The themes aren't strictly guarded by the thought police or anything. They're really more like ideas or launching points for discussions.

```
╔══════════════════════════════════════════╗
║     *Chrysalis* Communications Menu        ║
║   [H]otkeys  [E]xit  [J]ump  [G]oodbye     ║
║                                            ║
║ [W] = Who Else Is Online Now               ║
║ [U] = Users Who Have Called Recently       ║
║ [Q] = Quick Connex Profile Searches        ║
║          Chat Conferences Available        ║
║ [I] = Instructions for conferencing        ║
║                                            ║
║ [A] = InterChange  (General chat area)     ║
║ [B] = Teen Forum   (Teen members area)     ║
║ [C] = Adult Forum  (Adult members area)    ║
║ [D] = CrossFire    (Free form debates)     ║
║ [K] = Young Adult  (16-24 year olds)       ║
║ [N] = Mayhem       (Anonymous area)        ║
║ [O] = Paging Area  (Paging only)           ║
║ [P] = Platinum     (Members only)          ║
║ [R] = InterGame    (Interactive games)     ║
║ [S] = Whispers     (Women only)            ║
║ [U] = Whiskers     (Men only)              ║
║ [Y] = Beliefs      (Religious chat)        ║
║                                            ║
║  Line: 50 | 38,400 Baud | Time: 10:01      ║
╚══════════════════════════════════════════╝
```

Figure 11-2:
Chat with a theme, as defined by the BBS.

  ✓ **Nonstructured:** These rooms are created when two or more people want to Chat. There is no theme, no mission, no purpose save that assigned to it by those participating. Once they're done talking, the room goes away. Very Zen.

A BBS doesn't have to choose one way or the other. It can have both a set of always-ready, predefined rooms as well as the option to create private areas, free from prying eyes.

Entering the Chat Menu

In Chatting, there's a chicken-or-the-egg issue. In order to have a meaningful Chat, there has to be someone else online with whom you can chat. The first step to Chatting is checking out who else is online to see if there are any candidates to invite to a *tête-à-tête*.

Some BBSs make you choose Chat first, before you know who else is online, and then, from the Chat Menu, let you use a command, usually called Who's Online. Others put the Who's Online command in the Main Menu and let you check out Who's Online before deciding to Chat.

Some BBSs, like the one in Figure 11-3, give you both options and let *you* decide how to approach the issue.

Figure 11-3:
The Swamp
BBS's Main
Menu lets
you either
check out
the users
online or go
straight into
the Chat
menu.

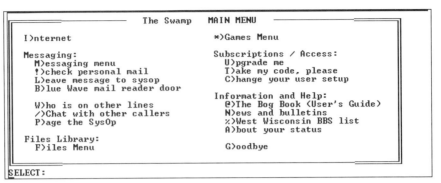

```
                          The Swamp    MAIN MENU

   I)nternet                           *)Games Menu

   Messaging:                          Subscriptions / Access:
     M)essaging menu                     U)pgrade me
     !)check personal mail               T)ake my code, please
     L)eave message to sysop             C)hange your user setup
     B)lue Wave mail reader door
                                       Information and Help:
     W)ho is on other lines              @)The Bog Book (User's Guide)
     /)Chat with other callers           N)ews and bulletins
     P)age the SysOp                      %)West Wisconsin BBS list
                                         A)bout your status
   Files Library:
     F)iles Menu                          G)oodbye

 SELECT :
```

The problem with chicken-or-egg discussions is that you go round and round and never come up with an answer. For the sake of moving forward, let's choose to go into the *Chat Menu* — which also may appear as *Talk To Other Nodes* — and check it out.

> ✔ If you're using a structured system, the next step is to go to the room that interests you. In Figure 11-2, you may want to go to the beliefs forum by pressing Y and then Enter. If you're looking for a nonstructured system, you might try the Traders' Connection, Figure 11-4, which lets you list available rooms to enter.

Figure 11-4:
Someone's
knockin' at
my door.
Hey,
where's that
"do not
disturb"
sign?

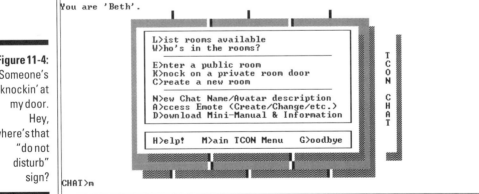

```
 You are 'Beth'.

        L)ist rooms available
        W)ho's in the rooms?
                                                 T
        E)nter a public room                     C
        K)nock on a private room door            O
        C)reate a new room                       N

        N)ew Chat Name/Avatar description         C
        A)ccess Emote (Create/Change/etc.)        H
        D)ownload Mini-Manual & Information        A
                                                   T
        H)elp!   M)ain TCON Menu   G)oodbye

 CHAT>m
```

✓ Or you can now find the Who's Online command and issue it — usually by typing W and pressing Enter — to get a list of those people currently on the system, which would look something like Figure 11-5.

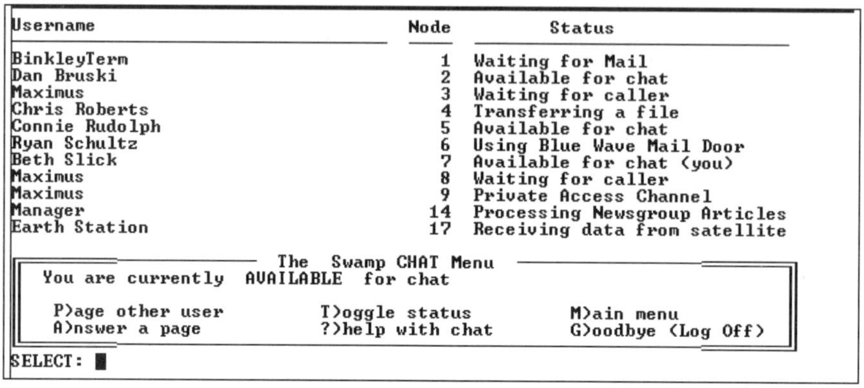

Figure 11-5:
The Swamp
BBS, with its
simple, clear
Chat Menu,
automatically
tells you
who's online
when you
enter.

```
Username                          Node        Status
BinkleyTerm                          1    Waiting for Mail
Dan Bruski                           2    Available for chat
Maximus                              3    Waiting for caller
Chris Roberts                        4    Transferring a file
Connie Rudolph                       5    Available for chat
Ryan Schultz                         6    Using Blue Wave Mail Door
Beth Slick                           7    Available for chat (you)
Maximus                              8    Waiting for caller
Maximus                              9    Private Access Channel
Manager                             14    Processing Newsgroup Articles
Earth Station                       17    Receiving data from satellite
                          ───── The  Swamp CHAT Menu ─────
    You are currently  AVAILABLE  for chat

    P)age other user        T)oggle status        M)ain menu
    A)nswer a page          ?)help with chat      G)oodbye (Log Off)

SELECT: █
```

Although every system looks different, you shouldn't be too surprised, by now, to learn that even things like the Who's Online list has elements you can count on to be there from BBS to BBS:

✓ **User's name or alias:** This is the name of the person online, or the alias. Even systems that don't allow aliases or secret names when you log on will allow *handles* or secret names in Chat. It's kind of a tradition.

✓ **Node or line number:** Each person who calls in connects with the BBS on a different line or *node*. You need to know the line or node number someone is on, generally, to get the computer to talk to that person for you. Sometimes the name is enough. Sometimes you need to know their account. Whatever it is you need to know is displayed on the Who's Online screen, like the one in Figure 11-6.

✓ **Status:** What are they doing right now? This is important because if the people you want to Chat with are in the middle of downloading, they probably can't Chat with you right now. They can't even see that you want to Chat.

✓ **Chat Status:** Some people do not want to Chat. This may either be indicated in their general Status, as in Figure 11-5, or there may be an actual Chat Status column which tells you whether the person is at all amenable to the notion of Chatting. You can always put yourself in Greta Garbo mode and indicate you *vant to be ahlone* by turning your Chat status to Off, Un-available, or Ignore. In Figure 11-5, in the box at the bottom, you can see I'm available for Chat, but pressing T would Toggle, or change, that status.

Figure 11-6:
Another
BBS,
another
Who's
Online
screen.
Though not
exactly the
same as
Figure 11-5,
you can see
the two are
basically the
same.

```
Who's on the system...
User             Ln Location        Doing?         Announcement
--------------------------------------------------------------------
BOB WILLIAMS     01 %X0D%I'll Be Righ Game/Sur
JOHN CFULLER     02 %X40%SHELBYVILLE% DL Files
JOHN REED        04 %X1B%The Digital  DL Files
BETH SLICK       07 VENICE, CA        WhoIsOn
PETE SCHNEIDER   12 %X47%OS/2 Warp%X0 Intrchg
MIKE CHAMBERS    16 %X0A%Nashville On  At Menu        Shark Attack!!!!
BRAD FRY         39 BRENTWOOD,TN       Game/Sur
BOBBY RAFFERTY   40 OLNEY, MD          ReadMsgs
MATHEW BINKLEY   45 Ashland City, TN   Intrchg
DAVID REEVES     47 NASHVILLE,TN.      Game/Sur
GEN-X COMMUNICAT 48 NASHVILLE, TN      WriteMsg
JASON RICE       53 %X0C%Dickson, TN%  Intrchg

Press any key to continue...█
```

If you're a woman, and you leave your Chat status on, chances are quite high you'll receive many invitations to Chat — women make up less than 20 percent of the online population. If you find this attention annoying, turn your Chat status to Off until you're ready to Chat. If the word Available appears next to your name, then it's not too surprising that others will assume you are.

If you see someone online that you want to Chat with, but their status is turned off, write them a quick E-Mail introducing yourself and telling them why you want to Chat. Maybe you can start a correspondence which will eventually evolve into a Chat session.

Hawkeye Habegger

"I keep a pretty close eye on what is happening on the BBS. When I first began, I watched it like a hawk. A user logged on one day with his real name, grabbed a file, and ran out of time. New users are limited on time and back then there was an allowable daily limit for new callers. I then watched, and two seconds later he was back again, this time under another name. A Sysop develops a sixth sense for false log ons. I broke into Chat and told the jerk that there was only one name allowed per user. We Chatted and I am not sure what transpired, but today we are best friends."

Don Habegger, Sysop, YA! WEBECAD! BBS

Paging

Okay, so you've selected the Chat partner of your dreams, and he or she is available and doesn't seem to be overly busy at the moment. The next step is to *page* the person with whom you'd like to Chat.

In Figure 11-7, I've initiated a page by selecting P for Page, and the system is asking which node I want to talk to.

```
Username                        Node        Status

BinkleyTerm                       1    Waiting for Mail
Dan Bruski                        2    Available for chat
Maximus                           3    Waiting for caller
Maximus                           4    Waiting for caller
Connie Rudolph                    5    Available for chat
Ryan Schultz                      6    Using Blue Wave Mail Door
Beth Slick                        7    Available for chat (you)
Maximus                           8    Waiting for caller
Maximus                           9    Private Access Channel
Manager                          14    Processing Newsgroup Articles
Earth Station                    17    Receiving data from satellite
                         The  Swamp CHAT Menu
  You are currently  AVAILABLE  for chat

    P)age other user       T)oggle status        M)ain menu
    A)nswer a page         ?)help with chat      G)oodbye (Log Off)

SELECT: p

Please enter the node number to page (?=list): █
```

Figure 11-7: If you want to page Beth Slick for a Chat, type the number 7 and press Enter.

Responding

After you issue the page command

✔ The person you're paging hears a beep and sees a message on the screen that you want to Chat with him or her.

✔ Also included in that page are instructions on how to join you in Chat. The command could be anything from pressing R and Enter to typing **GO CHAT 2** — to go to Chat room number two. Whatever the command, the page recipient is told what to do to take affirmative action.

Just because you page someone, that doesn't mean that the person will join you in Chat. People can just completely ignore you or even turn off their available sign. Don't let such a rejection wound your inner child. You have no idea whether that person was busy then and had no time to Chat or what.

However, pretend — happy, happy — that the person has been hoping you'd page and now eagerly follows the instructions and joins you in Chat.

Chatting Rooms

You have made it! You're in Chat! Figure 11-8 shows what I saw on America's Suggestion Box when I paged another caller and he joined me in Chat.

What we have is a basic Chat session, of the decidedly tame variety, filled with typos, interruptions and so forth.

```
UltraChat: ROBB M has been informed of your request.
You are now waiting for the other user.  A period will appear every 5 seconds
while you wait.  Press the Enter key at any time to return to chat...
..UltraChat: You are now in private chat.  Use /X to exit.
P:Hi!
P:Howdhy... what'sup
P:nothing
P:how's ife in California
P:It's warm... sunny... I live three blocks from beach so I get all the beach
P:traffic on days like today... it can get noisy...
P:the weather was miserable today
P:where are you calling from
P:long island
P:New York?
P:yes
P:'cause there are tons of Long Islands and Long Beaches that aren't... so I
P:just wanted to know.
P:oh
P:so what do yoiu  am d6
P:I am 60 miles out on NY city
P:I've never been... just finished writing a novel that takes place, for a few
P:chapters in New York... kind of interesting to write about someplace you've
P:never been.
P:yeah
```

1. **When the other person joins you in Chat, a message on the screen lets you know that the person is there.**

   Otherwise, the screen is blank.

2. **Say hello, press Enter twice and wait.**

3. **The other person says hello, presses Enter twice, and waits.**

   This is sort of like that classic opening move in chess. It's a required step that everyone goes through.

4. **Then continue your conversation, ending each thought with two Enters and allowing the other person to speak.**

   Repeat until tender enough to pierce with a fork.

Introducing Chatting Room commands

Chatting is easy. You just type.

There are some additional Chatting Room commands that may come in handy. And, if this is your first time in a cybertalk, you may not realize you need to know how to do these things until you need them.

Some systems have very nice Chat menus that guide you through the process. Typically, though, being told that /X gets you out of Chat — as in the top of Figure 11-8 — is the most help you get from the BBS.

If you don't know these commands on your BBS, be sure to ask your Chat partner for some pointers.

Although every system has something like these commands, the usual caveat applies. Commands vary widely from system to system. You have to look them up when you start playing with Chat. Or, if you wander around with a blank look on your face, you may be able to get someone to lend a hand.

Back in Figure 11-4, there was an option to download the Chat manual. If you see something like that, take advantage of it at once!

If you want to wing it, though, here's a hint. On many systems, the forward slash (/) is often used to activate the Enter Chat Menu command. And, once you're Chatting away, the forward slash is often used at the beginning of the line to indicate *here comes a command!*

Leaving

You would expect this section to appear after all the others, telling you, when finished, what command to issue to get out of Chat. However, if you don't figure this one out before going in or, at least, before your chatting partner leaves, you may find yourself alone in a room with no way out but hanging up!

The moment you get into Chat with someone, ask what the command is to exit. Once you know that — and have written it down — you can at least bail if your partner turns into less than what you had hoped.

If the worst happens — you're alone and you can't get out — here are some things to try. Type **/Q** at the very beginning of a line and press Enter. Or try typing exit alone on a line and pressing Enter. How about typing **/X** and pressing Enter? If none of these does the trick, try pressing Esc. Still nothing? How about pressing Ctrl+X or Ctrl+C? One of those ought to do it. Eventually, you have permission to panic and hang up on the BBS.

When you come back online, try to be less macho and more bookwormy before going back into Chat. Either read a bulletin on Chat, or ask a friend. Either way, know your stuff before you go back into a Chat session.

Getting help

To get a list of available commands, try typing at the beginning of a line /**H**, for Help, and pressing Enter. Also, just pressing **?** and Enter at the beginning of a line might do it.

Looking around

While you're gabbing away, don't forget that, unless you entered private Chat, whatever you're saying is being broadcast to anyone else in the room. You may not know they're out there by their breathing or shuffling of feet, but they are there. You can find out who's there much the same way you found out who was online when you decided to enter Chat. Try typing /**W** and pressing Enter. Remember to issue this command at the beginning of the line or it won't work.

Squelching others

You may not want to see messages from someone, so you have the option of selecting out the messages of any individual. Wouldn't it be nice if you could do that in real life? You have to know which node the blithering idiot is in, so issue the looking-around command first to get that info. Then, if the person's node number is 7, for example, type at the beginning of the line /**I,7,off** and press Enter. If the jerk is in node 45, then you would type /**I,45,off** and press Enter. The I stands for Ignore. If you forgive 45, you can issue the same command substituting *on* for *off* — /**I,45,on** and Enter.

Private message

If you want, you can send someone a note that no one else can see. You have to know that person's node first, of course — just as in the previous example. Then type /**S,N,message goes here** and press Enter. The S stands for Send. To send a message to our favorite 45, type /**S,45,All's forgiven.**

On some BBSs, you have to go to the Chat menu to use the Chat commands. In others, there are global commands you can use anywhere in the system to page, check status, and so on. Look for these shortcuts in bulletins, the BBS manual, or just ask someone who's using Chat.

Beyond Chatting

On many BBSs, the art of Chatting has been supplemented by an array of Chat features. Here are just a couple:

- **Online bios:** Write about yourself so that others can get a sense of who you are — and you can see who they are — before going into a Chat. The GLIB BBS keeps track of who has read your bio and lets you know, so you can check out their bios as well.

- **Prepared messages:** Your page call can be enhanced with an announcement that appears after the normal system Page.

As more and more technology is added, there will be more ways to enhance Chat sessions. Already, a commercial service called Prodigy is adding sound and pictures. If history is an example, BBSs won't be far behind in adding features like that to their systems.

Normally, this would be the point where I'd tell you how to exit Chat, but I did that already at the beginning of this section.

Is there a virtual doctor in the house?

"To enhance the Prodigy Medical Support BB on Prodigy, I recently added a live weekly guest program. On Monday nights at 8:30pm (ET), the "door's open" to the Medical Support Auditorium in the Chat area of Prodigy. Each week we feature a new guest and topic, ranging from every topic on the Medical Support BB to sessions on pet care and advice on choosing a rest home or nursing facility. All sessions are recorded and available later in the Chat Transcript area of Prodigy."

Nancy Eggleston, Sysop, Prodigy Medical Support BB

Chapter 12

Playing Games, Shopping, and Doors

- -

In This Chapter

▶ Playing games

▶ Going shopping

▶ Walking through the door

- -

*E*ver since fashion-conscious scientists dumped vacuum tubes for silicon chips, people have been working day and night to figure out more ways to have fun with computers. I know what you're thinking — what could possibly be more fun than downloading files or wrestling with E-Mail? It's hard to imagine, but just in case your computer and BBSing haven't eaten up enough of your time and money, there are a couple more opportunities to wreak havoc with your personal schedule and banking account!

Playing Games

Do you like to slip 75 cents into the old video machine in the Laundromat while waiting for your clothes to survive the spin cycle? Video games are fun, not only because you get to see your score improve, but also because you can see your standing among the other players rise.

That sense of competition is also part of the fun behind online games. It's not just you sitting at home dueling with the evil wizard, it's all the others who are also playing and posting their scores that makes each game unique and challenging.

But you don't have to be a warrior of evil wizards to play BBS games. You can find games ranging from Canadian Trivia to a BBS version of Monopoly, and every conceivable type of word game in between — even some silly, fun-for-everyone offerings, as in Figure 12-1.

Figure 12-1:
Win extra online time with a few correct answers on the YA! WEBECAD! BBS.

```
You will now be given a chance at our question of the day! If you are one
of the first Ten people to guess it right, you can win extra time in Time
Door! Check out Bulletin 27 for the latest winners and call back tomorrow
to see if you were one of the weiners!

Would you like to try our trivia Question of the Day?

[Y] - Yes, I want to try the question.
[N] - No, I don't want to try the question.
```

Single-user games

The first classification of games is single-user games. That's simply where you play by yourself, against the BBS computer. Trivia games, Hangman, card games, and those types of divertissements are the most common. Sometimes the games have lots of graphics, and sometimes they are very plain. Remember, it's what's inside the counts. Figure 12-2 shows a typical games menu.

Figure 12-2:
What's your pleasure. No-peeky Black Jack? The Nashville Exchange has many options for your playing pleasure. Betcha can't play just one!

```
        [*]Hang-up      [+]Elapsed Time      [-]Prev Menu

            *-*-*-*-*-*-* Games *-*-*-*-*-*-*
            <Games are restricted to Subscribers>

[U] Crypto Cruncher           ¦          [P] EasyQuiz
[R]ock & Roll Trivia          ¦   >>>> [!] Warlords
[X] Black Jack                ¦   >>>> [$] Warlords Scores
[K]ing of the Board           ¦          [T]owers of Hanoi
[G] Card Guppies              ¦          [H]orny Toad

[1] Guppies Current Month     ¦          [M]icro Trivia
[2] Guppies Previous Month    ¦          [%] Word Power
[3] Guppies High Scores       ¦          [C] Crossed Words

[O]il Baron                   ¦
[W]ord Scramble               ¦          [L] Graffiti Wall
[B]iorythm Calculator         ¦          [I] Chains Word Game

Command: █
```

Multiline games

The second classification of games is the Multi-User, or multiline, games. Not only do you play against the computer, but you're also battling other people who have happened to call in at the same time — sort of like a cyberpick-up game. Don't expect virtual-reality graphics here, folks. But you can expect to have some fun — if crushing evil empires and destroying armadas is your idea of a good time. Some people have their own groups of players who arrange to meet online to play together. Figure 12-3, the Games/SIG menu for Trader's Connection, reveals the categories of games available on this system.

Figure 12-3:
Everything from Adventure to the ever-popular Miscellaneous games beckons you to relax and have some fun.

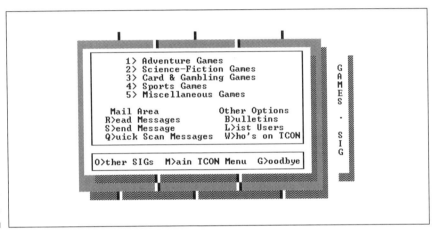

```
              1> Adventure Games
              2> Science-Fiction Games        G
              3> Card & Gambling Games        A
              4> Sports Games                 M
              5> Miscellaneous Games          E
                                              S
         Mail Area          Other Options     .
         R>ead Messages        B>ulletins
         S>end Message         L>ist Users    S
         Q>uick Scan Messages  W>ho's on TCON I
                                              G

         O>ther SIGs  M>ain TCON Menu  G>oodbye
```

Most of these games are complicated, and the rules have to be studied if you even hope to survive the first five minutes or move beyond the first dark cave. Be sure to download the manual.

MUD games

MUDs, MUs, and MUXs are all types of games found on the Internet. These bovine-like names all have to do with Multi-User and refer to areas, or domains, that are programmed by the players themselves. Anyone who wants can add a room, a building, or a zone for others to discover and explore. This is really interesting, but not exactly for beginners. Stick with the type preprogrammed single- and Multi-User BBS games for a little while before moving on to the advanced stuff. Or, and I can't resist saying this, you'll end up with MUD on your face. (Sorry. It was an impulse I could not control.)

No ice hockey in Texas

One member grew up in Maine and attended the University of Maine. He loves their hockey team and, since graduating, moved to Texas where he cannot obtain updates on how the Maine hockey team is doing. Well, he does now that he has

Prodigy. Members living in Maine are constantly posting notes about the Maine hockey team.

Lisa Anson, Board Leader, Prodigy Sports BB

Going Shopping

Shopping online? The big commercial services — CompuServe, America Online, Prodigy — have been selling goods via computers for years. I've even bought groceries and had them delivered via America Online. CompuServe was the first to come out with an electronic mall, selling computer- and noncomputer-related items. Vendors set up virtual shops there and let their customers place orders for such diverse things as flowers, airline tickets, books, videos, and candy.

Smaller BBSs are jumping on the bandwagon now — though the shopping mall notion is still in its infancy.

Selling advertising and "mall space" to local vendors is a way of off-setting the cost of running a system. Figures 12-4 and 12-5 hint at the wide variety of stuff available. Have plastic, will travel.

Figure 12-4:
Deep Cove's
Electronic
Mall has a
basic menu
from which
you can
select what
shop to visit.

```
Deep Cove BBS
DEEP COVE'S ELECTRONIC SUPER-MALL

<G>-Goodbye - Logoff System          <=>-Return to Deep Cove Main Menu
<O>-Operators Entrance               <V>-Vendors Entrance
<H>-How to become a Vendor?          <P>-Policies of Deep Cove's Mall
            <A>-Enter Main Mall Entrance (All Stores)

<1>-ZyXEL Intelligent Modem Store <2>-Deep Cove's Discount CD-ROMs
<3>-Complete Computer Solutions    <4>-The Graphics Shop
<5>-J&L Home Shopping:Coming Soon  <6>-"Show Me" Guide to the Internet
<7>-Angelo's FabriClean            <8>-One Stop CyberShop
<9>-The Allergy Specialists        <B>-
<C>-                               <D>-
<E>-                               <F>-
<I>-                               <J>-
<K>-                               <L>-
<M>-                               <N>-

Command:
```

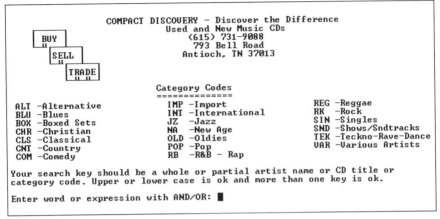

Figure 12-5:
The
Nashville
Exchange
proves that
CD doesn't
necessarily
mean
Change
Directory in
its online
Compact
Disk shop.

The shopping mall works best with products that don't require a value judgment prior to purchase. You don't want to buy a painting, a new perfume, or clothes that you can't see, for example, online. Buying books, magazine subscriptions, and national-brand items is your safest bet. But still be sure to check out the return guarantee.

Online shopping is another place that demands your vigilance. Keep your eyes open for people looking for a passive way to get your credit-card number. If you log onto Fly By Night BBS, don't give out your credit-card number on the first call. Check the BBS out with other users on other nearby systems first. They will know if Fly By Night is honest or not. If you log onto one of the Top 100, you know the system is on the up-and-up. With other systems, just beware.

Walking through the Door

Usually, you find games and shopping listed as simply another option on the Main Menu. But not always.

Sometimes you have to use the *door* option to access games and shopping.

Steven Spielberg was once asked what one, single image from all his movies was his favorite — or most illustrated his own philosophy. His reply was the moment in Close Encounters where the little boy, Barry, opens the door, and all that light comes flooding in through the other side. Spielberg liked it because it illustrated a willingness to "take a step toward what we don't understand."

I don't promise you a ride on a spaceship, but the BBS door command — sometimes known as the open or run command — lets you temporarily jump out of the BBS software and use another program on the BBS computer. For example: Want to read the daily newspaper? Newspapers are not part of a BBS system. To get to the newspaper program, you must leave the BBS.

When you open a door, be prepared for the possibility that the BBS screen will go away and you'll see a message about loading some sort of software. In a way, you are taking that step into another dimension. That's what a door is all about. Don't worry, you can come back whenever you like.

How you open a door depends on which BBS you're using. Here are a couple of the more popular approaches:

✔ Simply type the word **door** — or **open** or **run** — and press Enter. Faster than you can say "open sesame," you are asked which door you want to open and are shown a list. Type in the name or number of what you want and press Enter.

✔ You may need to look at the Main Menu and, following instructions, type something like **door mall** and press Enter. The door command opens the door, and the mall command selects which software to use.

In addition to games and shopping, you find some other types of programs once you step through that door. Don't be afraid to try a door.

Searching databases

A common use for doorways is to access databases. An encyclopedia may be available online through a door. Sometimes CD-ROM access is via a door. There has been a veritable explosion of information available on CD-ROM, ranging from demographics, magazine and newspaper text, medical and legal information, and on and on. Even the CIA Factbook is available through a searchable CD-ROM.

Reading magazines

Magazines and newspapers, including *USA Today* — in text-searchable format — may also be available through a door. With text-searchable format, you can search every single word in the whole newspaper — just like performing a search in a word processor. So, if you work on the Carrot Advisory Board, you can find out how many times carrot is used every day and in what context. This makes research a snap.

Making a love connection

A very popular doorway application is matchmaking software. You fill out a huge questionnaire asking some extremely personal questions, and the program helps find someone looking for what you have to offer and offering what you're looking for. Then you can send E-Mail or Chat if you're both online. What comes next is, of course, up to you.

Crash and burn, and pass the mustard

"ONIX holds an annual gathering at a huge picnic area — so big there are usually several groups holding picnics there at a time — in Valley Forge National Park. A user named Topgun — a member of ONIX since 1987 — attended his first picnic in 1992. Up to that point he had never met a single ONIX member face-to-face.

Topgun showed up, introduced himself, started chatting and eating the food provided. After about an hour, he overhead someone in the next group talking about the BBS. It was only then that he realized he'd spent the last hour hanging out with the wrong group and eating their food. At that point he came over to us and told everyone where he'd been and what had happened. Everyone had a huge laugh, including Topgun."

Jeff Miller, Sysop, ONIX

Chapter 13

Changing the System

. . . .

In This Chapter

▶ Assessing your setup

▶ Making needed changes

▶ Using other utility tools

. . . .

*Y*ou can make a difference. You can change the system.

At least, you can change a BBS system and how it works *for you*. I bet you didn't quite realize that the BBS, once it gets your name and password, changes itself slightly just for you. It's like those expensive cars that know how to adjust themselves for each passenger.

Assessing Your Setup

In the beginning, you have no choice but to accept a kind of one-size-fits-all BBS setup. But, as you get more mileage under the belt, you start to form opinions about what you like and dislike about how the system works. You may begin to rue the day you first logged on and replied yes or no to certain questions.

I'm here to tell you that you're not forever stuck with those replies. You can fine-tune the BBS to your exacting specifications.

You can make changes to virtually all those questions dealing with the look and the feel of the system. For example, you may decide you want graphics and colors. Or, because you've got a decent communications program that supports Zmodem, you want that to be the default. Yes, you can change all this.

Generally, you can expect to find the system-changing commands residing on the Main Menu under one of these choices — which are all basically the same thing:

✔ User Settings/Preferences

✔ Utilities or System Utilities

✔ Terminal Settings

The first step is to give the Main Menu command to activate the system utilities and arrive at something like Figure 13-1.

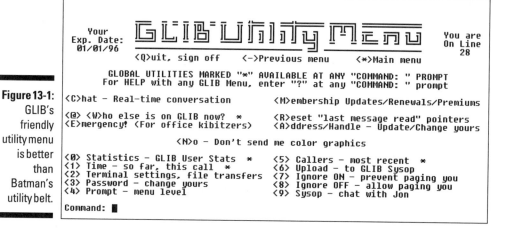

Figure 13-1: GLIB's friendly utility menu is better than Batman's utility belt.

```
    Your     GLIB Utility Menu          You are
 Exp. Date:                              On Line
  01/01/96                                  28
          <Q>uit, sign off    <->Previous menu    <*>Main menu
         GLOBAL UTILITIES MARKED "*" AVAILABLE AT ANY "COMMAND: " PROMPT
         For HELP with any GLIB Menu, enter "?" at any "COMMAND: " prompt

<C>hat - Real-time conversation              <M>embership Updates/Renewals/Premiums

<@> <W>ho else is on GLIB now? *             <R>eset "last message read" pointers
<E>mergency! <For office kibitzers>          <A>ddress/Handle - Update/Change yours

                       <N>o - Don't send me color graphics

<0> Statistics - GLIB User Stats  *     <5> Callers - most recent   *
<1> Time - so far, this call   *        <6> Upload - to GLIB Sysop
<2> Terminal settings, file transfers   <7> Ignore ON - prevent paging you
<3> Password - change yours             <8> Ignore OFF - allow paging you
<4> Prompt - menu level                 <9> Sysop - chat with Jon

Command: █
```

From the general utility menu, select the area in which you want to check your settings and, perhaps, make a change. You won't hurt anything by looking. If you want to go straight for the technical, choose Item 2 from Figure 13-1 — Terminal settings. You then get something like Figure 13-2.

Figure 13-2: These options should look vaguely familiar.

```
          User Setup Utility

Your Display     Capable of ANSI Graphics

<N>umber of Nulls Needed ..... 0                <?> HELP
<L>ine feeds needed? ......... Yes              <-> Previous Menu
<C>ase Display. Upper Only? .. No               <*> Main Menu
<A>NSI Graphics Display? ..... Yes
<W>idth of your Screen ....... 80
<S>creen Length (-More-) ..... 24
<E>xpert Menu Level .......... Full Menu Display
<U>pload Protocol ............ No Protocol Selected
<D>ownload Protocol .......... No Protocol Selected
<P>rompt for Prepared Text ... No
<F>ull Screen Edit Mode ...... Ask
Last Msg <R>ead Pointer ...... Lowest Message Read
<M>essage Entry Prompt ....... Line Number

Command: █
```

When you're staring at your settings, it's time to decide what, if anything, you want to change.

If you're afraid of making changes, then be sure to write down the current settings — before you change them. That way, you can always go back.

Making Needed Changes

There are four topics you should take a look at after your first hundred days online. You may want to consider fine-tuning these more critical items. If you are a card-carrying member of the If It's Not Broke, Don't Fix It Club, you can leave almost everything alone and go on your merry way. Except for one thing. Please consider changing your password, for the reasons coming up.

Generally, on all options, once you select the option that you want to change, the BBS prompts you every step of the way. Often the BBS gives you multiple-choice answers to select from. This is not the time to get creative.

Password

Changing your password every few months is considered a prudent idea by the prudent-idea committee. It's one way of making sure access to the BBS doesn't fall into enemy hands. You have to type in the old password first, and then the new password twice when prompted. Don't forget the new password. You don't want to get locked out of the system.

Protocol

If you've discovered that you have Zmodem — congratulations by the way — be sure to change your default upload and download protocol. By changing the default to Zmodem, you'll no longer be asked for a protocol when you download something. One of the great things about Zmodem is that the BBS talks directly to your computer and you never have to issue the download command. The file starts downloading all by itself. The other benefit of Zmodem is that, if the download is interrupted, you can call the BBS back and, when you start the download again, Zmodem knows how to pick up where you left off.

ANSI graphics

During any initial logon — like the one reproduced in Chapter 2 — you may choose not to use the BBS's graphics output capabilities. If you later change your mind, or if you've gone through the process in Appendix D to install your ANSI.SYS, then you can ask the BBS to display graphics/colors. If your BBS supports it, you can also change the foreground, background, and text colors of the BBS menus, as in Figure 13-3.

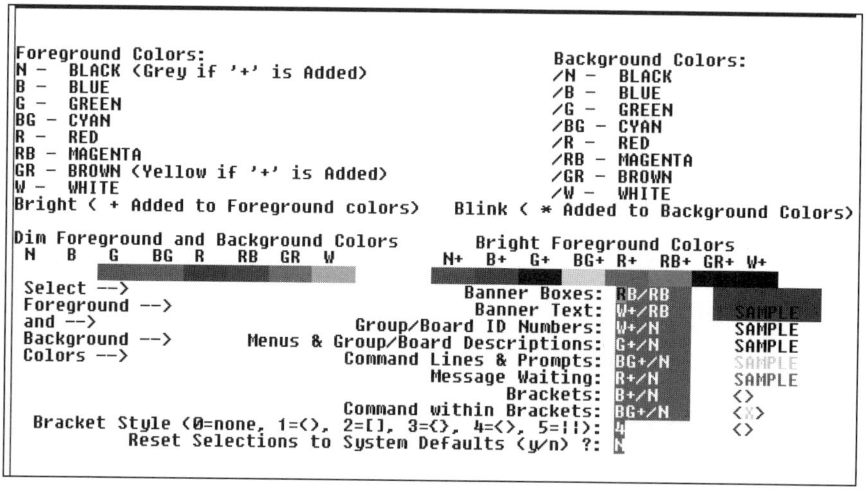

Figure 13-3:
Deep Cove Online has the advanced option of changing menu colors to taste.

```
Foreground Colors:                               Background Colors:
N  -  BLACK <Grey if '+' is Added>                /N -   BLACK
B  -  BLUE                                         /B -   BLUE
G  -  GREEN                                        /G -   GREEN
BG -  CYAN                                         /BG -  CYAN
R  -  RED                                          /R -   RED
RB -  MAGENTA                                      /RB -  MAGENTA
GR -  BROWN <Yellow if '+' is Added>              /GR -  BROWN
W  -  WHITE                                        /W -   WHITE
Bright < + Added to Foreground colors>      Blink < * Added to Background Colors)

Dim Foreground and Background Colors          Bright Foreground Colors
  N    B    G   BG   R   RB   GR   W        N+   B+   G+   BG+  R+   RB+  GR+  W+

Select -->                                  Banner Boxes:       RB/RB        SAMPLE
Foreground -->                              Banner Text:        W+/RB        SAMPLE
and -->                     Group/Board ID Numbers:             W+/N         SAMPLE
Background -->       Menus & Group/Board Descriptions:          G+/N         SAMPLE
Colors -->                   Command Lines & Prompts:           BG+/N        SAMPLE
                               Message Waiting:                 R+/N         SAMPLE
                                      Brackets:                 B+/N         <>
                           Command within Brackets:             BG+/N        <X>
Bracket Style <0=none, 1=<>, 2=[], 3=<>, 4=<>, 5=||>:           4            <>
           Reset Selections to System Defaults <y/n> ?:         N
```

Full-Screen Editor

If you're annoyed because every darn time you go to write a message, the BBS chimes in with questions about the full-screen editor, here's where you permanently — until you change it again — make your preference for the full-screen editor known.

Using Other Utilities

Because a utility is a small program that can adjust or examine a specific feature of another program, some BBSs opt to gather all of their utilities into one convenient workbench. Figure 13-4 shows a menu of very simple utilities; notice the range of items that are considered utilities. Other BBSs spread their utilities around so that they appear wherever the Sysop thinks you'll need them most.

Figure 13-4:
The
Nashville
Exchange
lets you
change your
settings as
well as find
caller
names — all
from the
utilities
menu.

```
========== Utilities ==========
[*]Hang-up [+]Elapsed Time [-]Prev Menu

[C]hange your password

[L]ocation - Change your listed location

[R]econfigure User Defaults - Scrn Width, Protocols etc.

[Y]our Statistics on TNE

[N]otePad - Personal Notepad & TODO Lister

[U]ser Look-Up - Search for Caller Names

Command: █
```

Time online

It's good to keep track of how much time you have left. Usually, the remaining time you have is displayed at the beginning of each prompt. If not, this is where you ask to see how much time you've spent online so far.

Your statistics

This is stuff like the number of times you've logged on, how much you've uploaded and how much you've downloaded. Some systems have rules that limit the volume of stuff you can download from the system. On these systems, you need to keep track of your upload-to-download ratio. If a BBS has a ten-to-one upload-to-download ratio, for example, that means for every ten bytes you download, you need to upload one. Here's where you can see how you're doing.

Who's online

Who's online, as discussed in Chapter 11 — the Chatting chapter — is sometimes a utility option and sometimes an option in its own right, sitting in a Chat menu. By the way, we're still waiting for the computer-age Abbott and Costello to come up with a "Who's Online" routine. Consider that a challenge.

Chat status

The utility menu is also one of the places where you can find your Chat status option. If you don't want to be invited to Chat, then be sure to set your status to Off, Ignore, or No — all words that mean *go away*.

Hheelllloo!!

"In setting up his communications program, one of our new users accidentally set his "local echo" to on by mistake, thus causing him to get ddoouubbllee lleettttteerrss with every keystroke. Instead of calling me, he immediately thought there was something wrong with his monitor. While still online, he twisted every dial on his monitor and when that didn't work, he broke out the screwdriver and aimed at the adjustment screws on the back. By the time he was done, he had unadjusted the monitor so badly that it had to be taken in for professional help. He is now one of our regulars, but we remind him about this every two months or so <G>!"

Don Presten, Sysop, West Coast Connection

The 5th Wave
By Rich Tennant

"QUICK KIDS! YOUR MOTHER'S FLAMING SOMEONE ON THE INTERNET!"

Chapter 14

Introducing the Internet Connection

· ·

In This Chapter

▶ The bad news

▶ The good news

▶ Coming to a BBS near you . . .

▶ Internet features

· ·

1 t seems as though every time you turn around, whether you're watching one of those tabloid news shows or a religious broadcast, someone is shoving an Internet address at you imploring you to send them some E-Mail. It's clear everyone is jumping on the Internet band wagon.

But, what the heck is the Internet?

It's almost easier to say what it *isn't*. The Internet isn't a service like Prodigy, America Online, or Compuserve. The Internet isn't run by any single company, and it's supposed to be a not-for-profit sort of thing — not surprising since it was invented by the U.S. government.

It might even be better to think of the Internet as a *method* for connecting a bunch of different computers, networks, and yes, BBSs, into a common system. The Internet works something like the BBS networks — where many BBSs exchange information — I mention in Chapter 10 on conferencing. The difference between BBS networks and Internet is that the systems connected to the Internet always remain connected, the information is exchanged on an ongoing basis, and people using the system can actually access any other computer on the system as though it were their own — within security limitations, of course.

The ongoing connection is achieved through a special kind of phone connection which costs a Sysop — or a business — some serious money. However, some companies and BBSs do get the phone line, add the hardware necessary, and hook up to the Internet. They, in turn, let us average types use the Internet through their setups. That's why they're called Internet providers, and we who use them are called $20 a month poorer.

Not every BBS can afford, or is interested in, providing full, live, real-time Internet. Fortunately, it's not an all-or-nothing deal. They can, however, provide *some* Internet services. For example, almost anyone can provide an E-Mail connection.

What does all that mean to you?

Not too much at first.

But the Internet is slowly moving into all of our lives. You'll see it referred to on BBSs, and typically Sysops ask for additional fees if they are providing live Internet service, to help cover their costs. What is the Internet and do you want to pay the higher fees for it? This chapter helps you to keep the Internet in perspective as well as gives an idea of what the fuss is all about.

The Bad News

If you've got the impression that the Internet is complicated, then so far you're right on the money. It's definitely not the place to start your online career. Why?

- ✔ First of all, the Internet uses an operating system called UNIX. In order to perform basic actions — like get a list of files — you have to learn some new commands. DIR doesn't work in UNIX. The equivalant is closer to ls-l and Enter. Yikes.

- ✔ It's best to kick off your training wheels using the several-hundred conferences available in BBS. After you've got that down, then try the 7,000 topics on the Internet. All the topics there, by the way, have wacky names like *alt.pets.training.bad.dog*. Try typing that three times real fast.

- ✔ While every conceivable kind of shareware is available on the Internet, it's a lot easier to find what you're looking for on a single BBS, than to hunt something down on the Internet that may be on one of the thousands of computers hooked up around the world.

- ✔ You may encounter a frosty factor on the Internet. Many old-timers there feel their system is being ruined by newcomers. They don't hide their resentment. Sometimes, raising your hand and asking for help will get you a hostile response — especially if *they* think you haven't done your homework. This is not to say that you won't find some very friendly and helpful folk; it's just that you'll also find some grouches.

✔ The Internet itself isn't even remotely user-friendly. Things are still described using acronyms and jargon words. If I were to ask someone how to get the just-released picture taken by the Hubble Telescope, I might be told, "FTP to FTP.HQ.NASA.GOV — NASA allows anonymous FTP — look in the pub/pao/presskit/1995 directory, set your transfer to binary, and then just use Get." And that's quite a detailed and helpful answer!

This should scare you into sticking with your local BBS, at least until you feel comfortable there. Once you start getting restless, you'll have the experience necessary to take on the Internet, *mano-a-mano*, without it scaring you for life.

The Good News

So maybe I went overboard, and you're now so put off by the Internet that you'll never go near it. Personally, I couldn't live without it. Okay, maybe a slight exaggeration. But now let's think about the fun stuff for a moment. I haven't even begun to scratch the surface of the Internet myself, but here's a few of the things I've used it for — other than sending E-Mail:

✔ Signed up to receive electronic press releases from NASA. They send me updates at least every other day. And yes, I have downloaded several Hubble photos.

✔ Chatted with the research scientists living in Antarctica.

✔ Used a program called Telnet to hook up to computers all around the world on the Internet and didn't pay any long distance charges.

✔ Downloaded a complete catalog of elephant jokes.

✔ Searched through the Library of Congress's card catalog.

✔ Performed research on a number of topics including job-hunting online, Egypt, and mutual funds.

✔ Read conversation in newsgroups entitled alt.fan.mandy-patinkin and alt.movies.joe-vs-volcano.

With all the attention that is being lavished on the Internet by the media — and with businesses sensing a chance to make some money — companies are writing books and software to tame the Internet.

One major improvement is the new graphical *interface* attached to a system called the World Wide Web. An interface is what's between you and the machine carrying out the command. In Windows, for example, if you click on the File Manager icon, the program springs to life. You don't need to know what the program's really called or that it's in the such-and-such directory and that you have to do x, y, or z to get it going.

Likewise, the World Wide Web interface on the Internet makes the whole massive system not only accessible, but inviting (see Figure 14-1). Every *page* of the World Wide Web (WWW) is linked to information on other computers. Not every part of the Internet is connected to the WWW, though. This setup must be done by hand—usually by a business (like the Rolling Stones tour page), or by someone with a hobby (like the Cardiff Movie database), or by an institution of higher learning (like the Shakespeare page).

What you see on the screen of a WWW page is a picture or an icon of something like the Rolling Stones or Shakespeare. When you click on this icon, the computer has been set up to perform all of that FTP, Telnet, and http stuff, so you don't have to know a thing about what's going on, just as you don't have to know what's going on with File Manager. You can use your mouse to point and click your way around the world.

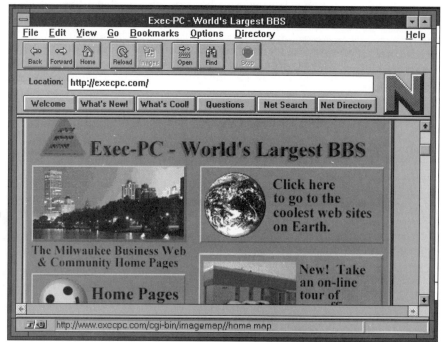

Figure 14-1:
Exec-PC's
World Wide
Web home
page,
available on
the Internet.

To use the WWW, you need to own something along the lines of a multimedia PC and have access to a special kind of Internet account called a PPP or SLIP — which I'm not going to explain. I just wanted you to know that it takes some effort to get a World Wide Web setup going. If you're curious, join a BBS that provides WWW services, and they'll help you along. If you're really into this stuff, pick up IDG's *Internet For Dummies* for a good overview.

Internet Features Coming to a BBS Near You...

Some very large BBSs are gravitating toward Internet connections. Worldwide interconnectivity certainly has an appealing ring to it, doesn't it?

If one of *your* goals is to hook up with the Internet, then you want a BBS which has that connection established. Here are some vocabulary words so you can tell who's on first when your favorite BBS starts to talk about Internet features:

✔ **Internet E-Mail:** This means you can send and receive E-Mail to and from anyone on the Internet — and on CompuServe, Prodigy, America Online, and the rest. This also means that you get an Internet address — which usually looks something like your.name@bbs.com. You can write to Microsoft's Bill Gates at billg@microsoft.com. or to the President of the United States at president@whitehouse.gov or even to me at bslick@netcom.com. The BBS shown in Figure 14-2 offers Internet E-Mail.

Figure 14-2: The Dance of Shiva BBS is one of many that offers Internet E-Mail.

✔ **Usenet Newsgroups:** These are the conferences on Internet. In Figure
14-3 — on the right — the conferences included on the BBS are listed. Did
you notice the asterisks in the list — you do remember about the wildcard
asterisk that stands for *anything*. There are hundreds of alt newsgroups
ranging from alt.animals.foxes to alt.personals.spanking to alt.zima. All of
these would be included in alt.*.

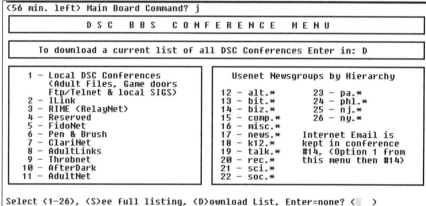

Figure 14-3:
DSC BBS
offers
Usenet
Newsgroups
which
attract
international
participation.

```
<56 min. left> Main Board Command? j

       D S C   B B S   C O N F E R E N C E   M E N U

   To download a current list of all DSC Conferences Enter in: D

  1 - Local DSC Conferences          Usenet Newsgroups by Hierarchy
      <Adult Files, Game doors
      Ftp/Telnet & local SIGS>    12 - alt.*     23 - pa.*
  2 - ILink                       13 - bit.*     24 - phl.*
  3 - RIME <RelayNet>             14 - biz.*     25 - nj.*
  4 - Reserved                    15 - comp.*    26 - ny.*
  5 - FidoNet                     16 - misc.*
  6 - Pen & Brush                 17 - news.*    Internet Email is
  7 - ClariNet                    18 - k12.*     kept in conference
  8 - AdultLinks                  19 - talk.*    #14. <Option 1 from
  9 - Throbnet                    20 - rec.*     this menu then #14)
 10 - AfterDark                   21 - sci.*
 11 - AdultNet                    22 - soc.*

Select <1-26>, <S>ee full listing, <D>ownload List, Enter=none? <   >
```

✔ **Telnet:** This means that you can connect to this BBS via the Internet. No
long distance fees — just a quick trip down the information superhighway.
Take a look at the listing in Appendix B to find out which BBSs on the Top
100 list have Telnet. More are joining every day. Check with your BBS for
details.

✔ **FTP:** This lets you log onto storage areas on the Internet — similar to the
file areas or file libraries on a BBS — and download files. FTP — File
Transfer Protocol — is confusing because it's used as both a noun (where
the files are stored) and a verb (transferring the files), often in the same
sentence. Remember, geeks have been in charge of this system for ages!

✔ **Gopher, Archie, Veronica, and Jughead:** Ripped from the headlines of
Archie comics, these are also names of search engines that find computers
on the Internet which have what you're looking for. For example, call up
Gopher and, when it asks what are you looking for, type in something like
organ transplants and press Enter. Then wait while Gopher searches the
Internet and comes back with a whole resource list.

✔ **World Wide Web:** As I mentioned before, the World Wide Web is definitely
where the coolest stuff on the Internet is being added. It takes a special
account and some work to get the World Wide Web going. A no-brainer
approach is to subscribe to the commercial service named Prodigy,
which — among other things — has a World Wide Web browser ready for
you to try right now. No doubt CompuServe and America Online will soon
have the same thing. All of these services will give you 30 days free.

Chapter 15
Reading Mail Offline

- -

In This Chapter

▶ Preparing for the installation
▶ Setting OLX up
▶ Configuring the online system
▶ Downloading the E-Mail packet
▶ Reading and replying on OLX
▶ Uploading your Reply packet

- -

*E*verything you've read so far may lead you to believe that you have to be online to read and respond to your E-Mail. The idea of reading and responding to E-Mail offline doesn't make any sense.

At first.

Once you get a little program known as an offline mail reader, however, the paradox resolves itself.

Using Offline Readers

Before we get into what an offline reader does for you, I hereby give you permission not to try using one until you've worked with a BBS for a few weeks and are comfortable with sending and receiving mail the old-fashioned way — while still online.

Don't get me wrong. Offline readers are a breeze. I just think that, with all the new concepts involved in BBSing, you might think that one more thing to know might be too much. You, of course, will have to be the final judge. I trust you.

On with the show!

The magic of the offline reader begins when you go online. Here's what it's like to use an offline reader — the details follow later:

- ✔ Instead of reading all your mail and your favorite conferences with one eye on the clock, confidently invoke a special command from the Main Menu.

- ✔ When this special command is issued, the BBS gathers all the new mail and new messages in your favorite conferences, stuffs them into a file, and downloads that file — known as a packet — to your computer.

- ✔ Then you hang up. Total online time — five to ten minutes.

- ✔ Next you invoke the offline mail-reader program. The reader knows how to interpret the packet you just downloaded and display the messages in exactly the same conferences they were collected from online. You can then read the E-Mail, reply, and so forth just as though you were still online. Except of course, since you're not online, you can take time to reply properly. No pressure.

- ✔ When you're done reading and replying to your E-Mail, then it's time to call the BBS again, issue a command, and then upload the replies you've written — which have been placed in a packet of their own. After the BBS gets the reply packet, it knows how to remove your replies and place them in the proper conferences.

- ✔ Then you hang up. Total online time, five minutes — max.

The advantages of using an offline reader are many:

- ✔ Your total online time is vastly reduced.

- ✔ The quality of your responses is improved.

- ✔ The number of messages you can now read is limited only by your desire — not by an arbitrary time limit.

- ✔ The offline reader does some things you can't do yourself, as you'll see. (This is a blatant attempt at getting your curiosity going.)

As usual, the most difficult part about using an offline reader is setting the thing up. However, you've already done things more difficult than setting up an offline reader — no matter how intimidating that sounds. Once you do set it up, though, you can casually mention to your friends that you've installed an offline mail reader and drive them nuts with jealousy.

Preparing for the Installation

The name of the offline mail reader I cover here is OLX — Offline Express. Actually, you'll be working with the *test-drive* version of OLX — OLX-TD. A test-drive version of a program is one that, although it works perfectly well, is not the current version of the program and doesn't have all the bells and whistles. If you were to register and pay for the program, you'd get the latest version and a — get this — *manual*. Oooh. Aahh!

Pretty tempting, huh?

Okay, team, eyes front. In order to pull off the OLX caper, we need to get some tools together on your computer.

✔ **PKZip and PkUnZip:** If you don't have these programs, follow the flashing cursor back over to Chapter 4 and do what it says to download your very own copies and then set them up. OLX needs these programs or it won't work.

✔ **OLX-TD.EXE:** Minor point, but you do need to get the OLX program in order to use it. On the bright side, it's a self-extracting file, so you won't have to fuss with unzipping it.

Here's how to get OLX:

1. **Get into your communications software program and add Mustang Software — makers of OLX — to your dialing directory.**

   Their BBS's phone number is 805/873-2400.

2. **Dial the number.**

3. **Once online, go through the brief logon process — providing them with your name and address. Eventually you arrive at the Main Menu.**

4. **Press O and Enter — for Other Info: Testdrives.**

   This version of OLX is what they call a test drive — a form of shareware.

5. **At the Testdrives Menu, press 6 and then Enter to get an informational screen about OLX.**

6. **When asked if you want to download the files, press Y and Enter if you want to download the file.**

7. **Select a download protocol — Zmodem, hopefully.**

8. **When the download process is initiated, issue your own download command, and then slect Zmodem as your protocol.**

9. **When the download is unloaded, be sure to press G, for Good-bye.**

10. **Then, press Enter when you're all finished and want to hang up.**

Once you have these programs, you're ready to move to the next phase.

Make sure you still know, and can type on demand, the name or path of your download directory — the place on the hard disk where files go when they are downloaded. OLX needs that information, so if you must look it up, now's the time to do so.

Putting the Offline Reader in Its Place

You've got your copy of OLX-TD.EXE sitting in your download directory where, right now, it's not doing anyone any good. Though, of course, I doff my hat to you for successfully downloading and getting it this far. Hopefully, downloading is becoming a matter-of-fact process for you.

What you're going to do in this section is make a home for OLX, move the file to the new home, and let the OLX program do it's self-extracting thing.

1. **Get to the DOS prompt.**

   If you're currently using a DOS program, exit the program. If you're using Windows, you can either exit Windows — save your files first, of course — or select **File** ⇨ **R**un from Program Manager and, in the Run dialog box, type **command** and press Enter. If you're running Windows 95, select Run from the Taskbar.

   One way or the other, get to the system prompt, so you see something like C:\.

2. **Type** CD\[name of download directory] **and press Enter.**

   This gets you to where OLX-TD landed when it was downloaded. If you didn't put it in the download directory, then substitute the program's present location for the name of the download directory.

3. **Once in the download directory, Type** MD \OLX **and press Enter.**

   If you did it right, you get no message from the computer, just the system prompt again.

4. **Now type** COPY OLX-TD.EXE \OLX **and press Enter.**

   This puts a copy of OLX-TD in its own directory.

5. **Type** CD\OLX **and press Enter.**

   This puts you in the directory where OLX-TD is going to be installed. Isn't this exciting?

6. **Type** OLX-TD **and press Enter.**

7. **Press Y and Enter after you're asked whether you are ready for OLX-TD to self-extract.**

   Now you get to see nine files magically appear from thin air. Take that, David Copperfield.

8. **When you see the C:\ prompt again, type** DEL SLMR2OLX.EXE **and press Enter.**

   This deletes a file you won't need.

If you want, at this point, you can print out the little manual that comes with OLX. Turn on your print and type **PRINT OLXTD.DOC** and press Enter. The computer will ask you a question — press Enter again.

Setting OLX Up

This is so easy to do, it's embarrassing.

1. **Type** OLXTD **and press Enter.**

   You get a screen like the one in Figure 15-1.

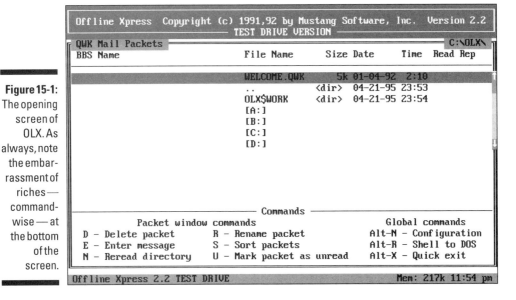

Figure 15-1: The opening screen of OLX. As always, note the embarrassment of riches — command-wise — at the bottom of the screen.

```
Offline Xpress  Copyright (c) 1991,92 by Mustang Software, Inc.  Version 2.2
                            TEST DRIVE VERSION
 QWK Mail Packets                                                    C:\OLX\
 BBS Name                         File Name    Size Date    Time  Read Rep

                               WELCOME.QWK       5k 01-04-92  2:10
                               ..            <dir>  04-21-95 23:53
                               OLX$WORK      <dir>  04-21-95 23:54
                               [A:]
                               [B:]
                               [C:]
                               [D:]



                             ── Commands ──
            Packet window commands                 Global commands
    D - Delete packet      R - Rename packet     Alt-N - Configuration
    E - Enter message      S - Sort packets      Alt-R - Shell to DOS
    N - Reread directory   U - Mark packet as unread  Alt-X - Quick exit
 Offline Xpress 2.2 TEST DRIVE                       Mem: 217k 11:54 pm
```

2. **Press Alt+N to enter the configuration program.**

3. **Move the cursor to highlight the word Directories, if it isn't already highlighted, and then press Enter.**

4. **Type the name of your download directory in the box to the right of where it says QWK directory.**

5. **Unless you have a special upload directory set up for some reason, also type the name of your download directory in the box to the right of where it says REP directory.**

6. **When you've got it right, press F10 to get back to something like Figure 15-1.**

Now you've done everything you need to do to get OLX ready to use. You're done setting it up.

At this point, I hope you will take a moment to run through the four-minute tutorial the people who brought you OLX have set up for you. All you have to do is make sure that your cursor is highlighting WELCOM.QWK and press Enter. Read and follow the instructions on the screen. In a few moments, you see the basics of using OLX.

When you're done with the OLX tutorial, press Alt+X to exit.

More than you want to know about offline readers

If you've worked with computers for more than one second, you know that, for every one way to do something, somebody else has figured out 15 other ways to do the same thing. Same goes for the whole issue of offline mail readers.

First of all, OLX—though a standard—is not the only offline mail reader around. Others include Robomail, Silver Xpress, QwkBasic, Speed Read, CmpQwk, QwkSlave, QwkTalk, and so forth. After you've become a whiz at OLX, you can check these other programs out to see if any scratch an offline itch.

Next, the way the packet file is put together by the BBS is compatible with the QWK format—

you may have noticed that many of the readers have QWK in their names. Every packet you receive will be called something.qwk. The QWK format is the most universally used. But it's not the only one. And I'll save you the agony of listing other formats.

However, OLX is recognized as a good reader; it's easy to use, it's easy to download, and it's easy to set up.

No matter which system you stay with at the end of the day, however, they all work basically the same.

Configuring the Online System

This definitely sounds worse than it is.

1. **Call up a BBS.**

   Nearly all BBSs have facilities for gathering offline mail. Certainly any of the ones in the Top 100 do.

2. **Once online, look at the Main Menu for anything that talks about setting up QWK, Mail Door, QSO or QMail.**

   Do you see a mention of configuring the mail door — or selecting conferences? If none of the mail options actually says *setup*, then choose the QWK mail option.

3. **Select your conferences.**

   The BBS shows you the list of the conferences it carries. Which ones do you normally join and read mail in? Those are the ones to select at this point. Don't worry, you can always amend your choices later.

4. **Set your last message pointers.**

   When asked about setting your last message pointers, take a look at the difference between where the system is planning to set your pointer and the highest message number. There could be a difference into the thousands. Maybe you should type a beginning number that's only 50 numbers smaller than the final number, so you don't download everything ever said on a particular conference.

5. **When you're finished selecting your options, the system generally returns you to the Main Menu.**

Downloading the E-Mail Packet

It is now the moment of truth. The moment you've been working toward. Will the BBS actually do what it's supposed to do and create the much-anticipated mail packet that includes the conference you just selected? We'll find out.

1. **Issue the QWK or mail-door command you see on the Main Menu.**

2. **On most BBSs, you see a short menu of items, including D for download; press D and then press Enter.**

   Figure 15-2 is what the BBS shared with me as it gathered messages for packet downloading.

```
(Z)ippy text search                              QWK Commands
(T)ransfer protocol          Live Internet       (QWK) transfer QWK mail
(TEST)/View(FP)Files      (telnet) / (Gopher)    (SELECT) Confs. for QWK
                          (finger) / (iwhois)    (QMAIL4) Qmail Subsystem
  Miscellaneous           (ftp) / (IRC) Chat
(C)omment to SysOp        (NETHELP) for INFO        Settings
(B)ulletins & Info                               (M) toggle color mode
(X)pert mode toggle            Other             (V)iew your statistics
(BANK) time bank          (CHAT) with other users (P)age length setting
(S)cript questionnaires   (NEWS) see system news (W)Set Pword/Alias/Info
(I)nitial logon screen    (OPEN) a (DOOR)        (UPDATE) your info
(G)oodbye/Hangup/logoff   (WHO) else is online   (ORDER) a subscription

(55 min. left) Main Board Command? qwk

QWK Commands: (D)ownload, (U)pload? d
(Ctrl-K) or (Ctrl-X) Aborts, (Ctrl-S) Suspends.
Scanning Main Board -> 3
Scanning Comedy (42) Conference -> 22
Scanning Movies (70) Conference -> 42
Scanning Writers (71) Conference -> 31
Total Messages Captured for Download -> 98
Creating QWK Packet, please wait...

ANSI    ONLINE  57600 8N1  [Alt+Z]-Menu  FDX 8 LF X ♪ ♫ CP LG ↑ PR  00:04:49
```

Figure 15-2:
The lower
half of this
DSC BBS
menu shows
the various
automatic
steps to
collect and
compress
files in three
conferences.

3. **If you haven't selected a default download protocol, then you are asked for your fave. Hopefully Zmodem.**

4. **When the BBS finishes its thing, log off and hang up.**

   That is, unless you want to hang out in one of the Chat areas. There's no offline substitute for chatting.

Reading and Replying on OLX

Now that you've got a packet of mail from the BBS, open it up and see what's inside.

1. **Get to the system prompt.**

   If you're in your communications program, exit it.

2. **Type** CD\OLX **and press Enter.**

   This gets you to the OLX directory — just like before.

3. **Type** OLXTD **and press Enter to start the OLX program.**

4. **Once in the program, the packet you just downloaded becomes visible.**

   If you called the DSC BBS, you see a DSC.QWK file with the current date and almost the current time. That's the file you just downloaded!

5. **Highlight that file and press Enter.**

6. **You get a little menu — as in Figure 15-3 — isn't it cute? Highlight the area that you want to look at and press Enter.**

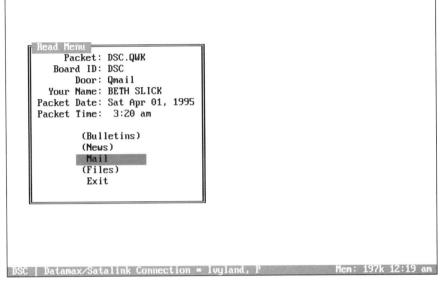

Figure 15-3:
You can now read your mail offline by selecting your area of interest and pressing Enter.

7. **Read and reply to messages.**

As you learned in the OLX Tutorial:

- Pressing Enter moves you forward through messages as you read them.

- Pressing Insert brings up a list of other areas to select from.

- Pressing R lets you reply to a message.

When you do press R, you get a block of Message Reply Info something like Figure 15-4. This is your chance to review your reply options such as who's getting the message, the security and so on. After you've been online a couple of times, all those options seem straightforward.

The only new thing here is the issue of the tagline — a sort of bumper sticker for your messages that is automatically generated by the OLX program (you can add your own later). If you've read any messages online, you've seen these taglines. Everyone enjoys them.

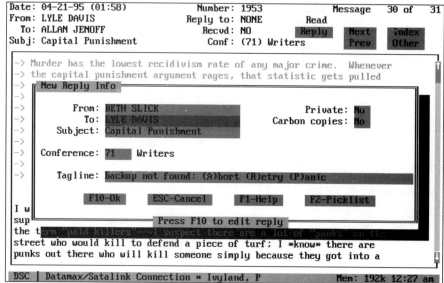

Figure 15-4:
The
Message
Reply Info
box lets you
fine-tune
your
message's
destination.

8. **Press F10 when you're finished editing the Message Reply Info.**

   OLX now sticks a copy of the message you're replying to on the screen.

9. **Use the commands at the bottom of the screen to wipe out what you don't need, and then you can write your message.**

   Are you having fun yet?

10. **When done, press F10.**

11. **When done reading and replying, press Alt+X to exit.**

    You have just finished creating a Reply packet. A file ending in REP now exists which contains the messages you just wrote. Just one more step and you're out of here.

Uploading Your Reply Packet

When you're in the mood to send the Reply Packet back up the line, then simply do it.

1. **Call the BBS and log on.**

2. **Type QWK or the door command from the Main Menu.**

3. Press U for Upload — or scan the options and find the one for uploading.

4. If prompted for a protocol choice, make one — Zmodem goes well with any meal.

5. Wait while the Reply packet is pulled into the BBS system, and its innards are distributed appropriately.

6. Log off and hang up.

Looking to the Future

The next time you call the BBS, all you have to do is select Downloading the Packet and continue from there. The BBS remembers your last-message-read position and conference selections.

Just because you've got the system set up a certain way, don't feel compelled to stick with that forever. You can add or remove conferences whenever the mood strikes.

No place like cyberhome

"The national online systems have a lot to offer. But you're only seeing half the picture if you limit yourself to those systems. The BBS community in your town has a huge resource of local/community-related information, messages, and other users. No National system can match the 'community' that you can get from a quality BBS in your area. Explore your cybervillage!"

Chuck Burke, Sysop, The Dance of Shiva BBS

Part III
I, Sysop

The 5th Wave
By Rich Tennant

"Now, when someone rings my doorbell, the current goes to a scanner that digitizes the audio impulses and sends the image to the PC where it's converted to a Pict file. The image is then animated, compressed, and sent via high-speed modem to an automated phone service that sends an e-mail message back to tell me someone was at my door 40 minutes ago."

In this part...

This section is, quite frankly, for the adventurous and the curious.

Beth has already shown you how to call a BBS and use it effectively and politely. If your interest in bulletin boards extends no further than that, then skip merrily on to Part IV. You won't be missing a thing. (Well, some good jokes — but nothing essential.)

If, on the other hand, the thought has crossed your mind that it might be fun to *run* a BBS…or that a bulletin board might serve as an interesting adjunct to your business or group…or, if you've begun to wonder what a BBS looks like from the *Sysop's* point of view, you're in the right place.

I'm Steve Gerber. I'll be your guide as you see how to use the host mode of your own communications program as a mini-BBS and then boldly go where no dummy has gone before — deep into the process of planning, installing, and setting up your own full-fledged Wildcat! BBS system.

Chapter 16

Hosting Your Own Mini-BBS

. . . .

In This Chapter

▶ Hosting a cyberparty

▶ Preparing your system

▶ Invoking the host

▶ Receiving guests

▶ Moving the party

. . . .

*H*ave you ever accessed your home computer from a laptop computer while on a business trip? Have you ever told your assistant to call up your home computer to download a report or to upload your new schedule? Have you ever wished your home computer could fax price lists on demand to your customers?

Is this beginning to sound like those phone company commercials where they try to take credit for inventions they didn't create?

Unlike those commercials, you already can call up, or have someone else call up, your home computer and send and receive files and faxes. The reality is that you're only about two keystrokes away from doing that this very day.

Hosting a CyberParty

Every decent modem-communications program has the power to turn your computer into a *host* computer. A host computer acts a lot like a BBS. That means if someone calls in, the host computer will automatically answer and ask the caller to log on. Once the caller has logged on, the host computer acts like a mini-BBS allowing such activities as

✔ Sending and receiving mail

✔ Uploading and downloading files

✔ Callback security

✔ Chat

A host computer also has some features not found exactly on most BBSs, such as

- Direct access to the host hard disk
- Ability to run programs on the host computer
- Ability to send and receive faxes

Each telecommunications program has its own set of host features. Yours may or may not sport the entire complement of options. If the manufacturer has gone to the bother of including a host mode at all, you can bank on at least having the ability to send and receive mail and files.

Even if you never plan on allowing people to call up your computer, knowing how to go into host mode can salvage a disaster — such as a disk or file left at home, or needing to send material to a colleague at the last minute. Take a few minutes now to prepare for that eventual emergency.

Preparing Your System

Spontaneity is fine if you're hosting a real party — call ten or twenty friends, order in some pizza, ice your favorite libations, crank up the tunes, and you're set. But becoming a cyberhost, though surprisingly easy, still requires a minor amount of preplanning.

Here's the fine print about host mode.

Because the host mode is strictly within the purview of the communications software you now own, the exact command to start host mode on your system is going to come from — you should pardon the expression — the manual. That's right, you'll have to take three deep breaths, give yourself a pep talk, and open the communications software manual or activate the software's Help feature. Either way, look up *host* or *host mode*. It's a nasty business, I know, but I'm sure you can handle it. If the manual is too daunting, give the manufacturer a call.

Here are the three things you'll need to find out from the host-mode section of your manual:

- **The command to set up the parameters of the host system:** There are a few decisions you have to make, like who gets to call into the system — guest list so to speak — and what parts of the computer they can use. Sometimes this is called *setup*, sometimes *configuration*.

✔ **Whether or not the host program takes care of turning on the modem's** *auto-answer* **feature:** Although your modem is already connected to the phone, you may have noticed that it typically doesn't try to answer when the phone rings. That's because the modem's auto-answer option is normally off. However, for this host mode business to work, the computer must answer the phone. If the instructions don't mention auto-answer, you're probably off the hook. So to speak. Otherwise, you'll have to look in your, gulp, modem manual to find out how to turn answer on.

✔ **The command to actually start the host mode.**

In Procomm Plus for Windows, selecting the *host* script file from the tool bar will kick you into host mode. In Qmodem for DOS, it's Alt+F5. Look in your manual to find what the host command is for you.

Making the guest list

Just to show you how incredibly clever they are, the modem-software makers have given you a few configuration options to puzzle over before going into host mode.

✔ **Who can call in:** You have the option to set up, in advance, the names and passwords of anyone who will be using your computer. You can choose to let anyone into your party or only those who have been invited in advance.

✔ **Who can get called back:** The ultimate security measure. Or paranoia. You set up not only the people who can call in, but also each of their own modem numbers. When they call in, the host program makes note of it and then hangs up on them. The caller then puts his modem into auto-answer, and the host calls the modem number associated with that person. This ensures that only the people on the list — not just someone knowing the name and password — can access the system.

✔ **Who can go where:** You can restrict access to your computer to only certain directories or give them free reign.

✔ **Who can shut it down:** At least one person should have the right to close down the host mode from a remote computer. That way the system won't be on all day long if you're not there to shut it down.

If you use Procomm Plus for Windows, you can set these options by selecting from the toolbar the script file *hostutil* (see Figure 16-1). If you use QmodemPro for DOS, you can find the setup screen under Config➪Host.

Answering the call

Breaking the news to the modem that it now has the increased responsibility of answering the phone usually falls to the host-mode program.

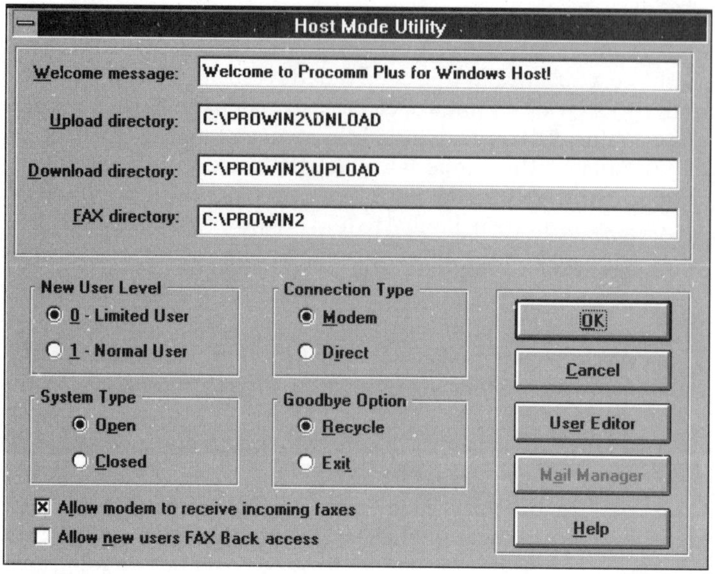

Figure 16-1:
Some
options for
setting up a
host system
with
Procomm
Plus for
Windows—
complete
with User
Editor
button to
predefine
callers and
their rights.

If, however, the manual tells you to set the modem to auto-answer, then that's what you must do. Either way, the manual will usually tell you *how* to set the modem to auto-answer. In Procomm Plus for Windows, for example, you enable auto-answer by selecting Auto-Answer from the Setup Menu and then picking whether you'll accept data (modem) calls, fax calls, or both.

If you don't set auto-answer now, and later find that the modem isn't responding to incoming calls, you may be forced to go native and type the auto-answer command yourself. Here's how:

1. **Activate the communications software, but don't go into host mode.**

2. **Underneath the OK that appears onscreen, type:** ATS0=2 **and press Enter.**

   To make sure you're reading that correctly, that's an uppercase A, uppercase T, uppercase S, the number zero, the equal sign, and the number 2. This tells the modem to answer on the second ring. If you change the two to a one, it'll answer on the first ring.

   This auto-answer setting will not permanently change how your modem works. You don't want the modem to answer the phone all the time. Most of your friends don't know how to speak modem-ese. You'll have to set auto-answer each time you're a host.

Normally, though, the host-mode program handles the auto-answer stuff for you. You probably won't even have to think about it.

Disarming call-waiting

Around here, the phone company charges for call-waiting *and* for cancel call-waiting. I never understood why it costs both to have a thing and not to have a thing. But I guess that's why I'm not a billion-dollar, multinational corporation, and they are. If you have both call-waiting and cancel call-waiting, you must invoke the cancel call-waiting command, whether you're online with a BBS or in host mode. Why? Because if you're in the middle of a session and someone else calls in, it'll knock everyone offline. Very frustrating.

The command to cancel call-waiting, if you have that feature, varies. If you have it, you should know what it is, because you're using it. If you don't know, ask the phone company. In these parts, the cancel call-waiting command is *70. They probably had a committee meeting to come up with that.

Once you know what your cancel call-waiting command is, you need to stick it in the modem's dial string. And, no, that's not talking dirty. It just means that if you normally enter a phone number as 5551212, you should instead use *705551212. Okay?

Invoking the Host

After all the preliminaries are over, it's time for the main course.

Hopefully, you've arranged for someone to call your host system and put it through its paces. If none of your friends are sufficiently advanced for such an effort, turn the host mode on at home, then go to work and try calling in from there. Just make sure you've given yourself the power to turn the system off remotely, or no one will be able to call your home all day long without getting a screeching modem on the other end of the line. It could scare your mother.

It's now or never. Invoke the host mode using the command you've learned from the manual.

- ✔ If you use Procomm Plus for Windows, the host command is a script file. Just drop down the Script File list and then select host.

- ✔ If you use QmodemPro for DOS, the host command is Alt+F5. If you prefer the long way around, use Alt+N to get to the menu, and select Host and then Start.

If everything's on track, after a few moments you see some sort of indication on the screen that the system is waiting for a call, as in Figure 16-2.

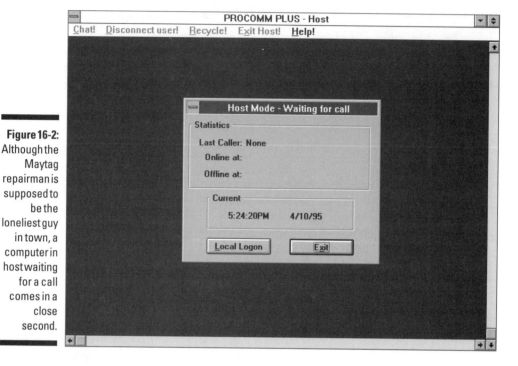

Figure 16-2:
Although the
Maytag
repairman is
supposed to
be the
loneliest guy
in town, a
computer in
host waiting
for a call
comes in a
close
second.

Now, hopefully, someone will call in.

Receiving Guests

When guests call, they are greeted with some kind of innocuous phrase like, "Welcome to the Host System." And then, just like on a regular BBS, they are asked for their name and password. Assuming they get that correct, they get a menu of options — as in Figure 16-3 or Figure 16-4 — and your host computer will work just like a BBS.

Once you or the guest are online in the host mode, you can carry out any of the commands in the menu. You can even write a message to someone else using the system, as in Figure 16-5.

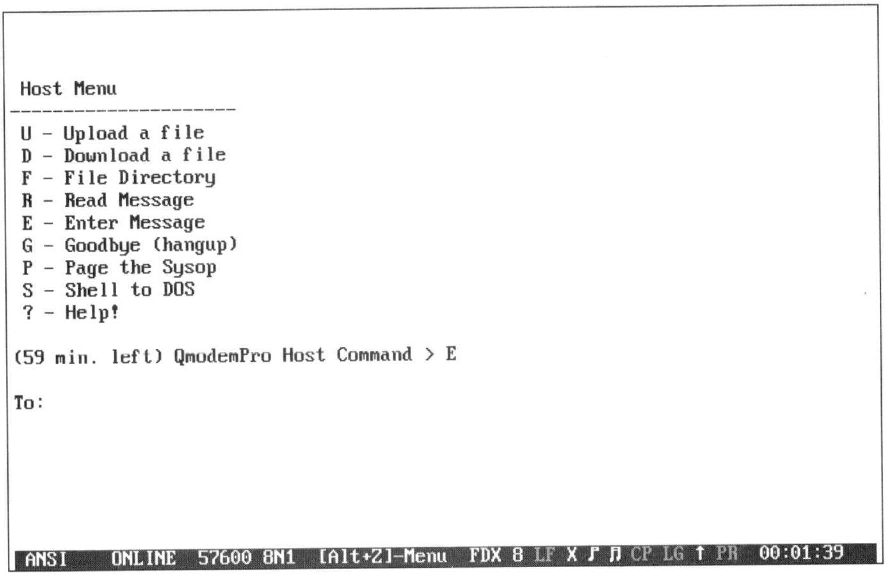

Figure 16-3:
A basic Host
Menu from
QmodemPro
for DOS
includes all-
time
classics
such as
Page the
Sysop. Fun
for the
whole
family.

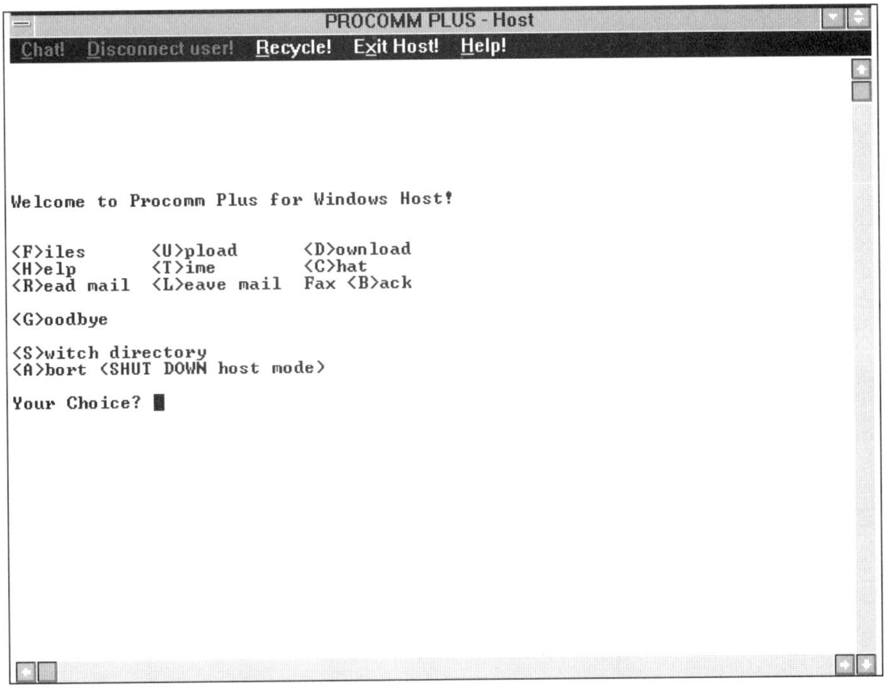

```
Host Menu
----------------------
U - Upload a file
D - Download a file
F - File Directory
R - Read Message
E - Enter Message
G - Goodbye (hangup)
P - Page the Sysop
S - Shell to DOS
? - Help!

(59 min. left) QmodemPro Host Command > E

To:
```

```
ANSI    ONLINE  57600 8N1  [Alt+Z]-Menu  FDX 8 LF X ♪ ♫ CP LG ↑ PR  00:01:39
```

Figure 16-4:
Procomm
Plus for
Windows
Host Menu
offers such
delicacies
as a Fax
Back option
and the
ability to
Shut Down
the Host
remotely.
Which is
kind of cold.

```
                        PROCOMM PLUS - Host
   Chat!  Disconnect user!  Recycle!  Exit Host!  Help!


Welcome to Procomm Plus for Windows Host!

<F>iles        <U>pload     <D>ownload
<H>elp         <T>ime       <C>hat
<R>ead mail    <L>eave mail Fax <B>ack

<G>oodbye

<S>witch directory
<A>bort <SHUT DOWN host mode>

Your Choice? █
```

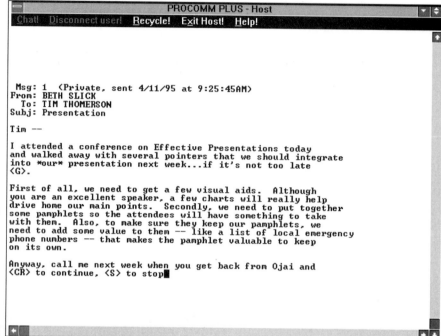

PROCOMM PLUS - Host

Chat! Disconnect user! Recycle! Exit Host! Help!

```
 Msg: 1 (Private, sent 4/11/95 at 9:25:45AM)
From: BETH SLICK
  To: TIM THOMERSON
Subj: Presentation

Tim --

I attended a conference on Effective Presentations today
and walked away with several pointers that we should integrate
into *our* presentation next week...if it's not too late
<G>.

First of all, we need to get a few visual aids.  Although
you are an excellent speaker, a few charts will really help
drive home our main points.  Secondly, we need to put together
some pamphlets so the attendees will have something to take
with them.  Also, to make sure they keep our pamphlets, we
need to add some value to them -- like a list of local emergency
phone numbers -- that makes the pamphlet valuable to keep
on its own.

Anyway, call me next week when you get back from Ojai and
<CR> to continue, <S> to stop█
```

Figure 16-5:
Leaving
E-Mail via a
host-mode
computer is
better than
voice mail.

Moving the Party

Host mode can be a lifesaver. Just remember, though, that host mode is to BBS software what Windows Notepad is to Word for Windows. In other words, don't try to make a chimpanzee do the job of King Kong.

If your goal in using host mode is to create a convenient way for you and someone else to send files back and forth, why not simply join a BBS that allows files to be attached to E-Mail — as described in Chapter 10. Or, taking that idea a step further, contact a local Sysop and strike up a deal to lease part of the BBS for your business. You can have a BBS-within-a-BBS for you and your associates.

If you find yourself straining against the inconvenience of a host-mode setup, and working with a local Sysop isn't feasible, then it's time to start thinking about starting your own BBS and becoming a Sysop. Or is it?

Chapter 17

Running Your Own BBS?

In This Chapter

▶ Ruling your own cyberspace realm

▶ Doing business electronically

▶ Reading, writing, and logging on

▶ Keeping yourself off the streets

▶ Abdicating the throne

▶ Cashing in — or costing out?

▶ Sharing, caring — and repressing your urge to kill

Most of us will never be able to sing like Pavarotti, draw Captain America like Jack Kirby, or play guitar like Jimi Hendrix. Those things take talent. The rest of us have to set our sights on more modest goals — say, absolute dominion over a small country.

In a very real sense, that's the power, and the responsibility, every Sysop assumes.

After you've logged onto a few boards, you'll probably notice that you relate to each one as a *place*, with its special landscape, its unique population, and its particular rules and customs. That's because every BBS is a kind of independent city-state, created in its Sysop's own image and governed according to the Sysop's own laws. In his little corner of the online universe, the Sysop is absolute monarch, supreme authority, and master of space and time.

Is it rational to think that you or I could wield such power? Would we even want to?

Put it this way: If all of human history offers any indication, absolute rule doesn't necessarily require talent; it just requires dedication and persistence. And power has its benevolent uses, some of which I am about to discuss.

Ruling Your Own Cyberspace Realm

You don't have to be a computer professional to run your own BBS. You don't even have to be a techie. When I set up my first board, I was just another cyber-klutz with a predicament on my hands.

My Problem

It was 1986 or so, and I was working for Sunbow Productions, a company that produces animated television series such as "G.I. Joe," "Transformers," and "My Little Pony," among others. I was employed as a story editor, not a telecommunications specialist; but I had begun to learn a little about computers and modems because we faced an unusual problem: Sunbow's main office was in New York, but most of the story editors (including me), the writers, and the film production facilities were located on, as they say, the Left Coast. Scripts written on Pacific time had to be read, critiqued, and returned to the story editors for revisions by personnel in an office three time zones away — and we were on a very tight production schedule.

Now remember, this was in the olden days, back before indoor plumbing and ubiquitous fax machines. Our options were limited. At first, we took the standard route and used the overnight delivery services such as Federal Express. That was fine, except that a writer might finish work at 3:00 a.m. (writers often work in their own personal time zones), collapse of exhaustion, and deliver the script to me late the next day, often *too* late to make the FedEx cutoff. We found ourselves still losing time in 24-hour blocks.

That led us to MCI Mail, which could receive a document by modem and deliver a hard copy to the addressee within two hours. That was better, much better — but the hard copy service was expensive, and I still had to get the script into the system no later than 1:00 p.m.; otherwise, the delivery would arrive at a New York office that had been deserted for the night.

The Solution

What we needed was a way for the writers to deliver their scripts to New York and Los Angeles *at the same time*, even if that time happened to be 3:00 a.m.

The solution, as you've probably guessed by now, was a BBS.

We named it after the villains' headquarters in the "G.I. Joe" series: Cobra Temple Alpha.

For modem-equipped writers, it was a dream come true. Even in the dead of night, they could upload their scripts to the board and stagger off to bed, secure in the knowledge that offices on both coasts could pick up their work first thing in the morning. Even our modemless writers rejoiced. I no longer had to yell and scream at them if they showed up at my door ten minutes too late for Federal Express. As long as they delivered their scripts on disk, I could post them on the board almost instantly. For the New York office, it meant they no longer had to spend the first three hours of their workday twiddling their thumbs and waiting for Los Angeles to wake up; they could pick up the scripts, as well as messages from the writers and story editors, at 9:00 a.m. *their* time.

The Sunbow BBS was the first in the animation industry. Since then, bulletin boards have become a fact of life in the biz. Even today, with fax machines readily accessible to every carbon-based life form on the planet, many production companies still favor BBSs because they can receive scripts and other documents in their original form, as word processor files, which they can load and edit on their own computers without retyping the stuff from scratch.

I was hooked

Sunbow eventually closed its Los Angeles office, but the BBS never quite disappeared. In the process of setting up and running the system, I got hooked on computer bulletin boards. Over the years, what was originally the Sunbow BBS has evolved from a private system for one company's writers into an open meeting place for writers who work in a variety of fields. It's known today as the Bingo Bango Bongo BBS, and its hard disk is spinning merrily away not six feet from where its absolute ruler, *moi*, is sitting. You can call it at (818) 842-2956. If you're a writer, or just enjoy schmoozing with writers, you'll be welcomed.

Doing Business Electronically

The Sunbow bulletin board solved a very particular problem for a company in a very specialized business, but it's far from the only way businesses and other organizations can use a BBS. For example:

> ✔ You head up a sales force that works mostly in the field. You could use a bulletin board to receive orders from anywhere in the country at any time of the day or night. Your file directories might contain up-to-the-minute specs, price schedules, and graphic images of every product your company offers.

✔ You run a business from your home. Would you like your clients or customers to be able to contact you at their convenience? If you're selling a product, wouldn't it be nifty if they could place credit card orders 24 hours a day — orders that you could acknowledge the very moment you receive them?

✔ You're working with a church or charitable organization. A BBS might be a great way to keep in touch with your volunteers, to disseminate information about your activities to the community at large, or to accept donations by credit card.

✔ Do you belong to a professional association, a union, or a guild? You could use a BBS to keep members abreast of developments in your field, publish minutes of your meetings, or distribute software of special interest to those in your occupation.

✔ What if you work in law enforcement? At city hall? In a state legislature? Wouldn't you like to make detailed information available to your community or constituents? Wouldn't you like to solicit feedback and suggestions from the people you serve and who depend on your services? And you — yeah, *you* — John or Jane Q. Citizen! Wouldn't you just *love* it if Mr. Mayor and Ms. County Supervisor made it easier for you to give 'em an earful?

✔ Oh, and speaking of ears, if you're in radio, you might want to follow the example of WTUE-FM in Dayton, Ohio. That station runs a BBS as an added service to its listeners, providing news about album releases, concert dates, rock-star gossip, and other items of interest. Incidentally, the service works both ways: Direct communication with the audience helps keep the station apprised of their listeners' ever-changing tastes with a specificity the *Billboard* charts could never provide. (Record stores, video stores, bookstores, boutique-style operations of all sorts — take note!)

Businesses, charities, and governments aren't the only organizations that can benefit from the use of a BBS. Bulletin boards are also very much at home in the halls of academe.

Reading, Writing, and Logging On

Are you a teacher? A principal? A high school newspaper editor? High schools and colleges are also natural settings for a BBS.

Some years back, I exchanged E-Mail messages with a high school teacher who was using a bulletin board to teach computer literacy and *conventional* literacy at the same time. His students could log onto the board to discuss school-related topics, upload their compositions, download homework assignments, and just chatter. Imagine — a place where passing notes was actually *encouraged* by the teacher!

It's not far-fetched, either, to suppose that students could use a BBS in conjunction with their school newspaper as an in-box for reporters' stories, an out-box for assignments, or even as the distribution point for an electronic edition.

What about extracurricular activities? Oh, sure, the schedule for club meetings, pep rallies, football games, and dances could be posted online, but that's only the beginning. Members of the French club could communicate *en français* in E-Mail messages. Members of the chess club could play online matches. Coaches could maintain an easily-accessible database of win-loss records for every team in the school's history.

At this point, I should stress that schools ought *not* to run a BBS on the same computer that they use to maintain student records and grades. If you don't believe us, scoot down to your local video store and rent a copy of *WarGames*. Yes, it's only a movie, but it illustrates at least one serious point: Any computer connected to a telephone line becomes, de facto, a tempting target for mischief-makers.

My own board participates in a mini-network that links three Los Angeles writers' boards with a film school in Edmonton, Alberta. Students who log onto the BBS in Edmonton have the rare opportunity to discuss and critique film and television with established professionals in the tinsel-and-glamour industry. (I don't know whether our mini-net has produced any Paddy Chayefskys yet, but I'm willing to bet that Edmonton will be graduating fewer starstruck wanna-bes and more hard-nosed realists than most other film schools.)

Keeping Yourself off the Streets

Allow me another confession here. A writer's existence is solitary and sedentary, and often his only companion is that intimidating blank sheet of paper — or, these days, a word processor screen that teems with mocking menus and taunting toolbars. I face many moments when I need to clear my head with some brief diversion. Leaving the house isn't an option; I know that I'll conveniently be too tired to work when I return. Reading a book is too involving; if I get caught up in a story, I won't put it down. Television is too passive. The telephone is altogether too interactive, and besides, I'd probably just be prattling away with some other writer who really ought to be working.

It's moments like these when I turn to the BBS. I can check my mail, browse some of the public forums, do a little Sysop housekeeping, see whether anyone's uploaded any interesting files, whatever. It keeps me from wandering too far from my work, lets me stay in touch with friends, and exercises a different part of my brain.

Frankly, this may be as good a reason as any for running a BBS.

Call running a BBS a hobby, a means to communicate with friends and colleagues, or a way to get out of *yourself* when you can't get out of the same four walls. Call it therapeutic. Call it *fun*. It's all those things.

But running a BBS is more, too. All of us lead busy lives. It's easy to lose touch with friends just because your schedule and their schedules never seem to mesh. Weirdly enough, in an era that's been termed postliterate, bulletin boards have contributed mightily to reviving the lost art of letter writing. The intimacy of personal correspondence has somehow survived the transition to E-Mail.

Maybe you're not quite the involuntary hermit I've become, but you've tired of model airplanes, or completed your baseball card collection, or you just can't work up the needed enthusiasm to finish sculpting that Neelix mask for the next Star Trek convention.

May the modem gods have mercy — you may be a candidate for Sysop-hood.

Or, not...

Abdicating the Throne

No doubt there are plenty of folks with plenty of good reasons to run a BBS. Unfortunately, a good reason isn't enough. Total power over a kingdom in cyberspace may sound enticing, but it's an awesome *responsibility*. And, as the saying goes, heavy hangs the head that wears the crown. Before you conclude it's your manifest destiny to yank Excalibur from that hunk of rock, it's time for a little reality check.

Cashing in — or costing out?

Although a BBS needn't cost an arm, a leg, and a mortgage on your firstborn to support, your available finances should factor into your decision. Setting up a BBS isn't cheap.

Advice to Aspiring Sysops

Sit down and think about it... _hard._ Ask yourself some questions. Can I afford to support even a small one-node board? Can I put up with a little extra stress? (Installing hardware can sometimes get on your nerves!) How long do I want to keep up this hobby? You don't want to open a BBS and then shut it down six months later. It will turn out to be a waste of your money and your time.

Ben Davis, Co-Sysop — ComputerSmart BBS (904) 272-8019

Hardware

You can't run your business and a BBS on the same computer. The board will need its own machine.

Bingo Bango Bongo runs on an ancient AST Premium 286 — actually, cannibalized components from _three_ of them — which has since been converted to a 386SX with an upgrade chip. The machine has only four megabytes of memory, a puny 80-megabyte hard disk that was original equipment on one of the three computers, and a primitive EGA-level graphics card. (What's an EGA card? Never mind. What matters is, they're probably not even manufactured anymore.) For now, I'm content with this system. My users, who number fewer than 200, are happy with it, too. By current standards, though, Bingo is a very, _very_ small BBS.

If you're willing to settle for ruling a sleepy, out-of-the-way cyberspace kingdom like mine, that retired computer gathering dust in the attic may be all the hardware you need. On the other hand, if you're going to run a BBS as a serious adjunct to your business, or if you dream of being the first kid on your block to compete head-to-head with CompuServe, you're going to want a great deal more horsepower.

How much more? Well, if Bingo is one extreme, consider the other:

The largest BBSs listed in _Boardwatch Magazine_'s Top 100 each represent investments by their Sysops in the tens, perhaps hundreds, of thousands of dollars. These systems run on multiple computers linked by local area networks and often support dozens of telephone lines for incoming calls — and _each line_ requires its own modem! (And you thought _you_ had problems getting _one_ measly modem to say "OK"!)

Most BBSs, of course, are neither as humble as Bingo nor as colossal as those Godzilla-sized boards. A typical BBS runs on a single computer and supports one to four phone lines. Even with the cost of a brand new machine, a new modem, BBS software, and the installation of a *dedicated* phone line (one used exclusively by the BBS), you can probably get a single-line board up and running for under $3,000.

That's a real bargain for a business with a problem like Sunbow's. I suspect we saved enough in lost time and overnight delivery charges to pay for the BBS in a month or two.

On the other hand, for the prospective hobbyist, it's $3,000 more than it costs *not* to start your own board — an alternative worth considering.

Software

Although most BBS software is priced very reasonably, you'll want to keep up with the latest version of your program. Some software publishers offer minor updates at no charge, but major new versions — the ones with all the new features you've just gotta have — come at a price.

Inevitably, you'll also want to purchase various accessories and utility programs to enhance and help manage the BBS. Most are shareware and are relatively inexpensive, but over time, even those ten- and twenty-dollar registrations begin to add up.

Hidden costs

There are also less obvious expenses associated with running a BBS. Last time I checked, phone service wasn't free. You have to pay at least a minimum charge for each line you install, even if it's never used for outgoing calls. In some areas of the country, the phone company requires bulletin boards to pay the higher phone rates that businesses pay, even if the board was never intended to turn a profit.

As time passes and technology marches relentlessly onward, every Sysop is tempted to upgrade the board's modems, add a CD-ROM to expand the file libraries, install a tape device for making automatic backups, and so on.

Finally, if you expect the cost of your BBS to be offset by all those user subscriptions that are bound to pour in, welcome to Fantasyland. Most of your callers will never subscribe. Even if you limit their time on the board as an inducement for them to cough up a few bucks, the vast majority will accept their deprivation with a shrug, use whatever time you do allow them, and then move on to the next board they don't support. Brutal, but true.

"The Time Tunnel"

Remember that TV series from the sixties about two guys plummeting help-lessly into a bottomless pit of time? It's a sensation that every Sysop knows well.

Perhaps even more costly than the hardware and software is the sheer number of *hours* a Sysop spends tending a BBS. If you think you can run a board in a few minutes of spare time each week, think again. Even a teensy-weensy system such as Bingo requires a half hour or so of care a day.

- ✔ New users log on and have to be upgraded.
- ✔ Someone discovers a file that's supposed to be available for download, but the system reports it missing from the hard disk.
- ✔ Mail from users has to be answered.

There are dozens of little housekeeping chores for every Sysop every day. For Sysops of the largest boards, the BBS can become a full-time job.

Denied its daily dose of TLC, the board starts to get sloppy. It may keep running for a while, especially if you've chosen a highly reliable BBS program, but entropy rapidly sets in. The board takes on the character of an attic or garage that hasn't been cleaned out for years. Users sense your lack of attention, and their own interest wanes. Eventually, they just stop calling.

Murphy's Law

You should be aware that Murphy probably had bulletin boards in mind when he formulated his famous law: Everything that *can* go wrong *will* go wrong, and at the worst possible moment.

The board's hard disk *will* crash when you can least afford the time or money to fix it. The newly-installed upgrade of that silly little blackjack game door *will* eat all the system files for no apparent reason. Your message base *will* get scrambled just because you ate trout for dinner. And if an asteroid hurtles out of the darkest reaches of interstellar space and slams into the earth, ground zero *will* be the BBS computer. Count on it.

And plan on spending countless happy hours — hours that *could* be spent with your significant other, or at the ballpark, or at the movies, or curled up with a John Grisham thriller, or blissfully asleep — establishing an intimate relation-ship with the innards of the machine.

If none of this daunts you and if your zeal to become a Sysop has only intensi-fied, you may actually be among the members of that lunatic fringe who qualify for the position.

Don't decide yet, though. Not until you hear the job description.

Sharing, caring—and repressing your urge to kill

You are lord and master of all you survey. You are all-powerful, all-knowing, all-wise.

You are Sysop.

And you get *no respect* — no respect at all!

The mildly depressing truth is, Sysops are the Rodney Dangerfields of royalty. Despite their dedication, despite their generosity, despite the truly impressive array of skills they have to develop, their work is mostly taken for granted. Job satisfaction usually consists of pride in their own accomplishment and, every so often, a brief thank-you note from a user.

That might be adequate if all a Sysop ever had to do was install a piece of software, turn on a modem, and keep them both running. But every Sysop, no matter how large or small the board, actually wears many hats and plays a multitude of roles, each of them absolutely essential to the success of a BBS.

✔ **One-person police force:** When a user logs on under half-a-dozen different aliases…when 14-year-old Timmy runs amok and tries to sneak a peek at the X-rated graphics files…when a *flame war* (an emotionally-charged flurry of inflammatory messages) breaks out in Conference 4…when a love-starved user leaves an indecent proposal in Mary Jo's E-Mail…when some inconsiderate lout lingers on the board, tying up the phone line, while he prowls the contents of every ZIP file on the system…who ya gonna call? Three guesses.

✔ **Mediator:** Self-expression and vigorous debate are part of the attraction of BBSing. Sometimes, however, debaters cross the line into invective and personal attack, and the Sysop has to step in — not merely to quell the riot, but to calm the passions of warring users and bring them back to the table in something resembling civilized discourse. *Every* Sysop, without exception, will confront this situation at least once. It requires the cool detachment of a shrink, the friendly ear of a bartender, and the restraint of a diplomat.

✔ **Caregiver:** It should come as no surprise that users think of the Sysop as the Human F1 Key. The larger the system, the more new users you'll have to contend with and the more time you'll spend explaining concepts you've already explained a few hundred times before.

✔ **Criminalist:** The penalties for violating software copyright laws can be extremely severe. A Sysop whose board carries illegal files — copies of commercial software such as WordPerfect or Windows 95, for example — may face the prospect of heavy fines, confiscation of the BBS hardware, and even a stretch in the pen. For that reason, every Sysop has to keep a microscopic eye on the board's file areas and ferret out any users who make unlawful uploads.

✔ **BBS software expert:** You may not know a Lotus 1-2-3 from a THX-1138, but you'd better resign yourself to learning your bulletin board software inside and out. Not only will you have to assist your users in operating it, you'll also need to know how to fix it when something goes wrong. (Yes, this means you'll have to read the manual. Probably more than once.)

✔ **Janitor:** This job just gets more glamorous by the minute, doesn't it? Even if you have a gigabyte hard drive in the BBS computer, you're going to run short on storage space eventually. Over time, every BBS accumulates multiple obsolete versions of uploaded software, five-year-old transcripts of Rush Limbaugh's meanest Clinton jokes, games that only run under DOS 2.0, and assorted other files that no one wants to download anymore. Somebody has to pick up the virtual mop and bucket and swab the place out. And baby, it's you. Sha-la-la-la-la-la-la.

One last thing to consider. If you're toying with the notion that you can set up a BBS and have someone else run the thing — forget it. I've set up boards for several other companies since the Sunbow days, and the pattern has always been the same. Even the folks who were most enthusiastic about using the system made _absolutely no effort_ to comprehend its inner workings. When I departed, the BBSs foundered, fell into disrepair, and ultimately ceased operation. No one else will care as much about your BBS as you do.

Okay, _now_ it's time to decide. If, having heard all this and taken it to heart, you still want to be a Sysop, you've probably caught the bug.

Read on, and I'll walk you through the installation process for Wildcat!, a best-selling BBS program. I'll also let you peek around the curtain to show you what a bulletin board looks like from the Sysop's point of view.

You "dropouts" are welcome to tag along too, by the way. You may appreciate your friendly neighborhood Sysop a little more when you discover what's going on behind the scenes of a BBS.

Advice to Aspiring Sysops: Part Deux

Plan carefully the focus of your bulletin board. Don't run one just for the sake of running one. Plan out the theme, what you're going to offer that others don't. Ask yourself, would you call your own board? Just as you would write a business plan when you start a business, write a bulletin board plan.

Peter Raymond, Sysop — The Ranch & Cattle Metro BBS (602) 943-1497

Become known and liked on other boards, so you will have a following when you start up. Answer all mail within 24 hours, and become active in your board's door games. Callers love to beat the Sysop.

Alyssa L. Baird, Sysop — LISA (702) 452-8309

The 5th Wave — By Rich Tennant

Chapter 18
Setting Up a Wildcat! BBS

. . . .

In This Chapter

▶ Planning your BBS

▶ Installing your BBS

▶ Making notes and MEMories

▶ Making wild(cat!)

. . . .

*F*irst I need to define the mission parameters.

What I do in this section is take you on a sight-seeing tour through the installation and setup of the essential features of a Wildcat! BBS. What I *don't* do is provide you with detailed, step-by-step instructions for setting up *every* feature, especially advanced features, or deal at all with the many add-on programs and Sysop utilities that are available for Wildcat!.

As you no doubt expect, I have my reasons for taking this approach and feel compelled to share them with you:

✔ You probably don't own a copy of Wildcat! yet, so advanced instructions won't be terribly useful to you at the moment.

✔ Wildcat! happens to be *my* favorite BBS program, but it may not be *yours*. You might select PCBoard, GAP, RBBS, or any one of a dozen other software packages. If you do, you'll need specific directions for *that* program, not Wildcat!. Because you and the manual will have to form an intimate bond sooner or later, you might as well start now.

✔ On the other hand, whether you choose Wildcat! or not, I want to give you a feel for what setting up a BBS is like. Wildcat!'s installation and configuration programs provide an excellent example. If you want even more information about setting up a BBS, check out IDG's *BBS SECRETS* by Ray Werner.

This concludes today's episode of "Convoluted Rationalizations."

Planning Your BBS

Before you so much as stick Disk 1 of the program into Drive A, you should have a plan for your BBS. What's the theme of your board? What are you going to offer that's different from other boards? What's unique about the way you're going to present it to your users? How is the board going to be organized?

The last thing the world needs is another BBS called Chock Full O' Neato Stuff, with conference titles such as Neato Word Processing Stuff, Neato Spreadsheet Stuff, Ultra-Neato Game Stuff — and file-area titles to match.

So assume for a moment that your passion is *movies* and that you want to run a board for others with like interests. You meditate transcendentally for a few hours at the shrine to Oscar you've constructed in your walk-in closet. The Muse strikes you! The name of your board will be The Me So Filmy BBS! (Anybody get the license number of that Muse?)

Organizing your board

Now that you have a name your users aren't likely to forget — whether they want to or not — it's time to think about the board's organization.

Keep in mind that the way you name the conference areas will, in effect, shape the discussion that takes place on your BBS. A conference called Films of the Italian Neorealists will probably elicit about three messages a year; whereas a conference called Classic Cinema is likely to attract a great deal of traffic, including the occasional message about Italian neorealism. Remember, too, that you want your conference names to be both interesting and clear. Why call a conference General Messages when you could dub it Lobby Chatter?

When you're finished, you might have a list that looks something like this:

1. Lobby Chatter
2. Classic Cinema
3. Coming Attractions
4. Picks & Pans
5. Videos & Laser Discs
6. Comments to the *Auteur*

Number 6 is your basic Comments to the Sysop conference, but you might as well keep the theme going.

Start small. With virtually any BBS software package, you can add new conferences as the need arises and delete the ones that aren't getting much traffic. After your board has been online for a few months, you'll know whether you need to consolidate some conferences or add more — or both.

Framing the file areas

Now it's time to think about file areas. Some things you should know before you start:

- ✔ File areas needn't correspond directly to the conferences.

- ✔ No matter what the theme of your board, it's always considerate to keep certain BBS-related programs, such as PKZip, on hand for your users.

- ✔ Uploads from users should probably be sent to a specific file area designated for that purpose. It'll be easier for you, as Sysop, to locate damaged files or unlawful uploads that way.

Because you're a considerate Sysop who wants to make life relatively easy on yourself, you now know what two of the file areas will be BBS utilities and New Uploads. The final list might turn out something like this:

1. BBS Utilities

2. Film-Related Software

3. Movie Graphics

4. News & Reviews

5. New Uploads

6. Prescan Mail Packets

Film-Related Software would include shareware film databases (yes, there are a couple), film-and-video cataloging programs, and so on. News & Reviews would be devoted to informational text files.

I've added that enigmatic Number 6 for technical reasons. I'll explain all about it when the time comes.

As you're working all this out, *write it down!* You'll need this information when you install your BBS.

Which is precisely what you're about to do. The moment of truth has arrived.

Feline taxonomy: The subspecies of Wildcat!

Mustang Software's Wildcat! BBS program is available in five different "subspecies." Wildcat! Single-Line, which currently retails at $129, supports only one BBS phone line. Wildcat! Multiline 10, priced at $249, and Multiline 48, priced at $499, handle up to ten and forty-eight lines, respectively. Wildcat! Multiline Platinum can accommodate up to *250 lines* and is priced at $799.

And then there's the lion king of the pack: The Wildcat! BBS Suite. This package includes the Multiline Platinum edition, an excellent Sysop utilities package (wcPRO), the Wildcat! programming language (wcCODE), and an Internet gateway (wcGATE), and retails for $999.

It's safe to say that most beginning Sysops would want to start with either the Single-Line or Multiline 10 edition. Most will also want wcPRO, which can be had for about $99 a la carte.

The prices quoted are subject to change, of course. (Isn't *everything* these days?)

I'm using the BBS Suite in this example, but don't let that concern you. The installation process for all five subspecies is virtually identical.

For further information about Wildcat! or Mustang Software's other products, which include the excellent QmodemPro for DOS and QmodemPro for Windows, call (805) 873-2500, or write to:

Mustang Software, Inc. P.O. Box 2264 Bakersfield, CA 93303

You can reach Mustang's own BBS at (805) 873-2400.

By the way, in case you were wondering: the exclamation point in "Wildcat!" *is* part of the name.

Installing Your BBS

Your Wildcat! package has arrived. You've demolished the shrink-wrap, opened the box, and removed the installation disks from their envelope. You're ready to embark on your great adventure. You sit down at the BBS computer — and realize you're staring at a DOS prompt. Wildcat!'s installation program *must* be run directly from DOS, and it's generally safer to run the setup program from DOS, as well. For most single-line systems, such as Me So Filmy, Wildcat! itself also runs directly from DOS. If you're already shuddering uncontrollably, stop here and read the section on "Remedial DOS" in Chapter 3. (I'll also seize this opportunity to insert a blatant plug for *DOS For Dummies,* 2nd Edition by Dan Gookin. It's the most reliable remedy known for symptoms of queasiness at the DOS prompt.)

If you're ready to continue, insert the Wildcat! disk labeled "Disk 1 Install" in your floppy drive.

Now you want to switch to the floppy drive that contains the Wildcat! disk. If you inserted the disk in Drive A, type **A:** and press Enter. (Type **B:** for Drive B, and so on.) The DOS prompt changes to A:\>, or something very much like it.

The name of the Wildcat! installation program is WINSTALL.EXE, so type **WINSTALL** and press Enter. The disk drive grinds for a few seconds, and then you see a screen that asks for the source drive.

Source drive isn't an ancient mystery like the source of the Nile or anything. WINSTALL just wants to confirm that you'll be installing the Wildcat! program from Drive A. If the drive letter in the box on the screen is the same as the drive letter you typed to get to the floppy drive, press Enter. If not, just type the correct letter and *then* press Enter to get the Wildcat! installation screen.

The Wildcat! installation screen

The Wildcat! installation screen is shown in Figure 18-1.

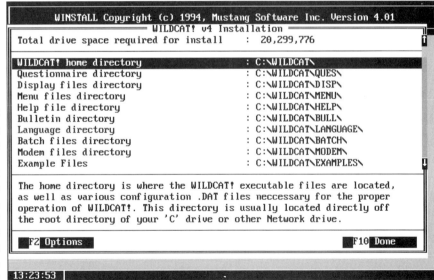

Figure 18-1:
The
Wildcat!
installation
screen. Now
WINSTALL
wants to
know where
to put which
files.

If this screen looks intimidating, just remember the *knee bone connected to the thigh bone* method of reading directory names. C:\WILDCAT means a directory called WILDCAT within the top (or *root*) directory of the hard disk. C:\WILDCAT\QUES means a directory called QUES within the directory called WILDCAT, which is within the top directory.

If you're still hesitant, press Esc and then Y to leave the WINSTALL program and take yet another look at the "Remedial DOS" section in Chapter 3. You can come back to WINSTALL and start the installation process again later.

What WINSTALL wants to know now is, "Where do you want me to put the various Wildcat! files on your disk?" The directory names are WINSTALL's own idea of where those files should go. In all probability, you won't come up with any better suggestions, so just let WINSTALL have its way. By the way, the directories in the list don't have to exist on your disk *before* you run WINSTALL. The program will create these directiories for you.

At this point, you may be asking yourself: What are all these directories *for?* Do I really *need* them? What's going to go *in* them?

Good and logical questions. Here's an explanantion of each one:

- **Wildcat! home directory**: This is where the main program files of your BBS will be stored.

- **Questionnaire directory**: Remember all the questions you answered when you first logged onto a BBS? (If you forgot, see Chapter 2.) That was a new-user questionnaire. BBS questionnaires can also be used to take product orders, BBS subscriptions, user polls, and so on. The files that contain those questionnaires will be stored here.

- **Display files directory**: When you log onto a board, you usually see some identifying screen welcoming you to the system. That's one type of display file, created by the Sysop. A typical BBS uses *several dozen* display files, some homemade, some packaged with the software. What they have in common is their overall purpose: to display on-screen information to the person calling the BBS.

- **Menu files directory**: Wildcat! can generate menus automatically, but they're a bit plain, so you can design your own menus to suit your taste and the theme of your board. Menu files are stored in this directory.

- **Help file directory**: Just what you'd expect. The online help files that Wildcat! displays to callers are kept in this directory. (Yes, technically these are display files, too, and you can customize them to your heart's content. Storing them separately just keeps the system more organized.)

- **Bulletin directory**: Bulletins are display files, too, of course, but they're also stored separately.

- **Language directory**: Wildcat!'s default language files go here. What's a default language, you ask? Well, for the BBS the default language is the language in which the various prompts and instructions are displayed. (Remember how other BBSs asked you to pick a language when you first logged on?) Unlike the messages you get from your word processor, though, Wildcat!'s prompts are stored in special files *separate* from the main programs. Wildcat! comes with a special utility program for editing prompt files, or creating additional ones. This program allows Sysops in non-English-speaking countries to translate the prompts for their users — and lets English-speaking Sysops offer a choice of languages. Additional language files would be stored in separate directories *within* the language directory: C:\WILDCAT\LANGUAGE\SANSKRIT, for example.

✔ **Batch files directory**: Okay, you're wondering what a batch file is, aren't you? I should have warned you that you'd have to get on a first-name basis with these little devils, too. In simplest terms, *batch files* are nothing more than text files containing a list of DOS commands. When you run a batch file, the computer carries out the DOS commands in the order listed. So a batch file is like a little program that you can create.

You already have at least one batch file, called AUTOEXEC.BAT, in the root directory of your computer. (All batch files end with the extension BAT.) AUTOEXEC is a special batch file that MS-DOS *exec*utes *auto*matically whenever you boot your computer. You can also create your own batch files—and run them exactly as if they were programs — by typing the name of the batch file and pressing Enter.

Other programs can also run batch files. Wildcat!, for example, uses them to operate doors, perform little chores between calls, and to run the board's *events* — scheduled maintenance, automated calls from the BBS to a network, and so on.

✔ **Modem files directory**: This directory is where Wildcat! stores its modem definition files. Don't let the terminology scare you. These files actually make your job a great deal easier. *Modem definition files* contain the sets of commands necessary to put Wildcat! on speaking terms with your modem. For most Sysops, that requires nothing more than picking the brand name of the modem from a list. Not bad, huh?

✔ **Example files**: These files aren't actually used for Wildcat!'s operation. They correspond to examples in the Wildcat! manual and you can use them for reference as you study the manual.

Look at Figure 18-1 again. See the scroll bar on the right side of the window? There are actually three more directories and types of files that aren't visible on this screen. These files are UUCP Communication Files (used for Internet mail), wcPRO FAX Support Files (used with a faxmodem to allow the BBS to fax bulletins and other text files to users), and Sample wcCODE Programs (utilities written in Wildcat!'s own programming language). Because all of these files are used in *very* advanced BBS operations, this is the first and last you'll hear about them in this book.

The WINSTALL window

When you understand what the various files and directories are for, you can choose what you want to install. Press F2 for Options. Up pops the window in Figure 18-2.

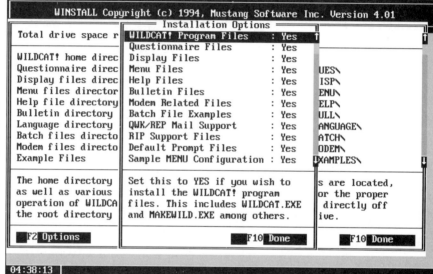

Figure 18-2:
So many
options, so
little time.
WINSTALL
wants to
know which
files you
want to
install.

Two new types of files appear on this list:

- **QWK/REP Mail Support files**: These are Wildcat!'s version of the Mail Doors you've encountered on other boards. They allow your callers to download mail in QWK packets, read and reply to their messages using an offline reader, and upload their replies in REP packets. You definitely want to install these files.

- **RIP Support Files**: *RIP* stands for *Remote Imaging Protocol*. As you might guess from the word *imaging*, these are display files, too, but a very special type. They're used to offer your callers the option of a *graphical interface* — sort of an ersatz Windows — that makes BBS commands selectable by mouse as well as the keyboard. Creating and editing RIP files is an advanced topic, way beyond the scope of the mission parameters, but it's something you'll want to investigate after your BBS has been online for a while.

You can move through the options in the pop-up window with up-arrow and down-arrow keys. If there were any options you *didn't* want to install, pressing Enter would change the *Yes* response in the right column to a *No*.

But be a sport about it, okay, and just install the whole enchilada. Press F10 for *Done*. That closes the pop-up window. Now press F10 again, and get this show on the road.

A series of screens tracks the progress of the installation, and WINSTALL prompts you whenever it needs the next disk.

When the installation is complete, WINSTALL pops up a window with Wildcat!'s README file, a text file containing information that became available after the manual went to press. You may not understand much of what's in this file, but look it over anyway. As you become more expert with your BBS, the information will be useful to you. You can scroll through it with the PgUp and PgDn keys. And, because you may want to refer to the README file later, press Alt+P to print the file.

Finally, press F10 to exit the WINSTALL program and return to the DOS prompt.

Congratulations! You've just installed your BBS!

At this point, though, it's only a standard installation of a prepackaged program. The next step begins its transformation from a no-name, no-personality system into the one-and-only Me So Filmy BBS.

Personality counts

Pick a theme for your BBS. Don't just say, "It's a general-interest board." Choose something meaningful. Give your callers a *reason* to call your board, then build on it. I have always been somewhat technically-minded myself, so I started my BBS as a "Technical Support Board," and I got dozens of callers with technical questions right off the bat. It gave my system a start without the normal begging for callers.

Tony Summy, Sysop—The Main Shop (714) 288-1320

Making Notes and MEMories

Before you begin your board's makeover, you need to know a few things.
Write down *all* of this information and keep it with your BBS plan.

- ✔ **The brand name, model, and top data speed of your modem**

  No major mysteries here. Just look at the box the modem came in. The
  brand name will be something like Hayes, Zoom, US Robotics, Intel, or
  Practical Peripherals. The model name will be something like Optima,
  Sportster, Turbo, or External Faxmodem. The modem's top speed will be
  a number like 28,800 (or 28.8), 14,400 (or 14.4), 9600, or 2400. If you have a
  faxmodem, make sure you find the modem's top *data* speed, not
  the fax speed.

- ✔ **Which serial port (also called COM port) your modem is connected to**

  If you're not sure, go to Appendix A and follow the instructions for
  "Hunting Down the Modem."

- ✔ **How much free memory your computer has available**

  If you're not sure, here's an easy way to find out:

  First, switch to the DOS directory of your hard disk. At the prompt, type
  CD \DOS and press Enter. (*CD* means *change directory*.) If the computer
  snarls `Invalid directory` at you, chances are that you've simply made a
  typo. Retype the command and press Enter again. When you've reached
  the DOS directory, the prompt will look something like this: `C:\DOS>`.

  Now, type **MEM** and press Enter. Some information, similar to that in
  Figure 18-3, scrolls onto the screen.

  You are only concerned about two lines on this screen. See the one that
  says `Extended (XMS)`? Jot down the number in the Free column on that
  line. In Figure 18-3, it's 5,738K. Scribble *XMS* after the number.

  Now check the line that says `Free Expanded (EMS)`. If that line doesn't
  appear at all on your screen, that's okay. It just means your computer's
  memory is configured a little differently. Jot down the number of K
  (kilobytes) on that line. In Figure 18-3, the number is 5,728K. Write *EMS*
  after this number.

Equipped with this information and your BBS plan, you're all set to give your
new board a personality transplant.

```
C:\DOS>mem

Memory Type       Total  =  Used  +  Free
-----------       -----     ----     ----
Conventional       640K      27K     613K
Upper              131K     101K      30K
Reserved           384K     384K       0K
Extended (XMS)*  15,229K   9,491K   5,738K
-----------       -----     ----     ----
Total memory     16,384K  10,003K   6,381K

Total under 1 MB   771K     128K     643K

Total Expanded (EMS)         15,680 (16,056,320 bytes)
Free Expanded (EMS)*         5,728K (5,865,472 bytes)

* EMM386 is using XMS memory to simulate EMS memory as needed.
  Free EMS memory may change as free XMS memory changes.

Largest executable program size    613K (627,632 bytes)
Largest free upper memory block     26K  (26,784 bytes)
MS-DOS is resident in the high memory area.

C:\DOS>
```

Figure 18-3:
The MEM command reveals the secrets of your computer's conventional, extended, and expanded memory. For repressed memory, consult a shrink.

Making Wild (cat!)

First, you have to switch to the Wildcat! home directory. At the DOS prompt, type **CD \WILDCAT** and press Enter. When you've reached the Wildcat! home directory, the DOS prompt will look something like this: `C:\WILDCAT>`.

The name of Wildcat!'s setup program is MAKEWILD.EXE. So type **MAKEWILD** and press Enter to start the program. After a moment, you see the Main Menu as pictured in Figure 18-4.

You move the highlight up and down the list of menu options with the up-arrow and down-arrow keys. To activate a menu option, you highlight it and press Enter.

Before you dive in, one quick note: Makewild isn't just for setting up Wildcat! the first time. Whenever you need to make changes to your BBS — adding or deleting conferences and file areas, installing a new modem, adding an additional phone line — Makewild is the program you'll use. Feel free to stroke the screen gently and tell the program how happy you are to make its acquaintance. (What's to lose — it works with plants, doesn't it?)

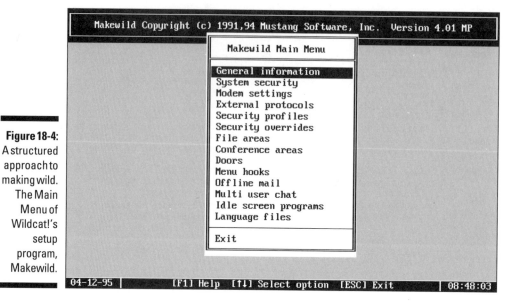

Figure 18-4:
A structured
approach to
making wild.
The Main
Menu of
Wildcat!'s
setup
program,
Makewild.

Ready? Start at the top. Highlight General information and press Enter.
Makewild's first General Information screen appears, lavishly depicted
in Figure 18-5.

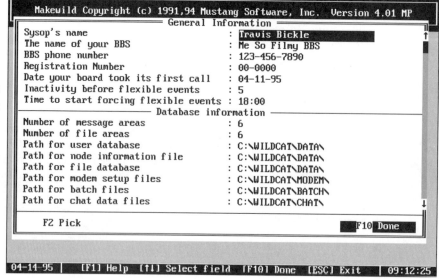

Figure 18-5:
Makewild's
first General
Information
screen.
Here's
where you
lay down
the blueprint
for your
BBS.

Creating your board's blueprint

Filling in Makewild's General Information section is akin to drawing blueprints for a building. As you progress, you'll be able to visualize the *shape* of the thing; you'll get a sense of its *size*; you'll be able to count the eaves and gables. What you *won't* see, not yet, is what color the house will be painted, what will be hanging over the mantelpiece, or whether the fixtures in the bathroom will be made of stainless steel or burnished brass. Without the blueprints, though, the foundation can't be laid and the frame can't be built.

Don't be put off by the amount of information Makewild needs. As you'll see, many of the default settings are just fine for your purposes, and even those you need to change usually require only a keystroke or two. The entire Wildcat! setup process really takes only about an hour. In fact, it takes longer to *explain* than it does to *do!*

Although the setup programs for other bulletin-board software may be organized somewhat differently, this *kind* of information is essential to setting up any BBS.

To move from one item to another in this section—and throughout Makewild—use the up-arrow and down-arrow keys. In those sections with multiple screens (by their scroll bars shall ye know them; note the right side of the General Information window), use the PgUp and PgDn keys to scroll from screen to screen.

The first General Information screen

When you first enter the General Information screen, you see that it doesn't quite match the one in Figure 18-5. Good old WINSTALL has inserted filler information in some of the items. The Sysop's name, for example, is listed as John Doe, and the name of your BBS reads Another Wildcat! BBS. You change these items simply by highlighting them and typing over whatever's there. (Actually, the filler answer disappears as soon as you press the first key to fill in new information.)

You should go through the items on this screen individually and fill them in. Keep your written BBS plan close at hand. You'll need it.

1. **Sysop's name**

   In this space, you type your real name, of course. Wildcat! uses this information in a number of interesting ways. For example, messages addressed merely to *Sysop* on the board, will be automatically routed to you, by name.

2. The name of your BBS

Here you type **Me So Filmy BBS** — or whatever you decide to call your board if you come to your senses.

3. BBS phone number

Type in the telephone number that users will call to reach your board.

4. Registration number

On a card that comes with your manual, find the registration number of your Wildcat! software. Type it here.

5. Date your board took its first call

Because you're setting up a brand new BBS, type today's date.

6. Inactivity before flexible events

And the inevitable question is, "Wha'?" No need for panic. Remember my discussion about Wildcat!'s running batch files to automate scheduled maintenance — and how those little chores were called *events*? That's what this is all about. Events can be scheduled in several different ways, one of which is *flexible*. If the board is *inactive* — that is, if no one calls — for a certain length of time, Wildcat! takes advantage of the lull to run a pending event. The default response is five minutes, and it's as good an answer as any.

7. Time to start forcing flexible events

If the board is extremely busy, a flexible event could be postponed *too* long, so that it never even runs on a given day. Wildcat! gets around that eventuality by *forcing* the execution of flexible events after a certain hour of the day. The default response is 18:00 — 6 p.m. — and again, it's as good a time as any.

8. Number of message areas

A *message area* and a *conference* are the same thing. In your BBS plan, you decided on six conferences, so that's the number you type in here.

9. Number of file areas

Consulting your BBS plan again, you see that you also decided on six of these. Press 6.

10. Path for user database

Path in this context is just another way of saying *directory*. And don't let the word *database* scare you. The *user database* is the file that Wildcat! uses to keep track of your callers, their security profiles (more about those shortly), their address and phone information, and the settings they chose for their calls to the BBS. By *settings* I mean color versus black-and-white, full-screen editor versus line editor, full menus versus expert menus, and so on. (You made all those choices for yourself when you called your first BBS, remember? The user database is where the BBS stores them.) The default response is C:\WILDCAT\DATA, and there's no reason to change it.

11. Path for node information file

For your purposes, a *node* is synonymous with a phone line into the BBS. If the BBS has one line, it has one node. If the board has six lines, it has six nodes. A *node information file* is something that Wildcat! creates to track each node and keep, the nodes from getting scrambled. Again, the default response is C:\WILDCAT\DATA, and again there's no reason to change it.

Even the single-line edition of Wildcat! actually provides for a *local node* (Node 0), which can be used by the Sysop, directly from the BBS computer, while a caller is on the board. To use Node 0, the BBS must be running in a DOS window under OS/2, Windows, or a text-based multitasking program called DESQview, which is published by Quarterdeck Office Systems.

12. Path for file database

If a *user* database keeps track of all the users on the board, guess what a *file* database is for. Correctamundo. The *file database* keeps track of the names, locations (on the disk), sizes, and so on of the files in the board's file areas. Same default response. Still no reason to change it.

13. Paths for modem setup files bath files

Wait! Didn't you already tell WINSTALL where to put the modem files? Yes, you did. At some point in the far-flung future, though, you may want to change that location — say, if you installed a second hard disk called Drive D and moved the whole BBS to that drive. So Makewild allows you to revise the information at any time. For now, leave these settings as they are.

14. Path for Chat data files

Wildcat! keeps records of user-to-user chats on multiline boards. Because Me So Filmy is a single-line board, this setting doesn't concern you.

Okay, take a deep breath. Relax. You've made it through the first General Information screen, and you've had to learn a great deal along the way. This might be an excellent opportunity to remember that all those Sysops whose boards you've been calling also had to learn all this stuff, and that you've been the beneficiary of their efforts. It's time for a moment of silent appreciation.

Second General Information screen

When you're done appreciating, press PgDn. You'll see the second of Makewild's General Information screens, pictured in Figure 18-6.

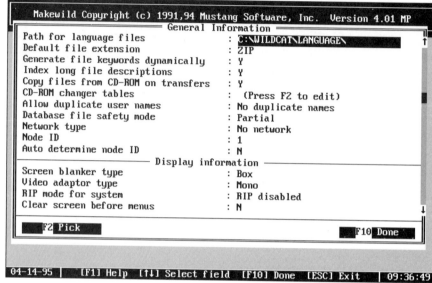

Figure 18-6:
Makewild's
second
General
Information
screen.
Number two
in a series of
three.
Collect 'em
all!

Once again, you must tackle each item in order.

1. Path for language files

Another setting from WINSTALL. Why mess?

2. Default file extension

This one is interesting. Most files on bulletin boards are, as you know, stored in the ZIP format. Wildcat! (and some other BBS programs) make it possible for callers to save some typing by employing a default file extension. To download the file TOPCOW12.ZIP, all the caller has to type at the download prompt is **TOPCOW12**. Wildcat! graciously fills in the .ZIP extension to complete the filename. Me So Filmy will be storing its files as ZIPs, so leave this setting alone.

3. Generate file keywords dynamically

Nah, you want your file keywords generated *lethargically*. But seriously, folks, Wildcat! can pluck words out of the descriptions that users enter for uploaded files and put them in the file database as *keywords* to be used when a caller is searching for files. The default response is Y, and it's a good one.

4. Index long file descriptions

To speed up file searches even more, Wildcat! can index every word of a long file description. This feature can be of great benefit to your callers, so you again accept the default Y.

5. Copy files from CD-ROM on transfers

I'm going to assume that Me So Filmy doesn't have a CD-ROM attached, so this item doesn't matter. Leave the setting as it is.

6. CD-ROM changer tables

Again, this setting doesn't apply to your little board. Moving right along...

7. Allow duplicate user names

Because Wildcat! assigns each user a separate *record number* — an individualized niche in the user database — it's possible to allow two or more callers to use identical names on the board. That sounds like a boon, but it has certain downsides, too. For now, trust me and don't change this setting. If and when you really set up your own Wildcat! board, consult the manual for details.

8. Database file safety mode

To see all three safety options, press F2. A little window pops up displaying the choices None, Partial, and Full. You move among these choices with the up-arrow and down-arrow keys. You make your selection by pressing Enter. (Just as you did on the Makewild Main Menu.) For a single-line board such as Me So Filmy, you can make do very nicely with None or Partial. Full is used almost exclusively for network installations.

9. Network type

No network. Zero. Zilch. Nada.

10. Node ID

That's actually *ID* as in *identity*, not *id* as in Freud. Because Me So Filmy is a one-line, one-node board, the default response is correct.

11. Auto determine node ID

This is an advanced setting that only applies to some multiline boards. Again, the default is correct.

12. Screen blanker type

Like Windows, Wildcat! has a built-in screen-saver. Unlike Windows, it won't display fish or flying toasters. Press F2 to see the screen-saver options: None, Box, and Blank out. If you choose None, the screen display always remains on. Box displays information about the last caller in a little rectangle that moves around an otherwise dark screen. Blank out turns off the BBS screen display completely. Whichever screen-saver method you choose, Wildcat! automatically reactivates the screen whenever a call is received.

13. Video adaptor type

Press F2 to open a pop-up window with the options Color, Mono, and Auto Detect, and the meaning of this setting becomes immediately clear. Keep in mind that this is the setting for *your* monitor, the one connected to the BBS computer. It has no effect on what your *callers* see. Even if the BBS computer has a monochrome monitor, callers can still ask for, and get, color. In most cases, Auto Detect is the best setting. Press Esc to un-pop the window without changing the setting.

14. RIP mode for system

Remember RIP, the BBS graphical interface? At your current level of expertise — which is to say, "none to speak of" — it's best to leave this setting as is, with RIP disabled. Just for fun, though, press F2 to look at the choices in the pop-up window. The third one — Forced RIP — sounds like a felony offense, doesn't it? Press Esc to close the pop-up window.

15. Clear screen before menus

This option refers to the way your callers will see menus displayed on the BBS. If you answer Y, the screen will be wiped clean before each menu is displayed. If you answer N, menus and other text will be displayed as a continuous scroll. There's no right or wrong setting; it's strictly a matter of personal taste.

And so the sun sets on the second of Makewild's General Information screens.

Another deep breath is in order.

Third and final General Information screen

After you've had your deep breath, press PgDn and move on to the third and final screen of this section, pictured in Figure 18-7.

1. Default split screen chat

No doubt you expected to breeze past this one, figuring it only applied to multiline systems. Well, hoo-hah! Not so. This item refers to user-and-*Sysop* chat, which is possible even on single-line systems. Wildcat! can split the screen in two, providing a separate window for the user's typing and Sysop's typing. In almost all cases, you'll want to set this option to Y. The alternative is for the user and the Sysop to type in the same window — and sometimes *on the same line*, if both are tickling the keys fast and furiously. It's a mess.

2. Make bulletin menu optional

Another question of personal taste. If you answer N, your callers will see the bulletin menu on every call. If you answer Y, Wildcat! will check to see if any bulletins have been updated since their last call and ask the caller if he wants to see the menu.

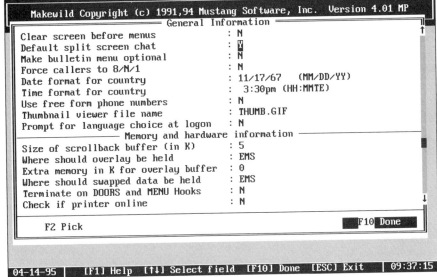

```
 Makewild Copyright (c) 1991,94 Mustang Software, Inc.  Version 4.01 MP
═══════════════════════ General Information ═══════════════════════
 Clear screen before menus              : N                          ↑
 Default split screen chat              : Y
 Make bulletin menu optional            : N
 Force callers to 8/N/1                 : N
 Date format for country                : 11/17/67   (MM/DD/YY)
 Time format for country                :  3:30pm (HH:MMTE)
 Use free form phone numbers            : N
 Thumbnail viewer file name             : THUMB.GIF
 Prompt for language choice at logon    : N
──────────────────── Memory and hardware information ────────────────────
 Size of scrollback buffer (in K)       : 5
 Where should overlay be held           : EMS
 Extra memory in K for overlay buffer   : 0
 Where should swapped data be held      : EMS
 Terminate on DOORS and MENU Hooks      : N
 Check if printer online                : N                          ↓

     F2 Pick                                          │F10│ Done

 04-14-95 │   [F1] Help  [↑↓] Select field  [F10] Done  [ESC] Exit  │ 09:37:15
```

Figure 18-7:
The third
and final
Makewild
General
Information
screen.
Decisions,
decisions.

3. Force callers to 8/N/1

In Chapter 23, one of the Top Ten Hints from Sysops is for callers to set up their communications software properly. Wildcat! can't actually change the *permanent* settings in a caller's communications program, but it *can* force the caller's program to correct itself while it's talking to your board. If most of your callers are DOS and Windows users, you might consider choosing Y. If you expect a significant number of Macintosh-equipped callers, though, leave it unchanged.

4. Date format for country

Six choices are available from an F2 pop-up window. Pick your favorite.

5. Time format for country

You can have Wildcat! display the time in either 12-hour or 24-hour (military time) format. And, for the 12-hour format, you can choose between two versions of the *a.m.* and *p.m.* suffixes. (One version displays only the *a* or *p*.) Again, it's up to you.

6. Use free form phone numbers

The default setting is N, meaning that callers have to enter their phone numbers in the standard format for the U.S. and Canada: ###-###-####. Translated, that's a three-digit area code, followed by a three-digit exchange, followed by a four-digit number. Wildcat! inserts the dashes for your callers as they type the numbers. If you expect a significant number of callers from outside North America, choose Y for free-form (unformatted) phone numbers. Otherwise, N is the more convenient setting.

7. Thumbnail viewer file name

Wildcat! allows callers to queue up a list of picture files they might want to download; then it uses a program called GIFSCOPE to assemble all those pictures into *one* GIF file that contains a thumbnail of each picture! Callers can download the thumbnail composite first and preview the pictures before downloading the actual—and much larger—files. Wildcat! and GIFSCOPE give the preview file whatever name you choose. You can stick with the default, THUMB.GIF, or give the file a name such as MESOFILM.GIF, which clearly identifies it as having come from your board.

8. Prompt for language choice at logon

This means *every* logon, not just the user's first call. In most cases, you'll want callers to make their language choice on their first call and change it, if necessary, from Wildcat!'s User Settings menu. Choose N.

9. Size of scrollback buffer (in K)

You've probably used the buffer in your own communications program to look back over BBS text that's already scrolled off the screen. A Wildcat! Sysop can do the same—review a caller's activity on the board—without disturbing what the caller is doing. Each screen of scrollback requires about 2K (kilobytes) of memory. The maximum setting for this option is 60K. Increasing this number, though, also increases the amount of memory Wildcat! needs to run. Be judicious.

10. Where should overlay be held

To conserve memory, Wildcat! loads and unloads parts of itself into and out of the computer's main memory as they're needed. Those parts of the program are contained in something called an *overlay file*. You don't really need to know a whole lot about this entry—only that the overlay file exists, and that, if the BBS computer has enough free memory, the whole thing can be loaded there.

What's the point? Well, grabbing stuff from memory is much faster than grabbing it from the disk. Wildcat!, and therefore your BBS, will run faster if you have enough free memory to hold the entire overlay file.

Press F2 to pop up a window of choices. Check the numbers you jotted down when you ran MEM. If the EMS number was larger than, say, 650K, choose EMS. If there was no EMS number, and the XMS number was larger than 650K, choose XMS. Otherwise, choose Disk.

11. Extra memory in K for overlay buffer

This is another option for speeding up the operation of the BBS. Instead of holding the entire overlay file in memory, Wildcat! reads *large chunks* of it into memory and keeps them there for as long as they're needed. This setting has no effect if you chose to hold the *entire* overlay in EMS or XMS memory. If you choose Disk for the previous option, set this one at about 40K.

12. **Where should swapped data be held**

    This setting relates mainly to the advanced topics of doors and menu hooks — and thus exceeds the mission parameters of this book. For now, leave the setting as is.

13. **Terminate on DOORS and MENU Hooks**

    Ditto.

14. **Check if printer online**

    While a caller is online, Wildcat! creates an *activity log* — a text file summarizing what each caller does on the BBS. Wildcat! can print out this file in real time, while the caller is on the board. If you have a spare printer to connect to the BBS computer, and you really enjoy the clickety-clack or zwissh-zwissh sound of a printer in the background twenty-four hours a day, choose Y. Otherwise, choose N.

Didn't realize that a Sysop had so many decisions to make — even before the BBS ever gets online—did you? Well, you knew the job was dangerous when you took it. And besides, you've just completed the General Information section. There's no turning back now.

Take *several* deep breaths. You've earned them, kiddo. But don't pat yourself on the back just yet. First, press F10 to *save* your new settings and return to the Makewild Main Menu.

You'll be delighted to know, by the way, that you're now almost a third of the way through the setup process. Most of the other Main Menu selections are much shorter than the General Information section.

If you want to take a break before continuing, highlight Exit on the Main Menu and press Enter. Makewild asks if you want it to check for the existence of any directory paths you entered. Press Y. If Makewild finds a path that doesn't exist yet, it will ask whether you want to create it. Press A for *All* and let Makewild do the work for you. When it's done, a window pops up that says `Operation Finished`. Press Enter to leave Makewild and return to the DOS prompt.

Battening down the hatches

If you left Makewild to take a break, be sure to switch back to the Wildcat! home directory. Type **CD \WILDCAT** and press Enter. Then, type **MAKEWILD** and press Enter to restart the program.

When the Main Menu appears, highlight System Security and press Enter. The list of items pictured in Figure 18-8 appears. This screen is where you set security options that apply to *everyone* who calls your board.

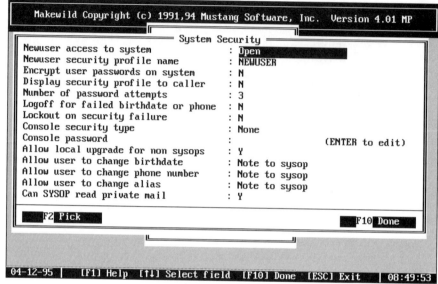

```
╔══════════════════════════════════════════════════════════════════╗
║ Makewild Copyright (c) 1991,94 Mustang Software, Inc.  Version 4.01 MP ║
╟──────────────────────────────────────────────────────────────────╢
║              ════════════ System Security ════════════            ║
║  Newuser access to system          : ▓Open▓                       ║
║  Newuser security profile name      : NEWUSER                     ║
║  Encrypt user passwords on system   : N                           ║
║  Display security profile to caller : N                           ║
║  Number of password attempts        : 3                           ║
║  Logoff for failed birthdate or phone : N                         ║
║  Lockout on security failure        : N                           ║
║  Console security type              : None                        ║
║  Console password                   :          (ENTER to edit)    ║
║  Allow local upgrade for non sysops : Y                           ║
║  Allow user to change birthdate     : Note to sysop               ║
║  Allow user to change phone number  : Note to sysop               ║
║  Allow user to change alias         : Note to sysop               ║
║  Can SYSOP read private mail        : Y                           ║
║ ▓F2▓ Pick                                        ▓F10▓ Done       ║
╚══════════════════════════════════════════════════════════════════╝
  04-12-95 │ [F1] Help  [↑↓] Select field  [F10] Done  [ESC] Exit │ 08:49:53
```

Figure 18-8:
Makewild's
System
Security
screen.
Wildcat!'s
answer to
The Club.

1. Newuser access to system

Press F2 to see a pop-up window with the four available options. *Open* means that anyone can log on as a new user. (You can still limit their access to any feature of the BBS, but that's handled elsewhere in Makewild. Stay tuned.) *Closed* means that *no one* can log on unless his or her name is already in the user database; callers who aren't in the database are automatically logged off. *Closed Comment* and *Closed Questionnaire* allow unrecognized callers to leave a comment to the Sysop or answer a questionnaire before Wildcat! bids them an automatic adieu. Me So Filmy is going to be a public board, so stick with Open, which is the default.

2. Newuser security profile name

I explain a little later what a security profile is. Here, you're just *naming* the profile for new callers. *Newuser* is as good a profile name as any, but it could just as easily be *Rutabaga* or anything else that strikes your fancy. Wildcat! automatically assigns this profile to any new user who logs onto the board.

3. Encrypt user passwords on system

This option adds an additional measure of security, but it could be *too* secure. Even the Sysop can't read user passwords once they've been encrypted, nor can the passwords be unencrypted. Leave this setting at N.

4. Display security profile to caller

If you set this option to Y, each caller can view the name of his security profile in Wildcat!'s User Settings menu. Because that profile name could be Rutabaga, and therefore not terribly meaningful to the caller, accept the default.

5. Number of password attempts

This option is a precaution to keep impostors from logging onto the board under other users' names. You can give your callers up to ten chances to type their password correctly when they log on. The default of three is usually sufficient, if the caller is who he or she claims to be.

6. Logoff for failed birthdate or phone

As a security measure, Wildcat! can store your callers' birthdate and phone number information and quiz them on it periodically. If they fail, and this option is set to Y, they'll be logged off the system automatically. The choice is yours.

7. Lockout on security failure

This option takes the previous option a couple of steps further. If a caller fails to enter the correct password, birthdate, or phone number, the caller is *locked out* of the system and will be logged off automatically on every subsequent call, until the Sysop decides otherwise. This option is only necessary on the most private of private boards.

8. Console security type

Console means the computer running the BBS. Pressing F2 reveals that the choices are None, Console Password, and No Console. *Console Password* requires any *local user*— that is, anyone logging onto the board directly from the BBS computer — to type in a password before issuing a *console command*, such as turning on the printer or turning off input from the keyboard. *No Console* locks out *all* console commands except local logons and *system shutdown* (exiting the BBS program and returning to DOS). Unless your board is located in an office or some other public area where a computerwise joker might decide to get playful, leave this option set to *None*.

9. Console password

If you set the previous option to Console Password, you have to tell Makewild what that password is going to be. This option doesn't apply to Me So Filmy.

10. Allow local upgrade for non sysops

Anyone who logs onto the board locally can use a console command to upgrade his or her security level. For now, leave this option set to Y, or you won't be able to upgrade *yourself* to Sysop status the first time you log on.

11. **Allow user to change birthdate**

The three choices are Yes, No, and Note to Sysop. *Yes* allows users to make changes whenever they want. *No* prevents them from making any changes. *Note to Sysop* asks the user to explain the reason for the change and sends the request as a message to the Sysop. Note to Sysop is probably the best option to guard against the occasional prankster who's managed to discover another user's password.

12. **Allow user to change phone number**

Same choices as the previous option. Because people tend to change phone numbers more often than birthdates, you might want to set this option to Yes, but Note to Sysop is fine, too.

13. **Allow user to change alias**

Aliases are discussed in Chapter 2, in the section called "Donning a Secret Disguise." If you want to let your users playact the parts of several different "handles," choose Yes. If you want to restrict them to one alias at a time, choose No or Note to Sysop.

14. **Can sysop read private mail**

The Sysop can always read his or her *own* private mail. This item asks, "Do you want to be able to read your *users'* private mail?" It's a touchy question. Your answer depends entirely on how much privacy you want to accord your users while they're on the board. The default setting is Y, but on my own BBS, I've set this option to N. Also, remember that this setting will apply to *anyone* on your board who has Sysop status.

When all these settings are exactly as you want them, press F10 to return to the Main Menu.

Introducing Wildcat! to your modem

Highlight Modem Settings on the Main Menu and press Enter. The first Modem Settings screen appears, as in Figure 18-9.

The first Modem Settings screen

Prior to panicking at all this techie-looking stuff, check the notes you made on the name and model of your modem. Then press F3. The pop-up window appears that lists the modem files that came with Wildcat!

If you find your modem in the list — and you probably will — highlight the name of the file and press Enter to load the file.

If not, choose either STD-1.MDM or STD-2.MDM or try leaving the settings at the default (Generic Hayes Compatible) as I did in Figure 18-9. In all likelihood, one of these sets of settings will work with your modem.

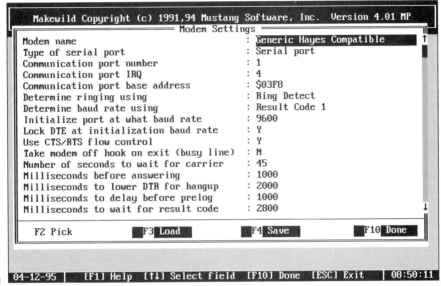

```
  Makewild Copyright (c) 1991,94 Mustang Software, Inc.   Version 4.01 MP
═══════════════════════════════ Modem Settings ═══════════════════════════════
 Modem name                            : Generic Hayes Compatible       ↑
 Type of serial port                   : Serial port
 Communication port number             : 1
 Communication port IRQ                : 4
 Communication port base address       : $03F8
 Determine ringing using               : Ring Detect
 Determine baud rate using             : Result Code 1
 Initialize port at what baud rate     : 9600
 Lock DTE at initialization baud rate  : Y
 Use CTS/RTS flow control              : Y
 Take modem off hook on exit (busy line) : N
 Number of seconds to wait for carrier : 45
 Milliseconds before answering         : 1000
 Milliseconds to lower DTR for hangup  : 2000
 Milliseconds to delay before prelog   : 1000
 Milliseconds to wait for result code  : 2800        ↓

   F2 Pick          F3 Load           F4 Save            F10 Done

 04-12-95 │  [F1] Help  [↑↓] Select field  [F10] Done  [ESC] Exit  │ 08:50:11
```

Figure 18-9:
Makewild's
first Modem
Settings
screen.
Don't
freak—this
may be
easier than
it looks.

If, in defiance of the odds, your modem isn't on the list, if neither of the STD modem files works for you, and if the generic settings don't work, either — you're still not up the creek. Call the Mustang Software BBS and do a quick check of the Wildcat! Modem Files area. Additional modem files are posted on the board very frequently, both by Mustang personnel and by other Sysops. If you find a file for your modem, you can download it from Mustang's board, copy it to your Wildcat! modem files directory, and load it directly into Makewild with the F3 key, just as if it had come with the software.

(If even *that* doesn't work, you have to call Mustang on the phone. The good news is, you'll find their tech-support people very helpful.)

When you've loaded your modem file, you notice that *most* of the other settings on the screen change to the appropriate values for that modem. A few exceptions exist, however: the settings for Communication port number, Communication port IRQ, and Communication port base address. Fortunately, unless your computer is *very* oddly configured, you only need to know the answer to the first of these. It's the COM port number you wrote down when you ran Microsoft Diagnostics (MSD).

If your modem isn't connected to COM1, use the down-arrow key to move to the Communication port number option. Type the number of the correct COM port. Now use the down-arrow key to move to the Communication port IRQ option. Like magic, the IRQ and base address settings change to match the new COM port number!

The second Modem Settings screen

Press F4 to save your new settings. Then press PgDn to move to the next screen, as shown in Figure 18-10.

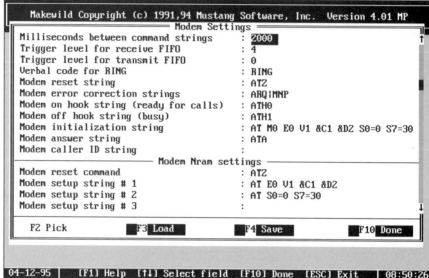

Figure 18-10: Makewild's second Modem Settings screen. You'll make few if any changes here. Fee FIFO fum.

```
    Makewild Copyright (c) 1991,94 Mustang Software, Inc.  Version 4.01 MP
                            ═══ Modem Settings ═══
   Milliseconds between command strings       : 2000
   Trigger level for receive FIFO             : 4
   Trigger level for transmit FIFO            : 0
   Verbal code for RING                       : RING
   Modem reset string                         : ATZ
   Modem error correction strings             : ARQ!MNP
   Modem on hook string (ready for calls)     : ATH0
   Modem off hook string (busy)               : ATH1
   Modem initialization string                : AT M0 E0 V1 &C1 &D2 S0=0 S7=30
   Modem answer string                        : ATA
   Modem caller ID string                     :
                        ─── Modem Nram settings ───
   Modem reset command                        : ATZ
   Modem setup string # 1                     : AT E0 V1 &C1 &D2
   Modem setup string # 2                     : AT S0=0 S7=30
   Modem setup string # 3                     :

    F2 Pick              F3 Load              F4 Save              F10 Done

  04-12-95 |    [F1] Help  [↑↓] Select field  [F10] Done  [ESC] Exit  |  08:50:26
```

FIFO? Nram? ARQ and MNP? Yeah, yeah — I know. They sound like characters from *Lord of the Rings*. For now, don't worry about what these settings mean. They also came from your modem file, and they're also probably correct. You should check the *Modem initialization string*—the series of commands that Wildcat! will send to your modem every time you start up the board and every time a caller logs off — to make sure that M0 is in there someplace. The M0 command turns off the modem's speaker, so that you won't hear a blast of noise every time a caller logs onto your board. If M0 already appears in the initialization string, you don't have to do anything. If not, use the down-arrow key to move to the Modem initialization string setting. Press the End key to move to the end of the command, type a space, type **M0** — that's a capital M and the number zero — and then press Enter. Press F4 to save your settings.

The third and fourth Modem Settings screens

It's very unlikely you'll have to change anything on these screens, but I want you to know they are there. They list baud rates and connect strings. For your edification, *baud rate* refers to the speed of a modem. A *connect string* is the sequence of letters and/or numbers that the modem sends to Wildcat! when it makes a connection with a caller's modem.

Press F10 to save your settings and return to the Main Menu.

Reaching outside Wildcat!

You're going to skip the next choice on Makewild's Main Menu, the somewhat advanced topic of External Protocols. For future reference, however, I thought you might like to know what they are.

An *external protocol* is a way of uploading and downloading files, which runs from another program, outside Wildcat!. Usually, the BBS "calls" that other program with a batch file.

Like most BBS software, Wildcat! has a wide variety of highly reliable built-in protocols.

If you develop an interest in external protocols, you can always come back to Makewild and add them to your board. Remember, Makewild is for updating and revising your Wildcat! BBS, not just installing it for the first time.

Profiling your users

Highlight Security Profiles on the Main Menu and press Enter to see the pop-up window illustrated in Figure 18-11.

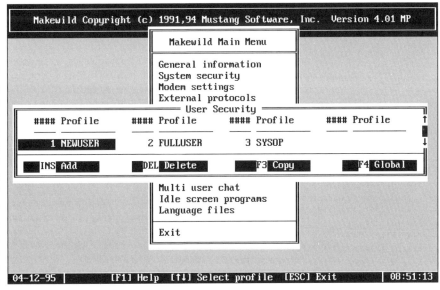

Figure 18-11: Makewild's User Security window. Me So Filmy has three levels of user access — NEWUSER, FULLUSER, and you, SYSOP.

The three security profiles shown — NEWUSER, FULLUSER, and SYSOP — are Makewild's defaults. For a fledgling BBS that's open to the public, these three are all you need. To edit the FULLUSER security profile, highlight it using the right-arrow or left-arrow keys and press Enter. Another window pops up, as shown in Figure 18-12.

Figure 18-12: Makewild's first Edit Security Profile window. I'm editing the profile called FULLUSER.

1. **The first line in this window is self-explanatory, but what in blazes is...**

2. **Expired profile name**

    Well, hypothetically, say that Me So Filmy was going to be a subscription board and that you had chosen to define an additional security profile called HALFUSER. You could set a date in the user database for each user's subscription to expire. When that date rolled around, the user would automatically be demoted from FULLUSER to HALFUSER.

    Okay, that sounds neat. But if the expiration date is set in the user database, why is there a line for an **Expire date** in this window? That's because you can also *plan* obsolescence into a user profile. Suppose, for example, that a small group of users was working on a project that required access to a special conference area. You'd define an additional user profile called, say, SPECIAL for those users. The project ends on a date-certain, and you want the users' additional access to end on that date also. You would enter that date here, and set the Expired profile name to NEWUSER or FULLUSER or whatever access level you wanted.

3. Security display file

You can create a special logon screen that is only displayed to users who match a certain security profile. This file could be called FULLUSER.BBS, for example.

4. Menu display set

Wildcat! generates its own menus, but the Sysop has the option to override them with more attractive, individualized menu display files. These Sysop-created menus are organized in sets of (usually) three: a main menu, a message menu, and a files menu; each set has its own identifying number. In my example, the menu set for the FULLUSER security profile would consist of files called MAIN5.BBS, MSG5.BBS, and FILE5.BBS — which is why I've entered the number 5 on this line.

5. Maximum logon time

The amount of time, in minutes, that a user can consume on the board *for each call.*

6. Daily time limit

The amount of time, in minutes, that a user can consume on the board *per day.* In this example, I've set both the daily limit and log-on limits to 60, but the two numbers don't have to be the same. You might want to allow each caller 90 minutes a day, but only 30 minutes per call, for example, so that one user can't hog the board for long periods of time while everyone else gets a busy signal.

7. Maximum up/down file ratio

Some Sysops like to discourage file hogs by requiring that the user make a certain number of uploads in exchange for a certain number of downloads. If you set this number to 10, for example, the user would be required to upload a file before he or she could download his or her 11th file from the board.

8. Maximum up/down K ratio

Same principle, different measurement. Instead of the number of files, you can require that the user upload a file for however many kilobytes, up to 255, of your stuff he or she has snagged.

9. Download warning action

Pressing F2 reveals three options — Nothing, Warning, and Disable. If you choose Nothing, users are able to continue downloads over their limits. Choose Warning, and the user sees a display file that lets him know he's pushing the envelope. If you choose Disable, Wildcat! prevents the user from downloading over the limit you've specified.

10. Maximum daily download files

This setting limits user downloads by the number of files per day, regardless of the file sizes, rather than by time or upload ratio. Zero allows an unlimited number of files. What can I say — you're a very benevolent Sysop.

11. Upload compensation

Some Sysops grant their users additional time on the board as an added reward for uploading. If you set this option to 2, the user would be granted two minutes on the board for every one spent uploading.

12. Allow upload overwrites

If this option is set to Y, users can upload new files with names identical to files they've uploaded earlier, replacing the earlier file. This setting does *not* allow users to overwrite *other* users' uploads, only their own.

13. Allow uploader to modify file info

This option allows callers to edit the descriptions and freshen the date and size information of files they uploaded. Again, it does *not* permit callers to alter information about *other* users' uploads.

14. Duplicate upload action

Press F2 to see the three options. *No duplicate files* rejects an upload if the file's name already exists in the file database. *Warn of duplicate files* advises the caller that the filename already exists but allows the caller to upload the file under a different name. *Ignore duplicate files* allows the caller to rename the upload *or* overwrite the original file, providing the caller uploaded the original file and that Allow upload overwrites has been set to Y.

To see the rest of the settings on this screen, press PgDn. You see the additional options illustrated in Figure 18-13.

15. Allow fast login

If this option is set to Y, Wildcat! allows users to skip your board's opening screens and go directly to the mail door (by typing an exclamation point before their first name) or to the Main Menu (by typing an asterisk before their first name).

16. Verify birthday after # calls

Remember how I told you that Wildcat! could quiz your users on their birthdates and phone numbers for added security? Here's where you tell the program how often you want to conduct that inquisition. If you set this option to 30, for example, Wildcat! asks the caller to type in his birthdate on every 30th call.

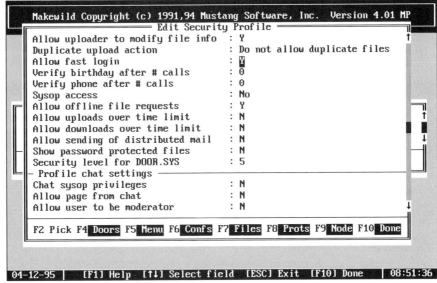

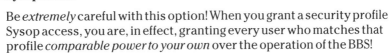

Figure 18-13:
Makewild's
second Edit
Security
Profile
screen.

17. Verify phone after # calls

Same as above, but this option asks the user for his or her phone number.

18. Sysop access

Be *extremely* careful with this option! When you grant a security profile Sysop access, you are, in effect, granting every user who matches that profile *comparable power to your own* over the operation of the BBS!

Press F2 to see the four options. *No* means *no,* and for most security profiles, this is the recommended setting. *Yes* gives users access to the Sysop menu — and, potentially, other users' private mail — but does not allow them to upgrade themselves to Master Sysop status. *Master* gives users access to virtually every aspect of the BBS. The fourth option, *Net Status,* is only used for other BBSs that may call yours to exchange mail. (Advanced topic. Exceeds mission parameters. That is all.)

19. Allow offline file requests

Wildcat! allows the Sysop to list a file in the file database without its being present on the hard disk or on a CD-ROM. This action allows the Sysop to store less-popular files on backup tapes or floppy disks, leaving room on the hard disk for more frequently downloaded files. If this option is set to Y, and a user tries to download a file listed as *offline,* Wildcat! automatically sends a message to the Sysop requesting that the file be put back online for the user.

20. Allow uploads over time limit

If this option is set to N, Wildcat! logs a caller off, even if the caller's upload hasn't been completed. This is a judgment call. If you have events that *must* run at a particular time, there may be good reason to leave it as is. If not, and you're feeling magnanimous, change the setting to Y.

21. Allow downloads over time limit

The same option as the preceding one, but it applies to downloads.

22. Allow sending of distributed mail

Wildcat! can allow a caller to send a message to a group of other callers all at once. Leave this set to N until you're very familiar with Wildcat!'s operations.

23. Show password protected files

Yep, files can have passwords, too. They can be assigned by the Sysop or by the caller who uploads the file. If this option is set to N, Wildcat! will not display any password-protected files when callers who match the FULLUSER profile list a file area or conduct a file search. If the option is set to Y, the names and descriptions of password-protected files will be visible. The user would still need to *know* the password, however, to download the file or view it online.

24. Security level for DOOR.SYS

Advanced topic. Exceeds mission parameters. For now, just set it at the number corresponding to the profile's menu set; in this case 5.

25. Profile chat settings

These settings only apply to multiline boards, which Me So Filmy isn't.

So — are you finished editing this security profile? Well, no. You're not. See those F-key buttons at the bottom of the screen in Figure 18-13? Each of them contains yet *more* options to further define each security profile.

- ✔ I'll skip the F4 (Doors) button, citing my usual lame excuse.

- ✔ F8 (Prots) sets security profile access to the various file transfer protocols. Makewild's default is to make *all* protocols available to the user, and there's no good reason to change it.

- ✔ F9 (Node) controls the security profile's access to the nodes of a multiline board. It doesn't apply to Me So Filmy.

Take a quick look, though, at the remaining buttons.

- ✔ F5 (Menu) has nothing to do with the Makewild menu. It controls the security profile's access to the commands on the BBS menu. Press F5. The window in Figure 18-14 pops up.

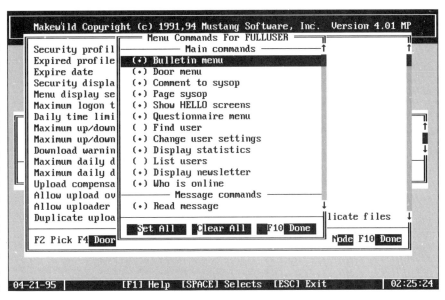

Figure 18-14:
Makewild
lets you
determine
which BBS
menu
commands
will be
available to
which
users,
based on
their
security
profile.

You move through the menu choices with the up-arrow and down-arrow keys. To toggle a menu section on or off, you press the spacebar. I won't go through each and every menu choice. I wanted to show you, though, just how much control a Sysop can exercise over what a user can or can't do on the BBS.

Press F10 (Done) to return to the Edit Security Profile screen.

✔ Press F6 (Confs) to see the pop-up window shown in Figure 18-15.

This window controls the conference access for each security profile. You move through the list of conferences with the arrow keys. You set the security profile's options for each conference by pressing R for Read, W for Write, and J for Join. You can set all three options by pressing S for Set All, or clear all three options by pressing C.

Now, what exactly does all this signify? It's simple, actually. If the R option is set, any user who's been assigned the FULLUSER profile can read the messages in that conference. If the W option is set, the user can write messages in that conference. If the J option is set, the user can join the conference. You can set any combination of R, W, and J for each conference. If *none* of the three is set for a given conference, that conference will be *completely invisible* to the user.

Press F10 to return to the Edit Security Profile screen.

Figure 18-15:
Makewild
also lets the
Sysop
choose
which
conferences
a user can
enter.

✔ Press F7 files to see the File Area Access pop-up window that appears in Figure 18-16.

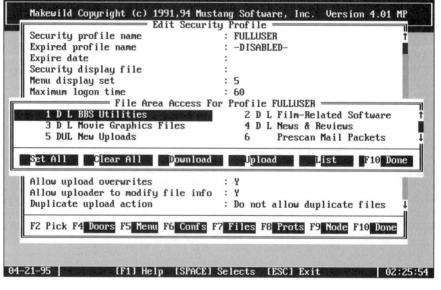

Figure 18-16:
Makewild
isn't finished
yet! The
Sysop can
also control
which file
areas are
available to
each user
profile.

This window works exactly the same way as the Conference Access window. Only the options and the letters that invoke them are different. Instead of R, W, and J, you have D, U, and L.

If you want users assigned the FULLUSER profile to be able to download from a particular file area, highlight that file area and then press *D*. If you want them to be able to upload to that area, press *U*. If you want them to be able to list the files in that area, press *L*.

Again, any combination of the D, U, and L options can be set for each file area. You'll notice in Figure 18-16, for example, that I've only allowed uploads to the New Uploads file area.

When you've finished, press F10 to save your settings and return to the Edit Security Profile screen. Press F10 again to get back to the User Security window (refer to Figure 18-11). When you've finished setting the options for all three security profiles, press F10 one more time to return to Makewild's Main Menu.

Invoking manual override

The Security Overrides selection on the Makewild Main Menu allows you to further modify your users' access to the BBS by creating *secondary profiles* which can be assigned to individual users as you see fit. These secondary profiles allow the assigned users additional access to BBS features. You can't use secondary profiles to deny a user access to privileges you've already granted in the main security profile. This is a somewhat advanced topic, so my discussion of it begins and ends here.

Fiddling with file areas

Highlight the File Areas selection on the Main Menu and press Enter. You are greeted by a list of your board's file areas (or some default names that Makewild has entered for you). To select a file area for editing, highlight the area by moving the arrow keys, and then press Enter. The BBS Utilities file area serves as an example.

Lo! Presto! Thou dost see the screen which appeareth in Figureth 18-17!

(Okay, I admit it. There are only so many ways to call your attention to a figure, and this one was a stretch. When I cross the line between the pleasantly absurd and the outright annoying, I trust you'll let me know.)

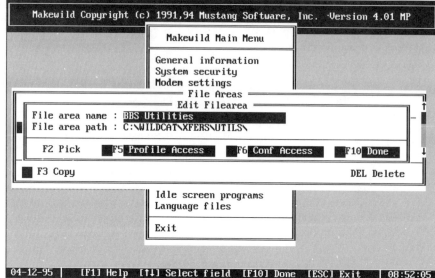

Figure 18-17:
Makewild's
Edit Filearea
window. No,
I don't know
why
"Filearea"
suddenly
became one
word. Blame
it on the
blistering
desert sun
over
Bakersfield.

The File area name option is highlighted by default. To change the name, simply type **BBS Utilities** over the placeholder inserted by Makewild. Press Tab to move to the File area path option. You want each path name to be one that you would recognize immediately from, say, the Windows File Manager or XTree. In this particular case, C:\WILDCAT\XFERS\UTILS — Makewild's placeholder — will do just spiffily. (If you wanted to change the path name, you would type over Makewild's suggestion.)

So now Makewild knows what you want to call the file area, and Wildcat! knows where to look for the files listed there. But you're not finished yet.

Profile Access window

See the buttons across the bottom of the window? Press F5 for Profile Access to see the pop-up window in Figure 18-22.

Look familiar? It should. It's essentially the obverse of the window in Figure 18-16. In that one, you determined each security profile's access to each file area. In this one, you're determining each file area's access to each security profile. This is a roundabout way of saying that the two windows do exactly the same thing but from different points of view.

Any settings you change in the File Area Access window of the Security Profile section will be reflected in this window and vice-versa — and the two windows work exactly the same way.

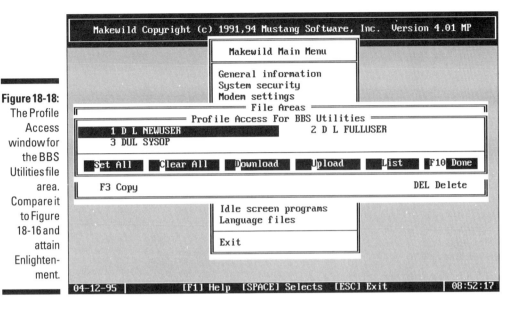

Makewild Copyright (c) 1991,94 Mustang Software, Inc.   Version 4.01 MP

Makewild Main Menu

General information
System security
Modem settings

File Areas
Profile Access For BBS Utilities

1 D L NEWUSER   2 D L FULLUSER
3 DUL SYSOP

Set All   Clear All   Download   Upload   List   F10 Done

F3 Copy   DEL Delete

Idle screen programs
Language files

Exit

04-12-95 | [F1] Help [SPACE] Selects [ESC] Exit   08:52:17

Figure 18-18:
The Profile
Access
window for
the BBS
Utilities file
area.
Compare it
to Figure
18-16 and
attain
Enlighten-
ment.

Why the duplication? Convenience, mainly. Say you add a new file area to the board. Off the top of your head, it might not occur to you that the Security Profile settings would have to change in order to let your users get at these new files. With the Profile Access window, you have all of your security profiles available, so you can make any relevant changes on the spot.

Because you're still happy with your settings for this file area, press F10 to save them and return to the Edit Filearea window.

Conference Area Access window

Can you guess what the F6 (Conf Access) button does? Try it. Press F6. You get the pop-up window shown in Figure 18-19.

Your callers' access to file areas can also be limited by which conference area they've currently joined. In this example, I've made the BBS Utilities file area available from every conference on the board. In most instances, with most file areas, that's what you'll do, too. But occasionally, very good reasons exist to enforce a stricter level of security on *some* file areas.

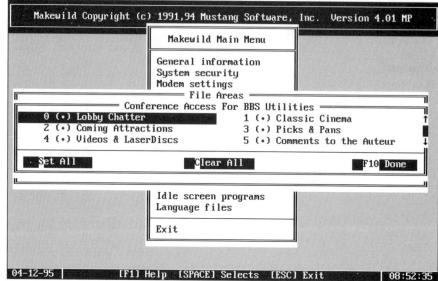

Figure 18-19:
The
Conference
Area
Access
window for
the BBS
Utilities
directory.
As Sysop,
it's your
decision
who can get
thence from
whence.

Remember the discussion of that hypothetical group of users working on a limited-time project? You could create a special conference and file area specifically for their use; from this window, you could make sure that their files could be accessed *only* from their message area. In effect, you'd be setting up a roadblock to those files from every other conference. (You can easily imagine how useful this capability would be in a business situation, too. Sales data, for example, could be made available to executives and salespeople from a *Personnel Only* conference and file area, although those areas would remain completely invisible to customers who call the board.)

To select a conference area to change, use the arrow keys to highlight it. Then press the spacebar to toggle the setting on and off. The little dot in the parentheses will blink out if access from a particular conference is turned off.

You're happy with these settings, though, so press F10 to return to the Edit Filearea window. Then press F10 again to return to the list of file areas.

Two buttons that I've yet to discuss appear in the Edit Filearea window (refer to Figure 18-17). Pressing F3 allows you to *copy* your settings from one file area to another file area or to several other file areas. Pressing Delete lets you wipe out a file area from the board's configuration. (Makewild warns you first, of course, so that you don't delete a file area accidentally.)

To return to the Makewild Main Menu press — uh. Okay, so no software is perfect. Mustang forgot the *Done* button on this screen. Fortunately, you can draw on your rapidly-growing store of experience and press F10 to get back to the Makewild Main Menu.

Cranking up your conferences

Highlight the Conference areas selection on the Main Menu and press Enter. You see a list of conference areas. The first time you call up this list, you see some placeholder conference names inserted by Makewild. As with the file areas, you change the conference names to match your BBS plan. Use Conference 0 (Lobby Chatter) as an example. Highlight the conference name using the arrow keys and press enter. You see the Editing Conference screen that appears in Figure 18-20.

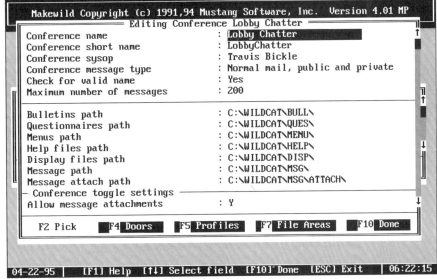

Figure 18-20:
Makewild's
first Editing
Conference
screen.
Here's
where you
shape the
discussion.

```
 Makewild Copyright (c) 1991,94 Mustang Software, Inc.  Version 4.01 MP
═══════════════════ Editing Conference Lobby Chatter ═══════════════════
  Conference name                 : Lobby Chatter
  Conference short name           : LobbyChatter
  Conference sysop                : Travis Bickle
  Conference message type         : Normal mail, public and private
  Check for valid name            : Yes
  Maximum number of messages      : 200

  Bulletins path                  : C:\WILDCAT\BULL\
  Questionnaires path             : C:\WILDCAT\QUES\
  Menus path                      : C:\WILDCAT\MENU\
  Help files path                 : C:\WILDCAT\HELP\
  Display files path              : C:\WILDCAT\DISP\
  Message path                    : C:\WILDCAT\MSG\
  Message attach path             : C:\WILDCAT\MSG\ATTACH\
 ─ Conference toggle settings ─────────────────────────────────────────
  Allow message attachments       : Y

    F2 Pick       F4 Doors    F5 Profiles    F7 File Areas    F10 Done

 04-22-95  │  [F1] Help  [↑↓] Select field  [F10] Done  [ESC] Exit  │  06:22:15
```

✔ **Conference name option**: This option is highlighted by default. I've typed *Lobby Chatter* over Makewild's placeholder name.

✔ **Conference short name**: When you move to the next option, Conference short name, Makewild changes it *automatically* to conform to the full conference name. (The short name, by the way, is used by Wildcat!'s mail door.)

✔ **Conference sysop**: Each Wildcat! conference can have its own Sysop. Messages addressed to "Sysop" in that conference are automatically routed to the *conference Sysop* rather than the board's overall Sysop. Enter your name here if you want users to be able to send Sysop comments to you. If you'd rather not allow messages addressed to Sysop in this conference, leave this option blank.

✔ **Conference message type**: Press F2 to see the list of six options: Normal msgs, public and private; Normal msgs, public only; Normal msgs, private only; Fido Netmail msgs, private only; Internet Email, private only; Usenet Newsgroup, public to ALL. The three Normal options are self-explanatory, and one of them will almost always be the right choice. The Fido, Internet, and Usenet options are only used for specialized types of networked mail and don't affect Me So Filmy in this, its budding stage.

✔ **Check for valid name**: Press F2 to see the three options: Yes, No, and Prompt. If set to Yes, this option prevents callers from leaving messages to names that don't exist in the user database. If set to No, callers can leave messages to any name at all. If set to Prompt, Wildcat! will help the caller search for a similar name in the user database but will allow messages to be addressed to names not listed there. Because a message addressed to a misspelled user name — especially a private message — would never reach the addressee anyway, this option should be set to Yes for all local conferences. (That is, conferences that don't exchange mail with other BBS systems.)

✔ **Maximum number of messages**: This option is exactly what it seems to be. How many messages do you want Wildcat! to store in the conference at any one time? The default of 200 is a reasonable number for all but the most heavily trafficked conferences. When the 201st message is entered, the first message in the conference is automatically deleted to make room for number 201.

✔ **Various paths**: Each conference can also have its own path for conference-specific bulletins, questionnaires, menus, help files, display files, and its actual message files. These are *extremely* useful options for conferences that are not open to the public, and are even useful for some special-interest conferences that are open to the public. Lobby Chatter, though, is the wide-open public forum of Me So Filmy, and you want it to use the same files as the rest of the board, so leave these settings alone.

✔ **Message attach path**: Wildcat! allows callers to attach a file to a message. Attached files are downloaded with a command from the Read Message menu in Wildcat! or through the mail door as part of the caller's QWK packet. This setting specifies where those attached files should be stored. The default response, C:\WILDCAT\MSG\ATTACH is just fine.

✔ **Allow message attachments**: The only time you should set this option to N is for conferences that share messages with other BBSs.

Press PgDn to see the rest of the Editing Conference options, illustrated in Figure 18-21.

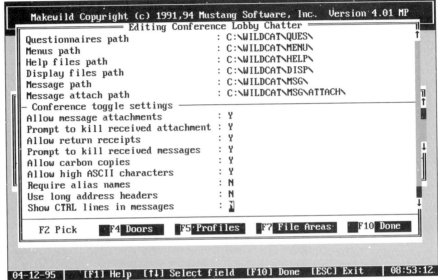

```
 Makewild Copyright (c) 1991,94 Mustang Software, Inc.  Version 4.01 MP
════════════════════ Editing Conference Lobby Chatter ═══════════════════
 Questionnaires path              : C:\WILDCAT\QUES\                      ↑
 Menus path                       : C:\WILDCAT\MENU\
 Help files path                  : C:\WILDCAT\HELP\
 Display files path               : C:\WILDCAT\DISP\
 Message path                     : C:\WILDCAT\MSG\
 Message attach path              : C:\WILDCAT\MSG\ATTACH\               ↑
 ─ Conference toggle settings ─
 Allow message attachments        : Y
 Prompt to kill received attachment : Y
 Allow return receipts            : Y
 Prompt to kill received messages : Y                                    ↓
 Allow carbon copies              : Y
 Allow high ASCII characters      : Y
 Require alias names              : N
 Use long address headers         : N
 Show CTRL lines in messages      : N                                    ↓

 F2 Pick    ▐F4▌ Doors    ▐F5▌Profiles   ▐F7▌ File Areas   ▐F10▌ Done
═══════════════════════════════════════════════════════════════════════
 04-12-95 │  [F1] Help  [↑↓] Select field  [F10] Done  [ESC] Exit │ 08:53:12
```

Figure 18-21:
Makewild's
second
screen of
Editing
Conference
options.

- **Prompt to kill received attachment**: This option allows the caller to delete an attached file after it's been downloaded. The default is Y, and you should stick with it.

- **Allow return receipts**: Wildcat! can automatically notify a caller when a message has been read by the addressee. These return receipts are addressed to the sender of the message from Wildcat! Mail Room and note the date and time the message was received. The default is Y, and it's fine for this conference. For conferences that exchange mail with other BBSs, you'd want to set this option to N.

- **Prompt to kill received messages**: If Y, Wildcat! will ask if the caller wants to delete a message after it's been read. Usually that default setting is fine, but there may be instances — particularly in public conferences where messages may be of interest to other callers — in which you'd rather *not* put that idea in the caller's head. There's no right or wrong setting for this option. It's up to you. (Callers can still delete their own mail with the Kill Message command on Wildcat!'s Message Menu.)

- **Allow carbon copies**: At the caller's request, Wildcat! can send a copy of a message to anyone else on the board. The only real downside to this option is that it can, if misused by callers, clutter a message file with useless copies. That doesn't happen often, though, so you can leave it set to Y. (In most conferences that share mail with other BBSs, you'd want to set it to N.)

✔ **Allow high ASCII characters**: *High ASCII characters* are the PC extended character set — the line drawing and accented characters. If most of your callers will be DOS or Windows users, it's safe to allow these characters in messages. If you expect a large number of non-DOS, non-Windows callers, set this option to N. (Some message-exchange networks — particularly Fidonet and Usenet — forbid the use of these characters. For conferences that exchange mail on those networks, this option should also be set to N.)

✔ **Require alias names**: If you set this option to Y, users who have not established alias names will be unable to send or receive messages in this conference. (They can still join the conference and *read* messages, however.) Obviously, this choice isn't what you want for Lobby Chatter, so leave this option set to N.

✔ **Use long address headers**: Wildcat! normally allows only 25 characters for message addressing to ensure compatibility with older offline mail readers and netmail programs. Some message networks, however, including the Internet, *require* longer address names. For conferences that will be exchanging mail on those networks, set this option to Y. For local conferences such as Lobby Chatter, the default setting of N is okay.

✔ **Show CTRL lines in messages**: This is an option that applies *only* to conferences shared with other BBSs. No need to change the default.

✔ **The inevitable F-key buttons**: Each of these buttons does exactly *what* you'd expect it to, in exactly the *way* you'd expect it to, based on everything you've seen in Makewild so far.

The F4 (Doors) button lets you designate which door programs will be accessible from the Lobby Chatter conference.

The F5 (Profiles) button lets you specify which security profiles will have access to which functions (Read, Write, and Join) in the conference. It's the obverse side of the window in Figure 18-15.

The F7 (File Areas) button lets you specify which file areas can be accessed from this conference.

When all the settings are exactly as you want them, press F10 (Done) to return to Makewild's Main Menu.

Opening doors

As discussed in Chapter 12, *doors* are add-on programs — games, subscription systems, order-taking systems, horoscopes, even news and weather reports — that the BBS runs from batch files. As time goes on, and you become more expert at running your board, you'll probably be tempted to add one or more doors to the system, but now isn't the time to consider this advanced topic.

Hooking the big one

A *menu hook* is similar to a door, but it can run an add-on program from *any* Wildcat! menu, whereas doors are listed on a separate Doors menu. Menu hooks can be exceptionally useful on the Sysop's menus. You could set up a hook, for example, that runs XTree or some other file manager, directly from Wildcat!'s Main Menu. Again, though, menu hooks are a somewhat advanced topic, and this isn't the time or the place. Perhaps you and I will meet again — someday, somewhere, in some other BBS book. (Cue the violins.)

QWKening your callers' mail

Highlight Offline mail on the Makewild Main Menu and press Enter. The Mail Door window as shown in Figure 18-22.

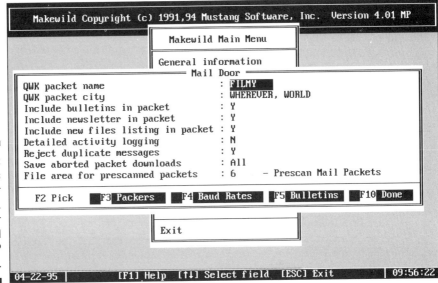

Figure 18-22: Makewild's Mail Door window. Name your QWK and make a REP for yourself.

Most of the options on this screen are self-explanatory, so I'll run through them very quickly.

- ✔ **QWK packet name**: In Chapter 15, you read that each BBS has its own distinctive mail packet name. Yours will be FILMY.QWK. (This also means, by the way, that the mail door will only accept reply packets named FILMY.REP.)

- ✔ **QWK packet city**: I've left this one at Makewild's silly default. You, of course, would type in the real geographical location of Me So Filmy.

- ✔ **Include bulletins in packet**: If Y, the mail door will collect any updated bulletins from the board and include them in the caller's FILMY.QWK.

- ✔ **Include newsletter in packet**: If Y, and if you've updated the board's newsletter since the caller's last mail packet, the mail door will include the newsletter in FILMY.QWK.

- ✔ **Include new files listing in packet**: If Y, the mail door will automatically get a list of any files uploaded to the board since the caller's last mail packet and include that list in FILMY.QWK.

- ✔ **Detailed activity logging**: The mail door creates a text file log of its activity. This option gives you a choice between two formats for that log. If you set it to Y, the log will contain detailed information about every message that every caller uploads or downloads. If you set it to N, the log records only the number of messages uploaded or downloaded. It's your choice, and it depends entirely on how closely you feel you need to watch the mail door.

- ✔ **Reject duplicate messages**: Leave this option set to Y. It prevents the caller from inadvertently uploading the same message twice to the BBS.

- ✔ **Save aborted packet downloads**: Press F2 to see the options, which are All, Net Status, and None. Every so often, a caller will get rudely dumped from the BBS in the midst of a download, due to telephone line noise or some other unexpected problem. If this disruption happens in the course of a QWK packet download, the mail door can save the caller's mail packet in a special file area until he or she calls back and downloads it success-fully. If you want to give your callers that ability, choose All. If not, choose None. Some networks exchange mail using the QWK packet format. If you want to confine this ability to other boards that call your BBS to exchange mail, choose Net Status.

- ✔ **File area for prescanned packets**: *Now* you know why you added that mysterious extra file area when you were working out your BBS plan. This file area is used *only* to store failed mail packet downloads or packets that have been prescanned for certain users — that is, prepared for the user before he or she calls in. (But that's another advanced topic.) *No* user other than the Sysop should have upload or download access to this file area. It exists solely for the use of the mail door.

The F-key buttons for the Mail Door screen are different from those you see elsewhere in Makewild. Here's a quick review of what they do:

✔ F3 gives you the File Packer Types window that allows you to select which methods of compressing QWK packets will be available to your users.

✔ Press F4 (Baud Rates) lets you determine how many messages callers can download based on the speed of their modems.

✔ F5 (Bulletins) lets you prevent lets you prevent individual bulletins from QWK packets.

Chatting, idling, and speaking in tongues

The remaining three options on the Makewild Main Menu are Multi user chat, Idle screen programs, and Language files. These are all advanced topics that fall outside the current mission parameters — but, because the subject hasn't come up before, I did want to explain exactly what an idle-screen program is.

Actually, I'd better start by explaining what an idle screen is. When there's no caller using the BBS — when it's idle, in other words — Wildcat! displays a static screen of BBS statistics and a list of available commands. That display is called the *idle screen*.

An *idle screen program,* then, is a program that can be run from the idle screen, without shutting down Wildcat!. (It's similar in concept to running a DOS program in a window, without having to exit Windows.) If you notice a flashing light on the modem, indicating an incoming call, you can quit the program, and Wildcat! pops right back up to answer the call.

Calling it quitsville

Highlight Exit on the Makewild Main Menu and press Enter. Makewild asks you again if you want to check any file paths you entered into the program. Press Y. If Makewild finds any paths that need to be created, you'll be prompted to let the program do it for you. Press A for All. When the Operation Finished window pops up, press Enter to return to the DOS prompt.

You did it! The Me So Filmy BBS is now fully configured and ready to go online!

Chapter 19

Exploring a BBS behind the Scenes

In This Chapter

▶ Taking command of your BBS

▶ Peering behind the curtain behind the curtain

▶ Custom tailoring your BBS

*Y*ou're about to peek behind the curtain at the nerve center of your cyberspace realm. The structure of what you'll see on this magical mystery tour will be somewhat different for each BBS program. *All* of them, however, like Wildcat!, provide the Sysop with some means to manage the board's users, files, and everyday maintenance.

Before we hop on the tour bus, we should point out that bulletin-board programs are different from almost any other type of software in one important respect. Like a celebrity who presents one face to the public and another in private, every BBS has a *hidden personality*. The face it shows to the world-at-large differs — sometimes just a little, sometimes markedly — from the one it exposes only to the Sysop.

From the caller's perspective, Wildcat! is structured around three basic menus: a Main Menu, a Message Menu, and a Files Menu. From the Sysop's point of view, Wildcat! has *four* primary menus. The fourth, as you might expect, is a *Sysop* Menu.

From that menu, the Sysop has direct access to the user database, the files database, the board's activity logs, the system's scheduled "events," and many other operational and informational functions associated with running the system. From that menu, the Sysop *rules*.

Taking Command of Your BBS

With your own BBS, Me So Filmy, set up and ready to run in Chapter 18, all that remains is to start the engine. If you've left the Wildcat! home directory, return there now by typing **CD \WILDCAT** and pressing Enter. The DOS prompt should look something like this: `C:\WILDCAT>`.

Wildcat! starts from a special batch file called CAT.BAT. So to "bring up the board," as Sysops say, type **CAT** and press Enter. After a few moments, you see the Wildcat! idle screen mentioned in Chapter 18. It looks something like the screen in Figure 19-1.

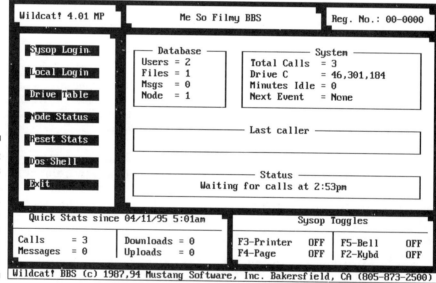

Figure 19-1: Wildcat!'s idle screen. Look out, world — Me So Filmy has just gone online!

The column at the left of the screen, under the box that says `Wildcat! 4.01 MP`, lists commands available directly from the idle screen. Each of these commands is invoked by holding down the Alt key and pressing the highlighted letter. The first thing you'll want to do is log on and upgrade yourself to Sysop status. So press Alt+L for Local Login.

The board doesn't know who you are yet, so don't be surprised when it treats you as a new user. It asks for your name, your city and state — all the usual stuff — and then has the audacity to inform you that you're not in the user database! Don't go ballistic. Just answer all of Wildcat!'s questions as if you were making your first call to any other BBS. In terms of our BBS-as-kingdom metaphor, you're now laying the groundwork for your coronation. You'll soon get your chance to show the board who's boss.

The New User Main Menu

When you've answered all the questions, Wildcat! delivers you to the rather meager Main Menu, shown in Figure 19-2.

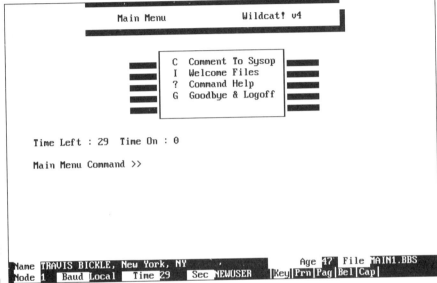

Figure 19-2:
Wildcat!'s
Main Menu
for the
NEWUSER
security
profile.
Stingy, but
secure.

Pay particular attention to the two lines at the bottom of the screen. Those are Wildcat!'s *status lines,* and they only appear on the *local console* (that is, the BBS computer). Outside callers never see them.

Most of the information on these two lines is self-explanatory—the caller's name, location, and age, for example. But check out at the last item on the first line. *File* indicates which file is currently being displayed to the caller. Here, it's MAIN1.BBS, part of a menu set that also includes MSG1.BBS and FILE1.BBS.

Take a look at the second status line. *Node* indicates which node of the BBS the caller is using. *Baud* indicates the speed of the caller's modem connection. (In this case, there's no baud number, just the designation *Local,* because we've logged on directly from the console.) *Time* indicates how many minutes the caller has remaining on the board. *Sec* is short for *security profile.* Because you've never called the board before, you have the default security profile, NEWUSER.

Beginning to see how the choices you make in MAKEWILD affect the way the board looks to a caller? For example, when we edited the FULLUSER security profile in MAKEWILD, we assigned it Menu Set 5. Although I didn't take you through the process for each security profile, it's clear from Figure 19-2 that the NEWUSER security profile was assigned Menu Set 1. You can further deduce that the maximum logon time for the NEWUSER profile is set to 30 minutes, one of which has already expired. And most of the Main Menu choices have been disabled for users with this security profile.

The five items at the right of the second status line — *Key* (Keyboard), *Prn* (Printer), *Pag* (Sysop Page), *Bel* (Bell), and *Cap* (Capture) — are all toggle switches activated by pressing F-keys at the console.

At the moment, only the keyboard is active. (It had better be. You're *using* it.) Briefly, here's what the other toggles are for:

- If Prn is toggled on, the printer spews out out the board's activity log in real time.

- If Pag is on, the caller can page the Sysop with the appropriate command from the Main Menu. (Not a new user, though. The menu doesn't grant the NEWUSER profile access to that command.)

- If Bel is turned on, the "system bell" — a fancy-shmancy name for those irritating beeps from the computer's speaker — would be audible. Turning this toggle off is like hitting the mute button on your TV remote.

- If Cap is switched on, the caller's activity on the board is recorded in a *capture file*, much like the ones your communications program creates, for later review by the Sysop.

But enough of this NEWUSER baloney! You're supposed to be absolute monarch! Maximum leader! You're right up there with Jupiter, Odin, Amon-Ra — maybe even Oprah! Well, here's where you stage your *coup d'état*.

The Security Change window

Press F9, known in certain esoteric rites as The Secret Scepter of Power. You'll see the Security Change window pop up over Wildcat!'s Main Menu, as in Figure 19-3.

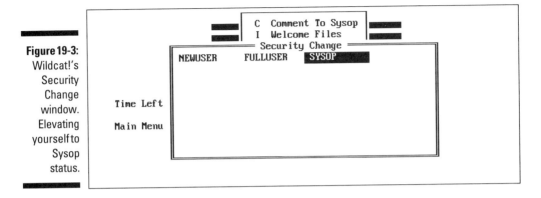

Figure 19-3:
Wildcat!'s
Security
Change
window.
Elevating
yourself to
Sysop
status.

Use the right-arrow key to highlight SYSOP. Press Enter. And —*voilà*!

Nothing happens.

That's because the board has to acclimate itself to your new security profile.
Press Enter again, and the kingdom is yours. You see a new, expanded Main
Menu like the one in Figure 19-4.

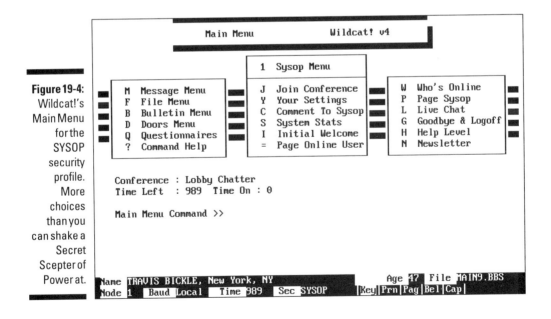

Figure 19-4:
Wildcat!'s
Main Menu
for the
SYSOP
security
profile.
More
choices
than you
can shake a
Secret
Scepter of
Power at.

Take a moment to gloat at the boost in your security level, menu set, and time left online.

Most of the commands in Figure 19-4 should be familiar to you from other BBSs. With but one exception, they're exactly the same commands your callers will see. Apart from a few extra Sysop bells and whistles, they work just as you'd expect them to.

There is, however, that lone command your callers *won't* see — the one placed imperiously atop the middle column, whence it gazes down upon all other commands, starkly elegant in the singularity of its designation: 1.

Is it an Aladdin's lamp, a Pandora's box — or both? I realize the suspense is killing you, so let's find out.

Gently lower that trembling finger toward the keyboard and press 1 to switch to the Sysop Menu. In a standard Wildcat! installation, it looks like the screen in Figure 19-5.

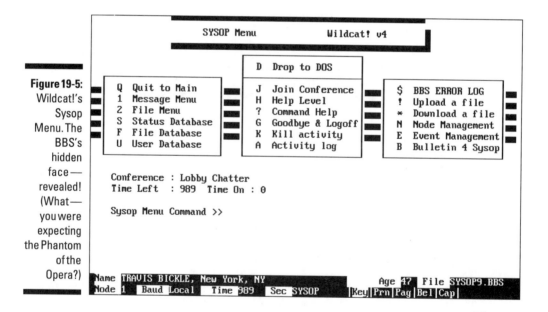

Figure 19-5: Wildcat!'s Sysop Menu. The BBS's hidden face — revealed! (What — you were expecting the Phantom of the Opera?)

```
              SYSOP Menu              Wildcat! v4

                          D   Drop to DOS

     Q   Quit to Main     J   Join Conference      $   BBS ERROR LOG
     1   Message Menu     H   Help Level           !   Upload a file
     2   File Menu        ?   Command Help         *   Download a file
     S   Status Database  G   Goodbye & Logoff     N   Node Management
     F   File Database    K   Kill activity        E   Event Management
     U   User Database    A   Activity log         B   Bulletin 4 Sysop

     Conference : Lobby Chatter
     Time Left  : 989  Time On : 0

     Sysop Menu Command >>



Name TRAVIS BICKLE, New York, NY              Age 47 File SYSOP9.BBS
Node 1   Baud Local    Time 989   Sec SYSOP    Key Prn Pag Bel Cap
```

Uh-oh. Not *exactly* what you expected, after that big build-up, huh — another curtain behind the curtain? No castle tower. No throne room. No dark, dank dungeon. No secret passageways. No sanctum sanctorum. Nothing — but another %#$& menu?!?

Well, yes. So far. But don't leap to any conclusions just yet.

SYSOP SEZ

Worlds in collision: A cyberspace kingdom meets the phone company

In 1989, when we moved our operation to a larger building, the phone company told us that we were not responsible for the cost of digging a mile-long trench through numerous well-manicured front lawns of our new neighbors in order to pull a 600-line phone cable to our new location. The total installation cost was agreed upon, in advance, to be $1200.

The trenching and cable laying started two weeks before we moved. When the cable was all the way to the new building, and we had moved in, the phone company called me and said they had made a mistake. They said I was responsible for "a little more of the cost of installation." I asked them how much that could be, a few hundred dollars? The nervous voice at the other end of the line said "$35,000." My only response was to scream into the phone, "WHAT?" He said he had checked the tariffs and there was nothing we could do about it.

Obviously, we could not afford this, and we wondered what the phone company was going to do about digging up everyone's lawn for a second time to remove the cable?

I called the Public Service Commission. They said they could do something about it. They took care of us, and two weeks later our phone company rep said we had the $1,200 agreement in writing, so that is what we had to pay.

This was one *major* brush with near disaster. It gives a whole new meaning to the words "get it in writing."

Before our latest move to a huge commercial building in 1994, we met with the phone company and told them about the problems in 1989. The next move went quite well — low cost, new trenching, this time with 600 phone lines plus fiber optic, no problem. We have many new friends at the phone company, and we all work together well.

Bob Mahoney, Sysop - Exec-PC BBS (414) 789-4500

Peering behind the Curtain behind the Curtain

Okay, it's true. The SYSOP Menu isn't entirely *terra incognita*. In fact, the first thing you notice is its similarity to BBS menus you've encountered before. You've got your commands for moving to other menus, your join conference command, your help command, your good-bye command. Nothing spectacular there.

Inspecting more closely, however, you discover there are also commands on the SYSOP Menu that *don't* appear anywhere else on the BBS. These commands are the secret passageways you've been looking for. They'll take you places where you've never been.

I can't explore all these passageways in a single chapter. That's a job better left to Wildcat!'s manual. I'll explain what each one is, though, and let you poke your nose into a few of the most interesting secret corridors of power.

"Status, Mr. Data...base?"— *Pressing S*

Gird yourself for another nonthrill. (I'm working up to the exciting stuff one step at a time.) The Status Database command on the SYSOP Menu could be called the Static Database command. When you press S to call it up, you see a screen similar to the one in Figure 19-6.

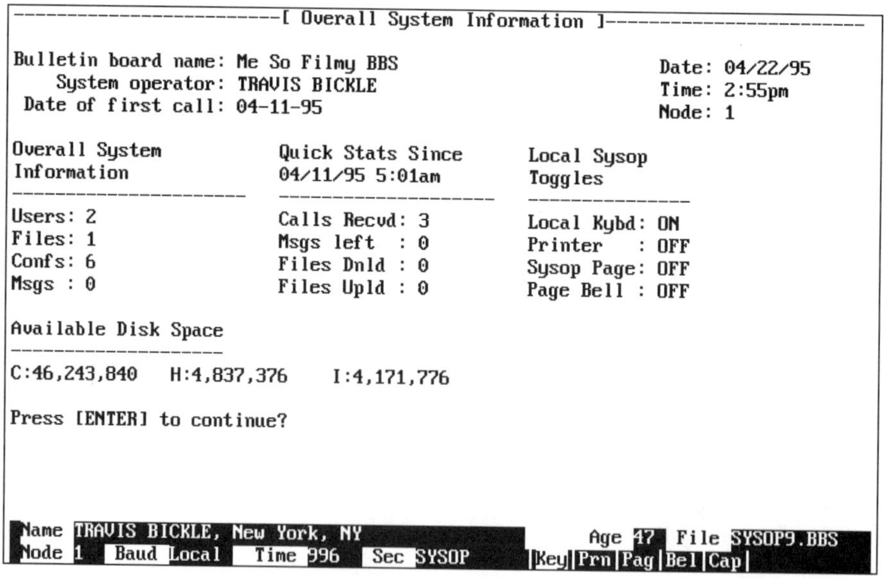

Figure 19-6:
Wildcat!'s
Overall
System
Information
screen. At-
a-glance
information
about the
board —
and not a lot
to do.

```
-----------------------[ Overall System Information ]-----------------------
Bulletin board name: Me So Filmy BBS                    Date: 04/22/95
     System operator: TRAVIS BICKLE                     Time: 2:55pm
  Date of first call: 04-11-95                          Node: 1

Overall System          Quick Stats Since          Local Sysop
Information             04/11/95 5:01am             Toggles
-------------------    ----------------------      ------------------
Users: 2               Calls Recvd: 3             Local Kybd: ON
Files: 1               Msgs left  : 0             Printer   : OFF
Confs: 6               Files Dnld : 0             Sysop Page: OFF
Msgs : 0               Files Upld : 0             Page Bell : OFF

Available Disk Space
--------------------
C:46,243,840   H:4,837,376     I:4,171,776

Press [ENTER] to continue?


Name TRAVIS BICKLE, New York, NY                       Age 47  File SYSOP9.BBS
Node 1   Baud Local   Time 996   Sec SYSOP        Key Prn Pag Bel Cap
```

All you can do with this screen is look at it. It's helpful, informative, and nice to have around, but most of what it has to say is stuff you already know. There's a second screen to this display that shows up after you press Enter. You can't do anything to that screen, either.

I trust that you've dawdled long enough at these static screens to satisfy whatever curiosity they may have piqued. You're probably ready for some _action_, right?

Good. Press Enter now to return to the SYSOP Menu. We're about to open one of those secret passageways.

Taking a walk on the file side — Pressing F

Maybe you've wondered where and how a BBS stores information about the files you upload and download. You already know that Wildcat! has something called a files database, but what exactly _is_ that? Press F on the SYSOP Menu — and step into my parlor. You see a screen something like the one in Figure 19-7.

By now, you've probably listed files on various BBSs a few dozen times. Perhaps you thought that what you saw in those listings was everything the board knew about the file. Not so, as Figure 19-7 makes abundantly clear.

Figure 19-7:
Inside
Wildcat!'s
file
database.
The dossier
on
CHAP17.ZIP.

```
Record #         : 1                      Match : NONE

[ 1] File name    : CHAP17.ZIP            [16] Times Dnld'd   : 1
[ 2] Date         : 04/21/95  6:04pm      [17] Cost           : 0
[ 3] Last access  : 04/22/95 11:12am      [18] On CD-ROM      : No
[ 4] Size         : 43368                 [19] No charge      : No
[ 5] Uploaded by  : BETH SLICK            [20] Never overwrite: No
[ 6] Password     : SCHRADER              [21] Never delete   : No
[ 7] Key 1        : CHAPTER               [22] U/L in progress: No
[ 8] Key 2        : 17                    [23] Stored offline : No
[ 9] Key 3        : BBS                   [24] Long desc.     : No
[10] Key 4        : DUMMIES               [25] Failed scan    : No
[11] Key 5        : WINWORD
[12] Key 6        : TRAVIS
[13] Area         : 5 - New Uploads
[14] Short desc.  : Chapter 17 of BBSs for Dummies -- for Travis from Beth
[15] Stored path  :

Edit   [1..25], [S]earch, [N]ext, [F]ind, [R]ead, [X]fer, [H]elp, Fr[e]shen,
[A]dd, [M]atch, [D]elete, [P]rev, [J]ump, [V]iew, [C]opy, [U]ser, [Q]uit?
```

By some astonishing coincidence, Chapter 17 of this very book has been uploaded to Me So Filmy by coauthor Beth Slick. Take a quick look at the information Wildcat! makes available to the Sysop about this one measly file:

- Item [1] is the filename. Pretty basic.

- Item [2] is the date the file was uploaded.

- Item [3] is the date the file was last *downloaded*.

- Item [4] is the file's size, in kilobytes.

- Item [5] is the uploader's name.

- Item [6] is the *file's* password, not Beth's. Because she didn't want just anybody to download it, Beth gave the file a password which, presumably, she had the good sense to share with the file's intended recipient in a private message.

- Items [7] through [12] are the keywords that Wildcat! generated dynamically (as opposed to lethargically, remember?) from the file's description.

- Item [13] tells us where the file is stored on the hard disk.

- Item [14] is the description of the file that Beth typed in when she uploaded it.

- Item [15] is a little Sysop secret. Although it's blank in this example, the "Stored path" field *could* contain the name of a directory path *other* than the one you entered in MAKEWILD for New Uploads. At the Sysop's discretion, the file can be kept in a different place on the hard drive but *listed* as if it were in C:\WILDCAT\XFERS\UPLOADS.

- Item [16] tells us the number of times the file has been downloaded.

- On a pay-per-file board, item [17] would specify the debit to a user's account for the download.

- Item [18] tells us if the file is stored on a CD-ROM.

- Item [19] doesn't refer to a monetary charge but to *time* deducted from the user's call. If there's "no charge" for the file, the caller would have as much time left on the board after downloading the file as before the download began. Sysops often set this option to *yes* for informational files — the rules of the BBS, for example — that they want every caller to download.

- If item [20] were set to *yes*, Wildcat! wouldn't allow Beth or even the Sysop to upload a file with the same name to the board, thereby replacing this file on this hard disk.

✔ If item [21] were set to *yes*, neither Wildcat! nor any of its Sysop utilities would be allowed to delete the file.

✔ U/L is shorthand for *upload*. Wildcat! enters the file into its database when the caller types in the name and file description and starts the upload. From item [22], the Sysop of a multiline board could see the database addition even before the entire file arrived.

✔ Remember how MAKEWILD asked if we wanted to allow requests for offline files? Item [23] indicates whether the file is stored somewhere other than on the BBS computer's hard drive or an available CD-ROM.

✔ Item [24] tells us whether Beth typed in a detailed description of the file, in addition to the short description in item [14].

✔ Many Sysops use virus-scanning software to check every file uploaded to the board. If the file fails the scan, Wildcat! makes note of it in item [25].

All of this information is completely subject to your whim as Sysop!

Look at the last two lines in Figure 19-7. See the one that starts "Edit [1..25]"? If you type in the number of the item you want to change, Wildcat! prompts you for the new information and lets you save the revised file record. And that's not all. Using the other commands listed on these two lines, you have total control of the files database. You can move backward and forward through the database, search for files, read text files online, view the contents of ZIP files, delete files, hop to the user record of the uploader, move files to different areas of the hard disk, and much, much more.

Granted, it isn't exactly Arnold Schwarzenegger's definition of "action," but, to a Sysop, having all this power at your fingertips is like owning your own Terminator.

So go ahead — enjoy it. Snarl "I'll be back!" at the files database. Then press Q to return to the Sysop Menu.

Browsing through your users' lives — Pressing U

Think the files database was impressive? Hah! The information that Wildcat! stores about your users would turn J. Edgar Hoover green. (If he isn't already.) And *you* never even had to resort to illegal wiretaps. Your callers gave you the information willingly and knowingly.

Lest you grow paranoid (as a caller) or megalomaniacal (as a Sysop), we should point out that most of this information is about your callers' interaction with the BBS. Unless callers bare their hearts to you in E-mail — and yes, it happens to every Sysop at least once — their private lives remain their own business.

So much for the preliminaries. Have a look at the Wildcat! user database. From the SYSOP Menu press U. You'll see a screen similar to the one in Figure 19-8.

Figure 19-8:
Wildcat's
user
database.
This is the
first screen
of three —
for each
caller!

```
Record number  : 2              Match : NONE              User ID : 2

[ 1] Name       : TRAVIS BICKLE            [18] Zip code   : 10011
[ 2] From       : New York, NY             [19] SecLevel   : SYSOP
[ 3] Phone [V]  : 212-555-5555             [20] ExpDate    : /  /
[ 4] Phone [D]  :                          [21] User since: 04/22/95
[ 5] Phone [F]  :               Age: 47    [22] D.O.B.     : 09/20/47
[ 6] Last call  : 04/22/95 2:47pm          [23] Memo date  : /  /
[ 7] Comment 1  : You talkin' to ME??      [24] # Calls    : 6
[ 8] Comment 2  :                          [25] Page avail : Yes
[ 9] Comment 3  :                          [26] Display    : No color
[10] Comment 4  :                          [27] E-prompt   : Yes
[11] Comment 5  :                          [28] Hot keys   : Yes
[12] Company    : Fresh Air Taxi Co.       [29] File disp  : Double line
[13] Address 1  : 631 Ninth Avenue         [30] Editor     : Full Screen
[14] Address 2  :                          [31] Protocol   : Zmodem
[15] City       : New York                 [32] N-mail bal : $      .00
[16] State      : NY                       [33] Acct bal   : $      .00
[17] Country    :                          [34] Help level : NOVICE

Edit [1..34], [F]ind, [N]ext, [M]atch, [J]ump, [D]elete, [E]xtra, [X] New Pwrd,
[U]ser Mail,   [C]onf,  [P]rev,  [W]rite, [H]elp, [S]earch, [A]dd,   [Q]uit?
```

There are so many items of information on Wildcat!'s three — count 'em! three! — user database screens that it would take another chapter to cover them in detail. As with the files database, I'll assume you're not interested in that kind of submicroscopic examination yet and just hit the high points, okay?

✔ Items [1] through [5] cover some basics. The user's name, location, and up to three phone numbers, one each for voice, data (a BBS, for example), and fax. Item [6] shows the date and time of the user's last call.

✔ Items [7] through [11] are comment lines that can contain any text you want, including comments typed by the user in response to one of Wildcat!'s questionnaires.

Quick aside here. You're in no way limited to the interrogation in Wildcat!'s default new user questionnaire. Each Sysop can use the MAKEQUES utility that comes with Wildcat! to create a custom questionnaire geared specifically to the focus of the BBS. On Me So Filmy, for example, you might want to ask new users to name their favorite film or favorite director, whether they own a VCR or a laser-disc player, or if they've ever heard of Italian neorealism. Responses to questions like these can be stored in the comment lines of the user record. Other types of questions — birthdates, phone numbers, the caller's preferred settings for the board — can also be sent directly from the questionnaire to the appropriate field of the user record.

✔ Items [12] through [18] are responses to the questions put to Mr. Bickle when he logged onto the board the first time.

✔ Item [19] is the user's security profile setting.

✔ Item [20] relates to the "Expired Profiles" discussed in Chapter 18. If Me So Filmy were a subscription board, this field would hold the date when the user's subscription was due to expire. On that date, Wildcat! would automatically demote the user to whatever "Expired Profile" we specified in MAKEWILD.

✔ Item [21] is the date of the user's *first* call to the board.

✔ Item [22] holds the user's date of birth, from which Wildcat! graciously calculates the user's age without our having to do any math.

✔ Item [23] again relates mainly to subscription boards. You might set this to a date 30 days in advance of the expiration date. Starting on that date, Wildcat! would display a file to the caller, warning that renewal time was just around the corner.

✔ Item [24] tells how many times the user has called the board.

✔ Item [25] relates to multiline boards. If Mr. Bickle doesn't care to be paged by other *users* (not the Sysop) for chat, he can change this setting to "No" from the Your Settings command on Wildcat!'s Main Menu.

✔ Item [26] simply specifies the user's preference for viewing the board in color, black-and-white, or RIP graphics.

✔ Item [27] is also a matter between the user and the board. If this is set to "Yes," Wildcat! will erase the "Continue" prompts from the screen after the user responds to them.

✔ Item [28] determines whether hot keys (shortcuts) can be used.

✔ Wildcat! has four different ways of listing file directories: a single-line mode; the default double-line mode; a full description mode, including any long description entered by the uploader; and a new ANSI mode that lists a screenful of files at a time and lets the user move through the list with the cursor keys. The user can elect to switch modes at any time with the Your settings command. The user's choice is reflected in item [29].

✔ Items [30] and [31] contain more options selected during the first logon procedure. By now, you've probably been asked a dozen times yourself for your preference in message editors and protocols.

✔ "N-mail bal" in item [32] is shorthand for "Net-mail Balance." Very advanced topic. Don't concern yourself.

✔ Remember how the files database asked for the cost of a file? On pay-per-file boards, Wildcat! would automatically deduct that cost from the user's account balance and post the adjusted balance in item [33].

✔ Item [34] reflects another user preference. As you probably know by now, bulletin boards can display their menu choices in a variety of different ways — full-screen menus, a line with nothing but the command letters, and, for really expert users, no menus at all. The NOVICE help level in Wildcat! indicates that the user wants full menus.

Check out the last two lines on the screen in Figure 19-8. Look familiar? As with the files database, *all the information on this screen is subject to change by the Sysop.*

You may be asking yourself, "Why would a Sysop want to change a user's name or address?" You wouldn't *have* to ask if you'd ever encountered a user from, say, New Yrok (if you can make it there, you'll make it anywehre) or one who's managed to convince the board his name is Danquayle (no last name, like Cher or Fabio).

Other user information might simply require updating from time to time, or you might want to make a little note to yourself about a problem user, or an especially helpful one, on a comment line.

The other commands on those last two lines allow the Sysop to move around the user database, view a list of users who match a certain security profile, delete users, change a user's password, add a new user to the board, and even write a message to the user whose record is displayed.

To move to the second screen of the user record, press E and then press Enter. You see a screen like the one in Figure 19-9.

Figure 19-9:
Wildcat!'s second user database screen. Some of the more potent Sysop options reside here.

```
TRAVIS BICKLE from New York, NY

[ 1] Computer Type   : Scorcese-XL        [17] Quote reply     : No
[ 2] Alias           : TAXIDRIVER         [18] Lines per page  : 23
[ 3] Title           :                    [19] Msgs written    : 1
[ 4] Sex             : Not disclosed      [20] Upload          : 0
[ 5] New files       : 01/01/80 12:00am   [21] Downloads       : 0
[ 6] Total upld Kb   : 0                  [22] Time left        : 995
[ 7] Total dnld Kb   : 0                  [23] Daily DL         : 0
[ 8] Minutes logged  : 30                 [24] Daily DK         : 0
[ 9] Novell name     :                    [25] Last conference : 0
[10] Secondary # 1   :                    [26] Locked out      : No
[11] Secondary # 2   :                    [27] Never delete    : No
[12] Secondary # 3   :                    [28] Logon siren on  : No
[13] Secondary # 4   :                    [29] Hide private    : No
[14] Secondary # 5   :                    [30] Hide deleted    : No
[15] Read mail mode  : Scroll             [31] User capture on : No
[16] Default language: Default            [32] Sorted lists    : No

Edit [1..32], [F]ind Alias, [S]earch Alias, [H]elp? [   ]
```

Lots more information. Lots more options — some of them nasty.

- ✔ Item [1] is a questionnaire answer, the caller's computer type.

- ✔ Item [2] is the alias, or "handle," chosen by the user for conferences in which aliases are permitted.

- ✔ Item [3], title, might also be an item from a questionnaire. If Travis had, for example, chosen the title "Homunculus," that word would appear in parentheses beside his name in the header of any message he writes.

- ✔ If the information for item [4], sex, isn't specifically requested in a questionnaire, Wildcat! automatically inserts "Not disclosed" in this field.

- ✔ Item [5] tells us when Travis did his last new-files listing.

- ✔ Items [6] and [7] tell us how many kilobytes he's uploaded and downloaded, respectively, since joining the board. Item [8] is the number of minutes he's spent on the board since his first call.

- ✔ Item [9] only applies to boards running on Novell networks.

- ✔ Items [10] through [14] are blank in our example, but they could contain names of secondary security profiles assigned to Travis. If you recall from Chapter 18, a secondary security profile provides a way to override settings in the user's primary security profile.

- ✔ Wildcat! offers callers three different modes for reading messages. The screen can be cleared after each message; messages can appear in a continuous scroll (the default, and Travis's choice); or callers can choose to scroll the message *text* while leaving the message *header* in place. The caller's choice is listed in item [15].

- ✔ Item [16] looks like a truism — the default language is the default — but this item lists the *user's* default language, not the board's.

- ✔ If item [17] were set to *Yes,* Wildcat! would insert the entire text of a message into Travis's *reply* to that message before he even begins typing. Travis could then insert his own ringing rejoinders between the blocks of "quoted" text. (Even with this option set to *No,* Travis can still quote all or part of the original message in his reply by using commands available in the message editor.)

- ✔ Item [18] tells how many lines of text Travis wants displayed on his screen at one time.

- ✔ Items [19] through [21] indicate how many messages Travis has written, and how many files he's uploaded and downloaded.

- ✔ Item [22] tells us how many minutes Travis has left on the board today.

- ✔ Items [23] and [24] indicate how many files and how many kilobytes Travis has downloaded today.

✔ Item [25] shows us which conference Travis was in when he logged off the board.

✔ If item [26] were set to *Yes,* Travis would not be allowed to log onto the board. Upon receiving his name and password, Wildcat! would display a file telling Travis that he's no longer welcome, and then the BBS's modem would hang up. *That'll* teach 'im!

✔ Some maintenance utilities allow the Sysop to purge the database of inactive users, those who haven't called in a specified period of time. If item [27] were set to *Yes,* Travis's record couldn't be deleted except by another Sysop, who would have to change this setting first.

✔ Want to keep an eye on problem users? Set item [28] to *Yes,* and Wildcat! will sound a five-second alarm whenever the caller logs on.

✔ Items [29] and [30] determine whether the user can read private mail or deleted messages addressed to others. If these options are set to *No,* then private and deleted messages are *not* hidden from the user.

✔ There are times when every Sysop would *like* to capture a user — and remand the person into custody of the proper authorities — but item [31] refers to a capture *file.* If this item is set to *Yes,* every move the user makes on the board is written to a file for later review by the Sysop. (Okay, so maybe you *do* have to resort to the occasional wiretap.)

✔ Item [32] lets the user view the list of conferences and file areas sorted alphabetically, rather than by number. (An anticlimax, if there ever was one.)

Once again, all this information can be revised by the Sysop.

The commands on the bottom line of the screen in Figure 19-9 are used to — of all things — hunt down user aliases. The difference between Find and Search is that the former requires the complete alias name. Search can track down all the aliases that contain a certain string of letters. For example, a Search for "tax" might turn up Taxidermist, Taxi Dancer, Taxman, and Ratta-Tat-Tax, as well as Travis's alias of Taxidriver.

The third screen in the user database concerns the user's status in various conferences. It also gives the Sysop the opportunity to show a granule of mercy by locking a caller out of a single conference, rather than the entire board. I'll skip the details of that screen, though, since we still have a significant stretch of territory to cover.

Press Enter to return to the first user database screen. Press Q and then press Enter again to return to the SYSOP Menu.

Following your users' footprints — Pressing A

I'm going to take the next two selections on the SYSOP Menu out of order for reasons that will shortly become obvious.

Press A to view Wildcat!'s *Activity log*. Because Me So Filmy hasn't experienced a real caller yet, I've appropriated an excerpt of my BBS's log for the example in Figure 19-10.

```
00:32 BUZZ DIXON [REGISTERED] - Northridge, CA at 9600 bps on Wed, 04/10/95
      * 8 Databits:YES, Detected:ANSI, MNP:YES, CONF:35, Time Limit:118
      * Voice #: 818-███-████ Data #:
      * Fast Login access allowed
      * MENU HOOK (MAIL.BAT) executed at 00:32
      * BUZZ DIXON returned from DOS or DOOR at 00:33
      * Search messages in conference 35
      * Read messages starting at 6635 in conference 35
      * Changed to conference 005 - Topic du Jour (BIW)
      * Search messages in conference 5
      * Search messages in conference 5
      * Changed to conference 025 - Wrestling (RIME)
      * Changed to conference 024 - 4DOS (RIME)
      * Changed to conference 023 - Politics (RIME)
      * Search messages in conference 23
      * Read messages starting at 30400 in conference 23
      * 7 line message left in 023 - Politics (RIME)
      * Changed to conference 022 - Horror (RIME)
      * Search messages in conference 22
00:50 Signed off NORMALLY.  Time Logged: 19 with 102 minutes remaining.
      ---------------------------------------------------------------------
02:30 EVENT (Run Batch) executed.
      ---------------------------------------------------------------------
02:43 READY FOR CALLS
```

Figure 19-10:
Excerpt from
a Wildcat!
activity log.
How the
Sysop
knows if
you've been
bad or good.

I'll attempt a quick translation of this excerpt.

Caller Buzz Dixon logged onto the board at 12:32 a.m. on April 10. His modem settings were correct. The last conference he'd joined was 35, and that's where the board would have taken him after the logon procedure. Mr. Dixon used the fast logon option described briefly in Chapter 18. We can tell he typed an exclamation point before his name, because that option took him to the Mail Door. (We know that from the name of the Menu Hook, MAIL.BAT, that the board executed next.) Mr. Dixon returned from the Mail Door after just one minute. Obviously, he was uploading replies, not downloading messages. He next did a search of the headers in conference 35 and, based on that search, chose to start reading with message number 6635. He then joined conference 5 and searched messages there twice. Whatever he was looking for, he probably didn't find it, since he read no messages before switching to conferences 25, 24, and finally 23, where he did yet another message search. Obviously, something piqued his interest in that conference; he began reading messages again with number 30400 and wrote a seven-line message, as well. He then switched to conference 22, searched the messages again, and apparently found nothing compelling. He logged off the board politely with the Good-bye command (that's what a "normal" sign-off is) at 12:50 a.m., having spent 19 minutes on the BBS.

The board was idle from 12:50 until 2:30 a.m., when a maintenance event ran automatically as scheduled. The event took 13 minutes to complete, after which the board came back online, "ready for calls."

End of translation.

Had Mr. Dixon read any bulletins, uploaded or downloaded files, listed new files since his last call, or tried to page the Sysop, those actions would also have been recorded in the log. In fact, just about every move Mr. Dixon — and *every* caller — makes while on the board is automatically recorded in the log.

By scanning the activity log every so often, you can track down problem users (or users having problems), gauge which conferences are attracting the most callers, discover which files are most and least popular, and so on. It's an invaluable resource and one that most Sysops consult very frequently.

Now, of course, you understand why we had to leapfrog the previous menu selection: Kill Activity. (Is it just me, or does that sound like supervised mayhem at a summer camp? "Okay, kids! Two o'clock! Kill Activity Time!") If you invoke that command by pressing K, the activity log gets *erased*. Which probably leaves you wondering why such a command even exists. Why would a Sysop want to eradicate this supposedly invaluable resource?

As is often the case with computers, the simplest answer is the right one: You've just seen for yourself how many lines of text can be generated during one 19-minute call. Imagine the size of the log file after *months* of BBS use. If, having reviewed the log, you find nothing untoward, you may very well want to erase it just to make a little extra room on the hard disk.

When you reach the end of the log file, Wildcat! prompts you to press Enter to continue. Do that and return to the SYSOP Menu.

*A fistful of commands — Pressing $, !, *, N, and B*

Hang onto your hats. I'm going to cover most of the commands in the far-right box of the SYSOP Menu at a whirlwind pace.

✔ ***BBS Error Log ($)*** displays a specialized log file of your board's misfortunes, major and minor. If the BBS *crashes* — stops dead in its tracks, in other words — this file can probably tell you what went wrong and whether you've got a mild annoyance or a full-blown catastrophe on your hands.

✔ **Upload a File (!)** lets the Sysop copy a file to the BBS from another directory or disk while at the console, using the same procedure that outside callers use for uploads. Nothing mysterious. It's just easier than filling in every field in the file database.

✔ **Download a File (*)** lets the Sysop copy a file *to* another disk or directory from the BBS.

✔ On multiline boards, **Node Management (N)** shows the status of each line and lets the Sysop change the console settings for that line.

✔ **Bulletin 4 Sysop (B)** isn't really a bulletin and doesn't perform any real function on the BBS. It displays some additional help files that come with Wildcat!, including a glossary of BBS terms and information about new features added to Wildcat!. It can be customized to display any file the Sysop wants.

Do I keep my promises, or what?

Overtaking events — Pressing E

As noted in Chapter 18, *events* are automated tasks, maintenance and the like, that the BBS runs on a schedule determined by you, the Sysop. If everything's working correctly, no human intervention is required once the initial setup of each event is completed.

By far, the two most common events run on every board deal with backing up essential files and calling other boards to pick up and deliver mail.

Press E from the SYSOP Menu, and you see a screen something like the one in Figure 19-11.

Figure 19-11:
Wildcat!'s
event list for
Me So
Filmy. One
predictably
dumb event.

```
 #  Description   Schedule Type  Start        Last Execute         Parameters
--- ----------- -------- ---- ------- -------------------- ----------
* 1 Run batch     SMTWTFS  Soft 12:01am Sat 04/22/95 3:01pm  DUMMIES.BAT
Current time:  Sat 04/22/95 3:01pm

Edit [A]dd, [E]dit, [R]un, [D]elete, [S]chedule, [H]elp, [Q]uit? [E]
Edit which event? [1  ]
```

Me So Filmy has only one event scheduled. The Description column tells you this event runs a batch file. The Schedule column tells you that the event runs every day. ("SMTWTFS" stands for Sunday, Monday, Tuesday, and so on.) The Type column identifies the event as "soft," meaning that the BBS will run it at the specified time if the board is idle or immediately after a call that runs past the specified time. The Start column, of course, shows the specified time. The Last Execute column tells us when the event was run most recently. The Parameters column shows us the name of the batch file Wildcat! will run, in this case DUMMIES.BAT.

The commands in the second-to-last line of this screen allow you to add new events, edit existing events, run an event on the spot, or delete an event. (Schedule simply redisplays the event listing after running one of the other choices.)

Taking the plunge to DOS — Pressing D

I've saved the Drop to DOS command for last. It's an advanced topic, but it should probably top your list of which advanced topics to tackle first.

From a local logon, you can leave Wildcat! and enter DOS anytime just by pressing Alt+D. That's not what the Drop to DOS command is for.

There may be times when *you* can only reach your BBS by modem — when you're on a business trip, for example, or if you're at work across town, and the BBS is located in your home. Suppose you had to get into DOS to fix some emergency or find some file that you need at the office.

That's what this command is for. It allows the Sysop to drop out of Wildcat! and into DOS even from a remote location.

The setup for this command is a bit complex, so we won't attempt to deal with the particulars here. Suffice it to say that you'll need a shareware program called Doorway, which you can find on the Mustang Software BBS and most other large bulletin boards. (A special version of Doorway is included in the Wildcat! BBS Suite package, discussed in Chapter 18.)

That concludes your tour of the SYSOP Menu. All that remains is to log off the board.

Be polite to yourself and your own board. Use the Good-bye command to log off. And keep in mind that a BBS program differs from almost any other type of software in a *second* important respect: *You don't shut the program down when you leave!* If you did, nobody else would be able to call in!

So press G to log off, wait a moment while Wildcat! handles some internal housekeeping, and then the familiar idle screen pops back up, telling you the board is waiting for calls.

Custom-tailoring your BBS

After you have your board up and running, you'll want to personalize it much, much further. In fact, you'll have to be careful that "tweaking" the system doesn't become an obsession, because many BBS programs — and Wildcat! in particular — let you modify almost every element of the board.

The menu sets that come with Wildcat! are nice enough, but you can create your own using Wildcat!'s wcDRAW program. You can change the names and call letters of the menu items. You can even use the MAKEMENU utility that comes with Wildcat! to alter the *structure* of the menus, making it possible, say, for your users to reach the Your Settings command from *any* menu, not just the Main Menu.

You'll want to customize the BBS's opening and closing screens, of course, to reflect the name of your board. You'll want to create your own bulletins for the system. You can even rewrite the prompt file so that Me So Filmy will ask users for commands in film jargon! (To the BBS, it's just another language — like the Star Trek prompts on Software Creations.)

The Secret Scepter of Power is in your hands. Rule wisely. Rule creatively. Rule compassionately.

Part IV
The Part of Tens

The 5th Wave   By Rich Tennant

Arthur inadvertently replaces his mouse pad with a Ouija board. For the rest of the day, he receives messages from the spectral world.

YOU WILL FORGET YOUR PASSWORD. YOUR HARD DISK WILL CRASH AAAHAHAHAHA

In this part...

*I*f this is your first ...*For Dummies* book, let me introduce you to the traditional Part of Tens — a collection of lists not unlike the ones on David Letterman's show. Except ours are in numerical order and have a much longer shelf life than Letterman's. And, while his lists are tossed out every night, ours are jammed with tips and information that might even take you into the next century. I love the sound of that.

Ladies and gentlemen, the Part of Tens.

Chapter 20

Top Ten Secret Commands

In This Chapter

▶ Pause (Ctrl+S)

▶ Restart (Ctrl+Q)

▶ Cancel (Ctrl+C)

▶ Abort (Ctrl+X)

▶ Suspend (Ctrl+K)

▶ Help (? or H)

▶ <CR> or Enter

▶ Top (* or 0)

▶ Backward and Forward (– and +)

▶ Global (/)

*O*kay, so the commands I'm about to share with you are not really *that* secret. But who would want to read a chapter entitled "Ten Commands You'd Know About Already if You Could Figure Out What They're Telling You on the Screen"?

One of the reasons these commands — though they are on the screen — remain secret or overlooked is because of the way they are presented. In Martian. You may see a message like `<CR> to Continue` or `^X Aborts`, and just ignore it, because it means nothing to you. It's so meaningless it doesn't even raise your curiosity.

A Bit of History

Incomprehensible messages appear now and again because most BBS software programs have their roots in the days of hobby computing. Getting online was a rite of passage, and only the technically adept could put the pieces together — literally — and successfully connect. While major strides to make BBSs easy for everyone have been made, the revenge of the nerds is present every now and then.

So, when you see `<CR> to Continue`, you're actually looking at a piece of history. CR stands for carriage return, which is what they called the Enter key on the first computers. Carriage return itself is a name leftover from manual typewriters, back in the days before typewriters used typing elements that were smart enough to scoot back and forth on their own. Sometimes on-screen instructions say to press Return. It's the same thing. When you see `Return to Continue`, it just means to press Enter to keep on going.

The other homage BBSs pay to days gone by is the ^ symbol, which — as I mentioned in an earlier chapter — means press the Ctrl key. `^X Aborts` means that to stop what's going on right now, press Ctrl+X. Another bit of history here: The first popular computers — other than Apples — that took the world by storm didn't even have an Alt key. Just the Ctrl key. That's why you'll never see a funny symbol for Alt.

Actually, now that I'm thinking about it, those early computer didn't even have function keys. We had to make our own function keys out of the numeric keypad. Of course, that was after we walked ten miles to school in the snow.

Here are some other keyboard semisecrets — a few of which are actual secrets. These secrets are a part of BBS lore handed down from one user to another. Once you know this stuff, you have to tell someone else. It's in the rules.

The Ten Commands

Here are the Top Ten Secret Commands.

Pause — Ctrl+S

If text is scrolling by faster than the speed limit, you can temporarily bring it to a screeching halt by pressing Ctrl+S. You can remember this because Ctrl+S stands for Suspend.

Restart — Ctrl+Q

Once you finish reading text, Ctrl+Q starts it up again. You can remember Ctrl+Q because Q stands for Quit Suspending. Honest.

Cancel — Ctrl+C

Ctrl+C is a time-honored cancel command. If something that you don't like is happening on the BBS, Ctrl+C is a good thing to try. It doesn't always work, but you won't be any worse off for trying it.

Abort — Ctrl+X

This is the traditional stop-the-download command. Just like you have to tell both the BBS and your communications software to *start* a download, you also have to tell both to stop a download. The abort command in your telecommunications software is usually available on the screen in the form of a cancel button. Once you cancel, though, you still have to press Ctrl+X, usually a few times, to get the BBS to stop sending. You get junky characters on-screen until you get the BBS's attention.

Suspend — Ctrl+K

When the BBS asks if you want to scan a message for mail, finishing the scan can take more time than you have patience — especially if it's been a long time between logons. If you suddenly change your mind and want the BBS to stop scanning, press Ctrl+K to handle the problem. Think of the command as Kill.

Help — ? or H

You should know, by now, that pressing question mark and Enter, or H and Enter, brings up a help screen for whatever you're doing. Many times, though, the screen won't tell you that a help screen is available. So, if you're confused, asking for help is always your first line of defense.

<CR> or Enter

Enter is a sort of all-purpose command that works in a lot of situations. Enter is mostly used to confirm a choice. I call it the Simon Says key, because nothing happens until you press Enter — Simon Says. However, Enter does a lot more than say go ahead.

✔ If you're on a blank line in a line editor, pressing another Enter is the signal that you're done.

✔ If you're looking at a menu, pressing Enter often backs you up a level.

✔ If you're reading E-Mail, pressing Enter takes you to the next message.

✔ Sometimes, pressing Enter is another way of aborting or stopping what's happening on the screen. I've used it to stop text that I had generated using a view command from scrolling.

✔ Generally, if things are out of control, try pressing Enter.

Top — * or 0

The asterisk and zero are two symbols used as shortcut keys to leapfrog from your current place in the BBS to the very top of the system. Keep a sharp eye on the menus for phrases like Go to Top, Jump to Main Menu, or simply Main Menu. This is especially helpful if you're not exactly sure where you are in the system. Going back to the top, or to the Main Menu, allows you to get your bearings and start again.

Backward and Forward — – and +

Look for plus or minus signs on menus or at the bottom of the screen when you're reading E-Mail. In menus, the minus sign is often a shortcut command to back up one level. In a message base, plus and minus keys are often used as navigation commands to travel forward or backward through the current message thread. That way, you can exclusively follow one conversation.

Global — /

The slash is often used as the first character in a global command. Not every BBS has global commands. A global command is something that works no matter where you are in a BBS. It's used to take you from one place to another on the system, bypassing menus and options. It's also used to start Chat sessions or give Chat commands. Global commands are powerful, timesaving shortcuts.

Read the screen

You can either call this the bonus secret or the ongoing nag. Either way, the best thing to do whenever you're unsure of what to do next is to look to the left of the cursor and read the screen. Your current options on how to proceed will usually be right there.

Chapter 21

Ten Files to Download First

In This Chapter

▶ PKZ204G.EXE

▶ DOSAV.EXE or WINAV.EXE

▶ QM46TD-1.EXE and QM46TD-2.EXE

▶ OLX-TD.EXE

▶ LIST90H.ZIP and WINLIST.ZIP

▶ VPIC61.ZIP

▶ SHEZ106.ZIP

▶ DRAGFL.ZIP

▶ WINPRN15.ZIP

▶ TIMESET7.ZIP

*T*his chapter is devoted to the Ten Files to Download First. The reason these are the files to get first is that they are absolutely critical, or at least very important, to managing your online life. Also, in the first few days of your online adventure, I want to make sure you have some exciting, top-of-the-online files to get you started. Even though all of these Ten Files to Download First are winners, each has its boosters and detractors, and other programs exist that do the same thing in a different way. It's kind of like deciding which is best, deep-dish or thin-crust pizza. It's all a matter of personal preference. And I guess that's what makes America great.

Other than the test-drive programs, the Ten Files to Download First are all *shareware*. That means that, if you download and keep them in your permanent library, the right thing to do is to pay the registration fee. Each program tells you how much its fee is and where to pay it. Don't worry about that at first. Shareware also means the filenames listed here may or may not be exactly the same by the time you start downloading. But the names won't be *completely* different. I mean, a file may be called KOOL13.ZIP today, and next week, when a new, enhanced version comes out — one that works under Windows 95 or something — it'll be called KOOL14.ZIP. Kool, of course, is a pretend name. There is, to my knowledge, no program called Kool.

If you use the BBS's search command, use wildcards to speed up the search. For example, search for KOOL*.ZIP, and the BBS search machine lets you know if any version of Kool exists on the system. The key is to replace the number part of the file names below with the asterisk.

PKZ204G.EXE

This is the unzipping program we downloaded in Chapter 4. If you didn't download it then, do it now. You won't be able to do anything with downloaded files ending in ZIP until you get this program, which decompresses zipped files . . . plus a whole lot more.

DOSAV.EXE or WINAV.EXE

These are the update-signature files that keep your Microsoft Anti-Virus system up-to-date. Alternatively, you can download SCN-217E.ZIP, which is the Virus Scan program from McAfee Associates. All these programs are covered in detail in Chapter 6. If you have yet to avail yourself of this basic preventive medicine, now is the time.

QM46TD-1.EXE and QM46TD-2.EXE

If you are using a crummy modem program and want one that's more friendly to use, you can download — or order via voice phone — a test-drive version of the Qmodem telecommunications program. A number of excellent shareware communications programs are out there, so if you get one of them instead, you'll be in good hands. However, since I had to pick one (the program is so big it is broken into two files), I selected my personal favorite and the one that's easiest to download. The people that make Qmodem have their own BBS.

To download the two files, call Mustang Software's BBS at 805/873-2400. After a brief logon process, you end up at the Main Menu. Press the letter O and Enter for Other Info: Testdrives. At the Testdrives Menu, press 4 and Enter to get an informational screen about Qmodem and reply by pressing Y and Enter if you want to download both files. You have to select a download protocol and the usual stuff. Be sure to press G, for Good-bye, and then press Enter when you're all finished and want to hang up.

OLX-TD.EXE

This is the offline mail reader discussed in Chapter 15. When your volume of mail to read reaches a certain peak, or your typing speed presses the need of replying off-the-clock, it's time to try an offline mail reader. Again, there are many offline readers, but you can't go wrong with OLX — Off-Line Express. Coincidentally, you can download this program from the Mustang Software BBS as well. The process is the same as in the previous instructions.

Call Mustang Software's BBS at 805/873-2400. After a brief logon process, you end up at the Main Menu. Press the letter O and Enter for Other Info: Testdrives. At the Testdrives Menu, press 6 and Enter to get an informational screen about OLX, and reply by pressing Y and Enter if you want to download the file. You have to select a download protocol and the usual stuff. Be sure to press G, for Good-bye, and then press Enter when you're finished and want to hang up.

LIST90H.ZIP and WINLIST.ZIP

List is a program that lets you view text files — like the README.TXT files — that come with every piece of software you will ever download. This program also organizes your directory and just does a whole lot more in the area of file-list management. This program has been around for a very long time and is usually referred to as "Vern Buerg's famous List program." The Windows version, Win List, requires that you also have just plain List. So, if you want to use the Windows version, you have to download them both.

VPIC61.ZIP

The answer is "file viewer." The question is, "What do I do with an image file once I download it?" Indeed, what is the point of downloading a picture of Roger Rabbit if you can't see the darn thing? With VPIC, you can view just about any type of image file in the known universe. Again, there are many, many viewers. This one can be found on most BBSs. If you can't find it, search for Viewer.

SHEZ106.ZIP

This is a shell for zipping. A shell program is designed to go around another program — like the shell of a snail goes around, essentially, a slug. Shez goes around the Zip brothers, making it easier to tag files for zipping and unzipping, to look inside a zipped file without unzipping it, and to selectively extract the files of your choice. But Shez also goes a lot further than that. You see, there are at least a half-dozen *other* programs that do what Zip does — though Zip is definitely king of the hill. If you ever have to learn about and deal with LZH, ZOO, PAK, ARJ, and the rest, Shez will be a shell for them as well.

DRAGFL.ZIP

Drag And File was acknowledged by PC Magazine as a majorly-great — not their words — shareware program. Basically, it combines the previous three programs into one and does a whole lot more. It works in Windows and replaces File Manager, if you want.

WINPRN15.ZIP

Win Print is a Windows program that makes it super-simple to print text files — those kind of README.TXT files you now have to deal with when you've downloaded something. The twist here is that, by using fonts in Windows, Win Print condenses the text so that you can print two, even four pages on one. The only limit here is your eyesight.

TIMESET7.ZIP

This one is a just-for-geek-fun program. This program uses your modem to call up the Naval Observatory's atomic clock and resets your computer system to the *exact* time. I don't exactly know why everyone I know that uses this, including me, thinks it's cool — maybe we're all special. Anyway, there it is.

Chapter 22
Ten Ways to Get Out of Trouble

In This Chapter

▶ Read

▶ Jump to the top

▶ Ask another user

▶ Voice support

▶ Use a screen command

▶ Try something different

▶ Visit the past

▶ Page the Sysop

▶ Leave a comment

▶ Hang up on the BBS

1 f you get stuck, this chapter offers some ways to unstick yourself.

How to get out of trouble depends a lot on how much trouble you've gotten yourself into. For most, being in trouble means you've zigged when you should have zagged, and now you don't know how to get out or to find what you're looking for.

If whatever you're typing appears on the screen but is completely ignored, your problem could be that line noise or some other act of fate — natural or otherwise — has tossed you off the system. Nothing works because you're not there any more. Here's how to check to make sure you're still hooked up:

✔ Someplace on your communications-software screen, the word *online* or *offline* is displayed. If you can find that, you're question's answered.

✔ If you have an external modem, is the OH light lit? If it is, you're still online.

✔ If your modem line goes through the phone, pick up the receiver and see if you get a dial tone (you're offline) or some weird noises (you're online).

If you're still online and having nice, normal problems like being lost and frustrated, here are a few things to try.

Read

The sad truth is that many answers are either there on the screen or available someplace else on the BBS — but people continue to ignore all the help that's provided. Look around you and learn from the people who have been doing this for a decade.

- **The prompts:** A BBS is an open-book test. Whenever there's a question, all your possible answers are displayed to the left of the cursor. If what you're typing doesn't appear on the screen, or you're getting beeped at, it's because you haven't entered a selection that was offered.

- **Help screens:** Obvious, yes, but often overlooked. If the computer is asking for a decision, and you have no idea what the choices mean, ask for help. The instructions for getting help usually appear someplace on the screen. Often, it's as simple as pressing a ? or an H.

- **Bulletins and FAQs:** Many Sysops slave for hours over a hot bulletin or fascinating FAQ — Frequently Asked Question — for callers to read online or download for closer study. Take a look at the bulletin menu on your favorite system. You may find the answers to all your major questions right there.

Jump to the Top

If you're helplessly caught in a sub-sub-menu maze or just don't even know where you are, then look on-screen for a command to return you to either the Main Menu or *the top*. Each system has a different command to return to the Main Menu — if it has one at all.

A sneaky way to get to the top menu is to issue the Goodbye or Logoff command, usually found on every menu. When you get the `are you sure you want to log off` question, choose No, and the system returns you to the Main Menu. Once you're back at the top, you have a fresh start. Maybe this time you'll take the right fork instead of the left.

Ask Another User

The Sysop isn't the only one who knows what's going on. Other users are reliable sources of information. On busy systems, Sysops rely on their callers to help each other. If something happened online that you don't understand, leave a public E-Mail message in the appropriate conference.

Don't feel intimidated by leaving a public question. Even if you think you've got the dumbest question ever, rest assured that no one will make fun of a *sincere, polite* inquiry. People online are BBS enthusiasts, eager to spread the word and help newcomers find their way. As you might expect, if you post a question that has a bad attitude and a nasty tone, others make it their duty to dump upon you mightily.

Once you've left your note, hundreds or maybe thousands of people read it. Someone will reply.

Voice Support

If you paid your subscription fee, you may be entitled to phone support. That's right, an actual conversation with another human. What *will* they think of next? But, even if you haven't paid your fee (yet), Sysops who list their voice numbers are willing to talk to you. If they aren't, you find out very quickly.

Use a Screen Command

See Chapter 21 for the top ten secret commands — keystroke actions that cover many situations. My favorite is ? for Help!

Try Something Different

Isn't there a saying about those who don't learn from their mistakes being doomed to repeat them? If something doesn't work, try something *different*. Make notes of what you're doing — the letters you're typing, and the times you pressed Enter. Then, try it again, taking a different route this time. That tack may not work either, but the goal is not to become mired in the same error loop. Make *new* mistakes.

Look at it this way, the more different mistakes you make, the fewer there are left to make before finding the answer. If you make the exact same mistake over and over, there is no progress.

Visit the Past

Most decent communications programs have the *scrollback buffer* feature. The scrollback buffer, if you haven't used it yet, captures everything that happens on the BBS — screen by screen and keystroke by keystroke — temporarily saving it. Most scrollback buffers hold only a dozen pages of stuff. And, as new stuff gets sucked into the front end of the buffer, older stuff gets pushed out the back. Automatically.

The contents of the scrollback buffer are a record of your recent past. What you just did is contained in the buffer. With that knowledge, you can find out how you got where you are. Or maybe the instructions the system gave you, which didn't mean anything at the time (like ESC to Exit), now tell you exactly what you need to know. Try going to the scrollback buffer for hints.

Page the Sysop

Paging the Sysop is like paging someone in the lobby of a hotel or at the airport. It's a way of calling out to people who don't know they are needed. What happens in a BBS when you page the Sysop is that a beep goes off letting the Sysop know that someone — like you — wants to chat with them. You should only page the Sysop when absolutely necessary. After all, when you page a Sysop, you're saying, "Hey, Sysop, drop everything you're doing and help me right now." If you are in a genuine predicament, though, that's what the Page the Sysop option is for.

Paging the Sysop is an especially helpful tool if you need to show your problem to the Sysop. The hardest thing in troubleshooting — for the technical support person — is envisioning what the person in trouble is seeing. Sometimes the caller doesn't have the vocabulary necessary to explain what's going on. As they say, a picture is worth a thousand bytes.

For the Page command to work, the Sysop has to be within earshot of the BBS computer and, of course, willing or able to drop everything and help you.

Leave a Comment

Whenever you exit the system, you are offered the chance to leave a comment to the Sysop. If you had a hard time with something online, and you don't know where to turn, leave a question. If appropriate, try to phrase the note in a way that is not accusatory.

> ✔ Not good: "Your stupid system wouldn't let me download!"
>
> ✔ Good: "I had a very difficult time downloading. After tagging the file, I selected Zmodem, but the system completely hung up. I'm using a Zoom Modem and Windows 3.1 terminal program. Is it you or me?"

After all, whom would you rather help out, the author of that first note or the author of the second? I'm not suggesting that you be overly nice in a fake sort of way. Just be careful not to dash off a caustic note in the heat of the moment.

Hang Up on the BBS

If everything is frozen on your computer, and nothing seems to work, it's time to pull the plug. Although hanging up on a system is not the preferred way of doing things, the BBS can take it. If you do it a lot, the others on the BBS may start to wonder what's wrong with you. But an occasional drop-out is expected.

When you're ready, press your computer's reset button — or turn the computer off and wait one minute before turning it back on. Another way to physically hang up on the BBS is to unplug the phone line that runs from the modem to the phone or to the wall. Wait a minute before plugging it back in. If you have an external modem, just turn it off and, after a few seconds, turn it back on.

After you've had a chance to catch your breath, go back online and download a bulletin, ask for help, call them on the voice phone or follow any of the previous suggestions. Remember, the main thing is to persist. I promise you'll eventually get what you want.

Chapter 23

Top Ten Hints from Sysops

In This Chapter

▶ Set your communications software properly

▶ Read the instructions on the screen

▶ Remember, the BBS is run by a hobbyist

▶ Be familiar with Zmodem

▶ Correct external high-speed modem dropouts

▶ Don't blame the Sysop for line noise

▶ You can't hurt the BBS

▶ Don't just log on and download files

▶ Use offline readers

▶ Give help to other users

▶ Bonus: Hints for dealing with Sysops

I asked the Sysops of the infamous Top 100 BBSs for any technical hints they could offer to anyone using a BBS. After all, they're the ones people have turned to over the years. If anyone knows what could go wrong, it's the Sysops.

Set Your Communications Software Properly

Oftentimes, the problems experienced by new users stem from unfamiliarity with telecommunications software and software that hasn't been properly set up. You can check the manual, check with whomever sold you the system, or even call a friend. The things you're looking to do are:

✔ Set your communications software to 8-N-1. This is the normal setting. Most software programs assume you want 8-N-1, but, if you're having trouble connecting, it's something to check. For those of you who insist on knowing what 8-N-1 means, it stands for eight data bits, no parity, one stop bit. Does that help?

✔ Select ANSI terminal emulation.

Read the Instructions on the Screen

Heads up! There is a lot of help available if you just pay attention. These Sysops have been running a BBS for a long time, and there is only a very slim chance that you are going to come up with a new question. Whatever you're having trouble with has been asked and answered dozens of times over the years. So check out the screen and the help files. Your answers might be right there.

✔ First of all, whenever the system asks you a question, you can press H or ? for help and get an explanation. Often, to the left of the cursor, are your choices.

✔ Read and study the help files in the bulletin menus. Help is also available in the form of files known as "FAQs" — short for Frequently Asked Questions — which clarify the basics.

Don't Be Afraid to Ask Questions

If you can't figure the situation out on your own, please do ask questions. Everyone remembers being a beginner, and, as long as you ask for help rather than demand it, you'll find plenty of assistance available. But also remember to rely on your fellow BBSers to help out. If no one can help, then go ahead and, from the Main Menu, Page the Sysop. If the Sysop is there, he or she will reply by typing a message on the screen asking if you rang. When you do ask questions, please be as concise and to-the-point as possible.

Remember, the BBS Is Run by a Hobbyist

It's easy to forget that the BBS isn't a setup like America Online or Prodigy. The vast majority of BBSs are run as a hobby by someone who loves computers and enjoys providing a gathering place for people. If the BBS goes down, or something goes wrong, Sysops depend on callers to let them know. The help is appreciated. Screaming complaints are not. Unfortunately, we live in a culture where it is often necessary to scream at low-wage, don't-care people who guard the front lines of big business in order to get attention. You needn't feel compelled to motivate the Sysop with such tactics. For the Sysop, it is a matter of pride that the BBS runs properly. All you have to do is point out the problem, and the Sysop will be on it as quickly as humanly possible.

Be Familiar with Zmodem

This falls under the "know thy modem software" category. Since virtually every telecommunications program now comes with Zmodem, you're going to be pretty hard-pressed to come up with excuses not to use Zmodem as your protocol *du jour*. Make sure you've got it and then use it.

Correct External High-Speed Modem Drop-Outs

You want a technical hint? This is about as technical as it gets. The good news is that you just got yourself a fancy external high-speed modem. The bad news is that it seems to be working unreliably. When you download, your modem often disconnects unexpectedly from the BBS. What gives? Well, a lot of computers have an old-fashioned serial port — that's where the modem plugs in. You need a new-fangled serial port equipped with what is called a 16550 UART chip. You can use Microsoft Diagnostics (MSD), as outlined in Appendix A, to find out whether you've got the 16550 UART chip, if this has been a problem for you.

Don't Blame the Sysop for Line Noise

One thing Sysops often get blamed for is *line noise*. When your connection with a BBS is unexpectedly terminated or dropped, more often than not it is caused by line noise, not a bad BBS setup. You've experienced line noise in voice calls — you know, when you get such a bad connection that you can't hear the other person? Line noise is caused by many things, including sunspots and wet weather. If you're experiencing any of those conditions, then line noise could be causing interference. Don't blame the Sysop for line noise, since a BBS has no more control over it than you do.

You Can't Hurt the BBS

Nothing you can do from your computer will hurt the BBS system. You can't cause the other system to crash and blow up. So, don't be shy. Try things out and have fun. Even if you have to hang up without logging off, you still won't damage anything.

Don't Just Download Files

Although some BBSs are set up exclusively for file grabbing, many are not. As much as computer people are sometimes characterized as socially awkward geeks, you may be surprised to learn that, for most Sysops, it's the people-factor that makes BBSing fun. Most Sysops prefer that you, as a guest on their system, spend some time mingling with the other partygoers, rather than spending your whole visit alone in a corner scarffing down the pâté.

Use Offline Readers

Check out Chapter 15 for the whys and wherefores of offline readers. Basically, using offline readers saves you time and long-distance charges, and moves you off the BBS quickly, so others have a chance to use the often-limited phone lines available to the system. If you're an E-Mail fan, this is definitely something to look into.

Give Help to Other Users

It will happen one day — sooner than you think. You'll see someone struggling to figure out a situation they've mired themselves in, and you'll know how to get them out. If you can help, don't be shy. Lend a hand to those who are newer to BBSing than you. Helping each other is a BBS tradition, and it's how you thank those who helped you. Besides, you'll learn more yourself by helping others.

Bonus: Hints for Dealing with Sysops

None of the Sysops would tell you this, but I will. Here are the secret tips that will make it easier for the Sysop to assist you when you ask for help:

- ✔ Be as concise and precise as possible.

  If the question is about downloading, don't start with: "I was online the other day and looked at list after list of files — did you know you have a lot of files? — and then, finally, after looking for ten or fifteen minutes, I found a file that looked good. Or at least that's what I thought. But my brother-in-law walked in and said . . ."

- ✔ Indicate that you are willing to work at finding a solution on your own: "I can't seem to download. Is there a bulletin or FAQ on this topic?"

- ✔ Indicate that you have made some effort on your own to discover the solution to the problem: "I read my manual and exchanged E-Mail with another person on this system, but I still can't seem to make it work."

- ✔ As a corollary to the previous point, don't mistake repetition for effort: "I hit Enter 100 times, and it never worked once."

Part V
Appendixes

The 5th Wave   **By Rich Tennant**

YOU'RE NOT A CYBERHOLIC... if you look for the Soup of the Day in the Format menu.

In this part...

The Appendixes are here to get you over the hump from wanting to make that first call on your own to actually doing it. In addition to the basics of finding your modem and installing ANSI.SYS, the appendixes also include the complete list of *Boardwatch Magazine's* Top 100 BBSs and a sampling of international BBSs for you to try. Consider that list as your launching pad into cyberspace. Bon Voyage!

Appendix A
Getting to the Starting Line

In This Appendix

▶ Picking a phone line

▶ Hunting down the modem

▶ Sleuthing out your software

▶ Dealing with the dialing directory

A s I mentioned in the Introduction, to go online you need a computer, a phone line, a modem, and modem software. Don't be embarrassed if you don't know whether you've got everything you need. Although you should, at least, feel a tad sheepish if you're confused about whether you do or do not own a computer. I'm going to trust you have a computer and concentrate on helping you find the other items.

What's not covered in this chapter is how to purchase, install, and configure a modem. Why not? Frankly, it would take another whole book to cover that topic properly. And I'm not exercising hyperbole, either. There are, in fact, two whole books, called *Modems For Dummies* and *MORE Modems For Dummies*, both also published by IDG Books Worldwide, which tackle that very issue.

Picking a Phone Line

You don't have to install a special phone line to use your modem. The phone line you already have will do just fine. If you have Call Waiting, though, you'll want to make sure you've also got Cancel Call Waiting — contact your phone company for that. If you don't turn off Call Waiting before you go online, and somebody calls, you'll find yourself off line in a flash. This always happens at the worst time. Guaranteed. If you become a serious cybersurfer, you'll want a second phone line, so you can be online and maintain voice communications with the outside world. Besides, how else will you be able to order pizza?

Even if you get Cancel Call Waiting, the phone company won't be much help in telling you what to do with that information — modem-wise. The code for Cancel Call Waiting is usually *70. So, if you're calling 555-1212 on your computer, then to Cancel Call Waiting you must add *70 to the front of the number being dial — like *70,555-1212. And, yes, that is a comma after the *70. That comma represents a pause to give the phone company a chance to turn off the Call Waiting before dialing the number. If you're wobbly about adding phone numbers to your communications software dialing directory, take a look at the section on "Dealing with the Dialing Directory" at the end of this chapter for a few clues.

Hunting Down the Modem

Modems — the devices that enable your computer to use the telephone to call another computer — come in many shapes, sizes, and speeds. However, at its most basic level, a modem is either *internal* (fits inside the computer) or *external* (is in a box that sits outside your computer).

Chances are, if you've got an external modem, it's that thing with a row lights in the front of it which is sitting right next to the computer. So, if you see something that matches that description, the answer is: "Yes, you've got a modem."

Finding an internal modem doesn't have to be a big deal just because it's hidden inside your computer. The easiest, most nontechnical, foolproof way to determine if you have an internal modem is simply to look at the back of your computer. Is there a phone line coming out of the machine? If not, is there a phone jack visible on the back of your computer? Either way, if the answer is affirmative, you've got a modem.

If, for some reason, looking at the back of your computer isn't possible, here are some more ways to discover whether or not a modem is installed. Each of these options is progressively more difficult and problematic.

- ✔ Look at your sales receipt or call the people who sold you the computer. They might know.
- ✔ Use Microsoft's MSD program.

   Just because you've never heard of Microsoft Diagnostics (MSD), doesn't mean you don't have it already sitting on your hard disk. For several years now, those sneaky devils at Microsoft have been secretly shipping MSD with many of their programs. It may already be on your computer. To use the MSD program, first get to a system prompt. In other words, save whatever you're doing and quit the program you're in. Quit Windows, even, if you're in it.

Once you're at the system prompt — it looks something like C : \ > — type **MSD** and press Enter.

If you typed MSD correctly, but you still see the phrase Bad Command or File Name, you don't have to read any further. It looks as though you don't have the MSD program.

If you do get the MSD opening screen, select COM Ports by pressing the letter C. (If you have an older version of the program, you may have to press Alt+S to select Serial Ports. Read the instructions on your screen.)

The next screen, Figure A-1, is kind of technical. All you have to know is that if one of your COM Ports answers Yes to Ring Indicator, Data Set Ready, and Clear to Send — you've got a modem! Make a note which COM Port your modem is using. If you see all No responses, you can deduce what that means.

To leave MSD, press Enter to close down the COM Ports screen, then press F3 to exit MSD altogether.

Figure A-1: Microsoft Diagnostics can locate an installed modem. Look for Yes answers on your COM Ports screen, like those under COM1:.

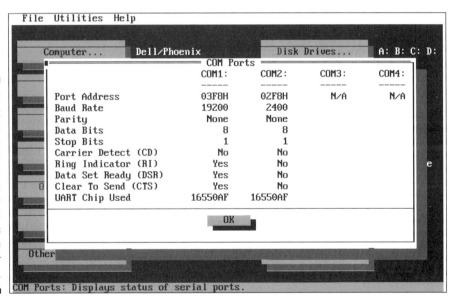

- Try asking Terminal.

  Terminal is the name of the Windows 3.1 modem software. Terminal is such a bad modem program that it would have won the award for most useless Windows accessory, if it weren't for the fact that the Windows built-in Calculator accessory sometimes gives wrong answers. If you use Windows 3.1, open the Accessories group and then double-click on the Terminal icon. If you're asked to select a default COM Port, try COM 1. If, when you get into the program, the word OK appears on-screen, you have a modem.

  If the word OK does not appear, select Settings⇨Communications⇨Connector and switch to COM 2, if COM 1 had been selected before — or vice versa. When you've selected the new COM setting, click on the OK button to close the Connector dialog box. At the blank Terminal screen, type **AT** and press Enter. Again, if the word OK appears, you've got a modem. Otherwise, it doesn't look too good.

  Either way, exit Terminal by selecting File⇨Exit.

Sleuthing Out Your Software

Okay, you've got a modem. Congrats. You're only part of the way there. In order to talk to the modem, you need modem software — also known as telecommunications software. The good news is that it's standard industry practice to include modem software with every modem purchase. Logically, therefore, if you have a modem, you should have modem software sitting around someplace, too. The comes-with-modem software is not exactly cutting edge, but it's better than nothing (and much better than Terminal). Here are some suggestions to determine what you've got:

- Look through your box of manuals. I know it's an ugly thought, but give it a try. If you've got the basic comes-with-it software, the manual will be very small. Look for software names like Bitcom and Quick-Link. If you have real modem software, the manual will be large, and the software names to look for are Qmodem, Procomm, Smartcom, and Crosstalk.

- Call whoever sold you the system and ask for help.

- Get into Windows and look for a Group Icon name that looks like it might be telecommunications software.

- Get into Windows File Manager by opening the Main Group and double-clicking on the File Manager icon. Travel up and down the directory tree — on the left — looking for directories with names like: PCPLUS, QMPRO, WINFAX, QL2, BITCOM, and TELIX. If you find something, make a note of it so you can use it later. To exit File Manager, press Alt+F4.

Dealing with the Dialing Directory

Okay, let's say you've found your phone line and your modem and started your communications software. Now what? Are you feeling like you're all dressed up with no place to go?

That's where the dialing directory comes into the picture. Each communications program — whether Windows, DOS, or Mac — has what's called a dialing directory. The dialing directory is the phone book for your communications software. This is where the phone numbers of BBSs are entered and saved.

Bringing up the dialing directory, selecting a destination to call, and then pressing Enter or clicking OK is usually the basic process for calling another computer.

Naturally, every piece of software has its own special way to activate the dialing directory. Often, though, the command is Alt+D. If you don't know what your command is, try Alt+D. Sometimes, as in Procomm Plus for Windows and other Windows programs, getting to the dialing directory is a matter of clicking on a phonebook icon.

Once the dialing directory is open, you usually find an option to *add*, *insert*, or *revise* the directory. This particular command is completely different from communications program to communications program, so you'll have to stare at the screen a bit until you see the option. Sometimes, you have to press a menu command first before those options are revealed. (Don't forget to use your system's help command.)

When the dialing directory finally opens itself up to you, as in Figure A-2, you'll find a simple fill-in-the-blank situation — name of place to call, phone number, and so on. Sometimes, you'll be prompted for *communications protocol*. If you are asked for this information, your answer is always 8-N-1. (That's eight data bits, No Parity, and one stop bit.)

When all that is entered, give the save or OK command, depending on your program.

And . . . you're right for lift-off into cyberspace.

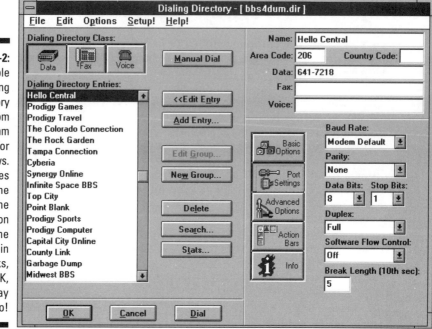

Figure A-2:
A sample
Dialing
Directory
from
Procomm
Plus for
Windows.
The names
are on the
left, and the
information
is on the
right. Fill in
the blanks,
click OK,
and away
you go!

Appendix B

The Complete Top 100 BBSs

*T*his is it. The complete list, which appeared in the September 1994 issue of *Boardwatch Magazine,* of the Top 100 BBSs

Before I let you loose on this list, here are a couple things to keep in mind:

- ✔ **Reader Survey:** This list was compiled as a result of a reader survey. In plain English, it's a popularity contest. Just as in voting on the best movie of the year, personal preference is the major factor. What I'm saying is that there was no scientific application of emperical data used to produce this list. Given the thousands of BBSs in existence, to be on this list at all is quite an achievement. And, just so you don't pass by the lower 50, I include some screen shots of a few of those systems interspersed in the next few pages.

- ✔ **Prodigy:** In order to access Prodigy Bulletin Boards, you have to join Prodigy — a commercial online service. If interested, call 800-775-7714. The words listed in the telephone number slot are the Jump words used to go to the bulletin board once you've joined Prodigy.

- ✔ **Telnet and WWW:** To access the Telnet or WWW address listed on the right, you must first be signed up with an Internet provider. If you aren't, don't worry about the Internet right now. However, those BBSs with Telnet addresses listed on the right can be accessed from anywhere in the world without incurring long-distance charges. Just log onto your local Internet account, type **telnet** [telnet address], and press Enter. To get onto Software Creations, after logging onto the Internet, for example, type **telnet swcbbs.com** and press Enter.

- ✔ **Changes:** At the time of the publication, all the phone numbers below were tested. A handful of the Top 100 aren't answering their phone anymore. They are so noted. By the time you get around to making a few calls, a few more systems may have fallen by the wayside or moved. Or features may have been added or removed. The only thing that's certain is that nothing stays the same. If you find a new number for any of these BBSs — or if you find your own favorite BBS — why not drop me a line and let me know. You can find me at bslick@netcom.com on the Internet. Meanwhile, keep your eyes peeled for the next list of the *Boardwatch Magazine* Top 100!

Okay, now go have fun! And play nice with the other kids!

Boardwatch Magazine Top 100 BBSs

Standing	BBS Name	Description	City, State	BBS Number	Telnet or WWW
1	Software Creations	Dedicated to the development and distribution of great software — home of the authors.	Clinton, MA	508/368-7139	swcbbs.com
2	EXEC-PC	World's largest BBS since 1983. Is trying to archive every single Shareware, free utility, and GIF image in the world.	New Berlin, WI	414/789-4360	bbs.execpc.com or http://execpc.com
3	GLIB (Gay and Lesbian Bureau)	A non profit information and communications resource primarily (but not exclusively) serving the gay, lesbian, and bisexual community.	Arlington, VA	703/578-4542	
4	Monterey Gaming System	Custom interactive gaming and multiuser conferences.	Monterey, CA	408/655-5555	
5	Blue Ridge Express	Three gigabyte files base and many discussion groups.	Richmond, VA	804/790-9600	
6	Deep Cove Online	News, publications, Internet E-Mail, shareware, games.	Surrey, BC	604/536-5885	deepcove.com
7†	AlphaOne Online	Adults only, bar atmosphere, matchmaking, personals, shareware.	Park Ridge, IL	708/827-3619	alphaone.com
8	America's Suggestion Box	General interest online information service and full Internet access provider.	Ronkonkoma, NY	516/471-8625	asb.com
9†	Lifestyle Online	Busiest and most active system for couples and singles to make contact via personal ads (no adult images).	East Setauket, NY	516/689-5390	lifestyle.com
10	Prodigy Genealogy	Information and help searching for people.			Genealogy BB
11	Chrysalis	Largest BBS in the state of Texas with 34 CD-ROMs online, Internet E-mail, online publications.	Plano, TX	214/690-9295	chrysalis.org
12†	Pleasure Dome BBS	Adults only, matchmaking, Internet E-mail, online games.	Virginia Beach, VA	804/490-5878	
13	The INDEX System	It's not just a BBS, it's an online community. G-Rated, but still tons of fun.	Woodstock, GA	404/924-8472	index.com
14	Pennsylvania Online	Family oriented, massive file library, Internet services.	Harrisburg, PA	717/657-8699	paonline.com

Standing	BBS Name	Description	City, State	BBS Number	Telnet or WWW
15	Springfield Public Access	Over 250,000 files, multiuser games, chat, Internet access, Virtual CommunityCenter™.	Springfield, MA	413/536-4365	the-spa.com
16	OS/2 Shareware	World's largest collection of OS/2 freeware, shareware, and public domain programs and information.	Fairfax, VA	703/385-4325	bbs.os2bbs.com
17	DSC	Shareware, Internet, Internet accounts.	Ivyland, PA	215/443-7390	dsc.voicenet.com
18	Wizard's Gate BBS	No fees, full access on first call, 12 gigabytes online	Columbus, OH	614/224-1635	
19	Aquila BBS	Chicago's largest BBS, family oriented, large file base.	Aurora, IL	708/820-8344	aquila.com
20	Nashville Exchange	Internet, shareware, online games.	Nashville, TN	615/383-0727	
21	deltaComm Online	Distribution and support for Telix.	Cary, NC	919/481-9399	
22	The File Shop BBS	US & World News, stock information, full Internet.	Kansas City, MO	913/262-7000	fileshop.com
23	Traders' Connection	World's largest classified ad database, chat, interactive games, magazines, 50 gigabytes of information.	Indianapolis, IN	317/359-5199	trader.com
24	PC-Ohio	Large message base, shareware, ads.	Cleveland, OH	216/381-3320	
25	Father & Son BBS	General BBS, messages, files, chat, E-mail.	Whitehall, PA	610/439-1509	
26	MicroFone InfoService	Since 1982, online games, Internet E-mail.	Metuchen, NJ	908/205-0189	
27	Doctor's Office	Nine Gigs online, chat, messages, games, matchmaker.	Vienna, VA	703/749-2860	docs.dgsys.com
28	ExecNet Information Systems	Internet, shareware, adult area.	Mount Vernon, NY	914/667-4066	gateway.execnet.com
29	City Lights	35,000 files, 100 online games, echoes.	Arden Hills, MN	612/633-1366	
30	The File Bank, Inc.	A full-service BBS offering hundreds of thousands of shareware files, hundreds of message areas, online games, and real-time chat.	Denver, CO	303/534-4646	

(continued)

Standing	BBS Name	Description	City, State	BBS Number	Telnet or WWW
31	Starship II BBS	Ten gigs online.	Lyndhurst, NJ	201/935-1485	
32	Network East	General access and a wide variety of online services, Internet E-Mail.	Rockville, MD	301/738-0000	
33	Atlanta Windows	Windows & OS/2 support, five Gigs online.	Woodstock, GA	404/516-0048	
34	The Swamp	Seeks to promote understanding in a friendly and trustworthy atmosphere. Internet, two gigs files online.	Riverfalls, WI	715/425-8865	
35	The Cracker Barrel BBS	Family oriented — run by father and son — Christian, medical and diabetes information.	Falmouth, VA	703/899-2285	
36	Odyssey	Online entertainment for adults over 18 years of age.	Monrovia, CA	818/358-6968	odyssey.ody.com
37	Crystal Quill	Works to provide a professionally run system with integrity to build a place where you can contact intelligent life.	Arlington, VA	703/241-7100	cq.cqi.com
38	Hello Central	We provide the finest recreational computer in a user-friendly, kid-free environment, somewhat like the bar Cheers on TV.	Bellevue, WA	206/641-7218	
39	Prodigy Games	Help on fantasy, sci-fi, coin-op, simulator.			Games BB
40	Prodigy Travel	Travel information and commentary.			Travel BB
41	Colorado Connection	BirdNet, 16 CD-ROMs, ASP BBS, Internet E-mail.	Arvada, CO	303/423-9775	
42	The Rock Garden	Online role-playing games, chat, strangest system on the air.	Phoenix, AZ	602/220-3000	garden.hvs.com
43	Tampa Connection	Matchmaking, full Internet, network chat.	Tampa, FL	813/961-8665	
44	Cyberia	General entertainment, online games, 3.3 gigs online, shareware, free communication software (717-840-0139).	York, PA	717/840-1444	Telnet soon
45	Synergy Online	Online games, chat system, 13 Gigs online.	Basking Ridge, NJ	201-331-1797	

Standing	BBS Name	Description	City, State	BBS Number	Telnet or WWW
46	Infinite Space BBS	Internet, Telnet, and nationwide chat system.	Orlando, FL	407/856-0021	
47	Top City	Chat, information, local radio stations online.	St. Paul, MN	612/225-1003	
48	Point Blank	Entertainment and business, chat, Internet E-Mail.	Plainview, NY	516/755-3000	
49	Prodigy Sports	All spectator sports such as hockey, baseball, basketball, football, figure skating, and gymnastics. Users include professionals.			Sports Play BB
50	Prodigy Computer	Hardware, software, news, hints, and tips.			Computer BB
51	Capital City Online	No answer.			

Figure B-1:
One bulletin on The Source BBS (#61) reveals the files winning the most-likely-to-be-downloaded award.

```
                              ┌─────────────────┐
                              │  The Source BBS │
                              └─────────────────┘
              Listing Of Most Popular Files Received Since 03/04/95

MEMBER.ZIP    Size:      5,769 ¦ REQUIRED for continued access to The
Date: 12/30/99  DL's:  2,664 ¦ Source.

NEWFILES.ZIP Size:     27,706 ¦ NEW FILES Uploaded in the past 15 days
Date: 03/18/95  DL's:  2,288 ¦

WINFILES.ZIP Size:     43,016 ¦ All files in the WINDOWS Directory, updated
Date: 03/18/95  DL's:    604 ¦ daily

210211.ZIP   Size:    249,586 ¦ Upgrade patch for PROCOMM PLUS for Windows
Date: 03/07/95  DL's:     21 ¦ V2.10 to V2.11.

CPUID95.ZIP  Size:     48,842 ¦ Intel Microprocessor Identification Utility
Date: 03/09/95  DL's:     19 ¦ February 1995:
[C]ontinue, [N]onStop, [S]top? [C]
```

Standing	BBS Name	Description	City, State	BBS Number	Telnet or WWW
52	County Link	46,000 files, FidoNet.	Columbia Stn, OH	216/236-6126	
53	Garbage Dump	National access from over 500 cities.	Albuquerque, NM	505/294-5675	
54	Midwest BBS	Internet E-mail, USA Today, shareware.	St. Charles, IL	708/513-1034	
55	Toledo's TBBS	A general board that claims to have it all, including Internet and CD-ROMs online in a professional atmosphere.	Temperence, MI	313/854-6001	toltbbs.com

(continued)

Standing	BBS Name	Description	City, State	BBS Number	Telnet or WWW
56†	Friendship Express BBS	Adults only, gay, lesbian, and other lifestyles.	Minneapolis, MN	612/566-5726	
57	Mercury Opus	Amiga, Mac, DOS, Windows, OS/2, adult files.	Largo, FL	813/321-0734	
58	BMUG Boston	Support BBS for the Mac Users Group.	Boston, MA	617/356-6336	
59†	Arka Amatuers	Adult chat, stories, shopping mall.	Fairfax, VA	703/352-8142	
60	Prodigy Crafts	Provides a place for people to go for ideas, inspiration, and support whether they are bragging on their project or bemoaning one that did not turn out.			Crafts BB

Figure B-2: The official Modemus Addictus Seal of Approval adorns TSCNet Online Services (#69) logoff screen.

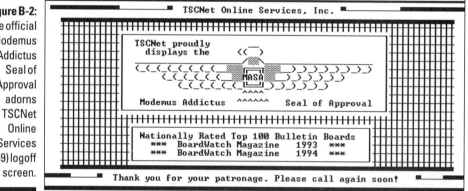

Standing	BBS Name	Description	City, State	BBS Number	Telnet or WWW
61	The Source	Irreverent source for new shareware Internet E-mail.	Redondo Bch, CA	310/371-3737	
62	Prodigy Hobbies	Contests, helpful hints, info on most hobbies.			Hobbies BB
63	YEBB	Educational and general BBS, sponsored by Sioux Falls school system.	Sioux Falls, SD	605/331-5831	605.331.5831
64	Pegasus Project	80,000 files, Internet T1 line (SLIP/PPP available), link by satellite connection, very large adult area. Call 813/481-9902 for free Pegasus-specific communications software, or download from BBS.	Cape Coral, FL	813/481-5575	pegproj.com

Standing	BBS Name	Description	City, State	BBS Number	Telnet or WWW
65	YA! WEBECAD!	CAD and graphics, 45 CD-ROMs, 11 gigabytes, 200,000 files online.	Evansville, IN	812/428-3870	
66	Eagles Nest Communications	Friendly, helpful BBS for the entire family, 89,000 files online, Internet.	Providence, RI	401/732-5290	enest.com
67	Radio Wave BBS	Provides information, messaging, and connectivity to the public in a friendly atmosphere. Internet, shareware.	Delren, NJ	609/764-0812	radiowave.com
68	Prodigy Music	Rock, alternative, metal, pop, blues, R&B, rap, hip hop, and reggae fans can chat with each other and post notes to music stars. Last year fans were able to communicate with Mick Jagger, Jimmy Page, and more. Contests.			Music BB

Figure B-3:
The West Coast Connection (#73) Main Menu uses whole word commands rather than just one-letter commands.

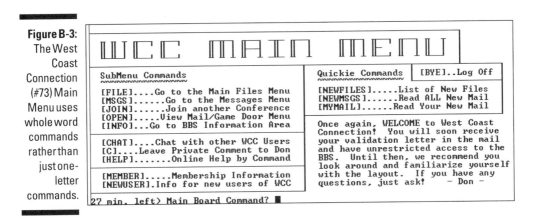

Standing	BBS Name	Description	City, State	BBS Number	Telnet or WWW
69	TSCNet	Makes callers feel like part of a cyberfamily while providing Internet, 13 gigabytes of files, and games. Annual Floppy-Disk-Throwing Party.	Silverdale, WA	360/613-0437	tscnet.com
70	Prodigy Medical	Medical support BB on Prodigy provides a meeting place to share and receive support and information on a wide variety of topics related to medical issues. Thirty topics.			Medical Support BB

(continued)

Standing	BBS Name	Description	City, State	BBS Number	Telnet or WWW
71	Windows Online	Provides shareware and support to Windows, Windows NT, DOS, and OS/2 users and network professionals. Own online magazine, WinOnLine Review.	Danville, CA	510/736-8343	http://www.cris.com/WOL
72	Digicom Info Network	Internet E-mail, FidoNet, Support BBS List.	Evansville, IN	812/479-1310	
73	West Coast Connection	Over 40,000 files, online games, 1000 message bases, Internet E-Mail, Pen and Brush Net.	El Cajon, CA	619/449-8333	
74	After The Bars	Gay and lesbian chat system, large database.	Chicago, IL	312/262-3626	
75	DLS InfoNet	Mission: To provide low cost Internet access for the masses. Shareware, Internet E-Mail, Usenet.	Littleton, CO	303/347-2921	
76	Hotlanta BBS	Social chat system for open-minded adults.	Atlanta, GA	404/518-3100	
77	Ultimate BBS	Large social chat system, files.	Mt. Pulaski, IL	217/792-3663	
78	Compass Rose	Social chat system, message, E-mail.	Davis, CA	916/447-0292	
79	Prodigy Teens	This is for teens to meet, find cyber Pen-Pals, discuss music, fashion, trends, politics, etc.			Teens BB

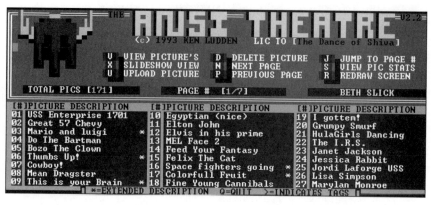

Figure B-4:
Have you seen ANSI Theatre on Dance of Shiva (#83)?

Standing	BBS Name	Description	City, State	BBS Number	Telnet or WWW
80	Perfect Vision Graphics	Graphics-oriented system offering thousands of original image scans from a wide range of subject matter — from science fiction and classic TV to supermodels.	Troy, OH	513/233-7993	
81	24th St. Exchange	A place to share ideas, information, well maintained and stocked with shareware, message bases, Internet E-Mail, and chat.	Sacramento, CA	916/448-2483	
82	Vegas Playground	BBS is a family-oriented, online community for the Las Vegas Valley area which includes games, message base, and monthly raffle for as-seen-on-TV prizes like Ginsu knives.	Las Vegas, NV	702/386-7979	
83	Dance of Shiva	Fun, graphics-oriented, cybervillage with 25 CD-ROMs, full Internet, and online periodicals.	Louisville, KY	502/899-7773	shivasys.com
84	Channel 1	Internet access, large file base of shareware.	Cambridge, MA	617/354-8873	
85	Mog-ur's EMS	Large file system, Internet, Usenet, 14 Networks.	Granada Hills, CA	818/366-1238	
86	The Godfather	Home of Emposium, CD-ROMs, GIFs, Usenet.	Tampa, FL	813/289-3314	
87	Fresno Public Access	Number disconnected.			

(continued)

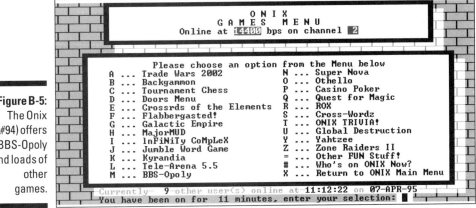

Figure B-5:
The Onix (#94) offers BBS-Opoly and loads of other games.

Standing	BBS Name	Description	City, State	BBS Number	Telnet or WWW
88	Rose and Crown	57 CD-ROMs online, Rime, GIFs, 100 disk CD changer.	Chattanooga, TN	615/892-0097	
89	Mico Message Service	Internet, shareware, chat, files.	Raleigh, NC	919/779-6674	
90	Tech Talk	10 Gigabytes, 60,000 files, Internet E-mail, Ultrachat.	Titusville, FL	407/635-8833	
91	MPCUG	3 Gigabytes online, files, Madison PC Users' Group.	Madison, WI	608/233-0286	
92	Kandy Shack	Large, nice file area, large message area.	Garden Grove, CA	714/636-2667	
93†	The Third Eye	Adults only, free speech, matchmaking.	Nashville, TN	615/227-6155	
94	ONIX	Friendly place for users to chat, socialize, and play interactive games with others. Live Internet.	Philadelphia, PA	215/883-1900	onix. comhttp://onix. com
95	Digital Vortex	Number disconnected.			
96	Linq	Bilingual — English and French — Linq is a cafe, bar, and library for adults over 18. Discussions range from general, politics, entertainment, and the erotic. Adult sections may be turned off at user's discretion.	Montreal, QB	514/522-3866	linq.com
97	Graphic Impulse BBS	General BBS leaning towards adult graphics, matchmaking, orginal scans.	Champaign, IL	217/398-4450	
98	In Through The Out Door	Something for everyone, user input appreciated, adult areas, online games, and E-Mail.	Muncie, IN	317/282-6862	
99	Titan BBS	Number disconnected.			
100	Possibilities	Online games, Ultrachat, messages, E-Mail, files.	Poway, CA	619/748-5264	

Appendix C

Putting the Global in Global Village

. . . .

In This Appendix
▶ A sampling of BBSs throughout the world
▶ The Association of Shareware Professionals

. . . .

*I*f you've ever been to Disneyland, you've seen or experienced the exhibit called, *It's a Small World.* Basically, it's a boat ride — in the sense that a *Tunnel of Love* is a boat ride — through a building containing tableau after tableau of animatronic children from around the world dressed in traditional costumes and all singing *It's a Small World After All* in their native languages. Although the exhibits are interesting, it's the tune that starts to grate at the nerves. The ride never seems to end.

It's impossible to walk away from that exhibit without the *Small World* theme song reverberating endlessly in your brain for days afterward. You wake up at 3 a.m. still humming the tune and hating yourself for it.

No matter how corny it sounds, though, it *is* a small world, and it's getting smaller every day. Of course, television brought global events to our doorstep long ago. But on CNN, only the anchors and reporters can send messages. BBSs and the Internet are available to everyday folks like you and me.

Getting the International Online

As you've seen in the previous chapters, Internet makes it possible to make connections across the street and around the globe at the same affordable price. As the technology becomes more available, more connections will be made — both human and electronic.

In the meantime, here is a list of *some* — just the barest sampling — of BBSs from around the world. If you log onto these systems, you'll find more lists of other international BBSs. Ask for recommendations. *Buena suerte, mazel tov, buena fortuna, viel glück,* and *amuse-toi bien!*

International BBSs

BBS NAME	Sysop Name	Phone
Australia		
Northern Computer Service	Mark Beel	+61-03-306-5130
Geowiz	Ray Firth	+011-02-457-0005
Prophet BBS	Larry Lewis	+61-2-835-1388
Electronic Oracle, The	Grayham Smith	+61-8-234-0791
Baud Room, The	Anthony Lloyd Zilles	+61-3-481-8022
Belgium		
Media Concept BBS	Dionysius Vander.Roost	+32-81-411300
Info-Center BBS	Freddy Verrezen	+32-14-311455
Full Connection BBS	Jose De Menezes Filho	+55-11-440-7204
Hot-Line BBS	Charles Miranda	+55-21-537-1603
Canada		
Online Systems of Canada	Bruce Asquith	519-657-7485
ToToche BBS	Patrick Asselin	514-326-8363
V-Net Online Services	Craig Behan	613-723-1740
Nucleus Information Serv	Dave Berzins	403-531-9353
CyberCity BBS	Luc Blais	819-684-8232
X-CONNECTIONS BBS	Pierre Burgoyne	819-776-0088
ComputerLink	Bill Campbell	416-233-5410
TEXADA Graphic WINDOWS	John A. Collins	604-486-7229
Synapse BBS	Daniel Coulombe	819-561-4321
Borderquest BBS	Nav Dhunay	403-262-5095
Silicon Tundra BBS	Richard Doiron	613-838-5341
Deep Cove BBS	Wayne Duval	604-536-5885
French Connexion, The	Phil French	416-632-5653
Trade Link	Karl Heigold	604-768-0988
Alpha City BBS	Rick Johnston	905-579-6302
Info-Source Canada	Terry Jonasson	204-667-0899
Superior Shareware	Jim Keigher	807-475-3099
Business Solutions BBS	Doug Lacombe	306-653-1664
OTB Communication System	David Lowry	416-844-2483
AIS Multiline	Chris Pinnell	604-489-4206
Acumen BBS	Dan Schmidt	807-626-9339
ATAB BBS	Donald C. Sheward	902-435-0751
T-8000 Info System	Brian G. Simpson	403-246-3374
The UpAllNite BBS	Martin Vanderzwan	519-351-4364
Late Nite Diversions	Jon Vidler	519-332-0241

BBS NAME	Sysop Name	Phone
Denmark		
Night Dream BBS	Thomas Jensen	+45-55340404
France		
Heremes Center BBS	Philippe Cheve	+331-69007672
Germany		
Hamster BBS	Hartmut W. Malzahn	+49-2371-14490
Silverado, The	David Silver	+49-6221-767992
Hong Kong		
iLink Information Service	Daniel Ng	+852-414-9393
Phone Magazine	Alsmond Yui	011-852-475-2772
India		
Live Wire BBS! Calcutta	Shamit Khemka	+91-33-248-1356
Live Wire BBS!	Suchit Nanda	+91-22-578-7812
Israel		
Channel V	Tal Reshef	+972-9-503801
Italy		
Prometheus	Federico Arezzo	+39-80-5515278
BBS2000	Giancarlo Cairella	+39-2-781147
/\ssisT-ON-LinE	Francesco Luconi	+39-55-2340486
Altair Data System	Paolo Zangheri	+39-2-642-0515
Japan		
JIX BBS	Paul Hardy	+06-351-6074
P&A BBS	Patrick Hochner	+81-425-46-9143
Malaysia		
PC Shop	Thim Liew	+60-3-957-4373
Mexico		
INTER-BBS Mexico Dls	Carlos Bazan	+52-5-251-6089
Netherlands		
MultiServer	Jos Bergman	+31-38-541358
HACOM BBS	Marcel Broekema	+31-33-801882
Knight Light PCB BBS	Willem Schotman	+31-13-678227
BBS Waterland	Joop Stokvis	+31-2990-40202
McBaud! BBS	Ron van Rossum	+31-10-475-2961

(Continued)

BBS NAME	Sysop Name	Phone
Portugal		
SkyLab BBS	Miguel Lupi Alves	+351-1-7269042
Visus BBS	Jose Camara	+351-1-7935839
B-Link BBS	Antonio M. Jorge	+351-1-4919755
Saudi Arabia		
MidEast Connection BBS	Mamdoh Al Oqiel	+966-1-441-0075
Darin	Jamil Sinan	+966-3-855-2131
Singapore		
Artist On-Line Info Sys	Anthony Chin	+65-456-1100
Interact BBS	Teo Chee Kian	+65-581-7024
Bobcat BBS System, The	Chan YK	+65-738-2509
Slovakia		
SAC BBS	Miroslav Trnka	+42-7-2048232
South Africa		
NCS Cape Town	Colyn Brookes	+21-930-2752
Spain		
Murphy BBS	Jordi J. Canals	+34-3-580-8515
Clavius	Margarita Marin	+34-1-3112371
Europa BBS	Francisco Martinez	+34-1-320-8460
Switzerland		
Active-Net BBS	Martin Altorfer	+41-552-61815
Nice Day BBS	Oliver Jenni	+41-61-4630321
Trinidad		
Opus Networx	Peter Wimbourne	809-628-5023
United Kingdom		
Shack BBS, The	Bill Butland	+44-903-268668
BixBox, The	Terry Dansey	+44-1634-20093
Hawk's Castle	Gerald Janes	+44-344-411621
WorldLink BBS Ltd.	John Kirkman	+44-332-830362
Shareware Support BBS	Adrian Mardlin	+44-494-431861
Worldlinlk BBS Ltd	Jonathan Moorhouse	+44-422-824949
ChatterBox	Mick Spice	+44-1732-845338
TTFBBS	Nick Thompson	+44-889-568625

That's one for you and one for me

"With the addition of Telnet capability in the spring of 1994, Crystal Quill began seeing a large number of logons from outside of the United States. There has been some difficulty in arranging appropriate payment for online subscriptions from foreign users due to currency differences. Two users solved this problem in quite a clever manner. One of our users wanted to subscribe to a BBS in Maloca, Poland, to which she telneted frequently from Crystal Quill. Another user from the Polish system had telneted to Crystal Quill and wanted to subscribe here. Rather than fight the mails and currency conversions, each user bought the other a subscription on their respective home systems, and the problem was solved!! Ingenious!"

Pamela Stewart, Sysop, Crystal Quill

And Now a Word for Our Sponsor...

The international BBS list was provided through the courtesy of the Association of Shareware Professionals, an organization which has set a standard code of ethics for shareware authors. These BBSs are ASP Associates and have agreed to abide by the ASP standards.

The Association of Shareware Professionals may be contacted at 545 Grover Rd., Muskegon, MI USA 49442-9427. If you prefer, they are also available via fax at 616-788-2765 or voice — normal business hours, EST — 616-788-5131. On CompuServe, GO ASPFORUM for the latest BBS list. Frankly, ASP is hard to miss because much of the software available for downloading will contain their logo and address.

This list is updated once a month by Richard Holler, ASP BBS Membership Committee Chairman. His voice number is 317-782-9903. BBS phone is 317-784-2147. CompuServe account, 73567,1547.

Talking Down Under

"There is a BBS in Australia called Kakadu Konnection (+61-89-480069). We often telnet into their BBS 192.94.208.15 and establish chat links. Our members enjoy chatting with Australian callers every once in a while."

Adam J. Viener, Sysop, Cyberia

Appendix D
I Want My ANSI.SYS!

In This Appendix
▶ Finding ANSI.SYS
▶ Installing ANSI.SYS
▶ Troubleshooting

1 f you say *yes* to graphics hoping to get cool, pinball-wizard type screens, but end up with a screen full of letters belonging to a Swedish movie — all Ä Ä Ä and ë ë ë and stuff like that — then your system is missing its ANSI driver.

An ANSI driver isn't one of those new, scientifically designed golf clubs. ANSI stands for American National Standards Institute, and the ANSI driver is a little piece of software that allows the use of clearing codes and escape sequences. And if none of that makes any sense to you, that's okay. What you really need to do is

1. **Determine if the file ANSI.SYS exists on your hard disk.**

2. **Edit your CONFIG.SYS file to include ANSI.SYS.**

3. **Faithfully defend the Constitution of the United States.**

I walk you through this process in the sections to come. It's not as bad as it sounds. Honest. It's much less dangerous than watching presidents Ford, Bush, and Clinton play golf.

Finding ANSI.SYS

Chances are quite good that you have the ANSI.SYS file on your hard disk. Chances are also quite good that ANSI.SYS is snoozing in your DOS directory. However, we need to know for sure that ANSI.SYS is where it's supposed to be before we go tell your CONFIG.SYS to wake him up. Here's one way:

1. **Get to a DOS prompt — something like** C:\ .

   If you're not using Windows, just quit your current program, after saving open files, of course, and you'll be at a system prompt.

   If you are in Windows, save first and then, from Program Manager, select File⇨**Run**. When the Run dialog box rears its ugly head, type **command** in the text box and click OK — or press Enter. That should pop you out to the system prompt. Alternatively, you can save yourself some keystrokes by double-clicking on the Main group icon and then double-clicking on the MS-DOS-prompt icon. Once you get to the system prompt, move on to Step 2.

2. **Type:** DIR C:\DOS\ANSI.SYS **and press Enter.**

   If your ANSI.SYS is where it should be, you see some nonsense about volumes having no label and then the word ANSI.SYS and some numbers and a date. This is good. You can fast forward to Installing ANSI.SYS. To return to Windows, type **exit** and press Enter.

   If you see the words File Not Found, guess what that means.

If you didn't locate ANSI.SYS in your DOS directory, and you use Windows, here's another way to locate ANSI.SYS. Save all your open files, then go to Program Manager and double-click the Main group. Double-click on File Manager, which looks like a file cabinet. Select File⇨**Search**. In the Search dialog box, type ANSI.SYS in the text box, make sure that Start From says C:\, and the Search All Subdirectories box is Xed — just like Figure D-1. When you've got it set just right, click OK or press Enter.

Figure D-1:
Who knows where ANSI.SYS is? The Windows Search knows.

Search		
Search For: `ansi.sys`		OK
Start From: `C:\`		Cancel
☒ Search All Subdirectories		Help

If ANSI.SYS is on the hard disk, you'll see where. Write that all down; there'll be a quiz later.

If ANSI.SYS is not on the hard disk, get a friend to help you — or call customer support from where you bought your computer. You'll need your original DOS disks. You do have a copy of DOS on disks, right?

Installing ANSI.SYS

Pretend you found ANSI.SYS in your DOS directory. To get those great-looking BBS screens, you have to modify one of the most important files on your computer. It's called CONFIG.SYS. Hope that doesn't make you nervous.

Before tramping your muddy feet through this important file, be smart and make a backup copy onto a floppy disk.

✔ If you're using DOS, go to a DOS prompt and, after putting a floppy disk into the A drive, type **COPY \CONFIG.SYS A:** and press Enter.

✔ Windows users can employ File Manager to copy CONFIG.SYS by selecting **File⇨Copy** and then typing **\CONFIG.SYS** in the From text box and **A:** in the To text box, and then pressing Enter or clicking OK to get the action rolling. You can even use Step 1 from the previous set of instructions either to get a DOS prompt, type **COPY \CONFIG.SYS A:**, and press Enter or to type the same command in the Run dialog box.

It is truly astonishing how many ways you can copy a file. The point is, if you haven't backed up your CONFIG.SYS file, you have no excuse.

Now that you're safely backed up:

1. **At the DOS prompt, type** EDIT \CONFIG.SYS **and press Enter.**

   As usual, to get to the DOS prompt, save your files and exit the program currently being used. Then type the EDIT command.

   Windows users can use Notepad to edit CONFIG.SYS if they prefer. Just double-click on the Main group and then double-click on the Notepad icon. Select **File⇨Open**. When you see the Open dialog box, go to the filename text box on the left, type **\CONFIG.SYS** and press Enter.

2. **Now that you're in CONFIG.SYS, just put your little cursor on the line directly underneath the line that says something like** buffers=30.

3. **Type** DEVICE=C:\DOS\ANSI.SYS **and press Enter.**

   The DEVICE=C:\DOS\ANSI.SYS should be on its own line.

   If your search for ANSI.SYS discovered it in a directory different from \DOS, then be sure to type that directory name instead of \DOS in the preceding step.

If you believe you've erased something or otherwise fouled up your CONFIG.SYS, then exit the file without saving it to put CONFIG.SYS back the way it was. In other words, select **File⇨Close** and, when asked if you want to save changes, respond with a resounding No. Then, go back to Step 1 and try again.

4. **Select File⇨Save.**

5. **Select File⇨Exit.**

Okay, you did it! To celebrate, get to the DOS prompt — quit Windows, quit your DOS programs, quit everything! Make sure that the floppy disk you used to back up CONFIG.SYS is out of the disk drive. Now, set off the fireworks and reboot the computer by simultaneously pressing Ctrl+Alt+Delete. If this famous three-fingered salute requires more manual dexterity than you can muster, then turn the computer off, wait one minute, then turn it back on.

At this point, if you did everything correctly, you are on the path to righteous graphics on BBSs.

Troubleshooting

In the Army it's called a SNAFU — Situation Normal, All Fouled Up. I suspect people in the service don't use *fouled*. But that's just a suspicion. In computers, the term is FUBAR — Fouled Up Beyond All Repair. I know for sure that computer people don't use the word *fouled*, but you get the idea.

If you made a typo in your CONFIG.SYS file and are now getting scary error message like `Unrecognized command` whenever you start the computer, take a deep breath. It's not the end of the world. Don't send in your $19.95 for a subscription to *Catastrophic Expectations*. We can fix this. Eat a candy bar first, if it helps, and meditate on the fact that it's great that you're expanding your horizons by editing your CONFIG.SYS.

When you're ready, simply go back to Step 1 and perform the edit CONFIG.SYS process all over again, making sure this time you type DEVICE instead of DELICE.

If you made a whopper of a typo, and the computer won't start . . . or if it does, nothing works, here's what you do:

1. **First make sure that your backup floppy disk isn't still in the drive when you reboot the computer.**

    That can stop any system cold. If a disk is in the drive, remove it and reboot the computer again by simultaneously pressing Ctrl+Alt+Delete.

2. **If the ol' disk-in-the-drive isn't the problem, reboot the computer again anyway and, when you see** `Starting MS-DOS`, **quickly press the F8 function key to bypass CONFIG.SYS.**

3. **At the C: prompt, stick the disk with the backup CONFIG.SYS into drive A, and then type** COPY A:\CONFIG.SYS C:\ **and press Enter.**

   Wait for the message about one file being copied to appear.

4. **Reboot the computer again by simultaneously pressing Ctrl+Alt+Delete.**

   This time you shouldn't see the error messages. You can start the edit process again, if you want.

Now you have FUBARN: Fouled Up Beyond Repair — Not. Happy computing.

Index

• Symbols •

8-N-1 (protocol), 19
^ (caret for Control key), 141, 302

• A •

Abort (Ctrl+X) command, 303
accounts, user, 28–29
acronyms, 83
adults-only BBSs, 6
aliases (handles), 34, 38
    see also nicknames
AlphaOne Online BBS, 161
angle brackets, 83–84
anonymity factor, 105
ANSI graphics, 188
ANSI.SYS file, 345–349
    installing, 347–348
    locating, 345–346
    troubleshooting, 348–349
anti-virus checking, 97–100
Aquila BBS, 149
    Main menu, 138
Archie, 196
Association of Shareware
        Professionals, 343
asterisk (*)
    as Top command, 304
    in place of underline, 82

• B •

Backward (–) command, 304
BBS (Bulletin Board System), 2, 9–14
    AlphaOne Online, 161
    anonymity factor, 105
    Aquila, 138, 149

assessing/changing system, 185–190
Bingo Bango Bongo, 221
Blue Ridge Express, 115
cannot be crashed from outside, 318
causes for concern, 103–109
chat lines, 79–81
Chrysalis, 166
components of, 10–14
content, 10–11
Dance of Shiva, 195
Deep Cove Online, 156, 180, 188
domestic listing, 329–338
doors, 181–183
DSC, 116, 204
E-Mail, 71–79
etiquette online, 81–84
Exec-PC, 113, 115
explained, 9–14
games, 177–180
GLIB (Gay/Lesbian Information Bureau),
        134, 137, 186, 303
hackers, 108–109
Index, 126
international listing, 339–343
Internet connection, 191–196
legal issues, 103–109
list of, 329–338
Micro Message, 13
mini, 211–218
Monterey Gaming System, 80
Nashville Exchange, 178, 181, 189
Network East, 152, 157
nicknames, 14
online etiquette, 81–84
operating costs, 10
owning/operating, 219–230
parental issues, 103–109
Pegasus Project, 13
phone lines, 226, 323–324

(continued)

BBS *(continued)*
 pitfalls, 103–109
 PKWare, 54–58
 scams, 104–105
  shopping online, 180–181
 Software Creations, 16, 20
 Springfield Public Access, 155
 stalking, 106
 structure, 12–14
 subscribing to, 27
 Sundown, 220–221
 Swamp, 12, 169–170
 Top 100 list, 16, 329–338
 Wildcat!, 231–275
 x-rated chat, 106
 YA! WEBECAD!, 178
Bingo Bango Bongo BBS, 221
Blue Ridge Express BBS, Main menu, 115
Boardwatch Magazine, Top 100 BBS list, 1,
  16, 329–338
book
 about, 2
 how to use, 3
 icons, 5–6
 overview, 4–5
 steps, 2–3
Boole, George, 123
Boolean file search, 122–123
boot disk, 101
Bulletin Listings menu, 30–31
Bulletin menu, 12
bulletins, reading, 310

• C •

call waiting, disabling, 323–324
Cancel (Ctrl+C) command, 303
captured files, 42
 pre-planning, 47–48
 printing, 50
 scrollback buffer, 49
 viewing/using, 50
caret (^) symbol as Control key, with
  E–Mail, 141

carriage return (CR), 302
channels, Chat session, 167
Chat lines (public forums), 10, 79–81
 acronyms, 83
 angle brackets, 83–84
 online etiquette, 81–84
 smileys/emoticons, 84
 x-rated, 106
Chat sessions, 165–176
 channels, 167
 Chat menu features, 168–172
 Chat room commands, 173–174
 classifying, 166–168
 conference, 167
 leaving, 174
 lobby, 167
 looking around, 175
 nonstructured rooms, 168
 online bios, 176
 online help, 175
 paging users, 172
 prepared messages, 176
 private chat, 167
 private messages, 175
 public chat, 167
 responding to page, 172
 rooms, 167, 173–175
 squelching/ignoring users, 175
 structured rooms, 167
Chat status utility, 189
children, parental issues, 107–108
Chrysalis BBS, Main menu, 166
command line, 3
commands
 <CR> or Enter key, 303–304
 Abort (Ctrl+X), 303
 Backward (–), 304
 Cancel (Ctrl+C), 303
 Forward (+), 304
 Global (/), 304
 Goodbye, 310
 Help (? or H+Enter), 303
 Help (Alt+F1), 3
 Logoff, 310

Page, 312
Pause (Ctrl+S), 302
Read The Screen, 304
Restart (Ctrl+Q), 302
Suspend (Ctrl+K), 303
Top (* or O+Enter), 304
comments, leaving, 313
communications software
    see also telecommunications software
    setting properly, 315–316
    dialing directory, 327–328
    identifying, 326
compressed files, 62–63
    see also PKZip/PKUnZip
computer viruses, see viruses
confabulation, 147
conferences, 10, 75–79, 147–164
    abandoning, 163
    acronyms, 84
    basics, 151–153
    characterizing, 148
    Chat sessions, 167
    choosing a topic, 155–157
    deleting messages, 159
    flame wars, 162
    Internet, 151
    joining, 152
    local, 149
    locating, 153–163
    lurkers, 152
    message gathering, 157–160
    network (echo), 149–150
    online etiquette, 81–84
    organization, 149–151
    posting E–Mail to, 75–79
    posting messages, 160–161
    private, 149
    reading messages, 158, 160
    reset last message read pointers, 159
    rules of debate, 162–163
    scanning messages, 158
    selecting, 163–164
    smileys/emoticons, 84

topics, 151
types of, 148
CONFIG.SYS file, 345–349
Control key (^), 141, 302
costs, hidden, 226
CR (carriage return), 302
crippleware, 58
cyberspace, exploring, 9–10

• D •

Dance of Shiva BBS, 195
data, capturing versus downloading, 42
databases, accessing through doors, 182
Deep Cove Online BBS, 156, 180, 188
default option, 20, 34
dialing directory, 327–328
directory
    DOS structure, 43–44
    download, 43, 45–46
domestic BBS listing, 329–338
doors, 181–183
    database access, 182
    love connections, 183
    magazines, 182
DOS
    directory structure, 43–44
    filename conventions, 44
    wildcards, 44–45
DOSAV.EXE file, 306
download directory, 43, 45–46
downloading
    deleting files, 127–129
    directory for, 43, 45–46
    files, 41–58, 305–308, 318
    protocol, 52
    tagged files, 125–126
DRAGFL.ZIP file, 308
DSC BBS, 204
    Main menu, 116

• E •

E-Mail (electronic mail), 11, 71–79, 131–146
  acronyms, 83–84
  angle brackets, 83–84
  attaching files, 144
  attaching/enclosing files with messages, 133–134
  BBS word-processor screen, 72–73
  carbon copies, 144
  caret (^) symbol with, 141
  editing messages, 140–141
  erasing messages, 134
  exchanging, 72–79
  forwarding messages, 144
  full-screen editor, 35–36, 139
  getting a receipt, 144
  line editor, 139, 141
  mailbox, 74
  marking messages for retrieval, 145
  message text prompt, 36
  message-handling commands, 133
  multiple messages, 135–136
  online etiquette, 81–84
  posting to a conference, 75–79
  printing on-screen messages, 134
  private, 74, 131
  public, 131
  reading offline, 197–207
  replying to messages, 134, 141–143
  responding to new, 132–136
  retrieving mail, 145–146
  saving versus sending, 73
  sending messages, 143–144
  smileys/emoticons, 84
  text editors, 139
  writing messages, 136–144
electronic business, BBS, 221–222
electronic mail *see* E-Mail
emoticons, 84
Enter key, as command, 303–304
Enter or <CR> command, 303

etiquette, online, 81–84
EXE file extension, 65
Exec-PC BBS, 113
Exec-PC BBS, Top menu, 115
external modem, 324

• F •

FAQ's (frequently asked questions), 12
file areas, 114
file collections, 114
file directories, 114
  topic search, 117–118
file extensions
  EXE, 65
  ZIP, 63
file libraries, 114
File menu, 114–116
file searches, 116–123
  Boolean, 122
  category, 120
  framing, 121–122
  locating search command, 120–121
  new, 118–119
  options, 121–122
  specific name, 120
  system statistics, 119
  topic, 117–118
  wildcard, 122
file transfer protocol (FTP), 196
filenames, DOS conventions, 44
files
  ANSI.SYS, 345–349
  attaching to E-Mail, 133–134
  capturing, 47–50
  capturing text to, 46–50
  compressing, 62–63
  CONFIG.SYS, 345–349
  deleting downloaded, 127–129
  DOSAV.EXE, 306
  downloading, 41–58, 305–308, 318
  DRAGFL.ZIP 308
  elements, 118–119

extracting, 64–65
finding/retrieving, 113–129
LIST90H.ZIP, 307
OLX–TD.EXE, 199–200, 307
PKZ204G.EXE, 61–70, 306
QM46TD–1.EXE, 306
QM46TD–2.EXE, 306
retrieving, 123–126
self–extracting, 65
SHEZ106.ZIP, 308
storing downloaded, 127
tagging, 125–126
TIMESET7.ZIP, 308
unzipping, 64–67
uploading, 59–60
VPIC61.ZIP, 307
wildcards to help search for, 306
WINAV.EXE, 306
WINLIST.ZIP, 307
WINPRN15.ZIP, 308
zipped, 61–64, 67–70
files to download first, 305–308
financial considerations, owning/
    operating, 224–227
flame wars, conferences, 162
Forward (+) command, 304
forward slash, (/) as Global command, 304
freeware, 10, 58
full-screen editor, 35–36, 188
    E-Mail, 139

• G •

games, 11, 177–180
    MUD, 179
    multiline, 179
    single-user, 178
GLIB (Gay/Lesbian Information Bureau)
        BBS 134, 303
    Main menu, 137
    Utility menu, 186
Global (/) command, 304
Goodbye command, 310

Gopher, 196
graphics, 36
    advantages/disadvantages, 21–22
    ANSI, 188
GUI (graphical user interface), 13

• H •

hackers, 108–109
handles (aliases), 34, 38
    see also nicknames
hang up on BBS, 313
hardware requirements, owning/operat-
    ing, 225–226
Help (? or H+Enter) command, 303
Help (Alt+F1) command, 3
Help screens, reading, 310
hints from Sysop
    ask questions, 316
    BBS is hobbyist, 318
    be polite, 316
    communicate with others
        on the BBS, 318
    communication software, 315–316
    help other users, 318
    high speed modems, 317
    know Zmodem, 317
    line noise, 317
    read screen instructions, 316
    use offline readers, 318
history, 301–302
host computer, mini-BBS, 211–218
hotkeys, 36–37
housekeeping chores, owning/
        operating, 227

• I •

icons, used in book, 5–6
Index BBS, 126
installation, Wildcat! BBS program,
    234–239

internal modem, 324
international BBS listing, 339–343
Internet, BBS access, 11
Internet conference, 151
Internet connection, 191–196
  advantages, 193–195
  Archie, 196
  disadvantages, 192–193
  E–Mail, 195
  features, 195–196
  FTP (file transfer protocol), 196
  Gopher, 196
  Jughead, 196
  offline readers, 197–198
  overview, 191–192
  Telnet, 196
  usenet newsgroups, 196
  Veronica, 196

• J •

Jughead, 196
jump to Top command, 310

• K •

Katz, Phil (PKZip), 63
key combinations
  ? or H+Enter (Help), 303
  Alt+F1 (Help), 3
  Ctrl+C (Cancel), 303
  Ctrl+K (Suspend), 303
  Ctrl+Q (Restart), 302
  Ctrl+S (Pause), 302
  Ctrl+X (Abort), 303
  Shift+PtrScr, 134

• L •

languages, selecting, 20
legal issues, 103–109

line editor, E-Mail, 139, 141
line noise, 317
LIST90H.ZIP file, 307
lobby, Chat session, 167
local conference, 149
logging off, 14, 31–32
logging on, 12, 15–40
  8-N-1 protocol, 19
  Bulletin Listings, 30–31
  connecting, 17–19
  connection noises, 17–18
  CPU information, 25–27
  default options, 20, 34
  dialing phone, 16–17
  disconnecting, 18
  first time, 15–32
  getting validated, 32–33
  graphics option, 21–22
  hanging up, 18
  introducing yourself to Sysop, 19–30
  language option, 20
  logging off, 31–32
  navigating, 28
  on-screen information, 23–24
  on-screen instructions, 19
  passwords, 24–25
  personal information, 25
  reading bulletins, 30–31
  registering, 22–24
  screen scrolling, 37–38
  second time, 38–40
  subscribing to a service, 27
  technical questions, 34–37
  unverified new user, 29–30
  user account, 28–29
  using aliases, 34
  variations in, 33–38
Logoff command, 310
love connections, accessing through
    doors, 183
lurkers, conference, 152

magazines, accessing through doors, 182
mailbox, E-Mail, 74
Main menu, 12–13
MajorBBS software, 33
material, capturing versus
    downloading, 42
McAfee AntiVirus program, 94–100
menus
  Bulletin, 12
  Bulletin Listings, 30–31
  File, 114–116
  Main, 12–13
message bases/menu, 148
message text prompt, 36
messages
  see also E-Mail/conferences
  writing E-Mail, 136–144
Micro Message Service BBS,
    Main menu, 13
Microsoft Anti-Virus program, 88–94,
    97–100
Microsoft Backup program, 88
Microsoft Diagnostics (MSD)
    program, 324–325
mini-BBS
  answering calls, 213–214
  auto-answer feature, 213
  disabling call-waiting, 215
  E-Mail via host mode, 218
  guest list, 213
  host computer, 211–212
  Host menu, 217
  host system parameters, 212
  hosting, 211–218
  invoking host mode, 215–216
  starting host mode, 213
  system preparation, 212–215
  welcome message, 216
minus sign (–), as Backward
    command, 304
modems
  dialing phone, 16–17

hanging up, 18
high speed, 317
identifying, 324–325
logging off, 31–32
types of, 324–326
Monterey Gaming System BBS,
    Chat menu, 80
MUD games, 179
multiline games, 179
Mustang Software, *see* Wildcat! BBS

Nashville Exchange BBS, 178, 181
  utilities menu, 189
network (echo) conference, 149–150
Network East BBS, 152, 157
new user
  getting validated, 32–33
  unverified, 29–30
newbies, 40
news/information services, 11
nicknames, 14
  see also handles/aliases
nulls, 37

• **O** •

Offline Express (OLX) program, 199–207
  configuring, 203
  downloading E-Mail packet, 203–204
  reading/replying to E-Mail, 204–206
  setting up, 201–202
  uploading reply packet, 206–207
offline readers, 199–207, 318
OLX program *see* Offline Express program
OLX-TD.EXE file, 199–200, 307
online, 1, 9
online etiquette, 81–84
options, default, 20, 34
owning/operating BBS, 219–228
  dedicated phone line, 226
  electronic business, 221–222

(continued)

owning/operating BBS *(continued)*
  financial considerations, 224–227
  hardware requirements, 225–226
  hidden costs, 226
  housekeeping chores, 227
  reasons for, 219–224
  settings for, 222–223
  software requirements, 226
  troubleshooting considerations, 227

• P •

page, on World Wide Web, 194
Page command, 312
page pausing, 35
paradigm shifts, 1
parental issues, 103–109
passwords
  changing, 187
  PIN (personal identification number), 24
  selecting, 24–25
  verifying, 25
Pause (Ctrl+S) command, 302
PCBoard software, 33
Pegasus Project BBS, Main menu, 13
personal information, 25
phone, dialing, 16–17
phone lines
  dedicated, 226
  types of, 323–324
PIN (personal identification number), 24
pitfalls, 103–109
PKUnZip program, 64–67
PKWare BBS, 54–58
PKZ204G.EXE file, 61–70, 306
PKZip program, 53, 61–70
  compressing files, 62–63
  creating directory for, 66–67
  EXE file extension, 65
  extracting files, 64–65
  self-extracting files, 65
  setting up, 67–70

ZIP file extension, 63
plus sign (+), as Forward command, 304
printing, captured files, 50
private
  chat, 167
  conference, 149
  E-Mail, 131
problem solving
  ask other users, 311
  bulletins, 310
  call voice support, 311
  disconnect, 313
  hang up on BBS, 313
  how to tell if you're online/offline, 309
  leave a comment, 313
  page Sysop, 312
  read Help screens, 310
  read prompts, 310
  return to top, 310
  use screen commands, 311
  use scrollback buffer feature, 312
programs
  see also software
  downloading, 305–308
  McAfee AntiVirus, 94–97
  Microsoft Anti-Virus, 88–94
  Microsoft Backup, 88
  Microsoft Diagnostics (MSD), 324–325
  OLX (Offline Express), 199–207
  PKUnZip, 64–67
  PKZip, 53, 61–70
  virus checker, 88–97
  Wildcat! BBS, 231–275
prompts, reading, 310
protocols
  8-N-1, 19
  changing, 187
  download, 52
  Zmodem, 187
public chat, 167
public E-Mail, 131
public forums (chat lines), 148

• Q •

QM46TD-1.EXE file, 306
QM46TD-2.EXE file, 306
questions
  See also technical questions
  ask other users, 311
  ask Sysop, 316

• R •

Read the Screen secret, 304
registering, 22–24
rescues, getting out of trouble, 309
Restart (Ctrl+Q) command, 302
rooms, Chat session, 167, 173–175
rules of debate, conferences, 162–163

• S •

scams, avoiding, 104–105
screen commands, using, 311
screens
  E-Mail word-processor, 72–73
  read instructions, 316
  Welcome, 12
scrollback buffer, 49, 312
searches
  file, 116–123
  using wildcards, 306
secret commands, top ten, 302–304
self-extracting files, 65
service, subscribing to, 27
set screen width, 35
settings for owning/operating BBS,
    222–223
shareware, 10, 58
  downloading, 305–306
  registering, 58
SHEZ106.ZIP file, 308
shopping online, 180–181
SIGS (Special Interest Groups), 148

single-user games, 178
smileys, 84
snail mail, 73
software
  see also programs
  communications, 315–316
  crippleware, 58
  freeware, 10, 58
  identifying communications, 326
  MajorBBS, 33
  McAfee AntiVirus, 94–97
  Microsoft Anti-Virus, 88–94
  Microsoft Backup, 88
  Microsoft Diagnostics (MSD), 324–325
  OLX (Offline Express), 199–207
  PCBoard, 33
  PKUnZip, 64–67
  PKZip, 53, 61–70
  required to own/operate BBS, 226
  shareware, 10, 58
  TBBS, 33
  telecommunications, 17
  virus checker, 88–97
  Wildcat! BBS, 33, 231–275
Software Creations BBS, 16
  Bulletin Listings menu, 30–31
  informational screen, 23
  logging onto, 15–32
  navigating, 28
  New Member's Main Menu, 30
  Startrek option, 20
  Subscriber's Main Menu, 39
  subscribing, 27
  Welcome screen, 22
Springfield Public Access BBS, 155
stalking, 106
statistics utility, 189
steps, terms used, 2–3
subscribing, 27
Sundown BBS, 220–221
Suspend (Ctrl+K) command, 303
Swamp BBS
  Bulletin menu, 12

(continued)

Swamp BBS *(continued)*
  Chat menu, 170
  Main menu, 169
symbols, ^ (caret), 141
Sysop
  BBS, 10
  customizing BBS, 297
  hints for dealing with, 319
  operating Wildcat! BBS, 277–297
  paging, 312
  responsibilities of, 228–229
  Wildcat! BBS idle screen, 278
  Wildcat! BBS New User Main Menu, 279
  Wildcat! BBS Security Change window,
      280–281
  Wildcat! BBS security profile, 281–282
  Wildcat! BBS status lines, 279–280
  Wildcat! BBS SYSOP menu, 282–297
Sysop, hints from
  ask questions, 316
  BBS is hobbyist, 318
  be polite, 316
  communicate with others
      on the BBS, 318
  communication software, 315–316
  help other users, 318
  high speed modems, 317
  know Zmodem, 317
  line noise, 317
  read screen instructions, 316
  use offline readers, 318
system, assessing, 185–190

• *T* •

tagged files, downloading, 125–126
TBBS software, 33
technical questions
  check out the top, 35
  full-screen editor, 35–36
  graphics, 36
  hotkeys, 36–37
  message text prompt, 36
  nulls, 37

  page pausing, 35
  set screen width, 35
telecommunications software
  see also communications software
  captured files, 46–50
  dialing directory, 17, 327–328
  dialing phone, 17
  download directory, 43, 45–46
  identifying, 326
  online help features, 18
  protocol, 19
  scrollback buffer, 49
ten files to download first, 305–308
  DOSAV.EXE, 306
  DRAGFL.ZIP 308
  LIST90H.ZIP, 307
  OLX–TD.EXE, 199–200, 307
  PKZ204G.EXE, 61–70, 306
  QM46TD–1.EXE, 306
  QM46TD–2.EXE, 306
  SHEZ106.ZIP, 308
  TIMESET7.ZIP, 308
  VPIC61.ZIP, 307
  WINAV.EXE, 306
  WINLIST.ZIP, 307
  WINPRN15.ZIP, 308
ten secret commands, 301–304
  <CR> or Enter key, 303–304
  Abort (Ctrl+X), 303
  Backward (–), 304
  Cancel (Ctrl+C), 303
  Forward (+), 304
  Global (/), 304
  Goodbye, 310
  Help (? or H+Enter), 303
  Help (Alt+F1), 3
  Logoff, 310
  Page, 312
  Pause (Ctrl+S), 302
  Read the screen, 304
  Restart (Ctrl+Q), 302
  Suspend (Ctrl+K), 303
  Top (* or O+Enter), 304
ten Sysop hints, 315–319

ask questions, 316
BBS is hobbyist, 318
be polite, 316
communicate with others
     on the BBS, 318
communication software, 315–316
help other users, 318
high speed modems, 317
know Zmodem, 317
line noise, 317
read screen instructions, 316
use offline readers, 318
ten ways to get out of trouble, 309–314
ask other users, 311
bulletins, 310
call voice support, 311
disconnect, 313
hang up on BBS, 313
how to tell if you're online/offline, 309
leave a comment, 313
page Sysop, 312
read Help screens, 310
read prompts, 310
return to top, 310
use screen commands, 311
use scrollback buffer feature, 312
terms, used in steps, 2–3
text editors, E-Mail, 139
text, capturing, 47–50
time online utility, 189
TIMESET7.ZIP file, 308
Top (* or O+Enter) command, 304
top, return to, 310
troubleshooting
ask other users, 311
bulletins, 310
call voice support, 311
considerations when
     owning/operating, 227
disconnect, 313
hang up on BBS, 313
how to tell if you're online/offline, 309
leave a comment, 313
page Sysop, 312

read Help screens, 310
read prompts, 310
return to top, 310
use screen commands, 311
use scrollback buffer feature, 312

• U •

UART 16550 chip, 317
unverified new user, 29–30
uploading files, 59–60
user account, 28–29
getting validated, 32–33
utilities, 188–189
chat status, 189
statistics, 189
time online, 189
who's online, 189

• V •

validation, 32–33
virus checker software, 88–100
viruses, 85–102
boot disk, 101
checking for, 97–100
overview, 86
preventive action, 86–88
red alert, 100–101
signature, 86
virus checkers, 88–97
VPIC61.ZIP file, 307

• W •

ways to get out of trouble, 309–314
Welcome screen, 12
who's online utility, 189
wildcard file search, 122–123
wildcards
DOS, 44–45
speed up searches, 306

Wildcats program, 33, 231–275
  activity log, 293–294
  batch files directory, 237
  blueprint, 243–251
  bulletin directory, 236

  chat features, 275
  Conference Access window, 267–268
  conference listings, 232–233
  conferences, 269–272
  configuration, 241–275
  directory structure, 235–237
  display files directory, 236
  doors, 272
  dropping to DOS, 296–297
  Edit Filearea window, 266
  Edit Security Profile windows, 258–265
  Editing Conference screens, 269–272
  event list, 295–296
  example files, 237
  exiting, 275
  external protocols, 257
  file areas, 233–234, 265–269
  files database, 285–287
  General Information screens, 242–251
  Help file directory, 236
  home directory, 236
  idle screen programs, 275, 278
  installation screen, 235
  installing, 234–239
  language directory, 236–237
  language files, 275
  Mail Door window, 273–275
  Makewild Main Menu, 242
  MAKEWILD.EXE file, 241
  manual security override, 265
  memory requirements, 240–241
  menu files directory, 236
  menu hook, 273
  modem files directory, 237
  modem information, 240
  modem settings, 254–257
  naming ideas, 232
  New User Main Menu, 279

  operating, 277–297
  organization, 232–233
  Overall System Information screen, 284
  overview, 231
  planning, 232–234
  Profile Access window, 266–267
  questionnaire directory, 236
  QWK/REP Mail Support Files, 238
  RIP Support Files, 238
  Sample wcCODE Programs, 237
  secondary profiles, 265
  Security Change window, 280–281
  security issues, 251–254
  security overrides, 265
  setup, 241–275
  source drive, 235
  status database, 284–285
  status lines, 279–380
  subspecies, 234
  SYSOP menu, 282–297
  SYSOP menu commands, 294–295
  sysop security profile, 281–282
  system security, 251–254
  user database, 287–292
  user profiles, 257–265
  User Security window, 257
  UUCP Communication Files, 237
  wcDRAW program, 297
  wcPRO FAX Support Files, 237
  WINSTALL window, 238–239
WINAV.EXE file, 306
WINLIST.ZIP file, 307
WINPRN15.ZIP file, 308
word-processor, E-Mail, 72–73
WWW (World Wide Web), 194–196

x-rated chat, 106

YA! WEBECAD! BBS, 178

• Z •

ZIP file extension, 63
zipped files, 61–70
Zmodem protocol, 187, 317

Title	Author	ISBN	Price
INTERNET / COMMUNICATIONS / NETWORKING			12/20/9
CompuServe For Dummies™	by Wallace Wang	1-56884-181-7	$19.95 USA/$26.95 Canada
Modems For Dummies™, 2nd Edition	by Tina Rathbone	1-56884-223-6	$19.99 USA/$26.99 Canada
Modems For Dummies™	by Tina Rathbone	1-56884-001-2	$19.95 USA/$26.95 Canada
MORE Internet For Dummies™	by John R. Levine & Margaret Levine Young	1-56884-164-7	$19.95 USA/$26.95 Canada
NetWare For Dummies™	by Ed Tittel & Deni Connor	1-56884-003-9	$19.95 USA/$26.95 Canada
Networking For Dummies™	by Doug Lowe	1-56884-079-9	$19.95 USA/$26.95 Canada
ProComm Plus 2 For Windows For Dummies™	by Wallace Wang	1-56884-219-8	$19.99 USA/$26.99 Canada
The Internet For Dummies™, 2nd Edition	by John R. Levine & Carol Baroudi	1-56884-222-8	$19.99 USA/$26.99 Canada
The Internet For Macs For Dummies™	by Charles Seiter	1-56884-184-1	$19.95 USA/$26.95 Canada
MACINTOSH			
Macs For Dummies®	by David Pogue	1-56884-173-6	$19.95 USA/$26.95 Canada
Macintosh System 7.5 For Dummies™	by Bob LeVitus	1-56884-197-3	$19.95 USA/$26.95 Canada
MORE Macs For Dummies™	by David Pogue	1-56884-087-X	$19.95 USA/$26.95 Canada
PageMaker 5 For Macs For Dummies™	by Galen Gruman	1-56884-178-7	$19.95 USA/$26.95 Canada
QuarkXPress 3.3 For Dummies™	by Galen Gruman & Barbara Assadi	1-56884-217-1	$19.99 USA/$26.99 Canada
Upgrading and Fixing Macs For Dummies™	by Kearney Rietmann & Frank Higgins	1-56884-189-2	$19.95 USA/$26.95 Canada
MULTIMEDIA			
Multimedia & CD-ROMs For Dummies™, Interactive Multimedia Value Pack	by Andy Rathbone	1-56884-225-2	$29.95 USA/$39.95 Canada
Multimedia & CD-ROMs For Dummies™	by Andy Rathbone	1-56884-089-6	$19.95 USA/$26.95 Canada
OPERATING SYSTEMS / DOS			
MORE DOS For Dummies™	by Dan Gookin	1-56884-046-2	$19.95 USA/$26.95 Canada
S.O.S. For DOS™	by Katherine Murray	1-56884-043-8	$12.95 USA/$16.95 Canada
OS/2 For Dummies™	by Andy Rathbone	1-878058-76-2	$19.95 USA/$26.95 Canada
UNIX			
UNIX For Dummies™	by John R. Levine & Margaret Levine Young	1-878058-58-4	$19.95 USA/$26.95 Canada
WINDOWS			
S.O.S. For Windows™	by Katherine Murray	1-56884-045-4	$12.95 USA/$16.95 Canada
MORE Windows 3.1 For Dummies™, 3rd Edition	by Andy Rathbone	1-56884-240-6	$19.99 USA/$26.99 Canada
PCs / HARDWARE			
Illustrated Computer Dictionary For Dummies™	by Dan Gookin, Wally Wang, & Chris Van Buren	1-56884-004-7	$12.95 USA/$16.95 Canada
Upgrading and Fixing PCs For Dummies™	by Andy Rathbone	1-56884-002-0	$19.95 USA/$26.95 Canada
PRESENTATION / AUTOCAD			
AutoCAD For Dummies™	by Bud Smith	1-56884-191-4	$19.95 USA/$26.95 Canada
PowerPoint 4 For Windows For Dummies™	by Doug Lowe	1-56884-161-2	$16.95 USA/$22.95 Canada
PROGRAMMING			
Borland C++ For Dummies™	by Michael Hyman	1-56884-162-0	$19.95 USA/$26.95 Canada
"Borland's New Language Product" For Dummies™	by Neil Rubenking	1-56884-200-7	$19.95 USA/$26.95 Canada
C For Dummies™	by Dan Gookin	1-878058-78-9	$19.95 USA/$26.95 Canada
C++ For Dummies™	by Stephen R. Davis	1-56884-163-9	$19.95 USA/$26.95 Canada
Mac Programming For Dummies™	by Dan Parks Sydow	1-56884-173-6	$19.95 USA/$26.95 Canada
QBasic Programming For Dummies™	by Douglas Hergert	1-56884-093-4	$19.95 USA/$26.95 Canada
Visual Basic "X" For Dummies™, 2nd Edition	by Wallace Wang	1-56884-230-9	$19.99 USA/$26.99 Canada
Visual Basic 3 For Dummies™	by Wallace Wang	1-56884-076-4	$19.95 USA/$26.95 Canada
SPREADSHEET			
1-2-3 For Dummies™	by Greg Harvey	1-878058-60-6	$16.95 USA/$21.95 Canada
1-2-3 For Windows 5 For Dummies™, 2nd Edition	by John Walkenbach	1-56884-216-3	$16.95 USA/$21.95 Canada
1-2-3 For Windows For Dummies™	by John Walkenbach	1-56884-052-7	$16.95 USA/$21.95 Canada
Excel 5 For Macs For Dummies™	by Greg Harvey	1-56884-186-8	$19.95 USA/$26.95 Canada
Excel For Dummies™, 2nd Edition	by Greg Harvey	1-56884-050-0	$16.95 USA/$21.95 Canada
MORE Excel 5 For Windows For Dummies™	by Greg Harvey	1-56884-207-4	$19.95 USA/$26.95 Canada
Quattro Pro 6 For Windows For Dummies™	by John Walkenbach	1-56884-174-4	$19.95 USA/$26.95 Canada
Quattro Pro For DOS For Dummies™	by John Walkenbach	1-56884-023-3	$16.95 USA/$21.95 Canada
UTILITIES / VCRs & CAMCORDERS			
Norton Utilities 8 For Dummies™	by Beth Slick	1-56884-166-3	$19.95 USA/$26.95 Canada
VCRs & Camcorders For Dummies™	by Andy Rathbone & Gordon McComb	1-56884-229-5	$14.99 USA/$20.99 Canada
WORD PROCESSING			
Ami Pro For Dummies™	by Jim Meade	1-56884-049-7	$19.95 USA/$26.95 Canada
MORE Word For Windows 6 For Dummies™	by Doug Lowe	1-56884-165-5	$19.93 USA/$26.95 Canada
MORE WordPerfect 6 For Windows For Dummies™	by Margaret Levine Young & David C. Kay	1-56884-206-6	$19.95 USA/$26.95 Canada
MORE WordPerfect 6 For DOS For Dummies™	by Wallace Wang, edited by Dan Gookin	1-56884-047-0	$19.95 USA/$26.95 Canada
S.O.S. For WordPerfect™	by Katherine Murray	1-56884-053-5	$12.95 USA/$16.95 Canada
Word 6 For Macs For Dummies™	by Dan Gookin	1-56884-190-6	$19.95 USA/$26.95 Canada
Word For Windows 6 For Dummies™	by Dan Gookin	1-56884-075-6	$16.95 USA/$21.95 Canada
Word For Windows For Dummies™	by Dan Gookin	1-878058-86-X	$16.95 USA/$21.95 Canada
WordPerfect 6 For Dummies™	by Dan Gookin	1-878058-77-0	$16.95 USA/$21.95 Canada
WordPerfect For Dummies™	by Dan Gookin	1-878058-52-5	$16.95 USA/$21.95 Canada
WordPerfect For Windows For Dummies™	by Margaret Levine Young & David C. Kay	1-56884-032-2	$16.95 USA/$21.95 Canada

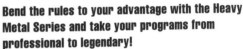

IDG BOOKS

Order Center: **(800) 762-2974** *(8 a.m.–6 p.m., EST, weekdays)*

12/20/9–

Quantity	ISBN	Title	Price	Total

Shipping & Handling Charges

	Description	First book	Each additional book	Total
Domestic	Normal	$4.50	$1.50	$
	Two Day Air	$8.50	$2.50	$
	Overnight	$18.00	$3.00	$
International	Surface	$8.00	$8.00	$
	Airmail	$16.00	$16.00	$
	DHL Air	$17.00	$17.00	$

*For large quantities call for shipping & handling charges.
**Prices are subject to change without notice.

Ship to:

Name _____

Company _____

Address _____

City/State/Zip _____

Daytime Phone _____

Payment: ☐ Check to IDG Books (US Funds Only)

☐ VISA ☐ MasterCard ☐ American Express

Card # _____ Expires _____

Signature _____

Subtotal _____

CA residents add
applicable sales tax _____

IN, MA, and MD
residents add
5% sales tax _____

IL residents add
6.25% sales tax _____

RI residents add
7% sales tax _____

TX residents add
8.25% sales tax _____

Shipping _____

Total _____

Please send this order form to:

IDG Books Worldwide
7260 Shadeland Station, Suite 100
Indianapolis, IN 46256

Allow up to 3 weeks for delivery.
Thank you!

IDG BOOKS WORLDWIDE REGISTRATION CARD

RETURN THIS REGISTRATION CARD FOR FREE CATALOG

Title of this book: BBSs For Dummies

My overall rating of this book: ❏ Very good [1]   ❏ Good [2]   ❏ Satisfactory [3]   ❏ Fair [4]   ❏ Poor [5]

How I first heard about this book:

❏ Found in bookstore; name: [6]

❏ Advertisement: [8]

❏ Word of mouth; heard about book from friend, co-worker, etc.: [10]

❏ Book review: [7]

❏ Catalog: [9]

❏ Other: [11]

What I liked most about this book:

What I would change, add, delete, etc., in future editions of this book:

Other comments:

Number of computer books I purchase in a year: ❏ 1 [12]   ❏ 2-5 [13]   ❏ 6-10 [14]   ❏ More than 10 [15]

I would characterize my computer skills as: ❏ Beginner [16]   ❏ Intermediate [17]   ❏ Advanced [18]   ❏ Professional [19]

I use ❏ DOS [20]   ❏ Windows [21]   ❏ OS/2 [22]   ❏ Unix [23]   ❏ Macintosh [24]   ❏ Other: [25]_____
(please specify)

I would be interested in new books on the following subjects:
(please check all that apply, and use the spaces provided to identify specific software)

❏ Word processing: [26]

❏ Data bases: [28]

❏ File Utilities: [30]

❏ Networking: [32]

❏ Other: [34]

❏ Spreadsheets: [27]

❏ Desktop publishing: [29]

❏ Money management: [31]

❏ Programming languages: [33]

I use a PC at (please check all that apply): ❏ home [35]   ❏ work [36]   ❏ school [37]   ❏ other: [38] _____

The disks I prefer to use are ❏ 5.25 [39]   ❏ 3.5 [40]   ❏ other: [41]_____

I have a CD ROM: ❏ yes [42]   ❏ no [43]

I plan to buy or upgrade computer hardware this year: ❏ yes [44]   ❏ no [45]

I plan to buy or upgrade computer software this year: ❏ yes [46]   ❏ no [47]

Name: _____   Business title: [48] _____   Type of Business: [49] _____

Address (❏ home [50] ❏ work [51]/Company name: _____)

Street/Suite# _____

City [52]/State [53]/Zipcode [54]: _____   Country [55] _____

❏ **I liked this book!** You may quote me by name in future
IDG Books Worldwide promotional materials.

My daytime phone number is _____

IDG BOOKS

THE WORLD OF COMPUTER KNOWLEDGE

 # YES!

Please keep me informed about IDG's World of Computer Knowledge.
Send me the latest IDG Books catalog.

 SECRETS™

 ...FOR DUMMIES™

COMPUTER
BOOK SERIES
FROM IDG

 MACWORLD MW AUTHORIZED EDITION

 AUTHORIZED PC WORLD EDITION